D0601879

SWORDS
and Hilt Weapons

Contributing authors

Michael D. Coe
Professor of Anthropology, Peabody Museum of Natural History, Yale University

Peter Connolly
Honorary Research Fellow of the Institute of Archaeology, University of London

Anthony Harding
Senior Lecturer in Archaeology, University of Durham

Victor Harris
Curator, Department of Japanese Antiquities, British Museum

Donald J. LaRocca
Assistant Curator, Arms and Armor Department, Metropolitan Museum of Art

Thom Richardson
Senior Curator of Armour, The Royal Armouries, H.M. Tower of London

Anthony North
Senior Research Assistant, Department of Metalwork, Victoria & Albert Museum

Christopher Spring
Research Assistant, Museum of Mankind, Ethnography Department of the British Museum

Frederick Wilkinson
President of the Arms and Armour Society

SWORDS
and Hilt Weapons

**BARNES
&NOBLE
BOOKS**
NEW YORK

Text copyright © Michael D. Coe, Peter Connolly, Anthony Harding,
Victor Harris, Donald J. Larocca, Thom Richardson, Anthony North,
Christopher Spring, Frederick Wilkinson 1989

Compilation copyright © Prion Books Limited 1989, 1993, 1996

This edition published by
Barnes & Noble, Inc.,
by arrangement with Prion Books Limited

1993 Barnes & Noble Books

All rights reserved. No part of this book may be reproduced, stored in a
retrieval system or transmitted in any form or by any means, electronic,
mechanical, photocopying or otherwise, without the prior permission of the
publisher and copyright owners.

10 9 8 7 6 5 4

ISBN 1–56619–249–8

Printed in Singapore by Imago

This book was devised and produced by Prion Books Limited,
32–34 Gordon House Road, London NW5 1LP

Contents

INTRODUCTION

Victor Harris

This book is about the history of swords and daggers throughout the world, but it is intended to be more than a history of the shapes and forms of the artefact. It aspires to give the reader a glimpse of that essential nature of the sword which has elevated it to a higher position than any other weapon in most societies throughout history.

The hilted cutting weapon must have developed from the chipped stone axe and the pointed stick, which were probably carried both as tools and weapons in the days before there was war. And then, around 3000 BC, the bronze blade was developed, to be followed by magical iron and heroic steel.

Sheathed in its scabbard, the sword might be an object of purely decorative beauty, the hilt chased in precious metals and inlaid with gems. Or its mounting might be of simple metal or wood, or cloth- or leather-clad. The hilt might be dressed with *memento mori*, signifying the death-dealing principle of the weapon. Or, with a cruciform hilt, the sword of the Christian knight might be an emblem of the very love of God.

At some times and in some nations the sword has been carried as an article of everyday wear. Elsewhere it has been kept above the mantle or over the lintel, away from the hands of children, awaiting the call to arms. And even today it is worn by soldiers as a badge of rank, kept lovingly by romantics nostalgic for days of glory, or collected by gentlemen as a thing of beauty and a stern reminder of the lore of ancient days.

But when the sword is drawn and hefted, the story is different. The bright blade is terrifying, the shape alerts strange senses to its functional elegance, and the sharp edge tells no compromise. Its purpose is to cut and kill. And that will impress even those who have no knowledge of nor interest in the history behind the weapon or the art or technology of the craftsman who made it.

Of course there is danger inherent in all blades. A blade must be tended painstakingly if the edge is to be kept keen, but even a dull blade must be treated with caution. Although the sword may have outlived its heyday as a weapon, its underlying dreadfulness cannot be ignored. As the Proverb says: 'To give a sword to a wood [mad] man is to give a sharp knife to a child.'

But what a delight in every boy's life is that first pen-knife, the coveted sharp and secret bright blade that belongs to no other! A long blade for everyday use, and a smaller sharp blade for an undefined future emergency. With that little knife one could cut string and carve wood, cut flutes out of cane, and whittle stick smooth and lovely. There was also the menace of the blade, and the fear of a cut and the bright red blood and even perhaps the thought of a secretly hoped-for white scar. There was a dignity inherent in the thing lacking in other toys. So too there is a dignity in swords and daggers, although the soldier's games are deadlier and his scars deeper than the schoolboy could imagine.

Sword and dagger conjure up similar dreams in distant cultures. The hilted weapon is the stuff of poems, and the symbol of a manly role in society. It has been so in all ages, through times of peace and of war. It is so for all peoples in all lands whether the brand has long outlived its practical usefulness or whether it is drawn daily in defence.

As a symbolic weapon the sword performs many functions without the spilling of blood. It is a mark of rule and is carried solemnly in civic procession as a symbol of law and administration. It is with the touch of a sword upon the shoulder that a knight is raised. And it is with the breaking of a sword that a man is disgraced. With the taking of a sword whole armies are given in surrender. In ancient Japan the sword was considered to embody the very soul of the samurai. The dagger was the implement of the highest etiquette – to atone for failure the samurai committed suicide by self-disembowelment and his lady pierced her jugular vein. Imitation swords have been used as currency, for healing, and all manner of ritual. In Africa, different types of ritual blades carried by the Asante people signify levels of authority, and the decorations on them are messages comprehensible only to those of the rank for which they are intended.

Sword dances survive which were once military exercises, like the reel of the Scottish Highlander over naked crossed broadswords. The magical nature of the sword is preserved in mummers' plays in the 'rose' or 'lock' of blades wedged together in knots over the head of mock decapitees.

For millennia the technology of the swordmaker was at the very forefront of science, and he was accorded a correspondingly important status in society. For armed might has always been the ultimate means of imposing authority, and the discovery of iron and steel established the sword as the ultimate cutting weapon.

The technology of strenthening the blade by 'pattern welding', that is by welding together strips of iron in various formations to produce a stronger blade, and adding carbon to the edge to make hard steel, developed in several cultures. The Vikings made swords of complex construction, and dressed them richly with precious metals. Fine-grained blades were made in Damascus and Syria, some with the Mohammed's Ladder pattern of folded iron in the blade. Half the world away in Japan a thousand years ago bright swords were made consisting of steel folded many times to produce thousands of layers, edge-hardened so that it could be honed razor-sharp.

Swords were passed from hand to hand as the greatest of presents, and from generation to generation as the most important possession of the family, or buried with the dead to provide protection in the afterlife. A fine blade is more permanent than the warriors who wield it. This theme recurs throughout heroic literature. We read, for example, in *Njal's Saga* of Sharphedin, trapped in fire with his legs burned below the knees, dead with open eyes, who drove his beloved axe deep into the wooden wall of the house in order to preserve the temper of its edge from the heat. And who can fail to thrill to Tennyson's description of Arthur's acquisition of Excalibur in 'The Passing of Arthur':

And Arthur rowed across and took it, rich
With jewels, elfin urim in the hilt,
Bewildering heart and eye – the blade so bright,
That men are blinded by it – on one side,
Graven in the oldest tongue of all this world,
"Take me", but turn the blade and ye shall see,
And written in the language that ye speak yourself,
"Cast me Away". And sad was Arthur. . . .

For swords survive their owners and move around the world to be mounted and remounted as customs change. I have by my side examples which serve as constant reminders of this intermarriage of the noble arm. An English soldier's plug bayonet, doubtless taken in battle two centuries ago, mounted with an ivory and brass hilt as a *skean dhu*, the 'black dagger' which the Scot carries in his sock. A Russian *shashqa* with a gilt hilt on an eighteenth-century European sabre, to which the head of Christ has been added, cut from the body of a fallen cavalryman on a twentieth-century battlefield where swords should have had no place. . . . And an early European broadsword mounted in India in *firangi* style.

As the instrument which takes or gives life, the sword is often embellished with a *memento mori* or a religious inscription. The names of saints are sometimes carved in the runnels of European rapiers; many Japanese blades bear Sanskrit invocations to Buddhist deities; 'magic numbers' are inlaid in gold near the top of Persian *shamshir* blades. Indeed for some races the sword is a magical implement used, like the *vajra*-hilted *purbhu* of Tibet, solely for religious ceremony. In ancient Japan the sword was the instrument of purification and exorcism in the Shinto religion.

In the West it is said that the pen is mightier than the sword. Napoleon Bonaparte is recorded as having said: 'There are only two powers in the world, the sword and the mind. In the long run the sword is always beaten by the mind.' But in Japan the proverb is 'bumbu no ichi', meaning 'pen and sword in accord'. For the Japanese swordsman fencing exercises were and are intellectual endeavours. He practices traditional techniques with the wooden sword until he is no longer fooled by his opponent, and comes to behave naturally, reaching with his sword into the true heart of things. The enlightened nineteenth-century Japanese swordsman Yamaoka Tesshu spoke of the true sword as being the sword of the mind, and fortified with that truth, he was invincible in combat. The study of swordplay therefore transcends mere skill in combat. The ultimate aim of swordsmanship is to 'defeat oneself' and rise above the ordinary concept of life and death. It is one of many paths which may be followed by the student of Zen.

In India and throughout the Buddhist East, as the attribute of bodhisattvas and deva kings, the sword represents the severance of the illusionary world from the ultimately real world. The cut itself is the key to spiritual enlightenment.

Small wonder then that the sword remains an emblem of temporal and spiritual excellence, and is still, even today, the focus for that most noble study, the search for the meaning of life and death. The sword represents man's striving, through technology and just dealing, to better himself and his society, and to quell that which walks as evil in our midst.

1 STONE, BRONZE AND IRON

Anthony Harding

Of all the multifold weapons of war and destruction, the sword more than any other epitomises the story of man's inhumanity to man. In every age and every era of technology – at least since the third millennium BC – our metaphors and aphorisms have reflected a situation in which the weapon of death, held in the hand and wielded face to face, was one with blade and handle, specially created for stabbing, thrusting, slashing and cutting.

Before metal was worked, wood and stone were shaped into offensive weapons, and one should not underestimate the power of such 'primitive' implements to cause harm. Dagger, dirk, rapier and sword all stem from the dark millennia prior to the invention of writing and the recording of events on clay or papyrus.

Not all ancient swords and daggers were designed to be used in battle – far from it. Just as many items of a modern soldier's equipment are purely ceremonial, so were many ancient weapons and pieces of armour. Their function was not to maim and kill but to display wealth, status and power, demonstrate artistic or technical skill, or strike terror, Goliath-style, into the opposition. We are apt to forget that such purposes must have played a major role in the creation and use of objects in the ancient past, but it is crucial that we remember it, as we shall shortly see.

The nomenclature of ancient weapons is a controversial area because there are no contemporary written records which give us clues as to how they were used. However, a number of authorities have divided ancient swords and daggers into groups according to their length. Colonel D.H. Gordon, a British army officer trained in sabre and bayonet fencing before World War I, made a special study of ancient swords and their probable functions, and suggested that weapons less than 14 ins/35.5 cm long should be classed as daggers, those 14–20 ins/35.5–51 cm long as dirks, those 20–28 ins/51–71 cm long as short swords, and anything over that length as long swords. In fact most prehistoric daggers are under 12 ins/30.5 cm in length and were clearly designed for stabbing or cutting at close quarters, but the precise function of longer weapons is more dependent on the form of their blade.

Narrow pointed blades, for example, commonly referred to as 'rapiers', were probably thrusting weapons. Wider, stouter blades, such as those found on weapons commonly referred to as 'cut-and-thrust' swords, would have been used for hacking and cutting as well as thrusting. However, ancient warfare was not always conducted using swords and daggers. The Assyrians, for example, relied on an entirely different panoply of arms.

Early hilt weapons

The earliest weapons intended for use against the person were of flint and other stones such as obsidian, sharpened to a fine edge by a process known as pressure flaking. This involved removing fine flakes of stone by applying pressure with a pointed piece of hard wood or antler. Even in the early part of the Upper Palaeolithic pressure-flaking was a fine art, enabling the flint-knapper to produce a cutting edge of carefully controlled form. The results of this expertise can be seen on the laurel-leaf points of the Solutrean period (named after the prehistoric site of La Solutré near Macon in Burgundy), but there is no certainty that such objects were used in fighting or indeed for any utilitarian purpose and no evidence that they were hafted or hilted. For this one has to wait until the Neolithic period and the advent of farming cultures.

A series of beautifully pressure-flaked projectile points and daggers were excavated from the early farming village of Çatal Hüyük in central Anatolia. One of the points, which had the remains of a leather sheath around it, may have been a primitive form of dagger, but the method of attaching a handle is not clear. The daggers – they are clearly daggers since they have broad tangs and the remnants of bone hilts fastened to them with lime, or lime and resin, and wound round with twine – are much more impressive. The blades are broad, pressure-flaked on one side and ground on the other. One example is complete, with a handle in the form of a snake, with pointillé decoration imitating a snake's scaly skin.

Such masterpieces of the knapper's art also occur in pre- and proto-Dynastic Egypt, unfortunately without precise archaeological contexts. From Gebel el-Arak north of Luxor comes a dagger with a bone handle decorated with elaborate scenes of human and animal figures. Another example has gold hilt plates, with snake motifs on one side and animals on the other. However the overall appearance of these weapons, with their flat, broad blades, suggests that they were for ceremonial use rather than hand-to-hand combat.

The first metal weapons

The first metal used with any frequency for making tools and weapons was unalloyed copper. Daggers made of copper are usually flat, with a simple tang, and reflect the relatively uncomplicated technology involved. With the advent of copper alloys, however, notably tin-bronze, the bronzesmith was able to achieve a much harder metal, especially when it was hot-forged. The Bronze Age, by which is meant the first fully metal-using era of human development, was therefore an age of great technical advances in the handling of weapon-making materials.

The early history of hilted weapons made from metal, in the early centres of civilization, is almost entirely concerned with short weapons, daggers in fact, although they have often been called swords. As we shall see, swords proper did not develop until the second millennium BC, and even when they did, some areas – notably Egypt – made little use of them until the Iron Age, preferring to retain an armoury based on the bow, the spear and special local forms. The dagger was only used for hand-to-hand fighting, presumably to deliver the *coup de grâce* against an opponent already in difficulties from the effects of longer-range weapons.

Short daggers of various forms appear widely through the Near East in the third and second millennia BC. In the highlands of Iran, prototype daggers were in use even during the fourth millennium. These early forms were tanged and often rivetted, the rivets attaching the grip to the tang. The grip would normally have been of organic materials such as wood and bone. An ivory grip survives on a dagger found at Kish near Babylon in Mesopotamia, for example. Graves of the Early Dynastic period in Mesopotamia quite frequently contained such daggers, usually

Above Flint dagger with bone hilt in the form of a snake, Çatal Hüyük, central Turkey, sixth millennium BC.

Opposite page Ivory-handled flint knife from Gebel el-Arak, Nile Valley, fourth millennium BC. The handle depicts a battle, apparently between Egyptians (shaven heads and arc-shaped boats) and easterners (with long hair and high-prowed boats).

Right Gold dagger and sheath from Tomb PG/580, one of the 'Royal Tombs' of Ur, southern Mesopotamia, mid-third millennium BC. The blade, handle decoration and sheath are of gold.

Below left Gold dagger and sheath from the tomb of Ahhotpe, mother of the Pharaoh Ahmosis I, at Thebes. The grip is of carved wood overlaid with silver, with triangular reservations for electrum, carnelian and lapis lazuli inserts. The blade is gold, with inlays of niello and gold wire bearing the name and titles of Ahmosis (ruled 1570–46 BC). The heads on the pommel may represent the goddess Hathor.

Below right Egyptian bronze dagger with ivory pommel, first half of second millennium BC.

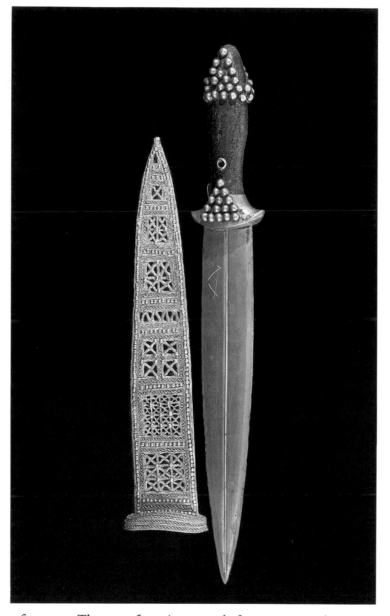

were found at Byblos in Lebanon in one of the hoards of material near the Obelisk Temple. These have hilts and scabbards decorated with processional scenes and heraldic animals. Three magnificent examples come from the tomb of Ahhotpe, mother of the Pharoah Ahmosis I (*c.*1570–1546 BC). One bears the cartouche of Ahmosis himself and is a kingly weapon in every sense. The wooden hilt has a sheet silver overlay with inlays of white gold, carnelian and lapis lazuli, the pommel has four female heads of inlaid gold sheet, the shoulder of the blade bears a bovine head in sheet gold, and the blade is of gold with an inlaid midrib. A leather sheath ornamented with sheet gold completes the effect. Because of its technical and esthetic resemblance to daggers found in the Shaft Graves of Mycenae, some authorities have suggested that it may have been made in the Aegean and sent to Egypt by way of trade or diplomatic exchange. A second blade in the Ahhotpe tomb is of a gold-bronze alloy, with a round-sectioned gold handle swelling out to a terminal disc. A third dagger, shorter than the other two, has rounded sides to the upper part of the blade to provide a comfortable grip, for there is no handle in the ordinary sense, just a large pommel attached to a wing-like termination. The blade is of gold-bronze, the 'handle' of gold, and the pommel of wood with silver overlay.

Still more magnificent are the daggers of Tutankhamun (d. *c.*1350 BC) one of gold, the other of iron. The gold blade is decorated with simple central grooves with a foliate and floral design at the head. The handle, which does not reveal the means by which it is fastened to the tang, is ornamented with alternating bands of geometric designs in granulated goldwork and naturalistic designs in gold cloisonné inset with precious stones and glass. Gold wire in a rope pattern at the base of the hilt conveys the impression of a twine binding of the kind used on flint daggers. The pommel bears the king's cartouches in gold, and gold cloisonné designs. The magnificent sheath is also of gold, with a feather pattern on one side and a scene of animals and stylized plants on the other. Some scholars detect foreign, perhaps Syrian or Aegean, influences on this piece.

Depicted in the famous rock reliefs at the sanctuary of Yazılıkaya, near the Hittite capital of Boğazköy in central Anatolia, is another kind of dagger or sword dating from the latter part of the second millennium. Not much of the blade is visible in the relief, which is carved so as to disappear into the ground, but the hilt is clearly formed of a human head and four crouching lions, two along the blade axis and two across it. These may have been representations of a Hittite underworld deity.

As can be seen, a considerable number of different dagger types of tanged and rivetted construction existed in the Ancient Near East. They were serviceable weapons, but not so serviceable that improvements could not be made. The next important step in the development of hand-to-hand weapons was a technical one, that of casting the hilt in one piece with the blade. This made the fastening of the grip or handle to the blade much more efficient

of copper. The use of precious metals for weapon-making was exceptional, although the Royal Tombs of Ur, dating from the latter part of the third millennium, contained two superb gold daggers. One has a handle of lapis lazuli decorated with tiny gold balls and a beautiful openwork sheath. The other has a handle with incurved sides, presumably to fit the hand, and a hemispherical pommel. A copper dagger from Ur terminates in a huge crescent-shaped pommel. Other forms have pointed blades and triangular tangs, or leaf-shaped blades reinforced with a midrib.

Short rivetted daggers of the kind described above are also found in Old Kingdom Egypt, Palestine and Syria, and continued in use through much of the second millennium. Some were extremely elaborate in their decoration. Several superb examples and durable, and led to the practice of hammering up the edges of the hilt into 'flanges'. Flange-hilted weapons, which make their first appearance in the early centuries of the second millennium, became common throughout the Eastern Mediterranean and Near East, and can be followed through to Late Bronze Age Iran, where the famous Luristan bronzes include versions of the form. In some cases, the handle was cast not as a flat flanged plate but as a solid metal projection round in cross-section, sometimes with a rounded or T-shaped termination for the addition of a pommel. A number of these all-in-one weapons cast in bronze, mostly without provenance but in one case allegedly from the Kermanshah cave, come from Luristan in northwestern Iran. Some bear the names of late second-millennium Babylonian kings and may therefore be Babylonian products; how they reached the remote fastnesses of Iran is a matter for speculation. They are distinguished by their crescentic T-shaped pommels and by having a nick or indentation on the edge of the upper part of the blade. Some also have shouldered hilts.

As already mentioned, short dagger-like weapons were the norm in Egypt and the Near East throughout the third millennium, but during the second millennium weapons of greater length started to develop, perhaps because of new fighting techniques associated with mounted warfare. The first signs of the change date back to the late third millennium and the royal tombs of Alaca Hüyük in central Anatolia. The longest of the swords found at Alaca Hüyük measures 32 ins/82 cm. Like its fellows it has a flat blade with straight sides and is rather too light, in addition to being poorly hafted, to have been very effective. These swords do, however, complement the many other beautiful and prestigious objects in the Alaca tombs, indicating the rise of a privileged class, perhaps expert in the arts of war.

After this period true swords are hard to find in the Near East. An early second-millennium piece from Byblos in Lebanon, found accompanied by a great many shorter tanged weapons, is 20½ ins/57 cm long and has a midrib to give it greater weight and rigidity. Long straight daggers or dirks have also been found in Middle Bronze Age tombs at Jericho on the north shore of the Dead Sea. But really the story of the sword begins in Crete. Later examples from Ugarit in Syria and elsewhere in the Near East are merely echoes of the Bronze Age world to the west and north.

We cannot leave the ancient Near East without mention of the 'sickle sword' or scimitar, and its more mundane relative, the curved sword. Representations of swords with curving blades, probably dating from the the third millennium in Babylonia, have been found at the Early Dynastic site of Tello. And from a tomb at Byblos in Lebanon dating from the reign of Amenemhet III (1842–1797 BC) have come several magnificent examples of the real thing. One has a bronze blade reinforced by a rib which ends in a gold uraeus or sacred serpent encrusted with silver, and a wooden hilt decorated with gold rosettes. At this time, however, curved blades seem to have been restricted to western Asia. Later, however, the Egyptians adopted them and the tomb of Tutankhamun (d. c.1350 BC) includes two splendid examples

Left Relief carving of a sword in the rock sanctuary at Yazılıkaya, near the Hittite capital of Boğazköy, central Turkey. The handle is in the form of a human head and four lions; the blade disappears into the ground and is thought to represent an underworld deity. Thirteenth century BC.

Below Sickle sword from Gezer, Palestine. Similar weapons are frequently depicted in Ancient Near Eastern art, and in Egypt served as a symbol of authority. Fourteenth century BC.

Bottom Gold dagger from the tomb of Tutankhamun, Valley of the Kings, Thebes. The blade is of gold, the handle of granulated goldwork and gold cloisonné inlaid with glass and precious stones. Fourteenth century BC.

Below right Dagger from a *tholos* tomb at Rutsi near Pylos (top) and two views of a similar weapon (below) from Shaft Grave IV at Mycenae. Both weapons date from the sixteenth century BC. The blades are of bronze, and were rivetted to handles of organic material, the rivets being capped with gold. The inlays, showing nautili swimming, a lion hunt and leopards attacking gazelles, are of gold, silver and niello. These superb weapons were clearly intended for display rather than fighting.

Below Painted stone depicting the Pharaoh Rameses III (ruled 1198–1166 BC) wielding a curved sword against the Canaanites.

with wooden hilt plates. Curved blades were obviously intended for delivering slashing blows, but the very gentle curve on one of Tutankhamun's blades suggests that it would have been useful for thrusting too. A version of the sickle sword also appears in Anatolia, where the marching warriors on the rock reliefs at Yazılıkaya have curved blades held up on their shoulders. The figures carved on the King's Gate at Boğazköy and on the facade at Alaca have sickle-type swords at their waists, with the extra Hittite embellishment of a curled-up tip.

The Aegean world

In complete contrast to the great cities and states of Egypt and the Near East, the glorious civilizations of Bronze Age Greece found that daggers or short swords were far from adequate for their needs. In the third millennium BC short rivetted daggers prevailed, but in the early centuries of the second millennium Greek smiths, perhaps obeying the same trend as that which influenced Levantine craftsmen, began to extend the length of their weapons very considerably.

These developments are hard to date precisely, but in Crete at least they seem to have coincided with the major advances in administration and settlement complexity generally referred to as the Palace Period. Swords excavated from the palace at Mallia in northern Crete, and from a cave-sanctuary at Arkalochori in the mountains of the central massif, were probably made in the seventeenth century BC, before the end of the First Palace Period, the first main phase of palace building. These magnificent weapons, some with hilt plates ornamented with sheet gold, are nearly 39 ins/100 cm long. But the deadliness of their appearance – a combination of a long narrow profile and a high stepped central reinforcement or midrib – is illusory. A small tang and two rivets in the shoulder are a precarious way of attaching a hilt if one intends to use a weapon with any force. So was display the primary function of these elegant weapons? At all events, the form rapidly became obsolete.

The absence of fortifications around Cretan palaces and the nature of Minoan life as depicted on wall paintings have usually been taken to mean that the Minoans were not greatly interested in fighting, or not greatly involved in it. But the recent discovery in a house at Knossos of the bones of four children bearing clear signs of cut marks – an indication of cannibalism? – is a sobering reminder that edged weapons were used against the person even by the 'civilized' Minoans. Perhaps the picture painted by Sir Arthur Evans and other Minoan archaeologists is rather too rosy.

In contrast to the 'peaceful' Minoans, the mainland Greeks or Mycenaeans who appeared around 1600 BC, and who took over as rulers of the Aegean from about 1450 BC, were distinctly warlike. Hunting and fighting scenes are depicted on many artefacts, on seals and rings for example, and weapons of all kinds, especially swords and daggers, appear in considerable quantity.

The bladed weapons found in the famous Shaft Graves of Mycenae, which date from the fifteenth and sixteenth centuries BC, are of three distinct kinds. First there are a number of long thin swords or 'rapiers' similar to those seen in Crete. These, like all the other Shaft Grave weapons, are elaborately decorated with gold on the hilt and upper blade, and sometimes with incised designs on the midrib. Then there are a number of shorter, tapering swords of lenticular or rhomboidal cross-section, with a quite distinct handle separated from the blade by a shoulder with pointed ends. The metal of the hilt and shoulder is hammered up into a flange in order to retain the hilt plates, which are further secured by a series of rivets. Finally there are the short daggers, with rivetted handles and stout tapering blades. Some of the blades are decorated with inlay work, which involved fastening gold and silver figures made of various alloys to thin plates of copper and filling the intervening spaces with niello, a black compound made of copper, lead and sulphur, then slotting the copper plates into recessed areas on the blade. Among the scenes depicted are a leopard stalking ducks in a papyrus swamp, a lion hunt, a lion attacking gazelles, leopards in a rocky landscape, and nautili swimming.

These beautiful objects, superb both technically and esthetically, make an important point in a very graphic way: weapons of

war often serve functions which are far from utilitarian. They also tell us that the princes of Mycenae commanded the services of the most skilled craftsmen of the age.

In the centuries which followed, the Mycenaeans, like their neighbours the Hittites, took care to defend themselves behind massive fortifications, the scale of which can still be seen at Mycenae and Tiryns. That they expected attacks is evident from the precautions they took against siege, including the elementary precaution of placing water supplies inside their citadels. They also developed full suits of armour, as the panoply from a tomb at Dendra not far from Mycenae shows. This is extremely cumbersome and heavy, and one hopes that the poor fellow who wore it did not also have to fight in it!

Swords of the period 1400–1200 BC, when Mycenaean influence was at its height in the Aegean and Eastern Mediterranean, invariably had an integral hilt of the flanged variety, and sometimes an integral pommel as well, or rather a T-shaped tang terminal to which a knob of ivory, stone or wood could be attached. Several variants developed on the general flanged hilt theme, notably 'horned' or rounded lobate shoulders at the junction of blade and hilt. Some of these long-bladed, flange-hilted weapons, including an example found in the *tholos* or beehive tomb at Dendra, were elaborately decorated. Some were also found accompanied by short broad-bladed daggers.

It was from the latter, it seems, that the standard short sword of the late Mycenean period (1200–1100 BC) developed. This had a broad blade 12–16 ins/30–40 cm long which tapered sharply towards the tip, square flanged shoulders, a straight flanged hilt, and an integral T-shaped pommel. It was not a glorious weapon, but it seems to have been popular over a wide area. An example is known from southern Italy and a fragment is even to be found in Truro Museum in Cornwall, allegedly found in a barrow near the Cornish village of Pelynt. Whether these weapons in foreign parts are the result of adventurers, far-flung trading enterprises, or modern collecting is hard to say, but there is good evidence, on other grounds, for a direct connection between Greece and the distant shores of Albion in the Bronze Age. Amber beads of British type have been found in the Shaft Graves of Mycenae, for example.

At all events these sturdy short swords marked the last gasp of purely indigenous sword development in Greece. Times were changing, and the next step in the story of the sword is a central European one.

The European dimension

The invention of the sword in Europe was, in all probability, quite separate from innovations in the Near East and the Aegean. Dating becomes more difficult as one moves away from the Eastern Mediterranean and from civilizations where written records enable an absolute chronology to be constructed, but 'barbarian' Europe's first swords were probably produced in east-

Left The Dendra 'panoply' (suit of armour) from a Mycenean chamber tomb of *c.*1400 BC. The helmet is made of boar's tusks and the cuirass is of bronze. Such heavy armour must have been awkward to fight in.

Left below Dagger with gold hilt excavated from a private house (Quartier Mu) at Mallia, Crete, Middle Minoan II period. The blade is fastened to the hilt by rivets, and the hilt itself, of organic material, is covered with a gold sleeve in openwork. A flat disc-like pommel completes the weapon.

Below Sword hilt from the beehive tomb at Dendra near Mycenae, *c.*1400 BC. The hilt plates and pommel are completely covered with elaborately ornamented gold sheet.

13

Right Flint dagger from Hindgavl, Denmark, probably third millennium BC. The exceptionally high quality of flint-working in the North enabled very effective weapons to be made in flint long after metal had become common further south.

Below Metal and flint swords from Denmark, second millennium BC. The longer weapon is a bronze sword from Torupgårde, Lolland; the other is a flint imitation of a metal sword, from Atte, Jutland. Such imitations were a response by the metal-less areas of the North to the new technology already available in the South.

central Europe around the middle of the second millennium BC, just as Mycenaean civilization began to dominate the Aegean.

As we have already seen, flint and other stones were used to make the earliest sharp-edged implements, and in areas where flint was abundant edged weapons were made in large quantities. In Denmark, for example, superbly worked flint blades made by pressure flaking were commonplace. In fact flint working was such an art and the tradition so deeply ingrained that the first metal daggers and swords imported into Northern Europe were slavishly copied in flint, even down to such details as rivets, which were purely skeuomorphic, imitating form but not function. Interestingly, Nordic flint weapons include copies of curved swords with curled-up tips, a quirk peculiar to the Hittites. Curved swords made of metal only occur in Scandinavia, one famous example from Rorby in Zealand being decorated with a ship, and in a single find at Nikolaev at the mouth of the Southern Bug river in the Ukraine.

By the time the Copper Age cultures of Europe – known to us principally by the types of pottery they made – came into being, flat tanged or rivetted copper daggers were used over a wide area. Although they were probably only marginally more effective than their flint or stone counterparts, they had the advantage of being less likely to chip, and they could be melted down and re-worked. The process of resharpening would have been more reliable too. Certainly the use and popularity of copper daggers increased dramatically through the third millennium and into the second.

By the Early Bronze Age, a number of area-specific tanged or rivetted forms were being produced in Europe. In many cases the blade was triangular, evenly tapering from hilt to blade tip, and fastened to the hilt by a row of rivets. In Northwest Europe the hilt was sometimes elaborately decorated. This is the case with several specimens found in France, at Saint-Adrien in Brittany for example. A most amazing hilt was also found on a weapon from the famous Bush Barrow grave near Stonehenge in southern England. Made of wood, it is decorated with thousands of tiny gold nails forming a zig-zag pattern. Indeed the nails are so small that it has been suggested that the maker may have used a rock crystal lens to bring them into focus as he worked. Elsewhere it was the practice to cast a metal hilt onto the blade, or decorate the blade with geometric designs. Representations of warriors, often very schematic, on statue-menhirs and other carved stones of the period give us some idea of the appearance of the Early Bronze Age man of war.

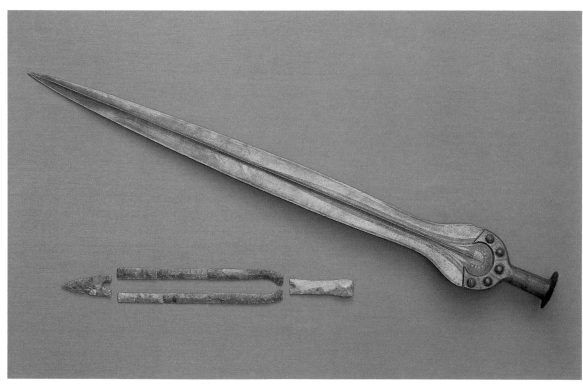

We cannot leave the subject of Early Bronze Age daggers without mentioning an extraordinary spin-off from the dagger – or was it from the battle axe? – and that is the Bronze Age 'halberd'. This was not a halberd in the proper sense, but a species of dagger mounted at right angles to its handle. The blade was heavy and usually asymmetrical, with a broad central raised rib and a triangular pattern of large rivet holes in the heel. In parts of northern Europe the hilt or haft was sometimes made of metal, with skeuomorphic bands around it to represent leather thongs. What are believed to be miniature copies of such weapons, perhaps toys, have been found in Early Bronze Age graves in southern England – with gold bindings! Of all the strange weapons of war ever invented, the Bronze Age halberd is surely one of the strangest. It must have been peculiarly useless in combat, for the blade is too stout for the tip to have been really sharp, and one would not have been able to wield the cutting edge effectively. Unsurprisingly, this extraordinary invention had a strictly limited life, appearing and disappearing in the early part of the second millennium.

From the small seeds of the rivetted dagger great things were to come. First of all, the blade grew longer, but without any fundamental change in the method of hilt attachment. Long weapons or 'rapiers' became common in many areas of Western Europe in the middle part of the European Bronze Age, that is during the middle centuries of the second millennium. But still the European smith had not solved the biggest headache of prehistoric sword-making: how was a durable join between hilt and blade to be achieved? We can easily guess – and the number of weapons with broken rivet holes is eloquent testimony to this – that the useful life of rivetted daggers, swords and rapiers must have been extremely short. If hilt and blade parted company in the heat of battle, the result was presumably fatal, or at least embarrassing. Effective hilt attachment was absolutely essential.

The method eventually hit upon was essentially the same as that adopted in the Aegean, to cast the blade and hilt in one piece, punching rivets through the hilt and shoulder and hammering up flanges to keep the hilt plates firmly in position. After an initial phase during which different forms of blade and tang were

Below left An elaborately decorated bronze sword from Hajdúsámson, Hungary (above) and 'halberds' of bronze from Dieskau, East Germany (below).

The sword, which dates from the middle of the second millennium BC, is decorated with engraved concentric arcs and the solid metal of the hilt is cast on and fastened by rivets. The halberds, which are of slightly earlier date, have metal handles cast onto the blade. Notice the skeuomorphic bindings.

Below 'Statue-stelae' from Pontevecchio, northwest Italy. These Early Bronze Age monuments depict two men and a woman in stylized form, the men with triangular-bladed daggers at the waist.

Right A collection of Late Bronze Age grip-tongue swords from Bavaria. The two swords on the left have solid metal hilts.

experimented with, the classic flange-hilted or 'grip-tongue' sword emerged. This had a long blade which swelled into a roughly triangular shoulder with a tongue-like grip projecting from it. Rivets, sometimes a dozen or more of them, were used to fasten the hilt plates to the shoulder and tongue. At the end of the grip the tongue often flared out in projections or 'ears' to take the pommel.

As time went on, European smiths began to experiment with variations on this theme. Instead of having parallel sides, blades sometimes swelled out in a broad leaf shape, giving extra weight and potency to blows struck with them. Around the coasts of Britain, France and Iberia a curious 'carp's tongue' blade profile developed – the inventive simile reflects the fact that many early typologists emanated from the hunting and fishing classes. The lower part of the blade, which was long, stout and straight-edged, tapered suddenly to a point.

Blade cross-sections also varied. The basic form was lenticular, but sometimes an angular or stepped central swelling was provided, often with grooves or 'blood channels' on either side of it, probably to reduce weight. The upper few inches of the blade edge were often milled – a primitive form of ricasso – to prevent an opponent's sword sliding up towards the hand, and in some areas blades were decorated with incised lines, usually concentric arcs forming geometric patterns.

Swords of the general kind described above became standard throughout Europe during the Late Bronze Age or Urnfield Period, when the phenomenon of cremation burial and the placing of ashes in urns became almost universal. From the Ukraine and Romania in the east to Ireland and Spain in the west, and from Sweden in the north to Italy in the south, everyone used a form of grip-tongue sword. And, interestingly, even Late Mycenaean Greece succumbed to the fashion. After 1200 BC the grip-tongue sword of 'European' type became the standard long sword in Greece, although local short swords continued to be made. Grip-tongue swords also appear in Cyprus and Egypt and at Ugarit in Syria. One example, from Tell Firaun in the Nile Delta, bears the cartouche of the Egyptian Pharoah Seti II (*c.* 1223–1217 BC). A similar find, or rather different form, was made at Ugarit, bearing the cartouche of Seti II's predecessor Merneptah (1236–1223 BC). However, there is some doubt as to whether this weapon is of European manufacture.

Scholars have long sought a satisfactory explanation for the wide dispersal of grip-tongue swords, and their occurrence in the rich civilizations of the Near East has led to speculation that European mercenaries might have taken them on campaigns in the Mediterranean. This was the period when Egyptian records refer to the Peoples of the Sea, groups of invaders who caused trouble throughout the Eastern Mediterranean, and who may have brought about the downfall of Ugarit, Tyre and Sidon, then part of the Egyptian Empire. Certainly they clashed with the Egyptians on at least two occasions, though on the first of these

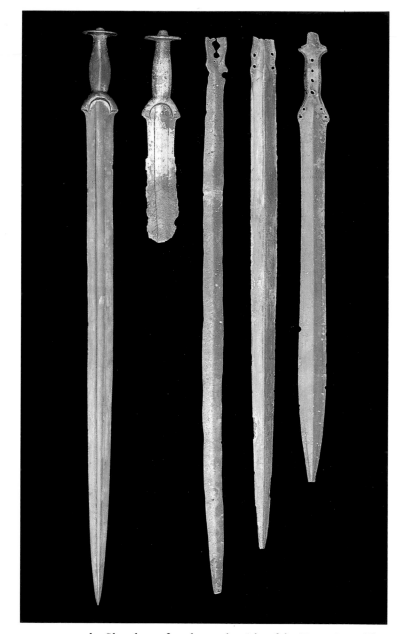

one group, the Shardana, fought on the side of the Egyptians. The presence of northern mercenaries in Egypt and the Levant, bearing their characteristic weaponry, is not implausible.

The grip-tongue sword was not the only achievement of the smiths of Bronze Age Europe. Technically more advanced was the metal-hilted sword which looked practically the same as the grip-tongue sword, even down to details such as skeuomorphic rivet heads, but it was hafted rather differently. A tube of metal of elliptical cross-section was cast onto the upper part of the blade so that it merged with the triangular shoulder. The end of the grip usually swelled to a disc, often with a projecting circular knob, button or bowl to stop the sword sliding out of the hand. At first the grip was decorated with incised geometric motifs, typically running spirals arranged in bands between raised ribs. Later other decorative techniques, such as openwork, were used, especially in Scandinavia. These metal-hilted swords often survive complete and undamaged, and give an impression of considerable technical mastery. The technique of over-casting, or joining two castings together, did indeed represent a significant step forward, and must have been much more reliable than the simple rivetting technique that preceded it.

Inter-group warfare was an important aspect of the Bronze Age, fortifications appearing in abundance from the beginning of the first millennium BC. These defensive works, often involving many thousands of man-hours in their construction, illustrate graphically how the development of ever more effective weaponry made it necessary to secure the home base.

The age of iron

It used to be thought that knowledge of iron-working was restricted to certain early cultures, notably the Hittites in Anatolia and the Philistines in the Levant. Today we know that such a picture is unrealistic. The technology for working iron was clearly present, although not widespread, in many of the states of the Near East. Iron objects were made and used throughout the Bronze Age, albeit in small numbers, but after 1200 BC the amount of iron available seems to have increased considerably, especially in Syria, Palestine, Cyprus and Greece. In Europe iron gradually became more common during the Late Bronze Age and universal after about 700 BC.

Iron is much more abundant than copper and more evenly distributed across the world. It can also be forged into much harder, sharper weapons than either copper or bronze. However, bronze continued to be used as the main material for objects requiring elaborate ornamentation. Iron objects may also have been decorated but the poor condition in which many survive makes this an unsafe assumption.

In many areas, early Iron Age swords differed little from those in use in the Bronze Age. In the Near East the evidence for the use of swords is somewhat contradictory. The books of the Bible relating to the settlement of Palestine and the founding of Jerusalem make frequent reference to swords. The left-handed Ehud 'made him a dagger [short sword] which had two edges, of a cubit in length, and did gird it under his raiment upon his right thigh'. His intention was to assassinate King Eglon of Moab with it, and Judges 3 goes on to give a very graphic account of the business. David uses Goliath's sword to cut off Goliath's head (1 Samuel 17.51), although unlike the Philistine champion's spear and armour, his sword is not described as anything special. Saul, routed by the Philistines, says to his armour-bearer: 'Draw thy sword and thrust me through with it lest these uncircumcised come and thrust me through and abuse me.' His armour-bearer refused, so Saul 'took a sword and fell upon it' (1 Samuel 31.4).

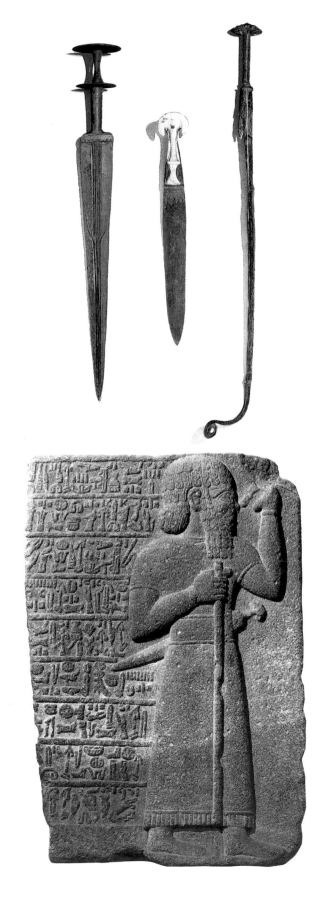

Left Three swords from northwest Iran (Luristan and Azerbaijan), tenth–ninth century BC. In these pieces the hilt is cast in one piece with the blade, a notable technical advance over tanged and rivetted handles.

Below Orthostat relief of the Neo-Hittite period (ninth–eighth century BC) from Carchemish, depicting King Katuwas holding a staff and wearing a sword on his left hip.

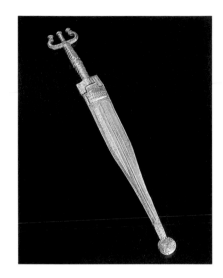

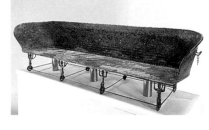

Yet there are few archaeological finds to bear out the Old Testament's constant references to 'smiting with the sword' or 'putting to the sword', even in the area of Philistine supremacy. Relief carvings on the funerary temple of Rameses III (d. 1153 BC) at Medinet Habu on the west bank of the Nile opposite Luxor show the Sea Peoples being defeated at a great battle in the Nile Delta. Some of the figures are carrying medium length swords with markedly triangular blades not dissimilar to certain archaeological examples which have a tapering blade with a high pointed midrib and a tongue-like tang. But really the amount of information provided by Egyptian reliefs is scanty compared with that given in Assyrian reliefs from the great palaces of Nimrud, Khorsabad and Nineveh, celebrating the conquests of the Assyrian kings between the early ninth and the late seventh century BC.

The Assyrians, the most advanced of the Near Eastern peoples in the arts of war in the Iron Age, made extensive use of swords and daggers as part of the regular armament of both cavalry and infantry. The most important offensive weapons were the spear, the bow and the sling, but the *namsaru*, a sword with a straight slender blade, is often depicted slung at the waist, occasionally supported by a shoulder strap. The finer details are hard to make out, but the hilts seem to be elaborately ornamented, and the scabbards terminate in chapes with scroll or lion designs on them. Swords only appear in scenes of hand-to-hand fighting, but this may be because the artists were keen to present an orderly picture of Assyrian military might, with well drilled ranks of soldiers marching into battle. The somewhat cruder sculptures of the same period from Neo-Hittite Carchemish and Zincirli also show warriors equipped with long swords.

In Greece the first Iron Age swords were much the same as their Late Bronze Age predecessors and probably similar to those depicted on a famous Geometric-period amphora from the Dipylon cemetery in Athens. This shows a whole funeral procession – the dead man on his bier, weeping relatives, rows of chariot-borne warriors – and a number of fairly short bladed weapons with pommels, although the latter are indicated merely by lines across the ends of the hilts. A few examples of single-edged weapons, perhaps forebears of the *kopis* of Classical times (see Chapter 2), survive from the Geometric period, although these may have been intended for domestic rather than military use.

Developments in Italy were more complex and varied than those in Greece, perhaps because of the rivalry of the various tribal groupings that emerged during the Iron Age. From these the Etruscan and Roman states eventually sprang. The great cemeteries of Etruria, dating from the tenth to the eight century BC, have produced many weapons, including swords. Grip-tongue swords of various kinds, both bronze and iron, were standard. These were usually quite short, with multiple lines following the blade edges, a grip profiled to fit the hand, and an integral T-shaped pommel. They also had elaborately ornamented scabbards, many of which survive. Geometric designs down the edges of scabbards, sometimes incorporating stylized animals and humans, are typical. As well as grip-tongue weapons there were also metal-hilted swords, some with simple disc pommels but many more with antennae-like pommels which echo contemporary pieces from north of the Alps.

By the seventh century, as Etruscan civilization began to form in central Italy, almost all weapons were being made of iron, some of it mined on the island of Elba, but corrosion and oxidization have taken their toll and it is often difficult to be sure of exact forms. All we can say is that straight swords generally gave way to daggers and to the curved slashing swords also known in Greece. Curved blades were no doubt a Persian influence, the Persian Empire being at its height and maximum extent in 500 BC.

Meanwhile, 'barbarian' or Celtic Europe developed its own distinctive weapon forms. Swords of the early Hallstatt period (700–600 BC), named after the Iron Age cemetery and nearby salt mines at Hallstatt near Salzburg in Austria, were essentially variants on Bronze Age themes, but longer and heavier, with elaborate pommels of roughly conical form. Most had sheaths, but usually only the bronze winged or pouch-like terminal or chape survives. Some of these swords are magnificent weapons, even though undecorated. To own one was a mark of warrior status. In the later Hallstatt period it became less common to bury swords with the dead. Shorter weapons, daggers, were provided instead. The blades were broad but thin, with a double edge, and like most iron weapons after 700 BC they were made from forged carbon steel and finished by grinding. Unfortunately many examples have corroded into the decorated scabbard in which they were buried. The pommel, attached to the thin tang of the blade, often takes the form of two up-curving arms or 'antennae' in the same plane as the blade. Some of these weapons occur in rich, princely graves, such as that excavated in 1978 at Hochdorf in Baden-Wurttemberg. Here, in about 550 BC, a Celtic chieftain was buried, with a gold band around his neck, a gold armlet, a belt and shoes embellished with gold, and an exquisite gold dagger. The couch he rested upon was made of bronze, embossed with ritual dance figures, some of them wielding swords.

During the La Tène period – finds from the Celtic settlement at La Tène, on the edge of Lake Neuchâtel in Switzerland, typify a rich civilization which lasted from about 500 BC until the first century BC – the Celtic genius for sophisticated curvilinear design and fantastic abstractions on natural themes began to assert itself. The standard La Tène period sword was of iron or steel, often pattern-welded by the skilled forging together of different strips of metal. It was also long, double-edged, straight-sided and rather slender, with a long narrow tang onto which were fitted a series of mountings in bronze, probably with organic materials in between. But the scabbards are the chief glory of these swords, decorated as they are with dragons, bird pairs, triskele and other geometric designs, floral and zoomorphic motifs . . . Most are of bronze, fitted with ferrules (small encircling iron bars), reinforcing plates, mouthguards, suspension loops and chapes.

These were the swords which carried the Celts north into Britain and Belgium. In 390 BC Celts from Gaul invaded Italy and sacked Rome, capital of the fledgling Roman Republic. The Greek historian Polybius, describing the Gauls (Celts) at the battle of Telamon in 225 BC, says: 'Very terrifying too were the appearance and the gestures of the naked warriors in front, all in the prime of life, and finely built men, and all in the leading companies richly adorned with gold torques and armlets.' Dionysius of Halicarnassus, another Greek historian living in Rome whose account of Roman history takes one up to 264 BC, tells us about the fighting style of the Gauls: '. . . they would raise their swords aloft and smite after the manner of wild boars, throwing the whole weight of their bodies into the blow like hewers of wood or men digging with mattocks, and again they would deliver crosswise blows aimed at no target, as if they intended to cut to pieces the entire bodies of their adversaries, protective armour and all . . . .' Celtic society was heroic and tribal, and the exploits of great warriors were celebrated in poetry and song, echoes of which survive in epics such as the Ulster Cycle, *Tain Bo Cuailgne* (The Cattle Raid of Cooley).

With the Celts our survey of the swords and hilt weapons of prehistory comes to an end, for already during the late Iron Age we are almost in history, and the story of the subsequent development of the sword becomes part of the story of the Greek and Roman worlds.

Left Hilt of a La Tène sword from Châtenay-Macheron (Haute Marne), La Tène II period (third–second century BC). Notice the human head between the pommel 'ears'.

Below left Sword and scabbard from La Tène, Lake Neuchâtel. Many such deposits have been found at the lake edge. The site may have been a bridge or platform from which arms were ritually thrown into the water.

Opposite page Artefacts from the princely grave at Hochdorf, Baden-Wurttemberg, second half of sixth century BC.

The dagger (top) has an iron blade, but the grip and sheath are of bronze overlaid with gold. The fineness of this piece suggests a display function.

The bronze and iron funerary couch (middle), now fully restored, is supported by eight hand-high female unicyclists riding iron casters. The repoussé warrior figures on the back panel of the couch (bottom) are engaged in a sword dance.

19

2 GREECE AND ROME

Peter Connolly

Right A group of three grip-tongue swords. The two on the left are bronze, late Mycenean (*c.*1200 BC), and come from Kallithea in Greece; blade length is 21½ ins/55 cm and 26½ ins/68 cm respectively. The sword on the right, from Kerameikos in Greece, is of iron and of later date (*c.*820 BC); blade length in this case is 28 ins/72 cm.

The two handles also belong to grip-tongue swords; the one on the left is of bone and comes from Italy, and the other is of bronze.

Far right An iron sword of hoplite type from Vergina, northern Greece (ancient Macedonia), late fourth century BC. Blade length is 16½ ins/42 cm and the hilt is decorated with sheet gold. Although clearly related to the Campovalano type, this is a much shorter and lighter weapon.

Right below Iron hoplite sword from Campovalano, Italy, sixth–fifth century BC. Blade length is 25 ins/63 cm and the handle is of grip-tongue type sandwiched between two pieces of bone and covered with a thin sheet of iron. The scabbard is of iron, decorated with bone inlay at the mouth and chape.

W hen Mycenaean civilization collapsed in the twelfth century BC, Greece entered a 'dark' age. But out of this enigmatic period emerged, four centuries later, a new civilization that was to outshine Mycenae, a civilization whose weapons were of iron rather than bronze. By the time the first Greek city states emerged, towards the end of the ninth century BC, bronze weapons had all but disappeared.

But iron was far more difficult to work than bronze and could not be cast. The technology of the age could do little more than reduce the ore to a rather impure metal laced with slag. Then the slag had to be beaten out before the metal could be forged into a satisfactory blade. During smelting, which was normally done with charcoal, a certain amount of carbon impregnated the iron, automatically converting parts of it to steel – steel is iron with a small percentage of carbon added. However, although the extra hardness of carbon-impregnated steel was recognized and appreciated, the impregnation process was very difficult to control. The result was usually a block of metal of very uneven consistency, varying from soft to hard more or less from one inch to the next. To achieve a more uniform consistency the smith was obliged to beat the metal into long strips, plait it, reheat it until it was white hot, beat it out into new strips, plait them, reheat them, and so on until he had obtained an evenly hard billet of metal. Traces of plaiting can be seen on many archaeological examples.

Archaic and Classical Greece

By the tenth century BC grip-tongue swords (also known, in archaeological circles, as Type 2 swords) were being made of iron. It will be remembered that the grip-tongue design originated in central Europe and made its first appearance in Greece towards the end of the thirteenth century BC. Grip-tongue weapons continued to be made through the 'dark' centuries, gradually evolving into the hoplite sword, the sword carried by the *hoplite* or heavily armed Greek foot-soldier of the Classical period.

The hoplite sword had a double-edged blade about 24 ins/60 cm long, waisted just below the hilt and then widening gradually,

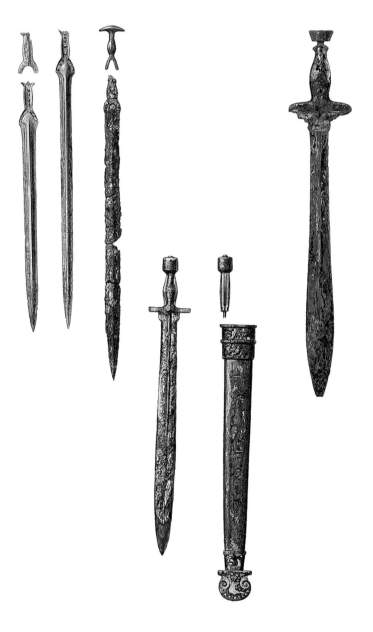

reaching its maximum width just over two-thirds of the way down and then tapering to a point. The tang was flat and very similar to its Bronze Age predecessor, being a complete cross-section of the hilt. The grip was formed by sandwiching the tang between two pieces of bone or wood and covering them, totally or partially, with a thin sheet of metal. The hoplite sword was essentially a slashing weapon, though some examples have long points and could have been very effective cut-and-thrust weapons, and was worn slung from a baldric over the right shoulder so that it hung almost horizontally on the left hip.

The hoplite sword, carried by Greek colonists throughout the length and breadth of the Mediterranean, was adopted by many indigenous peoples. In Italy it was almost universally accepted and remained in use until the Romans adopted the 'Spanish' sword in the third century BC. In fact the best examples of the hoplite sword come from the necropolis of Campovalano di Campli on the Adriatic side of Italy. These swords have iron scabbards inlaid with bone.

It is paradoxical that the most successful sword in the classical era should have been developed by a people who were not swordsmen. The sword was never more than a secondary or back-up weapon for the Greeks. Homer, writing in the eighth century BC, echoes the practices of his own day when he arms his heroes with throwing spears and slashing swords; once they had thrown their spears, they hacked and hewed with their swords.

During the seventh century BC the Greeks evolved the phalanx method of fighting, a method entirely suited to an emerging political system based on the city state. The thinking was that every able-bodied citizen should be able, with minimum training, to take up arms to defend his city. 'Defend' is the operative word here. Although the Greeks won several notable victories over the Persians by going over to the offensive, the phalanx, with its rigid, close-order formation of heavily armed spearmen equipped with large round shields, was essentially a defensive system. Even if the phalanx were forced to retreat, leaving the field to the enemy, casualties would be minimal provided the formation held. Greek spears had a spiked butt, so that if the point broke the

butt end could be used instead. Only if the butt broke would the sword be used. For the average phalangite, fighting with a sword was an act of desperation, for it involved opening up the shield wall. With the exception of the Spartans, few dared to fight in this way.

The hoplite sword appears frequently on Greek vases throughout the Archaic and Classical period, that is from 800–400 BC, but from about 500 BC a new type of sword quite unlike the hoplite weapon began to appear. This was the *kopis*, a single-edged weapon with a slightly S-shaped cutting edge. Few examples have been found in Greece but a large number have come to light in Italy and Corsica. Most of the vases that show this type of sword also come from Italy, which suggests an Italian origin, or perhaps an Asiatic one via Etruscan contacts in the East. Examples from the Etruscan colony of Aleria in Corsica have blades about 24 ins/60 cm long; broadest about three-quarters of the way down.

Above Alexander the Great (356–323 BC) shown on the Issus mosaic from Pompeii. On his left side one can see the handle of a typical hoplite sword, probably the short, light type similar to the example from Vergina.

Above Stages in the evolution of the *kopis*: an example from Corsica (left), from Greece (centre), and from Spain (right). The Corsican weapon is the earliest (sixth century BC) and the Spanish the latest (third–second century BC).

The early *kopis* was a hacking weapon about 24 ins/61 cm long; its successor was sabre-like, as in the Greek example above. In Spain the *kopis* developed into the shorter *falcata*.

Top A Greek vase from Nola in Campania, Italy, early fifth century BC. The kneeling warrior (left) wields a hoplite sword, while his standing companion (far left) wields the massive early *kopis*.

The *kopis* was a heavy hacking or chopping weapon and must have been devastating in hand-to-hand combat. By the same token, it was entirely unsuitable for phalangite tactics. In Italy it appears to have had a comparatively short life, probably disappearing before the middle of the fourth century BC, but in Greece it appears to have been used for much longer, probably mainly by cavalry, eventually evolving into a slimmer sabre-like weapon with a pommel in the shape of a bird's head. The Spaniards also adopted the *kopis*, eventually converting it into the short cut-and-thrust sword known as the *falcata*.

Both the hoplite sword and the *kopis* were adopted by the Macedonians. The hoplite type can be seen, worn by Alexander the Great, on the famous Issus mosaic from Pompeii. By this time, however, it had become much shorter, extant examples having a blade length of only 16–18 ins/40–45 cm. More than anything this reflected the Macedonians' total commitment to the spear and pike. In a pike phalanx there was even less opportunity for swordplay.

Etruscans and Latins

The development of the sword in Greece is clear-cut – there were really only two types, the two-edged hoplite sword and the single-edged *kopis* – and the dagger as a military weapon was virtually unknown. But in Italy, with its mixed population speaking several different languages, not all of them Indo-European, the situation was very different.

During the Early Iron Age a wide variety of swords and daggers, made of both iron and bronze, appear to have been in use. Some had clearly evolved from the same central European grip-tongue type that had been adopted by the Greeks, but others were indigenous. The swords ranged from long slashing weapons to shorter stabbing ones, with blade lengths varying

from 14 ins/35 cm to 26 ins/65 cm. Many of the longer examples had 'antennae' pommels, generally regarded as a Celtic invention.

The daggers of the Villanovan or proto-Etruscan period are of three types: those with leaf-shaped blades appear to have been the most common, others have straight-sided blades narrowing two-thirds of the way down to form a long diamond-sectioned stiletto-type point, and others have triangular blades, evenly tapering from hilt to point. Blades lengths vary, from 10 ins/25 cm to about 16 ins/40 cm. The grip, which was made of wood, bone or even stone, but never bronze, was capped by a T-shaped pommel. In fact 'T-shaped pommel' is something of a misnomer since it describes the splayed ends of the tang to which the pommel was attached rather than the pommel itself, which was usually a bulbous disc. Plenty of tangs survive, but few pommels.

The scabbards found with many of the shorter swords and daggers are made of beaten bronze, and have a cast bronze chape. Originally, they were probably lined with wood. One antennae sword found at Tarquinia in Etruria was still encased in a fragment of a wooden scabbard bound together with bronze wire. Such finds are rare but wood and leather were probably the commonest materials used for making scabbards. Punched decoration on some cast bronze scabbards imitates stitching on leather. The mouth of the scabbard, which was always made separately, is usually missing, which suggests that it was probably made of hide or wood. A few examples in bronze or bone have survived, however.

The military systems in use in Early Iron Age Italy were as diverse as the weaponry, ranging from the loosely-organized, fast-moving and lightly-armed infantry of the tribes occupying the central highlands to the rigid, heavily-armed phalanx of the Greeks who had colonized the coasts of the southern half of the peninsula.

In the seventh century BC the most powerful nation in Italy, the Etruscans, adopted the phalanx, putting themselves on an equal footing with the Greek colonists, their sworn enemies and competitors for the trade of the Western Mediterranean. The phalanx formed only the core of the Etruscan army, however; troops armed in native fashion fought alongside it, adding a degree of flexibility to the Greek system.

The hoplite sword was used everywhere in Italy, even among tribes which did not adopt the phalanx, and by the fifth century BC it and the massive *kopis*, which may have originated in Italy, had superseded all other types of sword. A hoplite sword can be seen slung across the chest of the famous Warrior of Capestrano, a primitive sixth-century statue. A small knife is attached to the front of the scabbard, a feature also found in warrior burials in the Abruzzi area.

Late in the seventh century BC the Etruscans forced their way south across the Tiber, bringing many of the Latin towns, including Rome, under their control. Then, in 509 BC, the Romans rose up against the tyrannical rule of Tarquinius Super-

bus and declared Rome a republic. They did not, however, rid themselves of the Etruscan phalanx system. It clearly had its uses and was retained, for a while at least.

Throughout the fifth century the Latin League, of which Rome was a member, successfully extended its territory to the north, south and east. Conflict with the eastern hill peoples, fighting in loose formation, probably forced the League to adopt more flexible methods of fighting, in which the sword was used to an extent unknown in Greece. Even so, the League was unprepared for what came next.

Towards the end of the fifth century BC the Celts began to arrive in northern Italy, bringing with them a style of fighting that was entirely foreign to both Greece and Italy. They drove the Etruscans out of the Po valley and advanced down the Adriatic coast as far as Ancona. Then, in 390 BC or thereabouts, they burst into central Italy, annihilated the army of the Latin League on the banks of the river Allia, and sacked Rome.

Left The sixth-century BC statue known as the Warrior of Capestrano after the town in central Italy where it was found. The figure has a hoplite type sword suspended from a chest harness, with the handle on the right breast. The position of the handle requires the sword to be drawn upwards, with the palm of the right hand facing forwards and the thumb down. This is the earliest representation of a sword in the traditional Roman position on the right side.

Far left Two daggers and two 'antennae' swords, Early Iron Age.

The two swords are from Fermo, central Italy. The example on the left, with a blade length of 17½ ins/45 cm, has clearly evolved from that Late Bronze Age grip–tongue type. The sword on the right has a bronze scabbard with decoration that appears to echo the stitching of leather-covered examples. Sword blades of this period were made of bronze or iron.

The dagger on the left is from the Etruscan town of Veii, just north of Rome; it has an iron blade about 10½ ins/27 cm long with a stiletto-type point, and a bone hilt and scabbard mouth of bone. The example on the right comes from Tarquinia in Etruria; it has a triangular bronze blade 12 ins/30 cm long and a bronze scabbard.

This defeat was make-or-break time for the Latins; they had to adapt or go under. The causes of the defeat on the Allia were quickly identified and a remedy sought. Individually the Celts were bigger than the Italians and had superior weapons produced by the best iron workers in Europe. The Celtic sword was capable of cutting right through the Italian shield. *En masse* the Celtic charge was so ferocious that the Italians could not withstand it.

It was to deal with the last two problems that the unique combination of *gladius* (sword), *pilum* (heavy javelin) and *scutum* (body shield) was developed. It was this system that conquered the Mediterranean world in the second and first centuries BC.

The change was gradual, and the ancient writers do not tell us how it took place. We know only that the round shield (the phalanx-type shield) was abandoned and that the curved oval shield and helmet were strengthened. It also seems likely that, at first, picked units (*maniples*) of the bravest men in the prime of life, armed with heavy javelin and sword, went out ahead of the main army to take the brunt of the Celtic charge. These front rankers became known as *principes*. The *principes* used their heavy javelins to break up the Celtic charge and then moved in to close quarters with their short thrusting swords.

The new legionary was trained to receive the blow of the Celtic slashing sword on his curved shield, which was strengthened at the top and bottom with a metal rim, and then to go in underneath with his short sword and thrust for the stomach. In this way he compensated for his shorter stature and reach, and took advantage of the fact that his adversary left himself wide open to attack when he raised his arm to strike a blow. If hard pressed, the front rankers would retreat, filtering back through the main body of the army which was still armed in defensive fashion with spear and large shield.

The Roman historian Livy (59 BC – AD 17) gives us a brief, albeit confused, glimpse of this changing system when, in about 340 BC, Rome took command of the Latin League. There were now two groups of swordsmen out ahead of the main body, the *principes* and the *hastati*. The latter appear to have brought the name of 'spearmen' with them in spite of their changed function. Nearly 40 per cent of the army was now equipped with sword and javelin, the rest with spears. However, tactics were still strongly defensive, with the swordsmen always ready to retire behind the spearmen if the going got too difficult.

Roman expansion

During the next sixty years Rome gradually conquered the whole of peninsular Italy, confining the Celts to the Po valley. Then interference in the politics of Sicily brought Rome face to face with her greatest adversary, Carthage. The Romans suffered disaster after disaster, losing nearly half a million men in the half century between 260 and 210 BC, but finally they emerged as masters of the Western Mediterranean. The Celts were driven from the Po valley and Greece was invaded during the early years of the second century BC. In two great battles, Cynoscephalae in 197 and Pydna in 168 BC, the supposedly invincible phalanx of the Macedonians was cut to pieces by the Roman legions. This greatly astonished the Greek world and proved conclusively that the sword was mightier than the spear.

The Greek historian Polybius, who was brought to Rome as a hostage after the battle of Pydna, gives the only comprehensive account of the Roman army of the Republican era, and all later historians must to some extent depend on his description. At the time he was writing (*c.*150 BC), swordsmen made up just over half the strength of a legion, which totalled about 4,200 men. Spearmen, who were mostly veterans and known as *triarii* or *pili*, represented only one-seventh of the total muster, the rest being light-armed troops. Defeats suffered during the Carthaginian wars compelled the Romans to retain some sort of defensive rear rank, but this continued to shrink as tactics became increasingly aggressive, so much so that in the space of fifty years the rear rank disappeared altogether, along with the light-armed troops. From about 100 BC onwards every man was armed with the short thrusting *gladius*, *pilum* and *scutum*, and this continued to be the case for the next 250 years.

Right Silver and iron sword from Atienza, Spain. Dating from the fourth century BC, this sword has all the characteristics – thrusting profile, slight waisting of the blade, long point, frame scabbard with suspension rings – of the later Roman *gladius hispaniensis* or Spanish sword.

Unfortunately we know little, if anything, about the development of the *gladius* during the last four pre-Christian centuries. Not one certain example exists. A fourth-century Etruscan wall painting in the Giglioli tomb at Tarquinia shows a number of *pila* ranged alongside a hoplite shield and sword, which may or may not imply that the Romans were still using the Greek sword at this period. Polybius refers to the sword used by the Roman army as the 'Spanish' sword, which implies a Spanish origin at some time prior to his own day.

The search for the Spanish ancestor of the Roman sword has been extremely difficult because the earliest archaeological examples of Roman swords only date from the first century BC, and come not from Italy but from the Rhineland. They have a long point and the majority are slightly waisted in the middle of the blade. A few swords of a similar type have been found in Spain but these date from the fourth or fifth century BC. The one thing that supports their claim to be the ancestors of the Roman *gladius* is that they have exactly the same type of scabbard, with four attachment rings. The Romans retained these four rings, although they did not use them in the way originally intended.

Polybius gives no clue to the date at which the 'Spanish' sword was adopted, but we can be reasonably sure that it was not as late as the Second Punic War (218–202 BC) when the Romans first invaded Spain, for Polybius lived in the house of Scipio Aemilianus, whose forebears had conquered southern Spain. If the Scipionic clan had had anything to do with introducing the Spanish sword, Polybius would almost certainly have mentioned it. We must assume, therefore, that it was adopted from Spanish mercenaries serving with the Carthaginians during the First Punic War or even earlier – many ancient peoples with territorial ambitions employed mercenaries – or that it was introduced by Spaniards serving in the armies of the Greeks or Etruscans in Italy.

The lack of evidence for the early Roman sword is made even more frustrating by the wealth of evidence for the early Roman dagger, which is never mentioned as a battle weapon. Daggers were common in Italy long before the Roman conquest. Several of pre-Roman date were found at Campovalano di Campli near Teramo in the Abruzzi. These have a leaf-shaped blade about 12 ins/30 cm long and a spiked tang with four antennae protruding from the pommel. The scabbards appear to have been made of wood completely covered with iron.

However, Roman daggers did not evolve directly from these. Like the sword, the traditional legionary dagger originated in Spain. The Spanish dagger, which has a leaf-shaped blade some 10 ins/25 cm long and a primitive flat-tanged double-disc handle, is well known from both native and Roman sites in Spain. Several examples were found at Numantia, the site of the famous Roman siege of 133 BC, and three handles dating from about 90 BC were found in the Roman camp at Caceres el Viejo. Another double-disc handle was recently found in the River Saône near Chalons,

where Caesar may have had a supply base. This last find, together with a blade found at Alesia, the site of Caesar's siege of Vercingetorix in 52 BC, establishes a direct link between the Spanish dagger and the kind of dagger used in the early years of the Empire. The latter differs only slightly from its Spanish prototype, having a pommel disc which flattens off at the top, with three purely decorative rivets in it, perhaps harking back to the earlier Italian antennae pommel. The wooden sheath, which had a metal frame, is now completely covered with bronze or iron and often highly decorated. It also has the four suspension rings of its Spanish predecessor, so that it could be worn, suspended horizontally, on either hip.

Returning to swords, however, we can be reasonably sure that the legionary sword of Caesar's day was very similar to the large numbers of long-pointed swords found in the Rhineland. These are referred to as Mainz-type swords. A Mainz-type sword recently found in the River Saône is probably Caesarian. Mainz-type swords have a blade 20–24 ins/50–60 cm long and 2–2½ ins/5–6 cm wide, and bear a slight resemblance to the hoplite sword in that the width of the blade increases slightly before tapering to the point, the taper beginning about three-quarters of the way down the blade. The tang is a Celtic-type spike around which the handle is fitted. This normally consists of three pieces: a thick rounded hilt, a grip with four ridges to fit the fingers, and a characteristic bulbous pommel.

One of the swords found in the Rhine near Mainz has an almost complete scabbard consisting of two pieces of thin wood sandwiched round the blade and clamped together by a semi-cylindri-

Far left A long, pointed *gladius hispaniensis* of the early first century AD found at Rheingönheim in Germany. Essentially a thrusting sword capable of rupturing mail, it has clearly evolved from the Atienza type. Blade length is 21½ ins/55 cm and the hilt is silver-plated.

Left A Spanish dagger of *c.*150 BC found at Numantia in northern Spain. Blade length is 6¾ ins/17 cm. This type of dagger was adopted by the Romans and appears on Roman sites from BC 133 onwards, the blade shape hardly changing at all until about 50 AD. The scabbard is of wood plated with bronze and held together by a bronze frame.

Above A *gladius hispaniensis*, complete with scabbard, found in the Rhine at Mainz. It has a blade length of 20½ ins/52 cm. The scabbard is made of wood faced on the front with a thin sheet of tinned bronze. Scabbards like this were held together by a bronze frame. In this case the frame and chape have been restored from other examples.

Right The tombstone of Annaius Daverzius, auxiliary infantryman of Cohors IIII Delmatarum, first half of the first century AD. The sword and dagger are worn on a separate belt. The dagger is attached by two frogs on the belt; these consist of a hook with a large terminal disc and are hinged to the belt plates. The sword is probably attached to the belt by straps and small buckles fastened to the four suspension rings. Several such small buckles have been found in conjunction with swords and belt plates.

cal bronze strip running down either side. The two side strips are held in position by a broad decorated plate wrapped around the top of the scabbard and three cast bronze strips, the upper two of which are fitted about a third of the way down the scabbard and hold the suspension rings. The third one is wrapped around the scabbard where it begins to taper to a point. The front of the scabbard is faced with a sheet of tinned bronze.

The four-ring suspension system inherited from the Spanish sword has led to an enormous amount of controversy as to how the Roman sword was worn. Before the introduction of plate armour (*lorica segmentata*) in about AD 50 the sword was definitely worn on the right hip, attached to a belt. This is shown quite clearly on several Roman tombstones, the best example being that of Annaius Daverzius, who wears two belts which cross in the centre at front and back, with a sword suspended from one and a dagger from the other. While one can see quite clearly the frogs to which the dagger is attached, there is no sign of an attachment for the sword. A sword recently found on the Greek island of Delos had two tiny buckles and a belt plate alonside the scabbard, suggesting that the scabbard was fastened to the belt by straps and buckles attached to the four scabbard rings.

Controversy has also raged as to whether the Roman sword was worn on the right or left side. The perpetrator of the 'left side' fallacy confidently declared that no sword longer than 20 ins/50 cm could be drawn from the right side while wearing *lorica segmentata* and that all swords longer than this were probably votive. Nevertheless the two great swordsmen of the ancient world, the Celt and the Roman, unquestionably wore their sword on the right hip. A man of average height can draw a sword with a blade of up to 34 ins/85 cm long from this position. In fact it is actually easier to draw a sword on the right side if one is carrying a large shield on the left arm. The suggestion that this could not be done while wearing *lorica segmentata*, because of the restriction caused by the shoulder guard, has been shown to be nonsense. The shoulder guard does not in any way restrict the necessary movement. If it had, it would also have restricted the throwing of the *pilum*.

A number of tombstones clearly show centurions wearing swords on their left side, but this had its drawbacks. When one of Caesar's legionary camps in Gaul was under siege in the winter of 54 BC a centurion named Titus Pullo, in an act of bravado, rushed out of the camp and threw his *pilum* at one of the enemy. He hit his mark, but the wounded Gaul's comrades hurled a volley of javelins back at him. One of these pierced his shield and stuck in his belt, knocking his scabbard out of position and making it impossible for him to draw his sword. He only survived because another centurion, Lucius Vorenus, rushed out and covered him while he freed his scabbard and drew his sword. The javelin had obviously knocked the scabbard backwards, with the result that the sword was just out of reach from either the front or back. Such a situation could not happen if the scabbard were on the right.

Imperial Rome

The semi-permanent camps established along the Rhine in the last decades of the first century BC by the Emperor Augustus provide us, for the first time, with a continuous archaeological record of Roman army equipment. The Rhine itself has also yielded important information, for although the camps provide a continuous record of occupancy, the best preserved artefacts, particularly those made of iron, are often those which come from rivers.

The Mainz-type sword, with its long point capable of piercing a mail shirt, continued in use throughout the first half of the first century AD. Dozens of examples have been found, including a superb specimen from Rheingonheim which has a handle sheathed in silver. This is clearly the work of a master craftsman. Another Mainz-type sword from Strasbourg is also a fine piece of craftsmanship. It has an elaborately decorated scabbard inscribed with the words 'Q. Nonienus Pudes ad ara f', meaning 'Quintus Nonienus Pudes made [this sword] at Cologne', the letters 'ad ara f' being an abbreviation of 'ad aram Ubiorum fecit'.

Around the middle of the first century AD two significant but apparently unconnected changes took place in Roman military equipment: plate armour was introduced and the Spanish sword, the sword that had conquered the world, was abandoned. The latter was replaced by a weapon with a narrower blade and a much shorter point. It is not known why this change took place, for although the archaeological record is excellent the literary sources are poor. However, the Spanish sword did have one weakness; the point stood up well to thrusting, but was liable to break if used for cutting and hacking. Adopted and developed during a period when Rome was fighting armoured enemies around the civilized Mediterranean, the armour-piercing capabilities of the Spanish sword became redundant against virtually unarmoured foes along the Rhine and Danube who fought at close quarters with slashing weapons. Against these uninhibited swordsmen the new sturdier cut-and-thrust sword was probably more effective.

The new sword, generally known as the Pompeian type after four examples found at Pompeii, bears some resemblance to its predecessor. It is about the same length, the handle is much the same and the method of suspension is identical. However the differences, besides those already mentioned, are considerable. The construction and decoration of the scabbard are quite different, for example. Gone is the metal rim of the Mainz-type scabbard, and the chape is now a separate unit. Perhaps the undulating edge of the Spanish sword cut into the scabbard; this could not happen with the straight-edged Pompeian sword.

The abrupt changeover to the new sword suggests that it had been in use for some time and undergone considerable evolution before it was adopted by the army. Gladiators are a common decorative motif on Pompeian-type scabbards, which may be a clue to the origin of the weapons they contained. Gladiators were primarily swordsmen, as their name implies. They did not wear

body armour and therefore had no need of a sword with armour-piercing capabilities, but they did require a sturdy cut-and-thrust weapon. In fact there was a considerable interchange of ideas between the army and the gladiatorial schools, Roman army training methods being derived from them. It may be no coincidence that four 'new' swords were found at Pompeii where so much gladiatorial equipment has been found.

It is perhaps significant that as the point of the Roman sword became shorter the point of the Roman dagger became longer. The dagger scabbard also changed, although it was still made of wood. The new scabbard, known as the Vindonissa type, had a simpler, flat, decorated bronze plate covering just the front of it, perhaps to make manufacture cheaper.

Experience gained from the use of reconstructed plate armour has shown that the sword cannot be worn on a belt as its weight causes the belt to slip down. It was therefore worn on a baldric slung over the left shoulder. This is well illustrated on Trajan's column (c.AD 110). A belt continued to be worn around the waist, probably fastened over the baldric to keep the sword scabbard in place on the right hip. The baldric would have performed the reciprocal action of preventing the belt slipping down. We do not know whether the dagger was ever worn with *lorica segmentata*. It is not shown at all on Trajan's column, where legionaries are depicted uniformly equipped with *lorica segmentata*, belt and baldric.

The second century AD was an era of great change. Soon after AD 100 the dagger disappears entirely from the archaeological record and by the middle of the century the short sword also disappears, to be replaced by a longer, slashing cavalry weapon. The large curved shield, the *scutum*, was also discarded and the sword scabbard moved to the left side. The new sword had a blade 26–28 ins/65–70 cm long, with a short point, and was called a *spatha*, hence *spada*, the modern Italian word for a sword.

Above Roman dagger from Hod Hill, Dorset, mid–first century AD. The pointed blade is 9 ins/23 cm long, and the weapon is typical of the middle and later part of the century. The introduction of the longer pointed dagger seems to have been associated with the adoption of the Pompeian sword.

Above left A short pointed Roman sword of Pompeian type (left) and a long pointed Roman dagger (right) with scabbard.

The sword dates from the late first century AD and was found at Newstead in Scotland. The blade is 19½ ins/49.5 cm long. The plaiting technique used in the forging of the blade is clearly visible.

The dagger, from Mainz in Germany, has the Vindonissa-type scabbard introduced towards the end of the first century AD. Made of wood, with a bronze facing plate, it was cheaper to produce than the bronze-frame scabbard.

The *spatha* was of Celtic origin. The Romans were exclusively infantrymen, relying on their allies for cavalry. During the Gallic War, Caesar raised huge bodies of cavalry in Gaul. The Gallic tribes were also the target of Augustus' recruiting efforts when he started to form regular cavalry units to serve alongside the legions operating in the Rhineland. These units were equipped in native fashion with mail shirt, helmet, oval shield and spear, and the long slashing sword that was to become the *spatha*, the primary weapon of the middle and later Empire.

There are no complete examples of early cavalry *spathae*. Although blades sometimes survive in almost perfect condition, scabbards and handles are always missing. Blades vary considerably in length. Two late first-century examples from Newstead in Scotland have a blade length of 24½ and 25 ins/62 and 63 cm and a width of about 1¼ ins/3 cm, but an example from Carnuntum on the Danube has a blade more than 32 ins/80 cm long and 1½ ins/4 cm wide.

First-century cavalry tombstones show scabbards and handles which are very similar to legionary types. Some tombstones, such as those of Titus Flavius Bassus and Gaius Romanius, buried in the Rhineland, clearly show rimmed scabbards of the Mainz type but with no cross bands or suspension rings, implying that the Celtic suspension loop was being used, but others, such as that of Quintus Carminius Ingenuus, also from the Rhineland, equally clearly show the traditional suspension rings. A few elongated chapes of the Pompeian type have been found on cavalry sites. These are probably from *spatha* scabbards, suggesting that auxiliary cavalry units copied legionary fashions.

Legionaries probably continued to use the four-ring attachment system for some time after they adopted the *spatha*, but gradually during the latter part of the second century the loop type became universal. During this period the Pompeian-style scabbard chape was replaced by a wide variety of chapes which remained in simultaneous use during the second half of the second century and the first half of the third. These range from close-fitting crescent-shaped types made of bronze to large disc-shaped ones made of iron and almost rectangular examples made of bone. The complex baldric system which accompanied the large disc chapes is shown on many Roman sculptures, and an almost complete example was found at Vimose in Denmark.

The dagger unexpectedly reappears in the third century. A large number found at Kunzing on the Danube illustrate the type, which clearly derives from that used in the first century. The blade is broader, with a spiked tang, the disc in the centre of the handle has disappeared, and there is now a triangular nick in the top of the pommel disc, but otherwise it is the same dagger. The scabbard, still with four attachment rings, is made of wood and held together by a metal frame which bears a remarkable resemblance to that found on the original Spanish dagger. It is scarcely likely that the Spanish dagger went out of use, to be reintroduced a century or so later. Somewhere in the Empire it must have continued in use and evolved into the third-century form. An example found at Copthall in London suggests that it must have been fairly widely used.

Above A typical Roman cavalry sword (*spatha*) from Rottweil, southern Germany, *c.*100 AD. Derived from the first-century BC Celtic sword, the *spatha* was a slashing weapon with a blade length of 25 ins/65 cm. The bronze chape, not shown to scale, comes from a smaller sword and is based on the Pompeian-style chape.

Right Tombstone of Gaius Romanius Capito, auxiliary cavalryman of the Norican Regiment, late first century AD. A long slashing *spatha* in a frame scabbard hangs, in Celtic fashion, at his right side.

Far right Roman dagger from Copthall Court, London, third century AD. It is considerably longer than first-century examples. The shape of the blade and the construction of the scabbard have more in common with the original Spanish dagger than with earlier Roman examples.

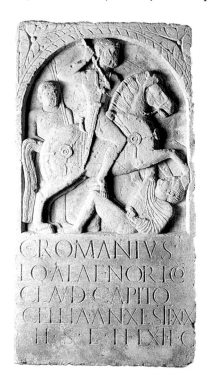

For more than two centuries the Romans and the Germans faced each other along the Rhine and Danube, but there was little interchange of weaponry. The Roman arms that turn up in Germany during the first, second and third centuries are generally looted. The Germans were armed primarily with spears and javelins and at first seemed content to remain so. But from the later part of the second century onwards, possibly stimulated by their experiences in the Marcomannic Wars, they began to adopt Roman weaponry. Swords clearly derived from Roman types begin to appear on Germanic sites with increasing frequency. This process of adoption accelerated during the third century, when it becomes virtually impossible to tell Roman from Germanic weapons. Often it is only the forger's stamp or an inscription that identifies a Roman weapon with certainty. The commonest type of sword during this period was the ring-pommelled type, with the tang bent round to form a large ring at the top of the grip, but it is impossible to say whether this modification was of Roman or German origin. Certainly both sides used it. A long narrow-bladed thrusting sword is also quite common in both Roman and Germanic contexts.

In the middle of the third century the Roman Empire began to crumble. Goths and Germans burst through the northern and western frontiers and inflicted a series of humiliating defeats on the Romans, and for a generation the Empire was in chaos, with armed bands marauding at will. But by the end of the century, order had been restored and Diocletian took over the reins of government.

Rome responded to the ever-present threat from the north and west by employing the invaders as mercenaries. The new recruits brought their own weaponry with them, and from then on it becomes almost impossible to differentiate between Roman and barbarian arms. A few examples of purely Roman character survive, such as the fourth-century *spatha* from Bonn which has a handle very similar to the first-century types. During this late period the sword was once again slung from the hip, using a narrow strap encircling the waist just below the belt. This fashion, probably adopted from the Parthians and Sassanians, can be seen clearly on the diptych of Stilicho in the cathedral treasury at Monza. Stilicho was a Roman general of Vandal origin.

On the death of the Emperor Theodosius in 395 the Empire was split into two, with Ravenna as the capital of the West and Constantinople the capital of the East. In 410, the Goths, already entrenched in various parts of the Empire, captured Rome.

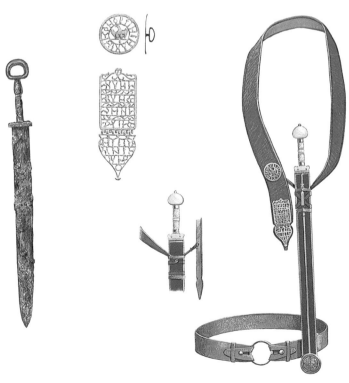

Above Diptych of Stilicho, showing its namesake in military attire, with shield, spear, and sword on the left hip. Stilicho was a Vandal chief who served as a general in the Roman army in the early part of the fifth century AD.

Left Tombstone of Aurelius Suro, a trumpeter (*bucinator*) in Legion I Adiutrix in the third century AD. This sculpture shows the broad baldric, characteristic of the period, suspending the sword on the left side.

Far left Ring-pommel sword from Hamfelde, Germany, and a reconstruction of a third-century AD sword, scabbard, baldric and belt (after J. Oldenstein).

The ring-pommel sword is a cross between the *spatha* and the *gladius*, with a broad slashing blade less than 20 ins/50 cm long. Examples have been found on Roman and Germanic sites of the third century AD, indicating that the type was used by both sides.

The other sword and its accoutrements come from sites in Germany and Denmark. The disc and hinged strap terminal (top left) come from Zugmantel in southern Germany; the broad leather strap is based on pieces found at Vimose in Denmark.

BARBARIANS AND CHRISTIANS

Anthony North

The decline of Rome and the increasing importance of the Eastern Roman Empire did not initially bring any great changes in the design of edged weapons. The slashing Roman cavalry sword or *spatha* was retained long after Rome fell, evolving eventually into the knightly sword of medieval times.

The history of the sword in the fifth century AD has been reasonably easy to establish thanks to a series of important finds made at Kragehul Mose in Denmark and Vendel in Sweden in the middle of the last century. These finds span nearly four hundred years, from the first century AD to the fifth, and include examples of the short Roman *gladius* and the long cavalry *spatha*. These and other objects were ritually deposited in pools and bogs and, although many were intentionally broken and bent before being consigned to oblivion, the peaty soil into which they fell proved an excellent preservative for both organic materials and metal.

Saxons and Vikings

We know, from a particularly well preserved weapon found at Kragehul in Denmark, that by the fifth century a new sword was beginning to evolve from the *spatha*, at least in Northern Europe. The blade of the Kragehul sword is 42 ins/105 cm long, straight and double-edged, and the grip has a distinctive waist with three horizontal raised ribs to fit the fingers, a feature found on many late Roman swords. The scabbard has a chape in the form of an open ring, with long shoes or plates enclosing either side of it, an openwork mount at the top, and a long vertical spine with a hook for attachment to a belt. Both the scabbard mounts and the hilt are of bronze. A number of similar swords with waisted grips have been found, dating from the second to the sixth century. Some have very elaborately worked gold hilts set with stones. A sixth-century sword found in Cumberland, England, for example, has a waisted horn grip with plates of gold and 'cloisons' containing cut garnets attached to it. It is possible, of course, that these were added to an already old weapon.

Perhaps one of the most luxurious swords to survive from the Anglo-Saxon period is the famous Sutton Hoo sword. The burial mound at Sutton Hoo, by the River Deben at Woodbridge,

Right Sword from Kragehul Mose Denmark, *c.*400 AD. The hilt is of bronze and the blade retains the original bronze scabbard mounts.

Suffolk, was excavated in 1939 and was found to contain a ship. Inside it were the possessions of a seventh-century East Anglian king. The sword was found badly crushed by many tons of earth, but enough of the blade survived to be X-rayed – it was found to be doubled-edged and pattern-welded, with a clear chevron pattern running down the centre. The scabbard was made of wood, lined with wool to prevent the blade rusting. However, the mounts of the sword are its chief glory, for they are of gold and cloisonné work. Garnets fill the cloisons on the pommel, and marvellously intricate and beautiful gold bosses ornament the scabbard. The small oval guard is made of two gold plates, filled originally with a light tin alloy. Archaeologists have concluded that this sumptuous weapon, together with a great gold buckle and a purse mount, formed part of a ceremonial regalia, probably that of King Redwald, who died in 624 or 625. The mound also contained other extraordinarily rich examples of Anglo-Saxon goldsmith's work.

From the many accounts of sword-giving in the Scandinavian sagas, it seems clear that swords were valuable family heirlooms, handed down from father to son. Much-prized specimens were decorated with gold and set with stones as a measure of their value. This respect for old weapons may have have had something to do with the fading of Roman influence and the dispersal of workshops and skilled craftsmen – it may not have been possible to have swords made or repaired locally by a skilled smith, for example – but it also stemmed from the intrinsic power of the sword itself. A sword used for heroic deeds acquired something beyond mere weight and dimensions.

The Vikings admired the sword above all other weapons, and gave their swords names such as 'Gramr' ('fierce'), 'Fotbitr' ('leg-biter') and 'Meofainn' ('ornamented down the middle', probably meaning that the blade was pattern-welded). In the oblique imagery of the sagas the sword becomes 'a lightning flash of blood'.

The settling of personal feuds by sword-fight is well documented in the sagas. Foote and Wilson, in their book *The Viking Achievement* draw attention to the *holmganga* or formal duel

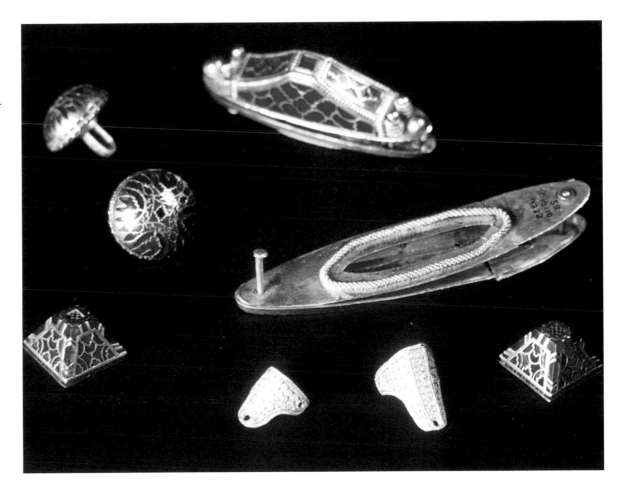

Above Gold filigree and cloisonné mounts from the sword and scabbard found in the Sutton Hoo ship burial. Anglo-Saxon, *c.*625.

Above right Hilt of a Viking sword from a ship burial at Ulltuna, Sweden, *c.*700. Pommel, guard and scabbard mounts are gilt bronze, decorated with interlaced patterns.

Right Bronze hilt of a Viking sword found at Broa, Gotland, Sweden, overlaid with geometric patterns in silver. It was probably made between 800 and 950.

described in *Kormaks Saga*. The word *holmganga* means 'island going'. for formal duels nearly always took place on small islands which imposed limitations of space on the combatants. The precise site of the combat was marked out by a square cloth pegged to the ground at each corner. Three furrows were then drawn around the cloth and the entire area was marked off by four posts linked by a rope. Each combatant had a second, who protected him with his shield. As in formal nineteenth-century German duels, the combatants took it in turn to strike each other. If one or other stepped out of the prescribed area, he was deemed to have run away. The purpose of the cloth was to show when blood was spilt, at which point the fight could be stopped, with honour satisfied. The fight could also be stopped by the wounded party agreeing to paying a sum of money to his opponent.

The Norse sagas are full of accounts of single combats using swords. The *Lausaviser*, for example, tells the story of the revenge of Einar, son of Ragnvald. Ragnvald, a Norwegian chieftain who ruled in Orkney in about 860, was burnt to death in his own house by two of Harald Fairhair's sons. Einar fought with one son, Halfdan Halegga, and killed him. When found the next morning on the side of a hill, the body had the shape of an eagle cut into its back with a sword – the ribs had been separated from the backbone and the lungs had been pulled out on either side to represent an eagle's wings. This was Einar's victory sacrifice to Odin.

Early eighth-century swords found in graves at Vendel in Sweden include a type in which the pommel and guard take the form of oval plates held together by four pins. A wedge-shaped cap is set on the pommel and the grip is narrow, ribbed, and decorated with interlace work and dragons. It was this type of sword which developed into the standard Anglo-Saxon sword. Many examples have rings or stones set into the hilt, which suggests that they were gifts from chieftains to retainers or worn as a mark of office.

Not all swords of the eighth and ninth centuries are double-edged. Straight single-edged blades with sharply tapering points have also been found, often in association with Norwegian sites. Included in this group is the *seax* or *sax*, a typically Scandinavian weapon whose origins appear to go back to the first, second and third centuries and a broad single-edged sword of the kind excavated at Vimose in Denmark. By 650, however, the *seax* had become a narrow single-edged weapon with the point set at a distinct angle to the blade. Early examples have grips formed of plaques rivetted through the tang, but later examples have grips which simply fit over the tang, a much stronger method of construction. Some have maker's names inscribed on them and inlaid decoration.

The swords the Vikings used from the eighth to the twelfth centuries show great originality in the decoration of their hilts – it is on the basis of their hilt form, and of course their provenance, that they are classified. The simple crossguard of the eighth and

ninth centuries was retained but new forms of pommel and decoration began to develop. Early pommels consisted of a pyramid-shaped block divided into three segments. Other early pommels, originally from Norway but carried by raiders to Ireland and the Western Isles of Scotland, were triangular. Later pommels tend to be divided vertically into many segments. There was also a tendency for the crossguard to become longer and thinner, and droop towards the blade.

Most Viking swords are broad double-edged weapons with a long channel down the centre, but single-edged blades with a back and no channel have also been found, many from Norway.

A remarkable series of swords from the Viking period, most of them found in Russia and dating from the ninth and tenth centuries, has been published recently. Several have blades inscribed with the name 'ULFBEHRT', a name already well known to weapons historians, and one is inscribed with the name 'LUNVELIT', which is most unusual. Crosses and geometrical designs also appear on many of the blades. The hilts are well preserved and most follow the usual Viking form, with a two-stage pommel sometimes divided into lobes and a short down-curving crossguard. The ornamentation of the hilts varies – some are decorated with relief interlace work, others with engraved and inlaid foliate scroll designs in niello – and shows a mixture of stylistic influences from steppe art to traditional Scandinavian designs.

The technology of Viking sword blades is of considerable interest. Pattern-welded blades had been made since the Late Iron Age, but the pattern-welding technique is particularly obvious in blades of Viking and Merovingian manufacture, and with X-rays it is possible to see such patterns even when a blade is in poor condition. A broad band of zig-zag swirls running down the centre of the blade is the commonest pattern. First the smith welded together long strips of iron and steel. Then he forged them into square-sectioned rods, which he twisted or folded and welded together in groups of three or four. These were used for the central core of the blade. The edges of the blade were then welded to it. After grinding and polishing, the twists and folds of the core pattern were brought out with acid.

It has been suggested that many pattern-welded blades of the Viking period were produced in a single centre somewhere in the Rhineland. Was it because this workshop was destroyed and its craftsmen dispersed that pattern-welded blades suddenly disappeared in the tenth century?

Inlaid inscriptions and other symbols are quite common on Viking blades, especially on swords from Norway, Ireland, Russia and Finland, although the habit of using iron for inlaid work is unusual. Roman smiths also marked their blades, often with small figures of gods, usually near the hilt. On Viking blades the inscriptions are usually the names of the owner or maker, inlaid in large letters in the central groove of the blade. The individual letters were made from small iron rods hammered into

Top Anglo-Saxon (Winchester style) *seax* blade from Sittingbourne, Kent, inlaid with copper, bronze and silver and decorated with niello.

Above Sword with 'brazil nut' pommel, German, tenth-eleventh century. The blade is inlaid with the name 'INGELRII'.

Above left Wood-carving from the portal of a stave church showing Regin the smith and Sigurd at the forge. Norwegian, twelfth century.

33

the blade when it was white hot; the blade was then re-heated and the letters re-hammered to seat them firmly. The same technique was used for inlaying animal symbols and also geometric designs thought to represent standards carried into battle.

Two names appear with some frequency on Viking blades, 'ULFBEHRT' and 'INGELRII', the latter in various spellings, but the date span covered by swords bearing one or other of these names makes it virtually impossible that they were the work of individual smiths. Perhaps the names indicate a factory or region, rather like the inscriptions 'Solingen' or 'Andrea Ferrara' on many later European blades. Inscriptions on later Viking swords, those of the eleventh century for example, tend to be less enigmatic: 'NISO ME FECIT' ('Niso made me') clearly refers to a maker. Runic inscriptions are generally confined to knife or *seax* blades, although they have been found on a few sword pommels. Owners' names usually appear on the crossguard rather than the blade; the guard of a sword from Balinderry in Ireland, for example, is inscribed 'HILTIPREHT' in large letters.

The hilts of Viking swords were almost never plain. Those which survive are decorated with motifs stamped into appliqué silver plate, with geometric designs inlaid into bronze pommels and guards, or, in the case of a number of late Viking swords from Sweden, with animals and interlace patterns worked in relief. A tenth-century sword found beneath Fetter Lane in London has a silver pommel divided into seven lobes at the top and skilfully

engraved with animals and foliage in niello, a style of decoration very similar to that found on metalwork from the Trewhiddle Hoard, discovered in Cornwall in 1774 and probably buried in 875 in fear of a Viking raid.

Elusive Byzantium

Whereas Roman and Scandinavian edged weapons survive in some quantity, those of the forces of Byzantium, the long-lived Eastern Roman Empire, have almost entirely disappeared. In fact, it is misleading to talk about 'Byzantine' weapons at all, since at the height of its power – from the ninth to the eleventh century – the Byzantine empire employed Scandinavian, Patzinakh, Russian, Turkish and even English mercenaries, all of whom used the equipment and weapons which suited them best. The celebrated Varangian Guard, a Viking elite corps which served the Empire in the tenth century, carried the broad Scandinavian axe and are referred to in contemporary sources as 'those who hang their swords from their right shoulders'.

Although very few Byzantine edged weapons have been identified, a number of contemporary writers describe various types of sword. The Emperor Maurice (539–602), author of a treatise on warfare called *Strategikon* written in the 580s or 590s, tells us that a long sword called a *spathion* was worn by cavalry. This was undoubtedly a direct descendant of the late Roman *spatha*. The treatise is a useful source for descriptions of Byzantine arms and armour since much of the equipment of contemporary soldiers is described in detail. By the tenth century, according to the *Tactica* of Emperor Leo VI (886–911), the *spathion* had developed into a weapon 'four spans in length' (about 36 ins/91 cm). It was, apparently, straight, double-edged and worn from a baldric.

A sword called a *paramerion* is also mentioned in the literature. This seems to have developed towards the end of the ninth century, and was a singled-edged weapon worn on the thigh, suspended from a waist belt. It may also have been curved, a form introduced by the Avars, a tribe from the Ukraine. There are also references to an edged weapon called a *rhomphaia*. A twelfth-century work, the *Alexiad* written by the Byzantine historian Anna Comnena (1083–1153), the eldest child of the Emperor Alexius I, refers to the emperor's retainers carrying 'great iron swords' when on imperial escort duty. There is argument about the exact nature of these weapons. Some authorities suggest that they were rather like a falchion with a curved blade, and others contend that they were not swords at all but pole-arms. To date, however, no examples of this putative weapon have been found or identified.

Some idea of the appearance of the edged weapons of Byzantium can be gained by examining contemporary illustrated manuscripts, ivories and similar artefacts. In the British Museum there is a gilt bronze plaque of St Theodore dating from the eleventh century which shows a sword, probably a *spathion*, with a small

Right Silver gilt pommel from a late eighth-century Anglo-Saxon sword found in Fetter Lane, London. The engraving shows an animal enmeshed in foliage.

pommel and a downward-curving crossguard with pierced terminals. There are a number of similar swords in the Askeri Museum in Istanbul, originally from the arsenal at Constantinople. Their date has not been firmly established but they could be of fourteenth-century manufacture. Many of the straight-bladed swords shown in ivory plaques have globe-shaped pommels, which may have been a distinctive Byzantine feature.

A sword which shows many Byzantine characteristics in form and decoration is the ceremonial sword in the regalia of the Holy Roman Emperor Frederick II of Hohenstaufen (1194–1250). The hilt and scabbard of this magnificent weapon are decorated with gold, enamel, pearls, filigree and rubies, very much in the style of other works of art known to be by Byzantine goldsmiths. The pommel of this sword has been changed at some period, probably about 1335, when a contemporary wheel-shaped pommel engraved with the Eagle and Lion of Bohemia was added. The scabbard bears the Imperial Eagle of Byzantium. It is possible that this illustrious weapon was a gift to Frederick II from one of the Byzantine emperors.

In the thirteenth and fourteenth centuries Genoese and Venetian mercenaries were called in to help defend Byzantium against a new threat, the Ottoman Turks. This led to a rapid introduction of Western edged weapons, with the result that by the time the Turks laid siege to Constantinople in 1453 the forces of Byzantium were fighting with many of the same weapons as their enemies.

In the arsenal of the Ottoman sultans at Istanbul are numerous Italian swords that might well, from their date, have been used by Venetian, Spanish and other allies of the Emperor against the besieging Turks. Among them are a number of Venetian swords with horizontally recurved quillons and square pommels, a group of swords with pronounced pear-shaped pommels and angular knucklebows, and a series of fifteenth-century cross-hilted swords. The arsenal also contains a series of swords with curious cap pommels and crudely made short quillons. A number of these odd-looking hilts are fitted with blades engraved with Arabic inscriptions dating them to the 1360s, but are otherwise very European in appearance. The hilts have certain points of similarity with those shown in contemporary Byzantine ivories and bronze plaques, so this group of swords may be authentically 'Byzantine'. One feature which argues against this, however, is the complete absence of any Greek inscriptions.

Ceremonial swords

With the exception of the weapons just referred to, the majority of weapons already mentioned in this chapter have come to light during excavations of tombs or battlefields. From the eleventh century onwards, however, an increasing number of weapons were preserved in church and state treasuries and arsenals, often because of their connection with a famous person. Most of them are regalia swords, forming part of the ceremonial instruments used at coronations or similar ceremonies.

One of the earliest attributable regalia swords is the sword of Charlemagne (950–1025) preserved in the Schatzkammer in Vienna. The blade is single-edged with a slight curve to it, and overlaid with copper decorated with dragons. The grip is set at an angle to the blade, a feature typical of early ninth-century Near Eastern swords, and bound with ray skin. The hilt and scabbard mounts are silver gilt, embossed with interlaced bands against a punched ground. The quillons are short and terminate in small knobs.

In several important ways this famous sword is reminiscent of early Islamic swords. The angled tang, the profile of the blade, the scabbard mounts and the form of the quillons are all features found on Near Eastern swords dating from the ninth century. The use of ray skin for the grip also hints at an Islamic origin. The sword has of course been repaired and restored on several occasions; the grip, for example, was probably re-mounted, with narrow bands of gold set with precious stones, in the fourteenth century.

Above Gilt bronze plaque of St Theodore, Byzantine, eleventh century. The warrior saint is dressed as a high-ranking officer, with a lamellar cuirass, and wears a sword with scrolling quillons.

Left Ceremonial sword of Frederick II of Hohenstaufen (1194–1250), crowned Holy Roman Emperor in 1220. The hilt and scabbard mounts are of gold, decorated with pearls and enamel. The pommel was replaced in the fourteenth century. Byzantine, *c*.1220.

There are parallels for the sword of Charlemagne from Russian sites. A tenth-century sword from the Dnieper has a similar blade profile, a similar guard, and a large cap-shaped pommel with a swelling at the top. As for the mounts, it is generally accepted that the closest parallels for these occur on a sword found in a warrior's grave at Geztered in Hungary. In this case the mounts are of gold, decorated with palmettes and scrolls against a punched ground. Swords from other Hungarian sites such as Tarcal and Tiszafüred have similar mounts, though made of silver.

Clearly the sword of Charlemagne is of great antiquity, and as befits a sword of great antiquity, several traditions are associated with it. According to one, the sword was presented to Charlemagne by the famous Caliph of Bagdad, Harun al-Rashid (785–809). According to another, the sword originally belonged to Attila the Hun (406–453). There is a third possibility, for those who do not like the first two: it was presented to a German prince by the widow of King András of Hungary for having helped her son to regain the throne in 1063. None of these exotic stories can be substantiated, however. All that can be said is that the sword was probably made in Russia or in Eastern Europe at some time during the ninth century.

By the beginning of the eleventh century European swords had undergone various changes. Lobed pommels lost their vertical divisions and took on a brazil nut shape, guards tended to be long and straight, and blades became much longer, with a gradually tapering double edge.

A number of swords with brazil nut pommels are known from excavations, but a particularly fine example of the type, preserved in excellent condition, can be seen in the Weltlichen Schatzkammer in Vienna. Known as the Sword of St Maurice, it was used as a ceremonial sword at the coronation of the German emperors. The gilded iron pommel, shaped like a brazil nut, is engraved with Latin inscriptions and the blade is marked with a cross within a circle. The scabbard is of olive wood, and the scabbard mounts are gold panels stamped with figures of an emperor divided by bands of cloisonné enamel. As with many regalia swords, this weapon has been altered during its long lifetime. The blade and scabbard are probably eleventh century, but the hilt, or rather the decoration on the hilt, dates from 1198–1218.

Another ceremonial sword preserved in excellent condition is the cross-hilted sword used at the coronations of the kings of France. This is also associated with Charlemagne and can be seen in the Galerie d'Apollon at the Louvre, Paris. It dates from the twelfth century and has a hilt of gold very similar to some late Viking hilts. The pommel is decorated with very Scandinavian-looking interlace relief, and the crossguard terminates in splendidly barbaric lions with gaping jaws.

In the Domkirch at Essen there is another fine sword of the period, also with gold mounts. The hilt is of eleventh century form with a bun-shaped pommel and a simple crossguard; made of gold, it is decorated with filigree and set with gold plates

stamped with vertical rows of animals and scrolls. On one side of the bottom scabbard chape are the figures of St Cosmas and St Damian, patron saints of the Domkirch, and on the other the inscription 'Gladius cum quo decollati fuerunt nostri patroni' ('The sword which which our patrons were beheaded'). The nature of the ornament, especially the use of gold filigree and the rectangular enamel panels on the crossguard, is very similar to the work of Byzantine goldsmiths. It is not known how the sword found its way to Essen, but on the basis of its enamelled gold work it probably came from Constantinople. Similar work can be seen in St Marks in Venice on objects known to have come from Constantinople.

Falchions and wheel pommels

The belief that sword hilts regularly changed their form throughout the medieval period, or that new styles quickly or universally replaced older ones, is largely mistaken. Developments varied very much from region to region, and a style of hilt abandoned in one country might well be retained for several generations in another. A good instance of such conservatism is the survival of a form of Viking hilt well into the thirteenth century. On a number of knightly effigies in the north of England one sees swords which have the lobed and vertically divided pommel typical of ninth- and tenth-century Scandinavian swords but also the long straight double-edged blade and long down-curving quillons typical of the thirteenth century.

However, a type of sword which appears to have been relatively common in the thirteenth century, judging from manu-

Above Sword of Charlemagne, Eastern European, ninth-century. The hilt and scabbard mounts are of gold; the grip, wrapped in fish skin, is set with stones mounted in silver-gilt; and the blade is inlaid with copper, gilded and engraved. The silver gilt collars set with stones are late medieval repairs.

Right Scene from the Bayeux Tapestry showing Norman horsemen with lances and swords attacking Harold's men, who are dismounted and fighting with axes and swords. English, *c.*1075.

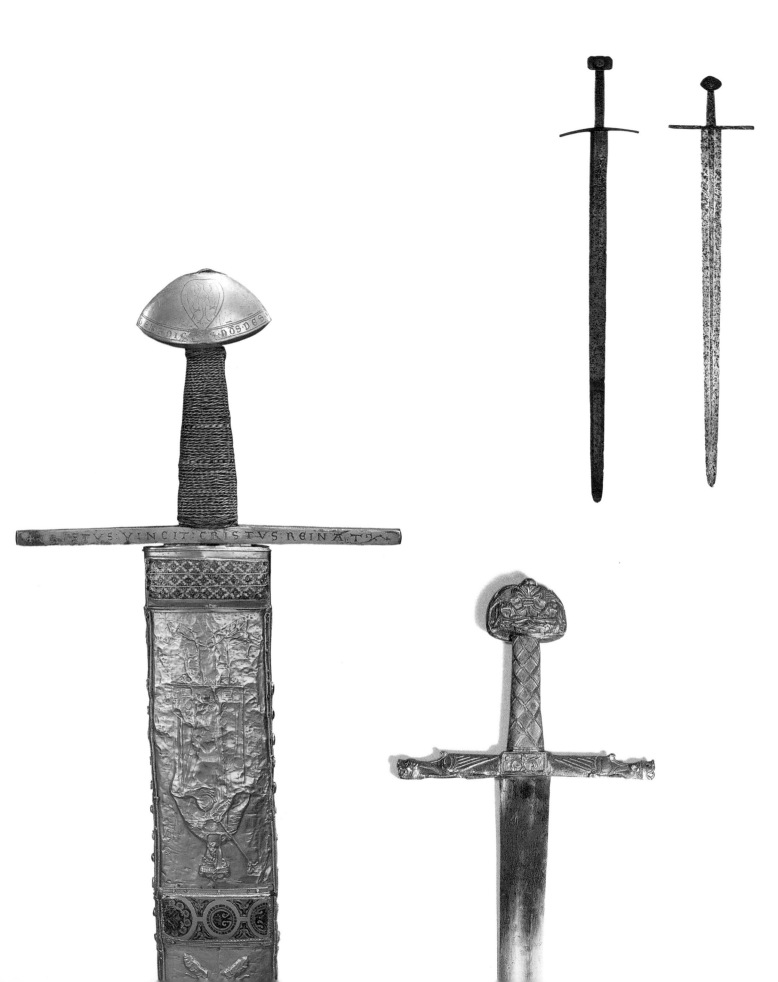

Above Sword with a hand-and-a-half grip (left) and an iron-hilted sword with a 'brazil nut' pommel (right). The latter is German, eleventh-twelfth century, and has maker's marks inlaid in latten along the blade. The hand-and-a-half weapon is Hungarian, fourteenth century.

Far left Sword of St Maurice, part of the German imperial regalia. The hilt is of gilded iron, engraved with texts and the arms of Otto IV (1198–1218), and the scabbard is mounted in stamped and enamelled gold. Scabbard and blade date from the first half of the eleventh century.

Left Cross-hilted Sword of Charlemagne, the coronation sword of the French kings, Northern European, twelfth century.

37

script illustrations, was the falchion, a broad cleaver-like weapon. Interestingly falchions are nearly always shown being brandished by pagans. Perhaps the illustrators were trying to show the curved broad-bladed swords used by the Saracens – some falchions are indeed very similar to Near Eastern weapons. The type is excellently represented by the Conyers Falchion from Durham Cathedral in northeast England. The broad cleaver-shaped blade is straight-backed and has channels or fullers running down it. The guard is a simple cross engraved with dragons and foliage, and the pommel is wheel-shaped and engraved with an eagle on one face and three lions on the other, the arms of the Holy Roman Empire and of England. Both guard and pommel are of copper gilt set with enamel. This very fine weapon was almost certainly made for Richard Earl of Cornwall, King of the Romans, between 1257 and 1272, and is probably English work. It used to be the sword of tenure of the Conyers family, demonstrating their right to hold lands at Sockburn in County Durham and was presented to every new Bishop of Durham on his accession to the diocese, a custom which lasted until 1860. The guard is badly scarred and scratched, which suggests considerable use at some time in its history, but otherwise the weapon is in fine condition. There are other falchions in existence, most of them excavated examples. One from Thorpe near Norwich, England, has a blade with a clipped point remarkably similar to contemporary Near Eastern blades. Again, a New Eastern prototype seems to be suggested.

The wheel-shaped pommel seems to have been introduced around 1100, and over the next 150 years became the norm throughout Europe. It almost certainly developed from the large cap-type pommel found somewhat earlier. At about the same time sword blades became longer – about 37 ins/95 cm was the average. The majority have a fairly broad straight blade, often with a single narrow fuller, clearly intended for cutting and hacking rather than thrusting. Usually the crossguard is a substantial straight bar, although on some early twelfth-century examples the guard turns sharply down at the ends, sometimes with animal motif terminals. In the latter half of the century quillons tend to have gently drooping ends. Twelfth-century pommels come in a variety of shapes – large mushroom-shaped knobs, brazil nut and ovoidal forms, and discs and wheels in the plane of the blade. In the last quarter of the century pommels in the form of truncated pyramids and vertically divided rectangles appear. Many of these forms continued in use after the twelfth century and are therefore inconclusive for dating purposes. To date a weapon accurately the shape of the blade and any inscription or decoration on the hilt must also be taken into account.

The twelfth and thirteenth centuries

By the middle of the thirteenth century the standard form of sword was about 36 ins/100 cm long, broad-bladed, with a double fuller running the length of the blade. Often the blade was inlaid with letters or symbols made of latten, an alloy resembling brass, the guard was a simple cross bar, and the pommel had a distinctive chamfer at the edge. A good example of the type, found in the River Witham in Lincolnshire, can be seen in the British Museum. Although the hilt is almost certainly English, the blade was probably made in Germany. Swords like it appear on many contemporary effigies.

After 1250 the evolution of the sword in Europe becomes rather easier to follow, partly because sword hilts are shown clearly in contemporary manuscripts and on effigies and partly because an increasing number of swords found their way into dynastic armouries, churches and monasteries where they were carefully preserved. The dynastic armouries of Dresden and Vienna, for example, contain many medieval swords in a marvel-

lous state of preservation. Battlefields of the period are generally a disappointing source for swords, implying that swords were both highly prized and expensive. Any battle site would have been speedily and thoroughly scoured for desirable weapons, leaving only those lodged in inaccessible places for later generations to find. A sword belonging to a famous person or with a hilt made from precious materials was a thing to cherish, and even venerate. The sword used to kill Thomas à Becket in 1170, for instance, was kept on a special altar in Canterbury Cathedral on the spot where he was martyred, and miniature replicas of the sword, in a scabbard, were sold to pilgrims. All traces of the altar, and other pilgrim relics at Canterbury, vanished with the religious reforms of Henry VIII.

The tombs of kings and princes have also yielded illustrious swords. Space does not allow me to quote more than one example, but the sword excavated from the tomb of Sancho IV of Castile is interesting. The hilt is clearly of Moorish or Near Eastern craftsmanship, the pommel being engraved with repeating invocations in the kind of Kufic script which appears on late thirteenth-century Islamic metal wares. The weapon was presumably made before Sancho IV's death in 1295 or thereabouts.

By the early fourteenth century sword blades had extended to about 50 ins/125 cm. To balance the extra weight the grip was made longer so that it could be held by both hands and the pommel was made larger and heavier. Blades were generally broad, parallel-edged and nipped in sharply at the point or sometimes gradually tapered towards the point. Running down the blade were multiple narrow channels or a single broad one. Double-edged blades were a great deal more common than single-edged. But still the emphasis was on the use of the edge of the blade rather than the point.

Throughout the fourteenth century, wheel pommels, often with a raised centre, continued to be popular, although the practice of inlaying or engraving them with heraldic devices became less common than previously. Although metal pommels continued to be the norm, a few examples in rock crystal and chalcedony have been found. After 1300 quillons tend to elongate and turn down towards the blade, sometimes with a small cusp projecting down the centre of the blade.

Opposite page, left and right
Wheel-pommel sword with blade inlaid in latten with Roman and Lombardic letters, English, *c.*1250–1330. Found in the River Witham in Lincolnshire in 1825, this is one of the finest English knightly swords to have survived from the Middle Ages.

Page from the Manesse Codex showing mounted knights fighting with swords. German, early fourteenth century.

Far left above Italian sword with an Arabic inscription on the blade recording its deposition in an arsenal by His Excellency As-Saifri al Ukuz in the year 769 AH (1367). The hilt is of steel and the wheel pommel is of latten.

Far left below Three two-handed swords, all of fourteenth-century date. The sword in the centre is Northern European, while those on the left and right are German. The weapon on the left has a facetted pommel, the original leather-bound grip, and letters and a maker's mark inlaid along the blade.

Left Sword and scabbard found near Westminster Bridge, London (left) and a baselard excavated at Bull Wharf, London (right).

The sword is English, made in about 1330. It has an iron hilt and is stamped with a maker's mark on the blade and hilt. The silver scabbard mounts are engraved with the owner's badge, a stag's head with the motto 'Wiste I' ('Knew I').

The baselard is also English, *c.*1380. The wooden hilt is mounted in iron and the single-edged blade is inlaid in latten with maker's marks.

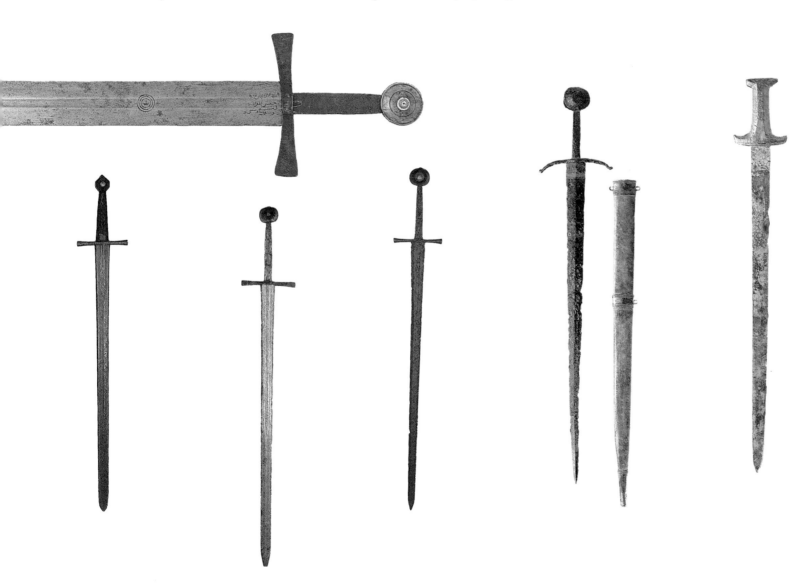

Right Sword of Sancho IV of Castile, Spanish, *c.*1295. The bronze hilt is engraved with pious invocations in Kufic script and the panels on the grip show the arms of Castile quartered with those of Leon.

Fragments from the Crusades

It is a constant source of disappointment to students of arms and armour that so little remains of the equipment of Christian and Muslim forces from the period of the Crusades. Although most of the period is well documented, only a few fragments, mostly excavated from Crusader castles, survive.

The period of the Crusades covered nearly two centuries. It commenced with announcement by Pope Urban II in 1095 of a crusade to free Jerusalem from Muslim rule. The military campaign took a year or so get under way, and resulted in notable victories such as that of Dorylaeum in 1097 and in long sieges such as that of Antioch in 1097/8. On 7 June 1099 the Crusaders reached Jerusalem and laid siege to the city, which eventually fell to them on Friday 15 July at the very hour when the crucifixion was thought to have taken place. At that moment Godfrey de Bouillon laid his siege tower against the walls adjacent to the Jewish quarter and Raymond de Saint-Gilles entered the city from the southwest.

Another seven crusades followed, as a result of which various Christian kingdoms, principalities and counties were established around the shores of the Eastern Mediterranean. Gradually, however, the combined forces of geography, and Islam proved too much. In May 1291 Acre, the strongest of all the Crusader cities, fell to the Muslims and the Latin kingdoms of the east collapsed.

In the Metropolitan Museum of Art in New York are some of the few fragments of arms and armour that can be definitely associated with the Crusades. A bronze sword pommel decorated with the arms of Pierre de Dreux, Duke of Britanny and Earl of Richmond, who went twice to the Holy Land in 1238 and 1249, was acquired in the 1920s from a bazaar in Damascus. In the same collection are a few fragment of mail excavated from Castle Montfort, sacked by Sultan Baybars in 1270. There are also a few dagger pommels decorated with enamelled coats-of-arms, probably of thirteenth-century date, which have been found in Syria. These are in various collections and museums and the similarity of their decoration suggests that they were all produced in the enamel workshops of Limoges in France.

It is from manuscripts and monuments that we gain the best idea of the appearance of the Crusader knight. Sources such as the Maciejowksi Bible, a French manuscript dating from about 1250, show knights wearing mail shirts and helmets. Their swords are clearly of the short broad-bladed thrusting variety, with straight quillons and disc or brazil nut pommels, but they are invariably shown being used as cutting weapons. The leather scabbard was worn low on the hip, hanging from a long belt. Daggers are very rarely shown.

Actual combats between the forces of Islam and Christendom are shown in various contemporary sources. One of the best known, although represented today only by a series of eighteenth-century engravings, are the thirteenth-century stained glass panels made for the church of Saint-Denis just outside Paris. Christian knights are shown wearing Norman-style helmets, mailcoats and shields, while the Saracens are equipped with lamellar armour, round-topped helmets and round shields. The swords of the Saracens are straight and tapering, with very small guards and pommels. Straight swords of similar design, and probably of twelfth- or thirteenth-century date, are preserved in the arsenal of the Sultans in Istanbul. Swords like these are more fully described in Chapter 11, but the point should be made that both straight and curved weapons were used by Muslim forces during the Crusading period.

The challenge of plate armour

With the development of plate armour towards the end of the thirteenth century swordsmiths were obliged to change the design of sword blades. Blades primarily designed for cutting and hacking were unable to penetrate plate armour. So the emphasis changed from cutting to thrusting. A more rigid blade was developed, diamond-shaped in cross section, reinforced by a raised ridge down the centre. This proved extremely effective and remained in use until well into the fifteenth century. Wheel-shaped pommels and down-curving quillons persisted throughout the fourteenth century. Pear-shaped and facetted pommels were introduced around 1400.

The development of the sword during the fourteenth century can be traced reasonably precisely thanks to a remarkable group of swords preserved by the Turks in the arsenal at Alexandria in Egypt. Many of these are of Western European origin. With marvellous foresight each weapon was inscribed with the date it was deposited and with the name of the governor ruling at the time. The contents of the arsenal were removed to Istanbul in 1514, and now form part of the collections on display in the Topkapı Palace. Most of the swords are fighting weapons ranging in date from the first half of the fourteenth century to about 1440 and they are in fine condition. Swords of Italian manufacture predominate but there are also German weapons. The hilts vary from the simple cruciform type with a wheel pommel to a Venetian-type hilt with a square or facetted pommel. Some have a small ring guard welded to one quillon, which is most significant, for it was from this simple extra guard that the complex rapier hilts of the sixteenth century evolved. This extra guard is shown on swords in illustrated manuscripts from about 1340 onwards but the earliest surviving swords with a ring guard are of slightly later date.

The fourteenth century also saw the introduction of bearing swords. These were, and are, very large ceremonial swords borne before rulers and other dignitaries on ceremonial occasions. On display in the Topkapı in Istanbul is a bearing sword of extraordinary dimensions, taken by the Turks in their campaigns against Hungary. The heraldic devices on it imply that its owner was Mathias Corvinus, king of Hungary from 1440 to 1490.

Bearing swords are not the only outsize weapons to be found in arsenals. In many armouries around the world there are huge swords associated with famous heroes and legendary dering-do. Visitors to Warwick Castle are always suitably impressed by the sword of Guy of Warwick and his gigantic 'porridge pot' of cast bronze. In Arundel Castle in Sussex is the mighty sword of the legendary hero Bevis of Hampton, fancifully described in Wright's *Antiquities of Arundel* as 'the identical sword worn by Bevis, formerly Governor of the castle, previous to the Norman Conquest'. In fact the Arundel Castle sword is a cross-hilted weapon of late fourteenth-century date and from the gashes on its edge has seen valiant service.

Above Sword with a hilt of pierced steel, one of a series of similar swords from the Armoury of the Council of Ten, Doges' Palace, Venice. Venetian *c*. 1470.

Left Page from a Spanish manuscript, the *Cantigas* of Alfonso the Wise, *c*. 1250, showing Christians fighting Moors. The forces of Islam are depicted as lightly armoured horsemen carrying shields (*adargas*) and long lances.

One of the most intriguing edged weapons 'discovered' in recent years belongs to Dublin Corporation. For many years it was generally assumed to be a civic sword of seventeenth-century date because of the seventeenth-century mounts on the scabbard. However Claude Blair has recently shown that the sword is both medieval and royal. It was in fact made in 1396 for Henry IV of England (1367–1413) by a goldsmith named Herman van Cleve. The blade is long and double-edged and the hilt is of hand-and-a-half proportions, with long quillons and a facetted pear-shaped pommel. Both the hilt and scabbard mounts are of silver gilt. Only one of the scabbard mounts, in the form of a garter engraved with forget-me-nots, is original. The hilt is also engraved with forget-me-nots. Engraved on the flap in the centre of the quillons and also on the original scabbard mount are the words 'SOUEREYNE SOUEREYNE' in Gothic letters. This motto, together with the forget-me-nots, was Henry's device before his accession to the throne in 1399. The sword was apparently given to a mayor of Dublin in 1403 when the King granted him the privilege of having a sword borne before him in procession.

The late Gothic style of ornament is widely found on sword hilts made in the first half of the fifteenth century. Hilts with wrythen pommels and quillons terminating in Gothic beasts and wrought with Gothic foliage are all found. As the century progressed, blades became somewhat narrower and shorter, consonant with a more thrusting style of swordsmanship. Wheel pommels persisted, much reduced in size, or were replaced by fish-tail and pear shapes or facetted forms, with regional variations becoming very noticeable around the middle of the century. The typical Venetian pommel, for example, was square and appears in conjunction with horizontally scrolling quillons. Another type of sword, also thought to be Venetian, had a curiously elongated pommel and a sharply angled knuckleguard, perhaps based on Turkish prototypes. By the 1460s swords with knuckleguards and ring guards on the quillons were becoming increasingly common. They were, as we shall see in the next chapter, the forebears of the rapier.

Knives and daggers

After the two Roman empires went their separate ways, daggers did not change radically for a considerable period. We know this from weapons excavated from fifth- and sixth-century sites. Two fine examples from a sixth-century Frankish site have short broad blades, oval cap pommels and waisted grips very much in the style of swords of the period. No doubt they survived because the mounts are of gold set with stones.

However by the ninth century the dagger version of the Scandinavian *seax* had been widely adopted in Northern Europe. This was simply a shorter, lighter version of the sword, with a wide single-edged blade tapering sharply to a point and a long flat tang to which the grip was fitted. The wide flat blade was an ideal

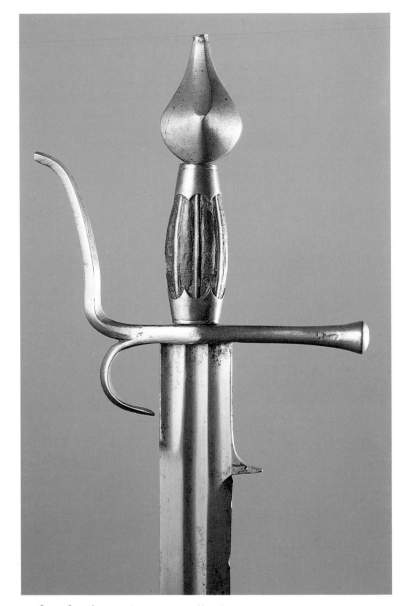

surface for decoration, especially for inlay. One tenth-century specimen has a blade inlaid with silver, brass, copper and niello and bears the name of its owner or maker.

When a short-bladed weapon like a knife was intended for use only as a cutting weapon, it was more practical to make it with a single edge only, and by forging the blade with a thick back edge the cutler was able to combine both weight and strength. Single-edged weapons are also easier to sharpen. Daggers with single-edged blades similar to those of the seventeenth and eighteenth centuries have been found in Swiss graves dating from as early as the tenth.

The practice of using small discs for the guards and pommels of daggers evolved much earlier than is generally realised. There are, for example, daggers from the Viking period which have hilts

Above The Great Dublin Civic Sword, once part of the personal armoury of Henry IV and granted as a bearing sword to the Mayor of Dublin in 1403. The hilt and one of the scabbard mounts are engraved with forget-me-nots, a device used by Henry before he became king.

Right Venetian broadsword with knucklebow and finger ring, made in about 1450. Many similar fine fighting swords are preserved in the armoury of the Council of Ten in the Doges' Palace, Venice.

mounted with oval discs, although traditionally the 'rondel' or 'roundel' dagger is regarded as having developed around 1300. On medieval rondel daggers the discs at the top and bottom of the tubular grip were plain or facetted and produced in a variety of materials, gilt copper being the most common. As with other medieval daggers, the quality of the workmanship varies considerably.

Other types of dagger hilt faithfully followed the design of contemporary sword hilts, with one exception, the 'antennae' hilt. Antennae-hilted daggers were a Celtic invention, a feature of the Hallstatt period (800–500 BC) when Celtic culture dominated Central and Western Europe. In a slightly altered form the antennae hilt was revived in the fourteenth century, with both pommel and guard being constructed of simple curved bars with scrolled ends.

One of the best known forms of medieval dagger is the baselard. This had a distinctive crosspiece at both the guard and pommel end, giving the hilt the appearance of a capital I. The type almost certainly originated in Switzerland and can be traced back to the thirteenth century. It seems to have been associated with the city of Basel, hence its name, but was widely carried throughout Europe, especially in the fourteenth and fifteenth centuries. As a satirical English song of the period says: 'There is no man worth a leke, Be he sturdy, be he meke, But he bear a basilard.' Versions with wood and bone hilts are common, but silver hilts were also made.

Another dagger typical of the Middle Ages is the ballock knife, euphemistically referred to by Victorian scholars as the 'kidney dagger'. 'Ballock' is a reference to the two spheres or rounded prominences which form the guard. The standard form had a wooden grip with a swelling pommel, although more illustrious examples are hilted in silver and often have a two-stage facetted blade. The ballock knife first appeared around 1300 and remained in use in some areas, notably in Scotland, until the seventeenth century. Ballock knives turn up in large numbers on medieval sites, and several hundred were found on the *Mary Rose*, wrecked off the Isle of Wight in 1545.

A large number of medieval daggers have been found in recent years by treasure-hunters working on the Thames foreshore in London, off Billingsgate and the City. These range from simple quillon daggers with crossbars resembling those on contemporary swords to elaborately mounted daggers with Gothic hilts. These are exciting finds for they represent types which have not survived elsewhere, and most have been preserved in excellent condition – the Thames mud quickly sealed them, keeping both wood and metal safe from deterioration. Some specimens are broken, and were probably thrown into the river as useless, but others are undamaged and of first-rate quality. In the Middle Ages, the Thames was London's main thoroughfare, plied by scores of boatmen and ferrymen. No doubt many valuables were lost by travellers getting in and out of boats, especially at night.

Above Baselard with rootwood hilt mounted in silver, Swiss (Basel?), c.1350. The ring on top of the pommel bears the letters 'HNAON', an owner's motto, and the blade is inlaid with a maker's mark.

Above left, left to right
Rondel dagger from the River Thames, English, late fourteenth century.
Dagger with lobed quillons, English, c.1400, also found in the River Thames.
Dagger from a grave near Avully, Geneva. The hilt is mounted in gold with stamped designs. Swiss, tenth–eleventh century.
Quillon dagger found in Lavenham Church, Suffolk. The single-edged blade is inlaid with a maker's mark and the hilt is of cast and engraved bronze. English, fifteenth century.

43

4 THE RENAISSANCE SPIRIT

Donald J. LaRocca

By the year 1300, after nearly four thousand years of continuous development, the sword in Europe reached its apogee as an instrument of war. Yet within less than three hundred years the armoured, sword-wielding soldier had ceased to be the most potent force on the battlefield. Even in the fourteenth century the sword was tactically less significant than projectile weapons such as the long bow, and from the late fifteenth century even the long bow was ousted by hand-held firearms.

The evolution of the sword and the dagger throughout the Renaissance period presents a fascinating and complex picture. Long-cherished forms were retained side by side with forms which changed from year to year, making exact chronologies sometimes difficult to establish. Blades, hilts and other features changed their form in response to changes in body armour, new military tactics or simply the dictates of fashion.

From cutting to thrusting

The general shape of the sword in the fourteenth century was cruciform, as it had been in the previous two centuries. But whereas earlier cross-hilted swords were primarily cutting weapons, those from the mid-thirteenth century onwards were equally suited to thrusting, and by the fourteenth century the strictly cutting sword of cruciform shape, with its parallel-edged blade and short point, went out of general use.

A sword designed primarily for thrusting, later known as the estoc or tuck, was apparently in use by the end of the thirteenth century. For splitting mail links or piercing the gaps between various pieces of armour a steeply pointed and stiff blade was needed. Thus, from the second quarter of the fourteenth century, we find blades with flattened diamond or lozenge cross-sections.

As the century advanced, plate armour became more and more sophisticated. Even in the early years of the century available defences for the limbs included skilfully shaped and articulated metal plates which encased the wearer from shoulder to wrist and from fork to foot. Fourteenth-century armour for the torso, as reconstructed from the few surviving fragmentary examples,

consisted of various forms of the coat-of-plates or brigandine (metal plates of various sizes attached to a jacket of reinforced fabric). This was the type of armour found in the mass graves of those who fell at the battle of Wisby, fought in Gotland in Sweden in 1361, and also in a cache of fourteenth-century armour found in a ruined castle in Chalcis on the Greek Island of Euboea in the nineteenth century. Solid breast-plates and back-plates were not introduced until the fifteenth century.

Against plate armour a thrusting sword was obviously more effective than a cutting one, so the fully armoured mounted man-at-arms of the fourteenth century might be equipped with a thrusting sword suspended from the front or side of his saddle, while on his hip he still carried the more versatile cut-and-thrust sword. In both cases the grip would frequently have been of hand-and-a-half proportions, long enough to grasp with two hands when necessary but primarily intended for one. The hand-and-a-half or bastard sword, which made its appearance in the middle of the twelfth century, was especially popular in the fourteenth and fifteenth, and continued in use in various forms into the seventeenth. Two-handed swords, which were only really effective if wielded with two hands, existed before the middle of the fourteenth century but surviving examples which predate the late fifteenth century are very rare.

Judging from period illustrations, the falchion continued to be widely used throughout the fourteenth century. Its broad chopping blade could be straight or curved, with a rounded, pointed or clipped tip. Some falchions, such as those illustrated in the mid-thirteenth century Maciejowski Bible, were obviously rather crude chopping weapons, wielded with two hands and fitted with a simple wooden grip rather like that of an ordinary spade. Others were hilted in the same fashion as contemporary swords. A regal if anachronistic example can be seen in the hand of Julius Caesar, depicted as an armoured and crowned French king in the 'Nine Heroes' tapestries in The Cloisters, New York. These tapestries were woven in about 1385.

Opposite page The Battle of Agincourt, an illumination from the St. Albans Chronicle, *c.*1450. Although painted more than a generation after Agincourt (1415), this scene gives a fair, albeit stylized, image of fifteenth-century warfare. Fully armoured men-at-arms engage with lance and sword while archers and pikemen fight on foot.

Towards the developed hilt

It is to fourteenth-century hilts that we must look for the first hints of the changes which led, eventually, to the complicated system of guards characteristic of sixteenth-century rapier hilts.

Fourteenth-century crossguards, or quillons, were either straight or curved towards the blade in an arched or drooping fashion. Both straight and curved forms are found with flattened, spatulate ends, although curled or scroll-like terminals are seldom found before the end of the century. The guard is sometimes wider at the centre – where the tang passes through it – but what is referred to as a quillon block or *écusson* is rare before the early fifteenth century. In cross-section the guard was square, round or polygonal.

The forefinger hook, consisting of a bar, rod or branch describing a short loop from the forward quillon to the blade, was added to protect the right forefinger when it was hooked over the forward quillon. This, more than any other feature of fourteenth-century hilts, is considered to be the first step in the evolution of the rapier hilt. The earliest known appearance of a forefinger hook is that depicted on a falchion in the left panel of 'The Crucifixion and the Lamentation' diptych by the Master of the Codex of St. George, painted in Siena, *c*.1340–1350. In this instance, and in other early sources, the forefinger hook is associated with a single-edged cutting sword, but from the middle to later part of the fifteenth century and throughout the sixteenth forefinger hooks also appear on straight and double-edged swords. A good early example can be seen on a sword in the Tower of London; an Arabic inscription on the blade includes the date 1432, but the guard with its forefinger ring probably dates from the fourteenth century.

Related to the guard with forefinger ring is the earlier innovation of an unsharpened area at the shoulder of the blade, against which the finger could rest. A rudimentary form of ricasso, as this unsharpened area is called, was in evidence by the mid-twelfth century. Some later blades have a crescentic cut-out in the shoulder of the blade to accommodate the forefinger.

45

Above This sword, possibly Italian, was one of a group of swords included in the annual tribute paid by King John II of Cyprus after his father's defeat by the Mamluk Sultan Al Ashraf Sayf al-Din Barsbay in 1452. Two very similar swords with forefinger rings, with the same Arabic inscription dated 1432, are preserved in Istanbul.

Above right A robust cut-and-thrust sword (top), made *c.*1350–1400, and a fourteenth-century ring-pommel sword (below). The pommel of the former is framed by inscribed silver bands which read 'sunt.hic.etiam. sua.praemia.laveli' ('here too virtue has its due reward'), a quotation from the *Aeneid*. The ring-pommel sword is a Swiss weapon and relatively short (only 27 ins/68 cm overall); its hilt may be a rare if not unique variant of the baselard. The grip consists of five plaques of ivy root separated by copper bands.

The next step towards a more developed hilt was the knuckle guard. In its earliest stages, this was formed simply by bending the forward quillon towards and sometimes parallel to the grip. This feature first appears on falchions and other cutting swords of the late fourteenth and early fifteenth centuries.

As for pommels, wheels and discs with flat or bevelled facets remained in active use from the twelfth to the sixteenth century. To these were added, in the late fourteenth century, triangular or wedge-shaped pommels with the narrow end towards the grip. Much rarer were spherical pommels or cube-shaped pommels with bevelled corners.

Throughout the Middle Ages sword grips seem to have consisted of twin pieces of wood fitted over the tang and secured with horizontal turns of twisted wire or with leather or fabric bound with a variety of criss-cross leather bands, strips of fabric, or wire. The fabric or leather was occasionally studded with decorative rivet heads. However, the majority of medieval and Renaissance swords in existence today have had their grips replaced or restored at least once after their working lifetime, and only swords which have been preserved undisturbed in treasuries or tombs, such as that of Cangrande della Scala in Verona, opened in 1921, allow us to correctly interpret the wealth of examples depicted in sculpture, painting, and the graphic arts of the period.

The fifteenth century

The first quarter of the fifteenth century saw the development of fully articulated, head-to-toe plate armour, which continued to be refined throughout the century. This elicited various responses from swordsmiths of the day, one of which was the short, stiff and steeply pointed thrusting sword or estoc. The *stocco* of Estore Visconti (d. 1413), now in Monza Cathedral, is one of the finest surviving swords of this type and gives us an image of, for instance, the swords used in the campaigns of Henry V in the latter half of the Hundred Years' War.

A cut-and-thrust sword of similar proportions but with a less acute blade was also used during the fifteenth century, as was a more slender, elongated type, usually with a hand-and-a-half grip and a weighty pommel to counterbalance the length of the blade. One also finds hand-and-a-half swords with much broader blades of diamond cross-section, stiff enough for thrusting but also suitable for cutting. Swords of this type, often fitted with a 'waisted' grip, were particularly popular in Europe north of the Alps in the second half of the century and are seen in such familiar images as Dürer's 'Knight, Death and the Devil' woodcut.

From the middle of the century onwards, hilt developments become more and more rapid. Quillons arched more strongly towards the blade and scrolled ends became more common. Straight quillons did not go out of fashion, but towards the end of the century they begin to recurve horizontally. The quillon block with a strong central point extended towards the blade had been quite common since the early part of the century.

By about 1450 knuckleguard and forefinger ring were combined on the same hilt, and a second finger ring was added, mirroring the first. These two loops or rings symmetrically flanking the shoulders of the blade are referred to by modern writers as 'the arms of the hilt'. By 1475, if not earlier, the knuckleguard was combined with the arms of the hilt, and shortly thereafter the ends of the arms of the hilt were fitted with transverse lugs or a short curved bar which passed horizontally from the end of one arm to the end of the other; this is known as a side ring. Then the knuckleguard, from being a simple bent quillon, became another branch in addition to the forward quillon and formed an arc from the quillon block to the pommel. Late in the century the hilt sprouted yet another guard in the form of a side ring, post or short block, protruding horizontally from the outer face of the quillon block; this was designed to protect the back of the hand.

And so, to all intents and purposes, the rapier hilt was born. However, at the end of the fifteenth century the developed hilt just described was usually mounted on a sturdy cut-and-thrust blade. This is rather at odds with the modern notion of the rapier as a slender thrusting instrument. Such rapiers did indeed develop in the course of the sixteenth century as the wearing of swords with civilian dress became fashionable, but in the third quarter of

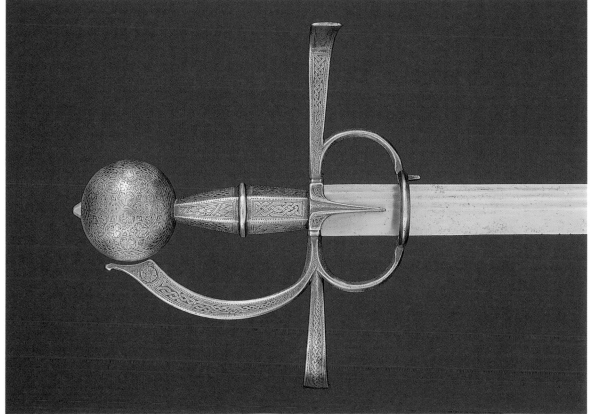

the fifteenth century, at least in Italy, the developed hilt fitted with a sturdy cut-and-thrust blade seems to have been favoured by the lightly armoured infantryman. The armoured cavalryman, with a metal gauntlet to protect his hand, stuck to the cruciform sword. However, this distinction was not universal. In Spain the early developed hilt seems to have been used by armoured cavalry as well, and was porbably carried to the New World by the troops of Cortés and De Soto.

As for the ricasso, seen with increasing frequency from the mid-fourteenth century onwards, this gradually became thicker and square in cross-section, and remained so for as long as straight sword blades continued to be used.

Many other sword types flourished in the fifteenth century. The falchion, also known as the *malchus* or *storta*, remained popular, although it was generally shorter and sometimes slimmer than the great chopper of the previous two centuries, and a more effective slashing weapon as a result. However, very few of the slender, almost sabre-like falchions survive, compared with the shorter variety. Both types were found mainly in Italy and France.

A later cousin of the early falchion was the German *Grosse Messer*, literally 'big knife', a very apt description. This had a long, slightly curved, single-edged blade, straight quillons – frequently with a side ring or lug on the quillon block – and a handle resembling an enlarged knife grip. Its use, and the use of related types, was generally confined to Germanic and Scandinavian countries. Other curved swords, or something approaching the sabre proper, were uncommon before the sixteenth century.

Throughout the century a great variety of civilian and infantry swords were used. These were usually shorter versions of the cavalry or knightly sword, often fitted with a single-edged blade. The most popular type was the hanger, to which we will revert later in this chapter. Another distinctive short weapon for use on foot was the Landsknecht sword or *Katzbalger* ('brawler' or, more literally, 'cat skinner'), favoured by German mercenaries from the later part of the century onwards. The characteristic features of this sword are a metal grip that flares out into an integral pommel, strongly recurved S-shaped quillons, and a short stout blade with parallel edges and a short point. In the sixteenth century, the terminals of the S-shaped quillons were occasionally extended to form a figure of eight. Landsknecht swords (and the related Landsknecht dagger) for officers and commanders could be richly ornamented, with chiselled, engraved or gilt hilts and etched blades.

Just as the *Katzbalger* is always associated with Germany, the *cinquedea* is considered distinctively Italian. The name refers to the width of the blade, five fingers, at the quillons. A highly original and handsome weapon, the *cinquedea* was developed in northern

Above Italian rapier, made in Venice in about 1490. The delicate engraved and blackened embellishment on the hilt of this sturdy, functional weapon is so similar to that on the *storta* shown on the next page that it is tempting to suggest that they once formed a pair, or were at least made in the same place and period.

Above left Detail from *Young Knight in a Landscape*, by Vittore Carpaccio (1460/65–c.1526). The confident young warrior wears a superb Italian light field armour made *alla tedesca* (in the German fashion) and stands ready to draw his finely made Katzbalger. It has been suggested that the knight is King Lajos II of Hungary, standing before the city of Ragusa (modern Dubrovnik) in 1520.

47

Below Two-handed sword, Italian (Venice?), *c.* 1570, made in the enduring form that characterized two-handed battle swords for over a century. Etched on the blade is a shield incorporating the arms of Hungary, Bohemia, Castile, Leon, Austria and Burgundy, suggesting that it may have been the weapon of a troop of ceremonial bodyguards.

Bottom A rare example of a *storta*, Italian (Venice), *c.* 1490. On the blade is an etched and gilt Latin inscription reminding the wielder that virtue is attained through God alone and ending with a plea not to be led into tribulations. The antecedents of the *storta* are to be found in the medieval falchion and in the single-edged sabre carried into Western Europe by nomadic warriors from the Eastern steppes.

Italy in the fifteenth century and remained in vogue into the early sixteenth. It appears to have been worn primarily with civilian dress. Both dagger- and sword-length *cinquedeas* exist, but the majority fall somewhere between a large dagger and a short sword. The flat tang is faced with two ivory plates pierced by inset filigree rosettes and secured by tubular rivets. The pommel cap and quillons are generally simple but are often chiselled, engraved or gilded. Equally distinctive is the facetted or fluted blade which typically bears a series of shallow channels in a sequence of four over three over two. Most *cinquedea* blades are etched and gilded, sometimes on a blued ground, with allegorical or mythological scenes and Latin mottoes.

The two-handed sword was a specialized and effective infantry weapon, and was recognized as such in the fifteenth and sixteenth centuries. Although large, measuring 60–70 ins/150–175 cm overall, it was not as hefty as it looked, weighing something of the order of 5–8 lbs/2.3–3.6 kg. In the hands of Swiss and German infantrymen it was lethal, and its use was considered a special skill, often meriting extra pay. Fifteenth-century examples usually have an expanded cruciform hilt, sometimes with side rings on one or both sides of the quillon block. This was the form which remained dominant in Italy during the sixteenth century, but in Germany a more flamboyant form developed. Two-handed swords typically have a generous ricasso to allow the blade to be safely gripped below the quillons and thus wielded more effectively at close quarters. Triangular or pointed projections, known as flukes, were added at the base of the ricasso to defend the hand.

The sixteenth century

One of the most remarkable things about the evolution of the rapier was its swiftness, and the explanation for this probably lies in the fact that from the late fifteenth century onwards the sword, and then the rapier, became an accepted part of civilian dress. Swords became more and more important as costume accessories and *ipso facto* subject to the vagaries of fashion. This is not to imply that the civilian rapier became a mere ornamental bauble,

eighteenth century. Rather, the sixteenth century marked a parting of the ways between those swords and rapiers suitable for use on the battlefield and those intended for civilian wear.

Variations of the cruciform hilt remained in wide use on military swords throughout the century. However, as the rapier became more fashionable, from about the second quarter of the century, so the practice of fitting military swords with rapier-type hilts became more common. One may generalize by saying that military weapons, of necessity, retained a robust cut-and-thrust blade, while civilian rapiers, at least by the middle of the sixteenth century, were fitted with a much slenderer blade, eminently suitable for a deadly thrust against an unarmoured opponent. Of course there are many exceptions to this generalization. In England, for instance, the long-standing popularity of sword and buckler for military and civilian wear delayed the wearing of the rapier alone until nearly the end of the century.

By the second quarter of the sixteenth century the side ring, found on the arms of the hilt from the 1480s, was sometimes found in conjunction with a second side ring mounted on the quillon block. At about the same time the outer face of the hilt sprouted a system of supplementary transverse bars or branches which passed from the root of the quillons to the knuckle guard and, in the opposite direction, to the arms of the hilt. The diagonal sweep of these transverse guards gives rise to the modern term 'swept-hilt' rapier. The inner face of the hilt followed suit, and by about 1575 the triple branch inner guard typical of most late rapiers was in place.

By the middle of the century, long, slender, straight quillons, frequently with recurved finials, became fashionable, but not to the exclusion of other types. By this time the arms of the hilt sometimes supported double side rings, one above the other, the uppermost being inclined toward the grip and sometimes joined to the knuckleguard by a transverse branch. Also it not unusual for one or both of these side rings to be filled by a pierced plate. By the end of the century a pierced plate was also occasionally found between two branches of the transverse inner guard. A solid plate, engraved rather than pierced, was also used in the side rings, especially on silver-hilted Saxon swords. The arms of the hilt terminated in various ways, including knobs (usually en suite with the quillon finials and the pommel), loops, or extensions which curved towards the grip or bent upright and parallel to it.

A great variety of pommels was used in the sixteenth century. As already mentioned, discs and wheels continued to be popular. The cockle-shell pommel introduced towards the end of the fifteenth century was used throughout the sixteenth and into the seventeenth. Spherical pommels, rare in earlier centuries, appeared in greater numbers, some squat, some mushroom-shaped, some almost cylindrical with rounded edges. Egg-shaped pommels, conical pommels and polygonal pommels were all tried, with their faces facetted, fluted, and enhanced in any one of a dozen other ways.

Above Italian rapier, *c.*1546. A matching weapon is preserved in the Real Armeria, Madrid. Both weapons apparently belong to an armour garniture commissioned by Emperor Charles V from the prestigious Negroli workshop in Milan.

Far left Right panel from the Paumgärtner Altar by Albrecht Dürer (1471–1528), showing St Eustachius in the no-nonsense fighting gear of a light cavalryman. On his right hip he wears a Landsknecht dagger and on his left a hand-and-a-half sword.

Left Cinquedea, Italian, *c.*1480–1500. The quintessential civilian side-arm of the High Renaissance in Italy, the *cinquedea* was worn on the right hip or at the small of the back with the hilt inclined to the right.

Below An extravagantly chiselled iron hilt, *c.*1560–70. A masterpiece of eccentric mannerist design, inspired by ornamentalists such as Virgil Solis, it demonstrates well the endless variety of decoration possible on a limited surface.

49

Above right Portrait of Stefano Sciarra Colonna by Angelo Bronzino (1503–72), painted in 1540. His sword is of cruciform type, with double side rings; his armour is subtly but richly decorated with gold damascening incorporating the column device of the Colonna.

A soldier of great renown and a member of one of the oldest and most illustrious Roman noble families, Stefano was initially an ardent Imperialist but later joined the Papal forces. During the Sack of Rome in 1527 he led the defence of the Vatican, enabling Pope Clement VII to escape to Castel San Angelo.

Right Rapier hilt of chiselled iron encrusted with silver, displaying a variety of military trophies and grotesque masks derived from the antique, possibly Italian, *c.*1555–60. The forward quillon has evolved into a transverse loop which joins the rear arm of the hilt, providing protection to the back of the hand and an additional surface for decoration.

As the preceding makes abundantly clear, greater variety than ever before was a characteristic feature of rapier design, particularly from the second quarter of the century onwards. This was also true, but perhaps to a slightly lesser extent, of cruciform swords during the same period. Cruciform hilts remained particularly popular on estocs for use in war, primarily against armoured opponents. In addition to the earlier thrusting blade, with a cross-section of flattened lozenge form, estoc blades of triangular and sometimes square cross-section, with concave sides, were in use throughout the sixteenth century. These very stiff blades were designed to puncture plate armour in much the same way as a crossbow bolt or the beak of a war hammer.

In general, cruciform war swords seem to have enjoyed longer popularity north of the Alps than in Italy or Spain. Whether fitted with a cut-and-thrust or rigid estoc-type blade, the hilt remained relatively simple; a pommel of conical outline and quillons arching slightly towards the blade were most common. Typically, there was a side ring from the quillon block, but in Germanic countries this was frequently replaced by a branch that ran from the mid-point of the forward quillon to the rear quillon, curving outwards at the quillon block.

Swords of the Saxon Reitschwert type represent what is probably the most fully evolved hilt that can still be termed 'cruciform'. They are also the most cohesive and well known subgroup of late cruciform swords. The type was established in Germany prior to the middle of the sixteenth century and remained in use in Saxony until the early seventeenth. In addition to the features described above, Reitschwert hilts often have spatulate quillons, arms of the hilt, a second side ring from the arms, and a diagonal inner guard or a thumb ring. Some of those made for the Saxon court are partially or wholly encased in engraved and blackened sheet silver.

Ceremonial swords

The most fundamental use which developed for the cruciform sword as the sixteenth century progressed was as a ceremonial or symbolic weapon. The sword had long symbolized authority. As the first weapon which was not simply a modified tool but one specifically designed as a killing instrument, the sword was the prerogative of warriors, the instrument used to enforce authority and its related privileges. As the warrior class evolved into a feudal aristocracy, the sword became a symbol of rank and status. The most highly decorated and sumptuous swords could only be afforded by the most powerful individuals and were reserved for important ceremonial occasions. Coronation ceremonies demanded the finest, most impressive regalia obtainable, and the sword was and remains a fundamental element of coronation regalia. Among the most notable examples are the twelfth-century gold hilt of the coronation sword of the kings of France, already mentioned in Chapter 3. The electoral sword of Frederick I of Saxony, given to him by Emperor Sigismund I of Germany in

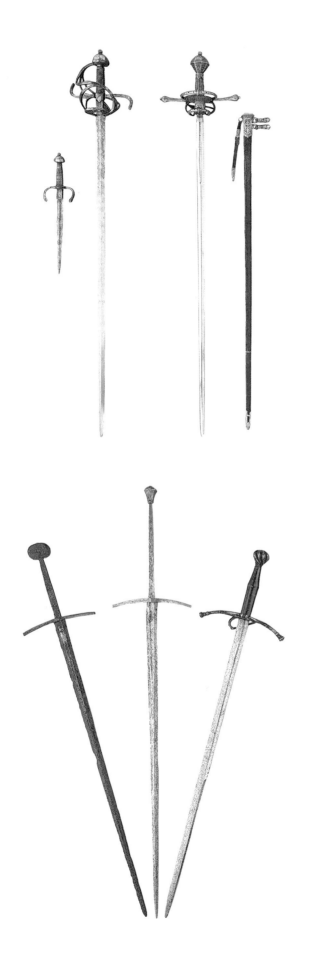

1425, has a cruciform hilt exquisitely decorated with rock crystal, silver gilt, gold and silver filigree; the silver-gilt and engraved sword made for the coronation of King Sigismund I of Poland in 1506 is also cruciform, as is the gilt and enamelled electoral sword of Augustus of Saxony, dated 1566.

Bearing swords, also cruciform, were carried point uppermost before kings and other august and powerful individuals. The posthumous biography of Richard Beauchamp, Earl of Warwick, records that he was given the honour of bearing the sword of Emperor Sigismund in procession before him. In the collection of the Tower of London is a fifteenth-century bearing sword of huge proportions (91 ins/228 cm from pommel to point) made, it is thought, for Henry V or perhaps for Edward, Prince of Wales.

Bearing swords were also bestowed as symbols of office. The sword of the Constables of France, now in the Musée de l'Armée in Paris, is a case in point. This sword, probably made in the second half of the fifteenth century, would have been presented by the king to each new Constable at his investiture; renowned soldiers such as Bertrand du Guesclin and Anne de Montmorency held the office of Constable during this period. The hilt decoration is intended to be read with the sword held point up, and the blade is extremely simple, a feature not uncommon on bearing swords.

Beginning in the fourteenth century, the mayors of several English cities were granted the right to have a sword borne before them on civic occasions. A number of these civic swords were gifts from the king himself. The privilege was gradually extended to other cities and was still being granted as late as the end of the seventeenth century. Perhaps the earliest civic sword still in existence is the sword of the city of Bristol, part of which is thought to date from 1373. Other civic swords survive in Lincoln, York and Coventry.

Throughout the Renaissance, and indeed until the early nineteenth century, the Pope presented swords more or less on a yearly basis to the most deserving defenders of the faith. These were two-handed swords, many of them exquisite examples of Italian, usually Roman, goldsmiths' work. The hilts and scabbards are sculpturally ornate, the former usually cast in silver and gilded. Presented en suite were a belt and a cap, intricately decorated with gold thread and pearls by professional embroiders whose work equalled that of the goldsmiths in splendour and delicacy. The presentation was made by the Pope in an elaborate ceremony held on Christmas Day. Due to the lavish use of precious materials and their delicate nature, papal swords and their accoutrements rarely survive together and intact. Archduke Ferdinand of Austria, honoured with the sword and cap in 1567 and again in 1581, was a famous collector of arms, armour and 'curiosa', and it is probably because of his collecting instincts that both of his presentations survive in a remarkably complete state.

Judicial beheading by means of the sword, as opposed to the axe, was favoured in France and central Europe throughout the

Left above A matching rapier and parrying dagger (left) and a more elaborate Reitschwert (right) with its original scabbard. Both weapons are Saxon, dating from the late sixteenth century.

The hilts of the rapier and parrying dagger are entirely covered with silver foil burnished over cross-hatching. The iron hilt of the Reitschwert is overlaid with pierced and engraved silver sheets.

Saxony was one of the leading silver-mining areas in Europe, which may account for the profusion and sustained popularity of silver-mounted Saxon swords.

Left Two hand-and-a-half swords (left and centre) and a German sword with a hilt typical of c.1500–20 but with an unusual blade (right).

The hand-and-a-half swords are possibly Flemish or English and date from the late fourteenth to the early fifteenth century. Such swords were capable of an effective cutting blow or, with their slender but stiff blades, of a thrust against the nearly complete plate armour of the period.

The blade on the German weapon is original; its back edge is sharpened for less than half its length, the remainder having a square shoulder like that of later sabre blades.

second of Henry VIII's six wives, disdained the axe and so a headsman practiced in the sword was brought from Saint-Omer, near Calais. While accounts of the event differ with respect to other details, all agree that the executioner was neat and efficient, performing his task with a single blow. The sword continued to be an instrument of execution until the early eighteenth century.

Tournament swords

The sword served the knightly classes not only in war and ceremony, but also in competitive sport. The tournament, introduced in the Middle Ages as a training for war, remained extremely popular during the Renaissance. In early medieval tournaments the arms and armour used varied little if at all from battlefield equipment, which made jousting and single combat singularly bloody and frequently deadly affairs, but by the end of the thirteenth century stricter rules were introduced and by the late fifteenth and sixteenth century the tournament had become less of a training for war and more of a symbolic and ceremony-laden sport.

Already by the middle of the thirteenth century there was a distinction between jousts *à plaisance* (jousts of peace) and jousts *à outrance* (jousts of war, or more literally jousts 'to the death'). Although details are lacking, the former must have required weapons that were in some way blunted or unsharpened. Although virtually no medieval tournament swords have survived, period documents and graphic sources have allowed us to reconstruct several types with varying degrees of certainty. Swords of whalebone and parchment were used in a tournament held by Edward I of England in 1278, but their exact appearance is unknown. By the mid-fifteenth century various types of long and short club were also used, with or instead of swords. *Le Livre des Tournois* of King René d'Anjou, a mid-fifteenth century compilation, shows tournament armour and weapons in great detail, and here the principal sword used for tournament on horseback was of cruciform shape, with a short triangular tip, blunted edges and a protective flap mounted over the quillons and extending towards the sword hand.

It appears that it was usual throughout the medieval and Renaissance period for tournament swords to be simply rebated war swords, such as those seen in Lucas Cranach's wonderfully detailed 'Third Tournament' woodcut of 1509. However, some idea of the probable variety of types is given in the *Freydal*, an early sixteenth-century manuscript illustrating the tournaments and feasts held at the court of Emperor Maximilian I. In addition to what appear to be one-handed, two-handed and bastard war swords suitable for cut and thrust, there are falchions or short sabre-like swords with extremely broad blades and clipped points, swords of the cut-and-thrust type but with blunted tips, and swords with double quillons which arch towards the blade and the grip. Aside from these, a great many unusual weapons not of the sword family are shown.

sixteenth and seventeenth centuries. Although derived from the two-handed war sword, the executioner's sword had become a rather specialized instrument by the second quarter of the sixteenth century. Typically the grip was straight, long enough to be comfortably grasped in both hands, the quillons were also straight, and the pommel was spherical or pear-shaped. The blade was straight, long, broad and flat, with little or no fuller, and rounded or nearly squared off at the tip – this more than anything else made its form and function unmistakable and immediately recognizable. Not infrequently it was decorated with scenes of execution or simply the implements of execution, such as the wheel, hook and gallows. Inscriptions on the blade, alone or in conjunction with the above, ranged from the poetic ('Maiden's love and bird songs are sweet and fleeting') to the moral ('When I raise my sword so God gives eternal life to this poor wretch'). Headsmen who had mastered the sword were considered skilled professionals, the best being specially commissioned to perform important executions. For her execution Anne Boleyn, the

Left Woodcut from *The Investiture of Ferdinand I*, 1530, by Jacob Breu the Elder (dates unknown). This extremely detailed and rare depiction of a major tournament in progress almost certainly represents an eye-witness account by the artist. Combat with sword and lance rages across the field. The Emperor Charles V is seen in the centre at full tilt, while his less fortunate brother Ferdinand I, King of Hungary and Bohemia, lies pinned beneath his horse in the background.

Opposite page Woodcut from *Der Weisskunig*, an allegorical biography of Emperor Maximilian, by Hans Burgkmair (1473–1531). In this episode from the history of the Peasants' War, the Emperor's Landsknechte look on as a professional headsman prepares to behead a rebellious peasant.

Above A scene from *The Hunts of Maximilian*, a series of tapestries made in Brussels in about 1530 after designs by Bernard van Orley (*c.* 1488–1541). This tapestry is entitled 'December' and shows the Emperor, armed with a sturdy boar sword and wearing full leg armour, bearing down on a wild boar which has been brought to bay by hunting dogs. The dog worrying at the boar's neck is also armoured.

Also rich in period detail is a series of woodcuts by Jacob Breu the Elder depicting the tournament given by Emperor Charles V 1530 at the investiture of his brother King Ferdinand I with the Habsburg territories in Austria. Contestants in the *Freiturnier* (fought in the open field with sword and lance) used rebated lances and two unusual types of curved single-edged short sword, one with a longish blade with a rounded tip, the other with a shorter, broader blade with a square tip. Whether curved tournament swords were used elsewhere is not known.

By the end of the sixteenth century most sword contests in tournaments took place on foot, with the combatants separated by a waist-high barrier. Generally the type of sword used in such contests had a light flexible blade with a round tip and, by the early seventeenth century, a basket hilt as well.

Hunting swords

Hunting was perhaps the most passionately pursued pastime of Europe's nobility from the Middle Ages through to the Industrial Revolution. From a very early date swords were worn as a side arm when hunting big game, but swords designed specifically for the hunt were apparently unknown before the fourteenth century. Short swords were worn by travellers and because of their manageable size were probably adopted for hunting. These tended to be either scaled-down versions of the typical cruciform war sword or straight single-edged weapons with a flat knife-like

grip and a knuckleguard. Fine examples of both types are shown in the famous 'Hunt of the Unicorn' tapestries (The Cloisters, New York), which date from the late fifteenth century.

The hanger, a short single-edged curved sword which became popular from the fifteenth century onwards, was modified for use as a hunting sword and remained the characteristic hunting sword until the late eighteenth century. An English form of the hanger was sometimes referred to as a woodknife, perhaps betraying its humble origins as a peasant knife. The blades of single-edged hunting swords were frequently given a saw-tooth pattern on the back edge, useful for cutting brush or sectioning game. By the late fifteenth century a full set of knives and other implements for dressing game were fitted into a single sheath, the whole kit being known as a garniture or *trousse*. This usually included a heavy cleaver (sometimes saw-backed), several small knives, a fork, a bodkin and sometimes a flat serving knife known as a *présentoir*.

By the fourteenth century large game such as deer and boar were hunted on horseback and on foot using a 'great hunting sword', which was strong enough to bear the charge of a large animal. Arguably the finest of all such swords was made for Emperor Maximilian I in 1496. Part of a garniture of swords, it is sumptuously decorated with silver, bronze, ivory, mother of pearl, etching, engraving and *goldschmelz* (gilt etching on a blued ground). Swords specifically intended for hunting boar appear in the first half of the fifteenth century. Their blades are of triangular, square or even octagonal section, as on contemporary estocs, stiff enough to withstand the onrush of a fierce and powerful boar. By about 1500 a wider, spear-like point was added and also a cross bar to prevent a transfixed animal running up the blade. Garnitures of hunting swords became more common after the middle of the century, and often consisted of a matching rapier, boar sword, hanger and trousse.

Daggers

The history and development of the dagger from 1300–1600 is at times quite close to that of the sword and at other times quite distinct from it. Whereas the knife was an accoutrement of all classes, the dagger had more specifically martial connotations. Interestingly, the dagger did not become a standard piece of knightly equipment until after 1250. This may have be due to the increased use of plate to reinforce and augment mail armour, and the need for a weapon which could puncture mail or pass between the various plates. Also, it became quite usual during the fourteenth century for cavalry to dismount and fight pitched battles, making a close quarters stabbing weapon more necessary than before.

A great variety of dagger types were used from the fourteenth through to the sixteenth century. Throughout the period one can generally find daggers with hilts which more or less correspond to those on contemporary swords. These are sometimes referred to as quillon daggers; roughly speaking, a quillon dagger is any

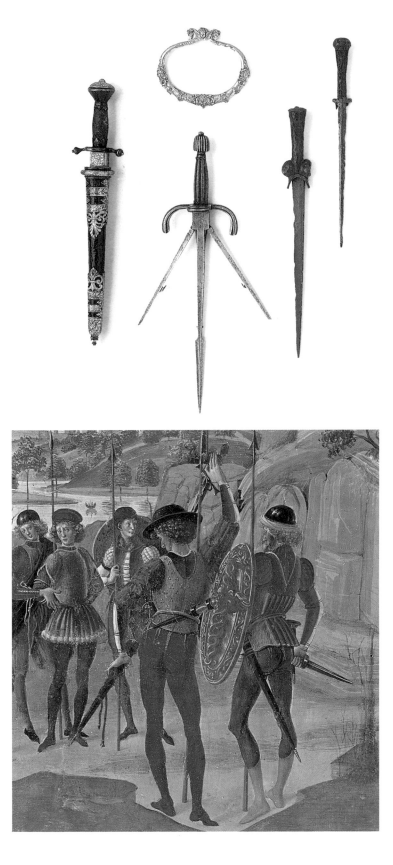

dagger with a cruciform hilt. However, several very popular daggers of the period owed little or nothing to contemporary sword hilts. Perhaps the most distinctive was the ballock dagger or ballock knife, already mentioned in Chapter 3. This developed towards the end of the thirteenth century and flourished until at least the seventeenth in countries north of the Alps, particularly in the Netherlands and England. It was both a military and a civilian weapon, and the anatomical verisimilitude of the hilt varied very greatly. The rondel dagger, also a medieval weapon, was used throughout the Renaissance and was frequently worn with armour. The distinctive roundels or discs of the pommel and guard are set at right angles to the grip, which is often decorated. Some of the finest examples have grips of carved horn set with gilt bronze mounts, and delicately etched blades.

The baselard, also mentioned in Chapter 3, was a popular and widely used form of dagger from the thirteenth to the early sixteenth centuries. It was apparently worn with civilian dress by all classes, from the lowest to the highest, and also with armour. The fashion was to wear it vertically, hanging through a loop from a waist belt or behind a belt purse, methods also seen with the ballock knife. More rarely it was suspended from a diagonal shoulder strap. Whether or not it originated in Basel, the baselard was certainly used in Switzerland and was probably the forerunner of the sixteenth-century Landsknecht sword and dagger (mentioned above) and of the more ornate Swiss dagger, sometimes referred to as a Holbein dagger.

The characteristic Swiss dagger of the sixteenth century had a sheath of cast silver or gilt bronze pierced with genre scenes, a popular theme being the 'Dance of Death'. Hans Holbein the Younger published several such sheath designs, hence the modern name 'Holbein dagger'.

The so-called ear dagger which became briefly popular across Western Europe in the sixteenth century was considered to be a Spanish invention, so it is probably no coincidence that the maker of one of the finest extant examples was the Spanish swordsmith Diego de Çaias, who served at the courts of François I and Henry II of France and Henry VIII of England. The ear dagger takes its name from the two splayed discs which form the pommel; the guard lacks quillon arms, and the grip is typically two plaques rivetted to a flat tang, as on the *cinquedea*.

Above Ear dagger signed 'ÇAIAS ME FE'. This weapon, made by the Spaniard Diego de Çaias in about 1530 while he was in the service of the French king François I, is perhaps the earliest known piece by him. A master sword cutler specializing in sumptuous gold and silver damascened decoration, de Çaias was in England by 1543 and is recorded as having made an estoc, three rapiers, two woodknives, four arming swords and three daggers for Henry VIII before the king's death in 1547.

Above left A gilt bronze purse frame (top) of a type frequently made *en suite* with rapier-and-dagger sets; a late sixteenth-century Saxon dagger (left), mounted with pierced and engraved silver sheets; a parrying dagger for the left hand (centre), with a spring-mounted triple blade designed to trap an opponent's sword; and two fifteenth-century ballock knives (right), the first of the more usual anatomical form, the second a rarer variety with triple nodes on the quillons and a triple-edged blade.

Below left Detail from *The Miracle of Saint Bernardino* by Bernardino Pintoricchio (*c.*1454–1513), showing the stylish costumes of Italian mercenaries of the period (about 1475) and two methods of wearing the rondel dagger. Note also the forefinger ring on the sword being sheathed by the soldier on the left.

55

Parrying daggers were used in conjunction with a sword or rapier. Their other name, left-hand or *main gauche* daggers, indicates their purpose even more clearly: they were held in the left hand and used to ward off or catch an opponent's blade. From the 1520s onwards it became customary to make parrying daggers en suite with rapiers, as matching sets. Most examples have typical dagger blades but towards the end of the century some were made with saw-like teeth designed to catch or even break an opponent's blade. A very few were spring-loaded so that at the touch of a lever they opened into a triple-bladed dagger.

Fencing

Duelling with sword and dagger was only one of many forms of fencing that developed as civilian wear of swords made duels between unarmoured opponents in non-military situations more common. By the turn of the sixteenth century, Italian fencing masters were renowned throughout Europe, and during the course of the century, as instruction in the art of fencing became a required part of a young nobleman's education, every self-respecting court in Europe sought the services of an Italian fencing master. It was not unusual for a young gentleman to travel to Italy to receive instruction.

One of the first influential fencing manuals was the *Opera Nova de Achille Marozzo Bolognese, Mastro Generale de l'Arte de l'Armi* (New Work by Achille Marrozzo of Bologna, Master General of the Art of Arms), published in 1536. Marozzo's work represents one of the earliest breaks with the freewheeling single combat tradition of the Middle Ages. In Marozzo the cut is as important as the thrust, opponents face each other squarely, and the attacker leads alternately with the right and left foot.

Further systematization is apparent in Camillo Agrippa's *Trattato di Scienza d'Arme e un dialogo in detta materia* (Treatise on the Science of Arms and a dialogue concerning the subject), published in 1553. Four on-guard postures are defined and the thrust is emphasized over the cut as a quicker and more effective in the attack. In addition, the on-guard postures always place the right foot foremost. Agrippa was also apparently the first to suggest that the left arm be held to the rear and up, in a posture similar to that used in modern fencing. But this stance, which effectively counterbalances the weight of the forward arm, was not consistently used until the rise of the French school in the early seventeenth century.

Like Marozzo, Agrippa includes in his last chapter techniques for duelling with sword and cloak, sword and shield, halberds, and daggers. He also gives advice on unarmed self-defence against the dagger, recommending several wrestling holds, some of which are included in his earlier chapters on swordplay.

In Giacomo di Grassi's *Ragione di adoprar sicuramente l'arme . . .* (Methods of the sure use of arms . . .), published in 1570, one finds the blade being used for both attack and parry, in other words for the riposte fundamental to modern fencing. Also in

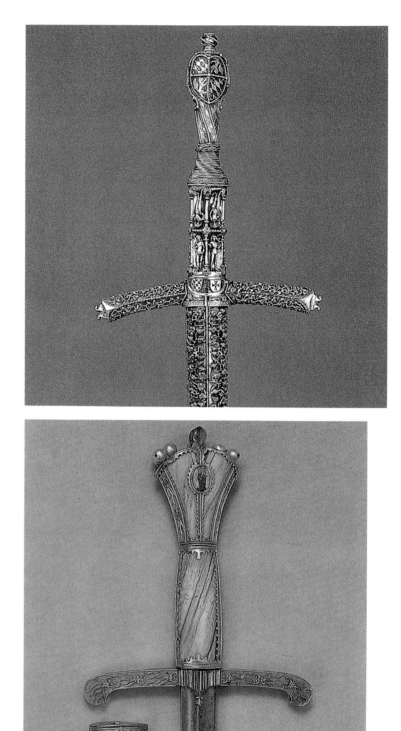

1570 Joachim Meyer, a student of Marozzo, published what was then the most scientific and thoroughly defined treatment of the subject in *Grundtliche Beschreibung der freyen ritterlichen und adelichen Kunst des Fechtens* (Thorough Description of the Free, Knightly and Noble Art of Fencing). His work represents the high point of the Italian-German school of fencing. An innovation seen for the first time in Meyer is the use of a geometric grid pattern placed on the floor beneath the fencer's feet to increase the precision of his movements. Meyer still used the cut but the thrust was clearly dominant.

In 1567 Charles IX established the Académie d'Armes in Paris and with it the French school, which was to dominate fencing in the seventeenth century.

The decorative arts

The decoration of edged weapons was always an important consideration and a symbol of the status of those who could afford fine arms. The decorative techniques used during the Renaissance were those also used in other areas of the arts: etching, engraving, nielloing, enamelling, carving, chiselling, inlaying, damascening, encrustation, gilding, silvering, and cast-

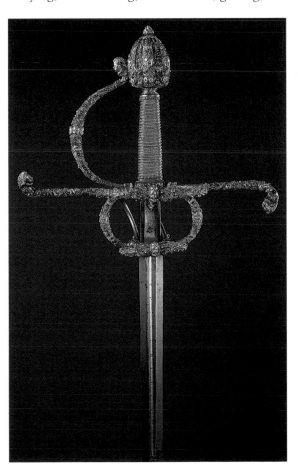

ing in bronze, gold and silver. Precious and semi-precious stones were used too. Materials such as bone, horn, ivory and tooled leather were regularly employed.

Superb examples of the stunning effects achieved by such techniques can be seen in the exotic ivory- and pearl-encrusted sword of Charles the Bold, Duke of Burgundy, made in about 1470 (Weltliche Schatzkammer, Vienna), the cast and gilt silver hilt and scabbard of the sword of Duke Christopher of Bavaria made in 1480 (Munich Schatzkammer), the delicately chiselled iron hilt in the Bavarian National Museum attributed variously to Othmar Wetter (d. 1589) and Thomas Rucker (*c.*1532–1606), and the sumptuous gold and enamel rapier of Emperor Maximilian II made in about 1550 (Waffensammlung, Vienna).

These swords and others bore witness not only to the high rank but also to the connoisseurship of their owners. The best available craftsmen were required to execute such masterpieces, and the task of designing them often fell to court artists whose remit was portraiture or architectural design. Sword designs exist from the hands of many well known artists and innumerable small masters. Albrecht Dürer, Hans Burgkmair, Urs Graf, Giulio Romano, Parmigianino and Hans Holbein in their careers all designed fine arms for the greatest rulers and patrons of Europe.

Opposite page, left and right
Design for a dagger by Hans Holbein the Younger (1497/8–1543). This design projects a weapon of unsurpassed beauty, presumably intended and perhaps executed for Holbein's patron, Henry VIII.

Hand-and-a-half sword (top right) made in about 1480 for Duke Christopher the Strong of Bavaria. The silhouette of the 'waisted' grip is typically German, otherwise the sword is an extraordinary example of fifteenth-century goldsmithing; the grip and sheath are silver gilt, with the arms of Bavaria, Pfalz and the Order of St George in enamel.

The sumptuous sword of Charles the Bold, Duke of Burgundy, made in 1467–77 (below). The core of the hilt is a narwhal tusk, framed in cusped bands of gold worked with the devices of the Order of the Golden Fleece. The pommel is surmounted by a ruby and pearls, symbolizing salvation.

Far left Rapier given by the Bohemian nobleman Wratislaw II to Maximilian II, King of Bohemia and later Holy Roman Emperor. The hilt, of finely cast and chased gold embellished with coloured enamel, is the work of a consummate but anonymous Spanish master, and the blade is by the famed Milanese maker Antonio Picinino. The weapon was made in about 1550.

Left 'Duelling with two-handed swords', scene from a treatise on fencing by Joachim Meyer, 1570. Like other fencing masters, Meyer did not confine himself solely to instruction in the use of the rapier, or rapier and dagger. The swords seen here are practice weapons with blunted blades which have a broad flaring area at the base combining flukes and ricasso.

5 FROM RAPIER TO SMALLSWORD

Anthony North

The seventeenth century was a most important one in the evolution of the sword in Europe, for by the 1630s the fashion for rapier and dagger play in fencing had considerably declined. A decade later the smallsword, in effect a light rapier, was introduced. In fact, from various advertisements in the 'lost' columns of journals such as *The London Gazette* it seems that, for a while at least, 'rapier' and 'smallsword' often meant the same thing. The smallsword rapidly became the most commonly worn sword in Europe and in some countries continued its career into the nineteenth century. Since the smallsword hilt developed directly from that of the rapier, it is appropriate that the two weapons should be discussed together. Other seventeenth-century developments are surveyed in Chapter 6.

Variations on the swept-hilt theme

By 1600 the type of rapier known as the swept-hilt rapier had become very fashionable. It was to remain in use until nearly the middle of the seventeenth century and was worn in most European countries. Consequently swept-hilt rapiers, particularly if they are undecorated, are extremely difficult to date and localize with any precision.

There were very many variations on the swept hilt theme. A type which, according to the evidence of portraits was specially fashionable around 1600, had a guard constructed of the usual S-shaped bars and a single long quillon, usually with a downward curve towards the blade. The outer guards were often of oval section, contrasting with the inner guards, which were usually rods of circular section, and offered scope for decoration. Many of the hilts in contemporary portraits were gilded or artificially coloured in some way. Over the centuries cleaning has tended to remove the original surface and many a swept hilt, now plain bright steel, was originally richly gilded, silvered or blued. These were comparatively easy methods of decorating a hilt, requiring simply an application of a gold amalgam, plating, or the use of chemicals. The more time-consuming decorative treatments of chiselling or engraving involved cutting metal away from the surface with a chisel or engraving tool, or inlaying precious metal

Right Detail from a painting by Frans Hals (1581/5–1666) showing an officer of the Corps of St Joris of Haarlem carrying a swept-hilt rapier in a broad sash.

into the surface. Hilts made of the softer metals could be cast in moulds and a small number of cast hilts in gold, silver and brass do indeed survive. In the Metropolitan Museum in New York there is a very fine swept hilt of cast bronze set with stones and gilded, dated 1606, made by a sword-cutler named Israel Schuech for one of the Electors of Saxony. Other unsigned hilts by the same maker are known.

The armoury in Dresden has an almost unparalleled collection of swept-hilt rapiers. These have been so carefully looked after since the day they were finished that they are preserved in virtually pristine condition. A number of duplicates were sold off earlier this century, giving museums and collectors the opportunity to acquire rarities from this hitherto closed collection. These included swept-hilt rapiers and accompanying daggers made for the Electoral Guard. The hilts on these weapons are very well made, but often quite plain, the decoration being limited to an engraved wave pattern, or to blueing and silvering. Various examples of the exceptionally fine work of hilt-maker Othmar Wetter (d. 1589) are preserved at Dresden and elsewhere.

Wetter was a master swordsmith, and worked initially for Duke Wilhelm V of Bavaria in Munich, becoming a master of the Munich guild in 1582. By 1590, however, he was working in Dresden, possibly having left Bavaria to escape religious persecution, for he was a Protestant. In Dresden he supplied hilts to the Elector Christian I and his court. A measure of the time it took him to make his extraordinarily delicate steel hilts is indicated by the record of payments made to him between 1591 and 1595; these show that, in that time, he completed only four hilts. When one looks at the minute figures, set within niches, chiselled so precisely into the steel, and at the beautiful engraving and gilding, one can understand why.

Another type of swept hilt, with two quillons rather than one, was used until the middle of the seventeenth century. In fact the double-quillon form can be traced back to before 1500. As the seventeenth century advanced swept hilts with double quillons gradually replaced the single-quillon type.

Left and below Two rapiers from the armoury of the Electors of Saxony, both made in Dresden. The weapon on the left, with a hilt of blued and chiselled steel, was made in about 1590. The hilt of the weapon below, of cast and chiselled gilt bronze set with precious stones and cameos, is dated 1606 and signed Israel Schuech.

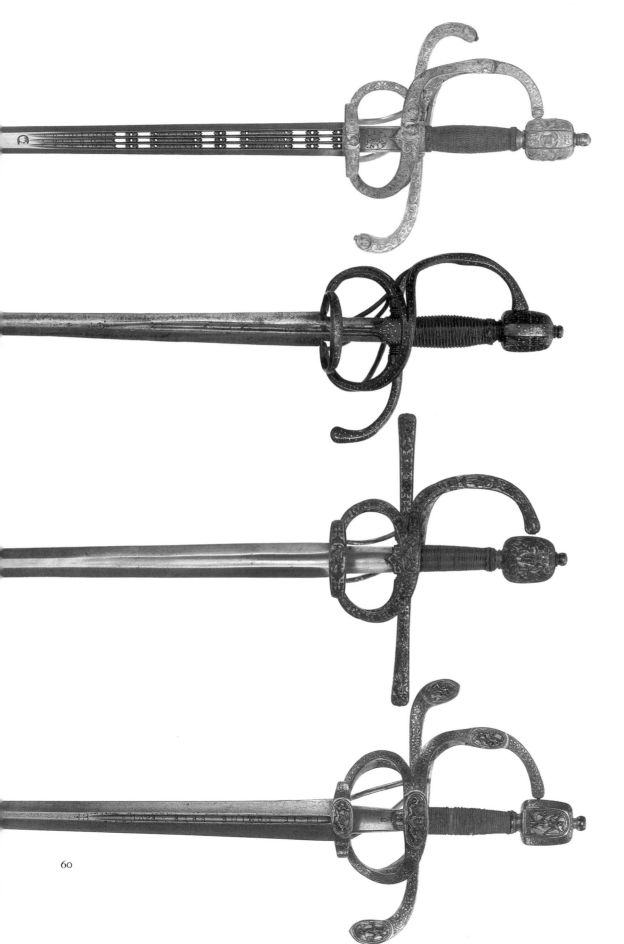

Although it is virtually impossible to attribute plain swept hilts to any particular country, as they were carried almost internationally, some national characteristics have been identified. It is virtually certain, for example, that a type of early seventeenth-century swept hilt with quillons terminating in oval plates and a short bar projecting outwards from the guard is English. One of the finest English rapiers of the period is of this form; finely damascened in gold and encrusted with silver, it was traditionally presented by Queen Elizabeth I to a member of the Wetherby family. On another typically English hilt of the period the bars of the guard have a prominent central ridge. However, the English did not take kindly to the rapier at first. George Silver, in his *Paradoxe of Defence* published in 1599, stated: 'If we will have true defence, we must seek it where it is, in short swords, short staves, the half pike, partisans, gleves, or such like weapons of perfect length, not in long swords, long rapiers, nor frog pricking poniards. But the rapier in reason ought not to be, nor suffered to be taught because it maketh men fearfull and unsafe in single combats and weak and unserviceable in the warres.'

Signatures and coats-of-arms on a hilt can also be a help in establishing nationality. A swept-hilt rapier damascened in silver and gold and bearing the device of Count Pio Capodilista (d. 1617) is almost certainly Italian, for example. French rapiers are a particular problem as so few portraits showing rapier hilts are available for study. In fact very few rapier hilts have been positively identified as French work, although certain swept-hilts decorated with fine silver chain work have been attributed to a French workshop.

Various other criteria can be helpful in dating swept-hilt rapiers, including the shape and construction of the bars forming the hilt, the way the quillons are constructed, and the shape of the pommel. Decoration can also be an important guide, but it has to be well preserved to be of real assistance, and in many cases it is much degraded.

The long curved bars which formed the guards of swept-hilt rapiers posed considerable design problems to the artist who decorated them, since all the ornament had to be arranged in a linear fashion. A school of craftsmen established at the end of the sixteenth century at the court of the Dukes of Bavaria in Munich excelled at chiselled hilt decoration. Three of the craftsmen who produced this kind of work are known, Emanuel Sadeler (d. 1610), Daniel Sadeler (d. *c.*1632) and Caspar Spät (d. 1691). Their work includes firearms, caskets, purse-mounts and fine swords and daggers.

It is virtually impossible to distinguish between the work of the two Sadelers as their work is not signed. However, Caspar Spät's signature is found on some fine guns. The work of the Munich school is characterized by the use of blued relief work against a gilt ground, Caspar Spät's predilection being for small overlapping scales decorated with gold dots. The Sadelers seem to have derived some of their ornament, especially the use of figures set

Opposite page, top to bottom
Another hilt by the Dresden sword-cutler Israel Schuech, made in about 1600 for the Elector Christian I. In this case the hilt is of cast and chased gilt bronze.

French rapier of about 1590. The hilt is of blued steel inlaid with silver in the form of piqué dots and silver wire.

Rapier by Daniel or Emanuel Sadeler, German *c.*1600. The hilt is of blued and gilded steel, chiselled in relief with designs after Etienne Delaune. The Sadelers worked for the Bavarian Electors at the Munich court.

South German (Augsburg) rapier, *c.*1590. The hilt is chiselled and gilded, with damascened decoration in gold and silver. The work is very fine and preserved in outstanding condition.

Left The so-called *Procession to Blackfriars*, depicting Queen Elizabeth I and members of her court, English School *c.*1600, attributed to Robert Peake the Elder. The gentlemen are wearing swept-hilt rapiers carried in sword-hangers suspended from the belt.

Below Italian rapier of about 1610. The hilt is of steel, demascened in gold and silver. On the ricasso are the arms of Count Pio Capodilista (d. 1617). It is rare for the arms of an individual to appear on a sword.

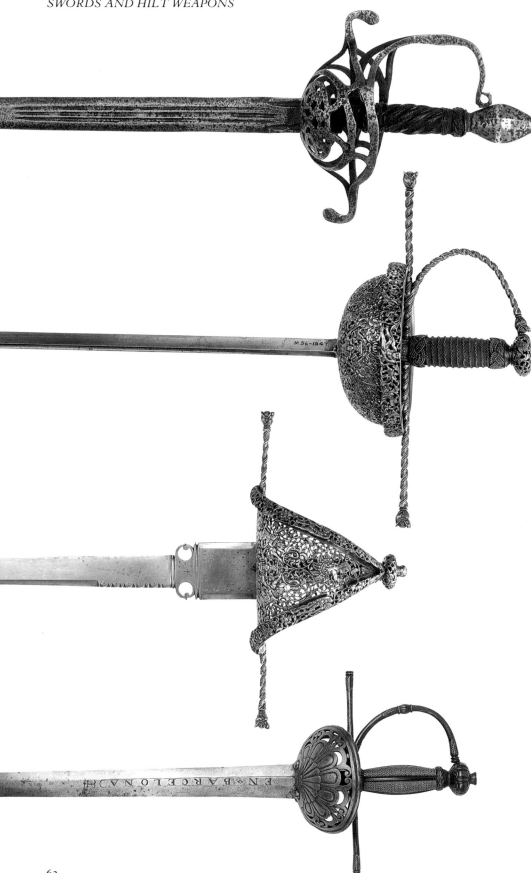

under canopies, from the graphic work of Etienne Delaune (c.1518–83). A splendid hilt given by the Emperor Rudoph II to the Saxon Elector Christian II in 1610 is chiselled with figures of Fortune, Leda and the Swan, and Neptune, with masks, fruit and flowers arranged between the main elements of the design. Daniel Sadeler is known to have worked for Rudolph II at the time this hilt was made, so it is likely that his was the hand responsible. Nearly all the surviving work of the Munich school was made for the Munich court, either for the dukes of Bavaria or as gifts.

Cup-hilt rapiers and other variants

From about 1610 it became customary to add additional protection for the hand in the form of a plate. This plate virtually filled the space between the bars and was usually pierced with ornamental designs, and by the 1620s had become a common feature of rapier hilts. It became the fashion to fit large solid fluted shells between the bars, and then fill the bars with a pierced plate, and by the 1630s the entire hand was protected, as if by a cup. It was from this form of hilt that the well-known cup-hilt rapier loved by all the Hollywood swordsmen developed.

Also from the 1620s a form of rapier hilt with very large plates and long recurved quillons became fashionable, especially in the Low Countries. Known as the 'Pappenheimer' hilt after Gottfried Heinrich, Graff Pappenheim, who is said to have carried one in the Thirty Years' War (1618–48), this type of hilt figures prominently in Dutch paintings of the 1630s and 1640s, especially in a series of paintings by Rotius in the museum at Hoorn in North Holland, which also show scarf swords and hangers. Many swords similar to those shown in these paintings have survived and sometimes a virtually identical pattern. Sometimes paintings show details which are now missing, such as a small by-knife fitted into the upper section of the scabbard or a particular type of scabbard hook.

The cup-hilt rapier mentioned above first appeared in about 1625 but, contrary to popular opinion, its use was comparatively limited. In England early cup hilts had a pierced cup guard linked to additional guards; a type using a scallop shell design was also fashionable. In about 1630 a form of cup hilt with a large dish-shaped guard and straight quillons became popular, principally in the Low Countries. This type was often fitted with an exceptionally long blade and, significantly, is often depicted in fencing books of the period.

The cup-hilt rapier, ancestor of the modern épée and fencing foil, reached its apogee in Spain and those territories under Spanish influence, such as Southern Italy and the Spanish Netherlands. The large deep cup forming the guard gave great scope for craftsmen who were skilled in piercing and chiselling steel. A few cup hilts are signed, almost invariably on the cup, and some are dated. Exceptionally gifted craftsmen included Antonio Cilenta of Naples, active around 1650, and Francisco Maria Rivolta, who worked in Milan in the 1670s. Very rarely one comes across a cup hilt which bears the name of an owner; an example in the Musée de l'Armée in Paris bears the name 'Miguel Anglada', together with the place of manufacture, 'Saragozza', and the date 1658. It is clear from portraits that cup-hilt rapiers were worn in Spain until almost the end of the eighteenth century.

A somewhat cruder version of the cup-hilt rapier was the Spanish *bilbo*, the name perhaps deriving from the city of Bilbao in northern Spain. Characteristically, *bilbo* hilts have plain solid shell guards extending up to the pommel. Very crudely made versions of the *bilbo* were favoured by Caribbean pirates towards the end of the seventeenth century. The writer has also seen a *bilbo* said to have been used in England during the Civil War; it was fitted with a much-used Solingen blade. A form of *bilbo* with

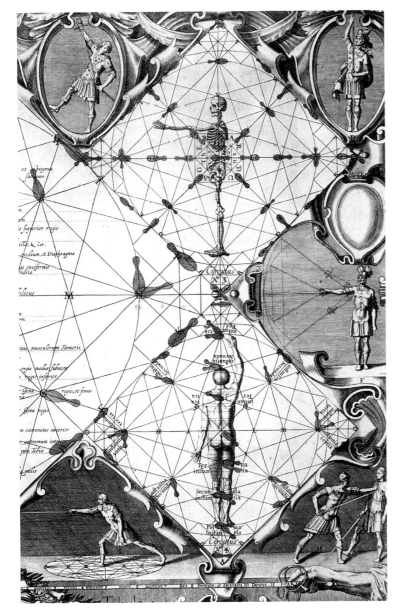

a very large double-edged blade became a standard military pattern in Spain during the eighteenth century. These large archaic weapons were still in use in the Napoleonic Wars and contrasted vividly with the elegant neo-classical hilts then in vogue throughout the rest of Europe.

Preserved in the Livrustkammaren in Stockholm are numerous swords dating from the Thirty Years' War (1618–48). Included in the group is the rapier carried by King Gustavus Adolphus of Sweden when he was killed at the battle of Lützen in 1632. It is a very simple and practical weapon with a plain substantial guard fitted with perforated oval plates. The blade is also plain, of diamond section, and tapers almost to a needle point. When a man's life depended on his sword, he nearly always chose a plain, well designed weapon rather than one adorned with sumptuous decoration.

Many of the highly decorated rapiers that survive would never have been risked in the field. Some hilts were undoubtedly made simply as another form of jewellery to be worn against dark costume. A very fine hilt from the 1630s in the Royal Collection at Windsor Castle is deeply chiselled with mythological scenes over its entire surface. The craftsman who made it is known by other chiselled hilts, but none are signed and the location of the workshop has not yet been firmly established; some authorities suggest a French source. The hilt at Windsor is said to have belonged to John Hampden (1595–1643), who died of wounds received at Chalgrove Field fighting against Prince Rupert of the Rhine. When a young man, he inherited considerable estates from his father and associated with men of fashion.

Opposite page, top to bottom
English rapier of about 1630. This plain but serviceable weapon is a cheaper version of the elaborately decorated rapiers fashionable during the period.

Matching Italian rapier (above) and left-hand dagger (below), with hilts of pierced and chiselled steel signed by Antonio di Cilenta of Naples. They were made in about 1650.

An unusually ornate Spanish *bilbo* with a pierced and embossed hilt. The blade is inscribed 'YOSEPH MARTI EN BARCELONA'. Marti was a member of the Barcelona blademakers' guild in 1716 and died in 1762. This weapon was probably made in about 1760.

Far left Page from the fencing book *Académie de L'Espée* by Girard Thibault of Antwerp, published in Leyden in 1630. Thibault devised a complicated fencing system based on a series of mysterious circles and squares.

Below Pappenheimer rapier, Flemish *c.*1620. The hilt is of steel, with silvering and punched decoration, and the blade bears the mark of the Stantler family of bladesmiths.

Above Gustavus Adolphus of Sweden at the Battle of Lützen, 6 November 1632, by Jan Marsen de Jonge. The king was killed by one of Count Wallenstein's cavalrymen as he lay wounded on the battlefield. The battle was fought in thick mist, a fact which the artist has understandably overlooked.

Above right French or German rapier, *c.*1635. The fine sword, now in the Royal Collection at Windsor Castle, is reputed to have belonged to John Hampden (d. 1643). The hilt is of steel, chiselled with pomegranates and biblical scenes. Note the unicorn on the ricasso.

Right The gilded iron hilt of the rapier carried by Gustavus Adolphus at Lützen. It is a German or Swedish weapon, made in about 1625.

Another style of hilt used in England in the early seventeenth century is also represented the Royal Collection at Windsor. It has thick rectangular bars chiselled, engraved and richly overlaid in silver, pierced apertures on the guard, and a pommel formed of openwork scrolls. The blade, which is by the Solingen maker Clemens Horn and dated 1617, bears the royal arms and has long been associated with King James I (1566–1625), although it is not shown in any of his portraits, which often show a rapier hilt set with precious stones. Unusually for a sword of this period, the original scabbard survives.

A survey of seventeenth-century portraits indicates that until about 1635 rapiers were generally worn with a dagger, the hilts of both often being decorated in the same manner. The dagger usually had quillons with large terminals, a central ring set with a plate guard to protect the thumb, and a pommel which matched that of the rapier, though naturally of smaller proportions. All the variety of ornament and design found on rapiers of the period is found on accompanying daggers. These were designed to be held in the left hand when fighting with the rapier. Daggers used with Spanish and Italian cup-hilt rapiers had a large plate, pierced and chiselled like the cup on the accompanying rapier, to protect the hand. Other forms of left-hand dagger had a comparatively simple crossguard with curving quillons and were fashionable throughout Western Europe in the first quarter of the century.

Swords were often made to the particular design of a client. Sometimes found, although they are comparatively rare, are rapiers designed to be used in the left hand. Even rarer are double-handed rapiers. In the armoury of the Counts Wrangel at Skokloster in Sweden there is a shallow cup-hilt rapier dating from the 1640s which has a very long narrow blade counterbalanced by two grips and two pommels set one above the other. This can only have been designed for a very formal fencing match and would have been totally impractical in the field.

Light rapiers

Towards the middle of the seventeenth century, numerous light short rapiers began to be fashionable, some with hilts which seem to have been modelled on those of contemporary quillon daggers. The guard was simply a cross with large terminals, often with a small ring set in the centre of the quillons, and the pommel usually matched the quillon terminals. Swords of this type are shown extensively in portraits of the period 1640–60 and are usually referred to as 'scarf swords', commonly being worn in a broad sash or scarf. Dutch admirals of the period of the Dutch Wars are frequently shown wearing scarf swords, as are many of the burghers who posed for the fine paintings of Dutch companies done in the middle of the century. Indeed many of these light rapiers seem to have been made solely for parade, since there are surviving examples with hilts of agate mounted in gold, ivory and delicately chiselled and pierced steel.

The craftsman Gottfried Leygebe (1630–83) of Nürnberg, who worked for the Elector of Brandenburg as a cutter of coin dies, a particularly exacting craft, produced some outstanding figurative hilts in steel for these light rapiers. He specialized in three-dimensional steel sculptures, and considering the intransigent nature of the material in which he worked, his skill is quite exceptional. He sometimes signed his work, usually on the base of the pommel.

Another form of light rapier fashionable from about 1630 onwards had a long loop guard attached to the outside of the hilt. It was light and convenient to wear and continued in fashion until the close of the eighteenth century. Additional protection for the hand was provided by a small shell set within the guard.

By 1640 hilts were being made which had a guard formed of a large double shell, with the blade passing through an aperture in the centre. This type of guard became a common feature of the later smallsword and continued in use until the nineteenth century. The single plate gave craftsmen a large surface to decorate and some of the earliest hilts of this form are very ornate – the angle at which the sword hung from the belt meant that the ornament could be easily seen. Early hilts of this type sometimes incorporated scenes of mounted warriors chiselled in very high relief at the front and low relief at the back. A very fine hilt of this type, chiselled in bright steel with equestrian figures, was presented to John Churchill, Duke of Marlborough, by the Emperor

Left English sword with a pierced, chiselled and engraved hilt encrusted with silver. The blade, by the Solingen maker Clemens Horn, bears the royal arms of the United Kingdom and the date 1617. By tradition the sword belonged to James I. Clemens Horn is known to have supplied a number of similar blades to James I.

Below Rapier for use with two hands, German *c*.1645. This very rare weapon, which would have been used for fencing or duelling, has been made more manageable by the addition of an extra grip and pommel. The blade is by the Solingen maker Meves Berns.

Charles VI (1711–40). The blade most often favoured on these early double-shell hilts was a long narrow one designed solely for thrusting.

Rapiers with double-shell guards became increasingly common from the 1640s onwards, the shell usually being set at the front of the hilt, separated from the grip by a square sleeve. Double-shell hilts are shown in many of the portraits of commanders of the English Civil War period. A variation on the type, incorporating pierced plates, was also carried by the town guard of Amsterdam. The military versions are plain and heavy, but those made for civilian use are often very ornate, with gold and silver overlay and more elaborate ornament such as piercing and chiselling. Some were designed without a knucklebow, although this extra guard was added at a later date to bring it into line with current fashion.

Rapier blades

It is virtually impossible to date a rapier blade with any accuracy, not least because blades were changed so regularly. Old blades were often refurbished and mounted up in more fashionable hilts, blades were also cut down and their profiles altered, and some blades show signs of later re-decoration. In the first quarter of the seventeenth century swept-hilt rapiers were fitted with fairly long blades, about 45 ins/114 cm on average. These were narrow and double-edged, with a long ricasso and a narrow channel down the centre, and designed solely for thrusting. A broader blade was also used during the period, with a double edge and several channels; the latter imparted strength as well as lightness, and probably had nothing to do with blood! Plain diamond-sectioned blades, long and narrow, are also found with swept hilts, but broader blades designed for cutting were also used, especially after the mid-1620s.

A large number of seventeenth-century rapier blades, especially those made in the first half of the century, are entirely plain. Some bear the name of the maker in small punched letters on the forte, and some are pierced with long slots and circular apertures at the forte. Some are dated, perhaps indicating when a batch was completed. Those which are decorated are usually etched or engraved, with scroll work, figurative subjects and mottoes often heightened with gilding. In a very few instances traces of blueing can still be seen. Very occasionally a blade bears a coat-of-arms.

There is some evidence that blades were carefully chosen to fit individual hilts. An early seventeenth-century swept-hilt rapier in the Victoria and Albert Museum has a guard which is chiselled and pierced with a distinctive chain design. The blade seems to have been deliberately selected to match the hilt, as the edge is cut with a series of undulations which echo the wavy profile of the hilt. The well-known Pappenheimer rapier was often fitted with a long blade with a raised median ridge.

After the 1640s there was a tendency for blades to become shorter, and many scarf swords and light rapiers were fitted with blades that had been cut down. There were exceptions, of course, such as the large dish-hilt rapiers of the 1660s, designed exclusively for fencing, which have blades of enormous length, usually very narrow or hollow-ground in profile. Similar narrow blades are occasionally found on other types of hilt, especially at the end of the seventeenth century. These weapons are usually very plain and may have been used for duelling.

Smallsword hilts

The origins of the smallsword are to be found in the light scarf sword or rapier with a double-shell guard and fully developed hilt. A. V. B. Norman, in his definitive study of rapiers and smallswords, has defined the smallsword as having the guard made as a separate element and the blade passing through an aperture in its centre. The quillon block acts as a sleeve to hold the shell guard against the blade. In its fully developed form the smallsword had two additional guards, known as the arms of the hilt, set in the quillon block, and a large curved knucklebow.

Certain fencing masters writing in the 1680s deprecated the practice of placing the fingers within the arms of the hilt where they could be injured when fighting at close quarters. This seems to indicate that these guards were originally intended as an additional grip rather than as a protection for the fingers.

Although the earliest recognizable smallswords date from about 1635, these elegant weapons did not really become fashionable until after 1660. However, the development of the smallsword in the latter part of the century was not one of regular change. In certain areas, notably in Scandinavia, old-fashioned hilts persisted well into the eighteenth century. The craftsmen of Brescia in northern Italy also stuck to the old pattern books, producing some very archaic ornament on hilts. Features such as

Left Portrait of John, Baron Belasyse, by Gilbert Jackson, English School, 1636. The rapier shown is of steel, chiselled with masks, the pommel in the shape of a man's head. Hilts decorated in this manner were fashionable up until the Civil War.

Far left This exceptionally fine steel hilt, chiselled in high relief with figures, masks and scrollwork, was probably made by one of the hilt-makers who worked for the French court in the Galeries du Louvre. Made in about 1650, it is one of the earliest datable smallswords and once belonged to John Churchill, Duke of Marlborough (1650–1722).

Opposite page Silver-hilted English smallsword bearing the London hallmarks for 1676/7 and the maker's mark WB.

the absence of a knucklebow, usually taken to indicate a comparatively early date, are in fact found on smallswords made well into the eighteenth century.

The smallsword had, by the last quarter of the seventeenth century, become the most fashionable type of sword in civilian and military use throughout most of Western Europe. Details of construction and ornament differed considerably, making it rather difficult to assign a hilt to a particular area and to give it a date. However, a considerable number of smallswords with hilts of silver have survived from the period after 1670. These often bear hallmarks and date letters, so a precise location and date can be assigned to them. A very small number of hilts made in gold have also survived, a few of them fully marked. As styles changed, old-fashioned hilts of precious metal were traded in for their bullion weight, which would then be set against the cost of a new hilt. This no doubt explains the relative rarity of hilts in precious metals compared with hilts of steel or other base metals. Hilts of gold must therefore have been rather more common than the small number of surviving examples would suggest.

Some idea of the cost of a silver-hilted smallsword can be gained by looking at contemporary diaries and manuscripts. When the lawyer Sir Dudley Ryder (1691–1756) was a student in 1717 he went to 'Mr Loveits to buy a sword, a silver gilt one for £3 4s. 6d. without the blade. My old one came to 4½ ounces of silver which made £1 4s. 9d at 5s. 6d per ounce'. (The bullion price of silver today is £3.30/$5.60 per ounce, much more affordable, comparatively speaking, than it was in Ryder's time.) This interesting entry in Ryder's diary shows that it was quite usual for a customer to purchase the hilt elements without a blade, this and the scabbard being supplied as a separate transaction, and to 'trade in' the precious metal of a hilt for its bullion value. Loveit is recorded as having premises in the Strand, London, around 1715. Ryder showed a sensible pride in his new purchase, noting: 'Having a new sword on, I could not help looking at it several times with a peculiar kind of pleasure. Sometimes it has made me uneasy to think that it was not so handsome as it might have been, that the carving is not well done. I am vexed with myself to find that my mind is too apt to be affected with such trifles.'

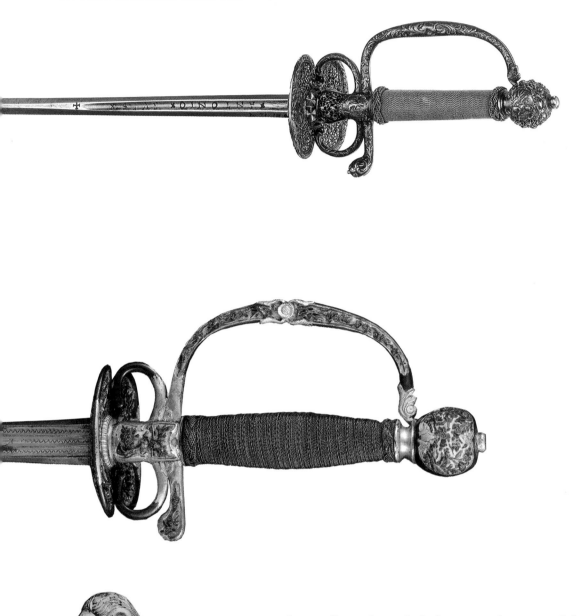

wares to Europe. These included some extraordinary sword hilts based upon contemporary European forms – local craftsmen clearly had European hilts to copy from – but decorated and constructed in exotic local and traditional styles. They thus represent a unique blend of East and West.

A very small number of carved and pierced ivory hilts decorated with cherubs and scrolling foliage have survived, dating from about 1700. The style of carving is very similar to that found on ivory wares from Ceylon, suggesting that they were made for Dutch traders. Both the traditional smallsword hilt, with its knucklebow and double-shell guard, and the simpler scarf sword hilt, with shell guard and quillons, are reproduced entirely in pierced and carved ivory. The prototypes for these delicate masterpieces were the pierced and chiselled steel and silver hilts produced in Holland and Northern Italy.

The Dutch also traded with Japan and as a result a variety of wares made by Japanese craftsmen were carried back to the West. These included hilts made of *shakudo*, a mixture of copper and gold, and patinated to a rich blue colour to contrast with the gilded panels of relief decoration set at intervals on the guard, knucklebow and pommel. As with the ivory hilts from Ceylon, contemporary Dutch hilts were the prototypes for these exotic pieces. The craftsmen who made them were specialists in *tsuba*, Japanese sword guards, and came from the area around Nagasaki. The majority of these exotic hilts echo standard smallsword or hunting sword hilts of the 1700s, but hilt forms of the 1750s were also copied.

Another curious group of smallsword hilts also identified as Eastern have a rather awkward design, with a very large knucklebow and an unusual square pommel. These are made of silvered or gilt brass, with applied or pierced floral ornament. Analysis of the brass alloy reveals a close resemblance to that used on brasswares from China and Japan.

Some very finely decorated hilts were also produced in India, probably for European officers, during the latter half of the eighteenth century. In some cases native craftsmen applied gold inlay to plain steel hilts of European manufacture; in others, all the elements of an existing hilt were copied locally. Delicate floral decoration was the favourite form of inlay, but figurative subjects were also attempted.

Some distinction should be made between the light decorative smallswords worn with civilian dress and the heavier, more solidly constructed weapons carried for war or while travelling. A considerable number of plain but very practical smallsword hilts of steel covered with black lacquer have survived. Various features such as the shape of the pommel, the large arms of the hilt, and the form of the shell guard suggest that these date from the first half of the eighteenth century. They are usually described as 'mourning swords' because of their black horsehair grips and sombre colouring. Most are fitted with plain, very workmanlike blades, and would have been ideal for self-defence.

On smallswords made before 1700 the arms of the hilt are usually quite large, and the knucklebow is usually straight, often with a central feature, usually an indented moulding or figurative design. Pommels could be globular, pear-shaped, or sometimes facetted. The ornament varied enormously from workshop to workshop, with both figurative and abstract designs being popular. Bold chiselled relief ornament was still fashionable on Dutch and German hilts of the seventeenth century; pierced lacework in steel, with small chiselled panels set at intervals on the hilt, was fashionable in Northern Italy towards the end of the century. Encrusted work in silver and gold was usually carried out on an artificially blued surface to enhance its effect.

As a result of trade with the Far East in the seventeenth century, Dutch mechants brought back an increasing number of exotic

Many of the military forms of smallsword are made of cast brass, sometimes gilded or silvered. Those dating from the early part of the eighteenth century are often very plain, the shells having substantial raised rims. Brass hilts with cast relief decoration were very popular in England from 1680–1700, judging from the large number that survive. Many are commemorative of William and Mary and carry profile busts crowned with laurel. The Labours of Hercules were also a popular motif. In the best examples, the workmanship is as good as that found on hilts of silver, but in general the use of worn moulds and poor casting techniques resulted in very crude decoration. The roughness was then disguised by heavy gilding. Most of these heavy, rather simply decorated hilts are fitted with very substantial blades and from the scarred appearance of both hilts and blades must have seen very hard service.

The development of the smallsword up to the 1740s can be traced with relative ease thanks to the number of silver hilts which bear hallmarks and date letters. In the 1720s and 1730s relief decoration in the form of classical figures set within foliage was fashionable. Here one can see the influence of designers such as Jean Berain (1637–1711) and Daniel Marot (1601–1718), with whom figures, foliage and strapwork were favourite motifs. A large number of very plain hilts of silver were also made in the first quarter of the century, the plain style being very fashionable in America where hilt-makers tended to rely on beauty of form and construction rather than on surface decoration. Unless a silver hilt is fully marked, it is often extremely difficult to distinguish between the work of American and English provincial hilt-makers.

In the second quarter of the eighteenth century there was a tendency for pommels to be pear-shaped and for the knucklebow to be a broad curve. The arms of the hilt continued to be large. Although designs for hilts in the rococo style of Meissonier (c.1693–1750) are known from as early as 1725, the style was not immediately reflected in sword hilts. French and German hilt-makers of the 1740s developed a style of decoration admirably suited to the sword, especially to steel hilts; this consisted of chiselling away the surface to leave the ornament in relief, then filling in the ground with gold foil, which was then matted with a fine punch. Many of the hunting scenes which form the repertoire of much of this type of ornament were based upon the graphic work of Jean-Baptiste Oudry (1686–1755) and his followers. These chiselled hilts vary considerably in quality, but the finest seem to have been the work of medallists. It is often possible to detect the work of two or even three craftsmen on the same hilt, which seems to indicate that a certain amount of mass-production was involved in their manufacture.

The scarf sword hilt continued to be produced throughout the first half of the eighteenth century. Because the simple knuckle-bow construction provided only a limited surface area for decoration, the grips of these attractive weapons were often made of

steel, which could be chiselled and gilded in the appropriate style. The grips of German and French scarf swords are often of porcelain and painted enamel, the blades fitted to them being narrow and flat rather than the usual hollow-ground triangular section found on larger hilts.

The rococo style became increasingly common after 1740. Sword hilts were heavily influenced by the style as it appeared on contemporary silverware, the wrythen swirls found on coffee pots, teapots and other vessels also being adopted by hilt-makers. The pommel and often the grip were formed as a series of long swirling spirals, with spiral roping appearing on the guard and knucklebow. This style was popular with military and naval officers; in fact, the smallsword carried by George Washington on the Braddock Expedition of 1755 is of this type.

A somewhat eccentric style of hilt with a heart-shaped shell guard, developed in the 1720s, became increasingly popular in the latter half of the century. Curiously, this was one of the forms copied by the Japanese for export to the West in the 1740s. The rococo style may have been the major influence in its development.

A fine silver hilt was very much part of a gentleman's everyday attire during the eighteenth century. James Boswell, the chronicler of the great Dr Johnson, gives an interesting account of a visit he made on 30 November 1762 to the shop of Mr Jefferys, sword-cutler to His Majesty. Although Boswell had left his money at home, he looked at a number of swords and picked out a handsome one at five guineas. 'Mr Jefferys', he said, 'I have not the money here to pay for it. Will you trust me?' Jefferys demurred at first, saying that he never gave credit to strangers, but after giving Boswell a keen glance, he relented. 'Come, Sir', he cried, 'I will trust you.' Boswell then supplied his name and address, chose a belt, and walked off with his fine new sword. Returning to pay Mr Jefferys the following day, he thanked him for his credit and proceeded to warn him of the dangers of giving credit to strangers. To which Jefferys graciously replied: 'Sir, we know our men. I would have trusted you with the value of a hundred pounds.' Boswell wrote that he 'thought this a good adventure' and much to his honour.

Smallsword blades

One of the features which distinguishes a smallsword from a rapier is the length and form of the blade. Early smallswords are usually fitted with narrow rapier blades which have been considerably shortened, or with the light double-edged blades supplied by Solingen cutlers. In about 1660, however, a new type of blade was introduced, almost certainly from Germany. This had a hollow-ground triangular section, combining strength with lightness, and was a masterpiece of design. The earliest examples of this type of blade were clearly intended to be used for cutting as well as thrusting, and have very wide edges, especially at the forte of the blade. However, the edges were usually very weak and

Opposite page, top to bottom
Smallsword with a chiselled and pierced steel hilt, northern Italian c.1700. This may be the work of a craftsman from Brescia, where the piercing and chiselling of steel was a speciality.

Smallsword with a *shakudo* hilt, Japanese c.1730. Hilts like this were copied from European prototypes but decorated in deliberately elaborate style for export to Holland.

Carved ivory hilt in the form of a lion, Sinhalese c.1660. This weapon was probably made for the Dutch East Indian Company.

Below Silver-hilted rapier, Dutch c.1660. The hilt takes the form of St George slaying the dragon; on the reverse are the initials PC, probably those of the original owner.

Below Hilt of the sword worn by Jean Cocteau as a member of the Académie Francaise. It was commissioned from the jeweller Cartier in 1955 and made to Cocteau's own very detailed design. The knucklebow represents the poet's flowing profile, the pommel the lyre of Orpheus; the grip, a pillar entwined with ribbon, denotes the theatre, and the quillons a chalk pencil. Like Cocteau's writings, the sword is signed with a six-pointed star, in this case executed in diamonds and rubies.

tended to crack and split. By 1700 blades had become much narrower and were designed solely for thrusting. Although they are usually quite wide at the forte, they taper sharply, giving strength where it was needed, for parrying an opponent's blade.

A type of blade fashionable from about 1675 onwards had a wide forte then tapered very suddenly to a narrow thrusting point. This was known as a *colichemarde*, a name said to derive from that of Johann Phillip, Count von Konigsmark, a Swedish soldier of fortune who was killed in a duel in 1686. For services to France, he was made a Maréchal of France by Louis XV, but at the time of his death he was in the service of the Venetian Republic. *Colichemarde* is not too implausible a gallicization of 'Konigsmark'. It is also worth noting that Sir William Hope, in his book *A new short and easy method of fencing* published in 1707, mentions a 'Konigsberg blade'.

Despite the above remarks, the variety of smallsword blades in the latter half of the seventeenth century was considerable, the narrow flat double-edged form still being used alongside the triangular type.

Decoration usually consisted of strapwork and figurative designs, usually etched, against a blued and gilt ground. Blades incorporating figures of the Twelve Apostles arranged along the length of the blade are recognized as the work of a particular German maker, as yet unidentified. The cutler's name and address or simply the place where the blade was made, such as Solingen, is usually given on the forte of the blade. There were also various forms of quality marks, such as small depressions or the words '*fin raison*' etched in the blade. Mottoes are also found, ranging from the Latin 'Recte faciendo, neminem timeas' ('By acting correctly you have nothing to fear') to the well-known 'Ne me tire pas sans raison. Ne me remette point sans honneur' ('Draw me not without reason. Sheath me not without honour').

Again, blades are notoriously difficult to date. Many a small-sword of the 1750s is fitted with a cut-down rapier blade of the 1640s which has been re-ground and trimmed to fit its new hilt.

Duels and duellers

The blade of a smallsword was deadly and a serious wound was almost invariably fatal. At least one newspaper account describes a customer being accidentally killed while trying out a new acquisition in a sword-seller's premises. An Irish writer, Joseph Hamilton, whose book of duelling *The Only Approved Guide through All the Stages of a Quarrel* was published in 1829, describes a smallsword known as 'Skiver the Pullet' used by an ancestor who 'had fought with it repeatedly and run through different parts of their persons several Scotch officers who had challenged him all at once, for some national reflection. It was a very long and narrow-bladed straight cut and thrust, as sharp as a razor, with a silver hilt, and a guard of leather inside it.'

The impression left by films and television is that all duels with the sword were very formal affairs. In fact contemporary accounts suggest that this was very far from the case. One of the most notorious duels with swords took place in Hyde Park in London on 15 November 1712. The cause of the quarrel between Charles Lord Mohun and the Duke of Hamilton was property in Cheshire. They fought at 7 o'clock in the morning and the savagery of their meeting shocked even their contemporaries. Jonathan Swift, the celebrated author of *Gulliver's Travels*, says in a letter to an acquaintance: 'The Lord Mohun died on the spot, but while the Duke was over him Mohun shortened his sword and stabbed him in the shoulder to the heart.' The Duke died nearby on the grass. An autopsy revealed that the Duke has been wounded in four places and Lord Mohun in three. The hands of both were badly cut where each had grasped the other's blade. They simply stabbed each other until they died.

A later duel with swords between Richard Brinsley Sheridan, the Irish playwright, and a Captain Matthews which took place at Kings Weston just outside Bath, Somerset, on 8 July 1772 was also somewhat informal. The two had fought before and were old enemies, and the duel quickly deteriorated into a wrestling match. For some reason their seconds did not intervene, and with broken swords the two contenders rolled about on the ground attempting to stab each other. Sheridan was wounded in the neck, and his opponent took off in a waiting post-chaise for London. One suspects that many duels romanticized in the nineteenth century by novelists such as Alexandre Dumas were very bloody, ill-tempered and savage affairs.

Duelling was not entirely the prerogative of men. The activities of the Chevalier Charles de Beaumont d'Eon (d. 1810) are well known, but another celebrated woman duellist was the actress La Maupin, born in Paris in 1673. She entered into a liaison with a fencing master called Sesane, who taught her all he knew. She is said to have killed three men after a quarrel at a ball, after which she retired to Brussels where she became the mistress of the Elector of Bavaria.

Smallsword ornament

Since many smallsword hilts were regarded almost as a form of jewellery, considerable effort and thought went into their design. Many of the engraved designs for the ornament on smallsword hilts survive. These are usually engraved on single sheets, and the ornament of the various elements of the hilt and scabbard are indicated, sometimes with alternatives. The majority of these designs, or at least the majority of those that have been published, come from German sources, many from Augsburg and Nürnberg. Designs by Georg Heumann of Nürnberg (1691–1759), for example, show hilts with scrolling foliage and trophies. Those of Jeremias Wacksmuth of Augsburg, produced in about 1750, show hilts with intense rococco ornament. There are also designs for sword hilts included in the repertoire of French enamellers and gold box makers, and a few hilts have survived from the middle of the eighteenth century which are clearly the work of jewellers rather than hilt makers. Such designs rarely indicate the material in which the hilt is to be made, although the appearance of a hilt in a set of goldsmith's work would naturally suggest a precious metal.

Exact matches between designs and surviving hilts are not often found. Elements are often taken from several designs and combined with other ornament, and there must also have been a certain amount of interchange between the separate elements of a hilt. If one looks at the Boulton and Watt pattern book of *c.*1775, for example, and then at surviving hilts in the Boulton and Watt style, one realises that hilts were assembled from different elements in many variations, no doubt to suit customers' tastes. A plain shell might be put with an ornate pommel, for example. As with designs for the work of gunsmiths, some designs must have been used long after they had gone out of fashion. This may account for the somewhat random ornament found on smallswords in the eighteenth century.

In the second half of the eighteenth century the hilt form of the smallsword underwent various changes. A style that became fashionable in England from about 1760 onwards had an oval shell guard, usually very finely pierced. There was also a general tendency for the arms of the hilt to become much smaller. In France, in the 1770s, some very fine chiselled hilts were made for presentation purposes, these usually have the lilies of France on the pommel or elsewhere on the hilt, and often the portrait bust of Louis XV in silver set into the pommel.

With the introduction of the neo-classical style in the 1770s there was a tendency for pommels to become urn-shaped. Some very fine neo-classical hilts in cut and polished steel, set with facetted beads or Wedgewood plaques, were made in a Birmingham factory set up by Matthew Boulton (1728–1809); swords were produced at the factory when he was in partnership with John Fothergill between 1762 and 1781 and with James Watt between 1775 and 1800. Their interest lies not only in their quality but in the fact that they were produced by sophisticated mass-production methods.

Perhaps the finest hilts in the neo-classical style were those produced for presentation purposes in the late eighteenth and early nineteenth centuries by goldsmiths and silversmiths. Presentation swords were given as rewards for naval or military successes and were lavishly enamelled. The imperial factory established by Nicolas-Noel Boutet in Versailles produced some very fine hilts of gold set with medallions and lapis lazuli for the French imperial court in the early years of the nineteenth century.

By this time a hilt consisting of a half-shell turned down toward the blade had become fashionable, although double-shell and oval forms continued to be produced and used during the period, especially for heavier military weapons.

The custom of wearing a sword in public had begun to decline in England by the 1750s, but in France it persisted until the early 1800s. In fact smallswords with cut steel hilts and long narrow

triangular blades, the direct descendants of more functional types, were worn as part of court dress in England until 1900. Their most recent manifestations are the swords produced by the jeweller Cartier and other artists for members of the Académie Française. Considerable imagination has gone into their design, the hilts reflecting the interests and talents of each Academician.

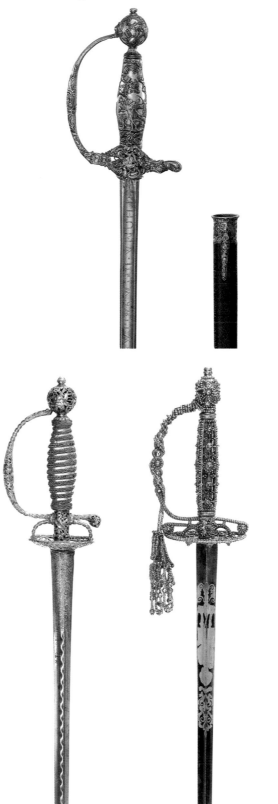

Left German smallsword made in about 1750. The hilt and scabbard mounts are of chiselled and gilt steel. The chiselling is of exceptional quality and may be the work of a craftsman trained as a medallist.

Below left The smallsword on the left is French, *c.*1770, and a very good example of a top quality sword preserved in outstanding condition. The hilt is of chiselled, pierced and gilded steel.

The smallsword on the right is English, made in about 1790. The cut steel hilt is set with polished steel studs and furnished with a sword-knot composed of cut steel beads. This sword once belonged to Admiral Leveson Gower (1740–92).

71

6 SEVENTEENTH-CENTURY EUROPE

Anthony North

The seventeenth century is a fascinating period for the study of European swords and daggers: new types of sword, including the smallsword, were developed; there were some curious revivals of swords last used in medieval times; and the dagger was abandoned as part of civilian dress. Yet throughout the period the sword remained an essential implement of war and was carried as an additional ornament with civilian costume.

The demise of the cross-hilt

By 1600 the old-fashioned cross-hilted sword was used almost exclusively for ceremonies and executions. A few light sixteenth-century cross-hilted swords are known, but they were not widely worn. The large bearing swords of the seventeenth century differed little from those of earlier times, having a long broad blade, scrolling or straight quillons, and a long grip. A very small number of swords made for war in the early part of the century have the wrythen pommel and quillons in the Gothic style, but these were no doubt produced to special order.

In England James I revived the ceremonies connected with the making of Knights of the Bath, and their medieval nature was emphasized by the wearing of the old-fashioned cross-hilted sword. Although straight and double-edged, this was much shorter and lighter than its medieval counterpart and seems to have caught on as a fashion, for portraits showing such swords can be found until about 1615. Several examples survive in English churches and a few are associated with English families.

The cross hilt was also the standard form for heading swords, swords used for executions. The blades of such swords are invariably broad and straight, usually engraved with suitably solemn designs and mottoes, and terminate in a rounded profile, since only the edge was used. The hilt is of simple cross form, generally straight and very plain. Perhaps the best assemblage of these sinister weapons is to be found in the castle of the Counts of Flanders in Ghent, Belgium. An interesting heading sword dated 1639 is preserved in the museum at Wiener Neustadt in Austria; it was used in 1671 by the headsman Niklas Mohr to execute two

Croatian noblemen, Franz Cristof Frangepan and Peter Zrinyi, who had intrigued with the Turks against the Austrians. The blade bears inscriptions in Latin, a religious text and verses about the treachery and execution of Frangepan and Zrinyi, and also gives the name of the maker, a bladesmith named Karl Hasch. The execution took place on 30 April 1671 in the City Arsenal of Wiener Neustadt. Cross-hilted heading swords were used in Northern Europe until the eighteenth century and even later in parts of Germany.

Another form of cross-hilted sword which lasted well into the seventeenth century, and in Germany and other Northern European countries until well into the eighteenth, was the large bearing sword carried on ceremonial occasions by a specially appointed officer. Seventeenth-century bearing swords generally have a very broad straight blade, often engraved with the insignia or coat-of-arms of the guild or city for which it was made, and a guard formed of elaborate scrolls.

Mention should also be made of the large two-handed claymores used in Scotland in the early part of the century. These are notoriously difficult to date, but it seems likely that the type with downward-curving quillons and two large shell guards continued in use throughout the seventeenth century, and may in fact be of later date than hitherto appreciated.

A type of cross hilt fashionable in Italy and Germany in the second quarter of the seventeenth century was the 'crab claw' hilt. The guard is formed of a shell-shaped plate and two sets of downward-curving quillons shaped like claws. This was usually fitted with a broad straight double-edged blade, and many surviving examples bear the marks of Northern Italian bladesmiths. On some examples, the shell guard extends back to the pommel as on standard Spanish and Italian *main gauche* daggers of the period.

Basket hilts

The basket hilt first developed in the early sixteenth century with the addition of extra guards to certain types of cross-hilted sword. By the middle of the century the hand was protected, and indeed completely surrounded, by a very complex arrangement of plates

Opposite page The Introduction by Gerard Terborch (1617–81). The man wears a breastplate and buff coat, and carries a silver-hilted rapier of a type which evolved into the smallsword.

Left Cross-hilted sword signed 'Clemens Horn me fecit Solingen', English, *c.*1610. The initials and devices on the blade indicate that the sword was made for Henry Frederick, Prince of Wales (d. 1612).

Below Rapier with steel 'crab claw' hilt, Italian, *c.*1600.

and bars lined with leather or fabric. The blades of such swords were almost invariably for cutting rather than thrusting.

Basket hilts continued to be used during the seventeenth century, especially in England and Scotland – some of the colonists who settled in Jamestown, Virginia, possessed basket hilts. Flat bars set with plates formed the guard, which was sometimes fitted with long recurved quillons. Hilts from the early part of the century have very elaborate baskets formed of flat ribbon-shaped bars and are usually fitted with broad double-edged blades. In contemporary inventories these are referred to as 'Irish hilts'. Plain military weapons as well as expensive costume swords survive, some of the latter heavily encrusted with silver and damascened in gold.

Basket hilts underwent various changes during the course of the century. A type with narrow bars and a horizontal wheel pommel, for instance, seems to have been fashionable both in Scotland and England around the middle of the century. Many examples from the latter half of the century have narrow bars set with small plates. The Scottish basket hilt, with its traditional heart-shaped piercings and large square plates, seems to have appeared in the second half of the century and remained in use for well over a hundred years.

English basket hilts of the same period are often neglected, unjustifiably, for they include some very fine and complex plate and bar constructions and unlike the usual Scottish hilts are often pierced and engraved in the form of trophies with the owner's crest. There was a tendency in the latter part of the century to fit English hilts with narrow single-edged blades, a significant number being fitted with fine Hounslow blades shortened and refurbished for the purpose. Some basket hilts which now appear plain may originally have been lacquered. A few still possess their original japanned decoration, with simple floral and leaf motifs.

Silver basket hilts must have been made during the seventeenth century but most of those which survive date from after 1700. Some of these seem to have been presented at race meetings. One of the plates of a Scottish silver basket hilt sold recently at auction is inscribed at length with details of a race held at Huntly Castle in Aberdeenshire in 1701, and the pommel of the same sword is engraved with the words: 'Taken at Dumblain by one of Evans Dragoons', indicating that it was captured in battle. Unfortunately, hilts as intriguingly informative as this are rare.

Dalmatian troops in the service of Venice also carried a form of basket hilt. Known as a *schiavona*, this had a cage-like basket of narrow bars and seems to have been introduced in the second half of the sixteenth century. It continued in use until the end of the eighteenth. Sixteenth- and seventeenth-century versions have simpler hilts than their later counterparts, with three curved guards on one side of the hilt and a shield-shaped pommel made of cast brass. Later versions tend to be better made, with the bars welded into one unit. A very large number of *schiavonas*, often bearing arsenal marks stamped on the pommels, are preserved in the Armoury of the Council of Ten in the Doges' Palace in Venice.

The 'mortuary hilt', probably the best known of all English seventeenth-century hilts, was yet another variant of the basket hilt. 'Mortuary' is a nineteenth-century coining and describes the supposed remblance of the portrait heads chiselled on such hilts to the head of the martyred King Charles I. The bowl-shaped guard extending back to the pommel suggests direct descent from the short hangers with double-shell guards and wide knuckle-bows produced by the Hounslow factory in the 1630s. In fact the earliest basket-hilted swords of this type have guards decorated with the same scallop shell design as that found on early London hangers.

The first mortuary-hilted swords appeared in about 1630, and were the standard weapon of both Royalist and Parliamentary cavalry during the Civil War. They were usually fitted with a long single-edged blade for cutting and thrusting, and like all basket hilts had a leather lining inside the basket. Their quality is variable; some have very crude guards, probably made by local blacksmiths, and others are of very accomplished workmanship. The better hilts are chiselled in relief with equestrian warriors or trophies, sometimes with a crest or coat-of-arms worked into the design. The finest are encrusted with silver or gilded.

Right Venetian broadsword or *schiavona*. The hilt is of steel, decorated with studs, the pommel is of brass, and blade is dated 1734. This type of sword was carried by Dalmatian troops in the service of the Venetian Republic. Pommels of cast bronze or silver are often found on such swords.

Mortuary hilts underwent minor changes in the century that followed, such as the addition of extra bars linking the bowl to the knuckleguard and the incorporation of small plates which projected down the blade. There was a vogue in the 1640s for chiselled portrait faces on the hilt – hence the term 'mortuary' – and in the 1650s and 1660s the guard became much shallower. One of the swords which belonged to Oliver Cromwell is of this type. It was probably a family weapon, since the guard is chiselled with the Cromwell arms. A similar sword now in the Royal Armouries in London is said to have been carried by Cromwell when he led the charge at Drogheda in Ireland in 1649. One of the best illustrations of a mortuary sword is that shown in the portrait of William Haseland, a veteran of both the Civil War and Marlborough's wars in the early part of the eighteenth century. The painting was done in 1730 and shows him in the uniform of a Chelsea Pensioner. Long cavalry swords of the kind he is holding were made in large quantities, with only minor changes, until after 1660.

A type of basket hilt was also used in Germany. Introduced in the late sixteenth century, it had a basket formed of a series of curved, looping bars, long recurved quillons and two massive plate guards. Sometimes the quillon ends and pommel are cut in a

Above Broadsword with pierced steel hilt, Northern European, *c.*1650. Practical fighting weapons such as this were widely used by cavalry in the second half of the seventeenth century.

Far left 'Civil War Window' in Farndon Church, Cheshire, showing soldiers and equipment of the Civil War period. Swords are worn slung from broad buff leather belts.

Left Portrait of Chelsea Pensioner William Haseland, painted in 1730. Haseland fought in the English Civil War and is said to have been 110 years old when this picture was painted. His sword is a basket-hilt dating from the 1640s.

Right Broadsword with cast brass hilt, English, *c.*1685. Mass-produced hilts like this were very popular for cavalry use in the late seventeenth century.

Below Sword with basket hilt of pierced steel, japanned and gilded with foliage patterns, English, *c.*1650. The grip is covered in fish skin and bound with copper wire. This is the weapon said to have been used by Oliver Cromwell when he led the final assault on Drogheda in 1649.

series of small raised studs. The blades found with such hilts are generally very broad, straight and single-edged.

Another form of basket hilt used extensively in Northern Europe in the early part of the seventeenth century had a large, solid plate enclosing the hand, with additional bars at the back, and long quillons. The very broad, curved blades sometimes found with such hilts suggest that they were cavalry weapons. Not infrequently the plates forming the main part of the hilt are pierced with heart-shaped apertures reminiscent of later Scottish basket hilts.

Brass hilts and increasing standardization

Before 1660 most military hilts were of steel but in the last quarter of the century brass began to be used because of its cheapness. A large number of brass hilts could be produced very quickly, and therefore cheaply, by casting them in a mould, then assembling them by brazing. This was a decided advantage for any supplier of swords to the armies of John Churchill, First Duke of Marlborough! Of course cast hilts led to a decline in standards of workmanship and were, understandably, deplored by craftsmen who worked in steel.

Military swords underwent a certain amount of standardization during the seventeenth century. It is quite common, for example, to find certain plain swept-hilts of the 1620s all the same, suggesting that they were made for a special troop or guard whose equipment was uniform. The steel hilts with perforated shell guards used by the Amsterdam town guard during the 1650s are a good example of this. Casting hilts in brass undoubtedly ushered in the idea of mass production. At their best, brass-hilted military swords were well made and very serviceable. At their worst they were crudely made and weak.

The Thirty Years' War (1618–48), in which the troops of Bohemia, the Rhineland Palatinate, Austria, Spain, Denmark, Sweden and France all became embroiled at one time or another, played a major part in spreading certain types of military hilt throughout Europe. One form extensively used by nearly all the protagonists had a guard filled with a pierced, heart-shaped shell and surrounded by a network of scrolling bars. Screws were used to attach the guard to the pommel. On many surviving specimens, no doubt those carried by officers, the hilt is gilded. Broad, straight, double-edged blades are the usual type found with such hilts. The result was a very strong and serviceable weapon, well made and well proportioned, and ideal for cavalry use. Many examples of the type are found in Dutch and German arsenals, some with fine blades which bear the portrait of the Swedish king Gustavus Adolphus, indicating that their owners were followers of the Protestant leader.

Curved swords

The advantages of curved swords for cavalry use had been appreciated since the sixteenth century. Numerous campaigns waged against the Turks in Eastern Europe during the seventeenth century meant that there was considerable influence from the Near East. Turkish arms and costume were very fashionable, and armouries such as Dresden and the Kremlin have large quantities of Turkish and Persian swords taken as trophies or presented as gifts. Turkish arms also figure prominently in the armouries of Poland, Hungary and Germany, all of whom were in direct conflict with the Turks during the seventeenth century. Both in shape and hilt form the sword of Eastern Europe was heavily influenced by Turkish and Persian designs. Indeed many of the blades are of Islamic origin. The typical Eastern-style hilt had a simple crossguard with very long langets or extensions running up the grip and down the blade. The blade was usually single-edged and curved, often multiply grooved, and had a substantial back to it. The grip closely followed contemporary Turkish and Persian fashion in that it was cut off short near the pommel, which was a cap set at an angle. A type of sword known as a *karabela*, widely used in Poland and Hungary during the seventeenth century, had a grip formed of plaques held by rivets to the tang and engraved with a vertical chevron pattern. The grip extended at a sharp angle at the pommel and the guard was a cross

Far left Hanger with horn grip mounted in pierced brass, Venetian, *c.*1620.

Left Hanger with a carved boxwood grip, English or German, *c.*1630. The blade is somewhat crudely inlaid in brass with the words 'EDWARDUS PRINS ANGLIE'. Similar antiquarian insciptions are to be found on the blades of seventeenth-century hunting swords.

Below left Hanger with a gilded iron hilt and a pommel in the form of a bird of prey, English or Scottish, *c.*1610.

with short langets. So great was the influence of Turkish designs that it is often difficult to distinguish between Turkish and European work. The blades of Eastern European swords often bear inscriptions engraved or inlaid in gold. These range from Latin invocations such as 'Arma ferunt Pacem' and 'Pro Gloria et Patria' to commemorative titles such as 'Sigismundus II Rex Poloniae'.

A variation of the *karabela* was also adopted for cavalry use, the crossguard being extended to form a substantial knucklebow and, probably under German influence, a large thumb ring being attached to the back of the hilt. Swords of this type, normally associated with the light cavalry or hussars who played a major role in defeating the Turks in the latter part of the century, were the direct predecessors of the curved cavalry swords carried by most European armies in the eighteenth and nineteenth centuries.

77

Curved swords were also used in Northern Europe. In the sixteenth century a type of sword with recurved quillons and a very distinctive pommel in the shape of a lion with gaping jaws had become fashionable in Switzerland. Its seventeenth-century counterpart retained the pommel almost without alteration, but the guard was fitted with large perforated plates on either side; the blade, which was long, slightly curved and single-edged, had multiple grooves towards the back edge. In the latter part of the century the guard became much shorter, often with a single quillon and a knucklebow, and on Swiss and German hilts the curious 'Gothic' lion pommel was retained until about 1700. Swords like these were designed to be used by cavalry, and so the point was very much subordinate to the edge. Many blades were engraved with naive flowers and figurative subjects, and the occasional Latin motto.

Another very serviceable curved sword of medieval origin still in use in the first half of the seventeenth century was the falchion. This remarkably long-lived weapon, with its simple recurved crossguard and short, heavy; cleaver-like blade, was used during the Thirty Years' War, possibly by troops arranging for transport and waggons; a falchion would have been very handy for cutting the traces of runaway horses, for example.

A type of falchion fashionable in Italy and Germany during the first quarter of the century had a very short broad blade with a single edge and clipped point, sometimes with a slight curve to it, sometimes straight with a thick back edge rather like a cleaver. The guard was generally very simple, made of S-shaped bars with down-turned quillons, and the knuckblebow stopped just short of the pommel, which was flat with a short extension at the back. To afford greater protection to the hand, large scallop shell guards were sometimes attached to the quillons.

There is an interesting link between these businesslike weapons and their shipboard counterparts. A falchion-type weapon with a large shell is shown being wielded by the buccaneers Lolonois and Rock Brasiliano in the frontispiece of a book by John Esquemel-ing called *Buccaniers of America* published in London in 1684. Another falchion-type naval sword, this time a real one in the Danish Royal Collection, was supposed to have been taken by Count Adler from a Turkish admiral and later used by King Christian V of Denmark during the Scanian War of 1676. Some Italian falchions of the period were clearly influenced by Venetian hilts, which leads one to suppose that falchion-type swords may have been used extensively by the Venetian fleet in its battles with the Ottomans during the seventeenth century. Because of their short length and heavy cutting edge such weapons would have been ideal in the confined space between decks.

One very unusual sword mentioned and described by several seventeenth-century German fencing manuals is the *Düsack*. This curious and very rare weapon was made from a single piece of steel and was shaped like a broad, curved, single-edged cutlass, one end being pierced with an oval aperture forming the grip and

loop guard. An illustration in the *Neu Kunstliches Fechtbuch* of Jacob Sutor, published in Baden in 1612, clearly shows that it was essentially a cutting weapon. Possibly it developed from an agricultural implement – it was always considered a peasant weapon. By the seventeenth century its use seems to have dwindled to that of an occasional weapon in formal fencing matches, but it was still being mentioned in fencing books published as late as 1699. Very few actual examples of the *Düsack* have survived, although occasionally they come to light when old German collections are put up for sale. Judging from the appearance of the fencers using the *Düsack*, it was a very heavy, clumsy weapon and extremely unsuitable for war.

Hangers

These comparatively short swords were very popular for both civilian and military use throughout the seventeenth century. Hangers used exclusively for hunting are described in Chapters 4 and 8. The numbers of hangers which survive indicate that this form of short sword was very widely carried, especially in England. An English form which has only recently been identi-fied and dates from the early years of the seventeenth century has a hilt of iron with a pommel in the shape of a bird or animal head; the quillons are strongly recurved, sometimes with a small shell attached. Randle Holme, in his book *The Academy of Armory*, published in 1682, notes that a hanger closely resembling this was also used in Scotland. The blades found with these hilts are very short and usually curved.

The Hounslow Sword Factory, to which reference has already been made, was established in 1629 a few miles to the west of London on Hounslow Heath. Among its products were a large number of hangers of distinctive design, with pommels of cast brass, usually silvered or gilded, and vertically fluted grips, often mounted with a vertical iron strap on either side. The guards vary in design but a large double scallop shell was very popular in the 1630s, although for the sake of convenience a portion of it was often cut off. As on early mortuary hilts, the guard was often engraved with lines imitating a shell. In fact the close resemblance between these guards suggests that the mortuary hilt might have been a Hounslow invention. Some early hangers have an ingenious screwed tube holding the hilt assembly together, which would have allowed a damaged blade to be quickly replaced. The blades are usually broad and short, and in the case of Hounslow-made examples straight. They are of special interest because many of them are signed and dated, and in a few instances even the name of the client is recorded. It has been suggested that many of the better quality Hounslow hangers were made for the captains of Trained Bands.

Just before the Civil War a hanger hilt with a much smaller shell and a distinctive cap and scroll pommel became fashionable. These are always thought of as exclusive to Hounslow but the fact that they appear in Dutch pictures and have also been found on the

Continent suggests that may also have been manufactured elsewhere. Hilts of this form seems to have remained in use until about 1660–70 when they were gradually replaced by a type with small shells and a large cap pommel.

Hangers with hilts of silver survive in considerable quantity from the 1660s onwards. One well-known example, with a hilt entirely cast in silver and a very English-looking pommel and shell, belonged to the Dutch admiral Cornelis Van Tromp (1629–91), perhaps given to him when he visited London in 1675.

A large number of brass-hilted hangers survive from the last quarter of the century, the shells often bearing portrait busts of William and Mary, patriotic motifs such as crowns and wreaths, or classical figures. As the hanger was the sort of weapon worn when walking about town or travelling, the hilt was often very decorative. Many were fitted with carved grips of bone or ivory, and some were mounted with agates and other semi-precious stones. There are some interesting references to lost hangers in the newspapers of the 1670s – swords were often stolen or left in coaches or taverns. An advertisement in the *Mercurius Publicus* of 5–13 August 1663 reads: 'Lost – a short hanger, a saw on the back, the handle of black seal's skin, twined round with a silver wire, the hilt silvered, with a knife and bodkin in the scabbard suitable'. Many hanger blades both curved and straight had a saw edge on the back. This was probably intended for use in the hunting field, but saw edges are so common on hangers of the period that they

must have been put to a wide range of other uses. The additional knife and bodkin fitted into a pocket on the scabbard and were simply useful occasional tools.

Advertisements of the period also make frequent mention of silver hilts, or hilts plated with silver. The majority of these were cast in a two-piece mould, then worked up using engraving tools and punches. The ground of the main design was nearly always worked over with a hollow punch to give it texture and make the design stand out more clearly. The simple knucklebow-and-single-quillon hilt in silver was very fashionable towards the end of the century. Certain patterns of hilt were made both in iron and silver. A Scottish hanger of the 1700s, for instance, is virtually identical to an iron hilt of the same date.

Silver hanger hilts usually bear a maker's mark and other hallmarks, but there was clearly a lack of regulation in the marking of hilts compared to the marking of other silver wares. An advertisement in the 10 October 1661 edition of the *Mercurius Publicus* warns readers: '. . . sword hilts which are commonly made and vended under the notion of cast silver hilts, having occasionally been brought by the Working Cutlers to the Test of Goldsmith Hall, London have been found by the said Test to be of a compounded and counterfeit metal and not sterling. Which thing induces us to suspect, that the most part of cast silver hilts, now exposed to sale, are of the like false and sophisticated composition.' This statement and the number of plated hilts that were produced in the last quarter of the century seem to indicate that the buying of a silver hilt was a somewhat hazardous proceeding.

Opposite page Carved ivory grip and cast brass guard of a hunting sword, Dutch, *c.*1700 (above) and a Hounslow hanger with 'IOHAN KINNDT 1634' inscribed on the blade (below). The hilt of the Hounslow weapon is steel overlaid with silver, with bone and mother-of-pearl inlay on the grip.

Left Hanger with steel hilt and pommel of silvered brass, English, *c.*1635. This hilt is characteristic of swords made at Hounslow; the blade can be unscrewed for easy replacement.

Below, left to right
Silver-hilted hanger marked 'KILMAURS' on the blade, Scottish, *c.*1690. Kilmaurs in Ayrshire was famous for its cutlery.

Chiselled steel rapier hilt signed 'GOTFRID LEIGEBE' on the base of the pommel, German, *c.*1670.

Cast and patinated bronze hilt attributed to the Florentine sculptor Pietro Tacca, Italian, *c.*1640.

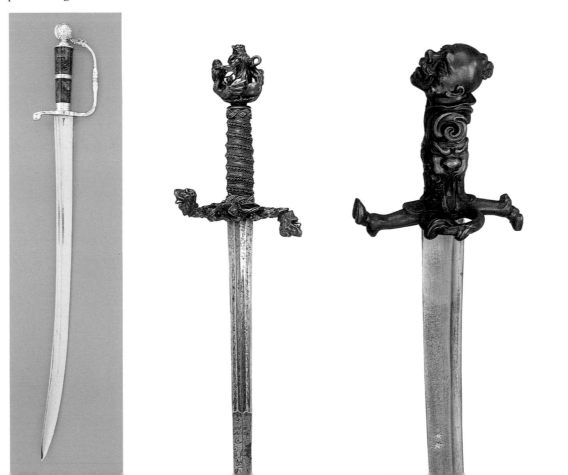

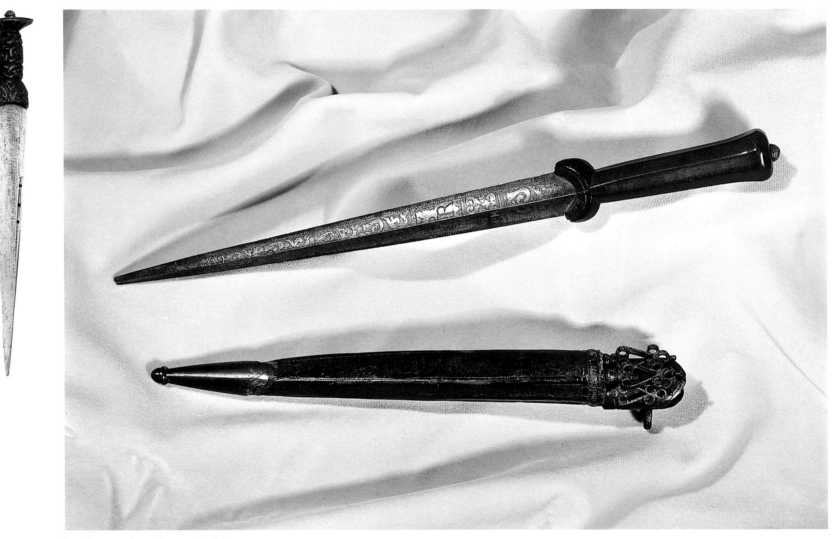

Sculptural and exotic hilts

The work of well-known craftsmen and artists such as the Sadeler brothers and Gottfried Leygebe has already been noted in connection with steel rapier hilts, but occasionally during the seventeenth century the work of well-known sulptors in bronze has also been identified. The Royal Armouries of H.M. Tower of London recently acquired a sword with a hilt which has been attributed to Pietro Tacca (1577–1640), a pupil of Giovanni da Bologna, sculptor to the Dukes of Tuscany. Since Tacca worked in Florence, it is tempting to suggest that the sword might have been made for Cosimo de Medici, Grand Duke of Tuscany, or one of his followers. The grip is in the form of a male head, the crossguard is shaped like the legs of a pig, and the side ring is sculpted into a pig's curly tail. It would be worthwhile surveying seventeenth-century sculptural hilts in bronze, silver and ivory and comparing them with the work of identified sculptors to see if more of their work as makers of sword hilts can be identified.

Some very exotic and curious swords are shown in a number of seventeenth-century portraits. Smallswords with hilts made by Japanese craftsmen are clearly recognizable, as are carved Indo-Portuguese hanger and smallsword hilts. A few portraits show distinctly oriental swords being worn with both civil and military costume. Colonel Alexander Popham of Littlecote in Wiltshire led a contingent of Parliamentary troops in the English Civil War and was afterwards painted wearing a short curved sword almost certainly made in Sri Lanka – the distinctive Sinhalese lion and *serendipaya* can clearly be seen on the hilt. Another curved sword of exotic origin appears in a portrait of the Salisbury family painted in the 1640s. Sir Thomas Salisbury (d. 1643) is shown wearing a *nimcha*, a curved sword indigenous to North Africa, especially to Morocco. Significantly the painting is a hunting piece and Sir Thomas may well have used the sword for hunting instead of the standard English hanger.

Dirks and stilettos

Although the practice of carrying a dagger with a rapier as part of everday costume was more or less discontinued from about 1640 onwards, daggers continued to be made throughout the century and some most interesting designs were produced. In Scotland the dirk, a direct descendant of the medieval ballock knife, acquired its traditional form. The earliest recognizable Scottish dirks retain the two lobes of medieval times at the junction of grip and blade, but the grip is decorated with bands of studs and interlaced work. By the end of the seventeenth century, hilts entirely covered with interlaced work were the norm. The blade was broad, single-edged and sometimes set with brass on the back edge. In the second half of the century brass was also used for the grip, often decorated with turned bands and engraved with formal leaf designs.

In recent years a number of interesting English daggers, all dating from around 1600, have been found on the foreshore of the River Thames. Most are left-hand weapons, with quillons and a thumb ring. The blades have a distinct central ridge and are usually inscribed and dated.

Another English type of dagger had flat spatulate quillons, a facetted blade with a saw back, and a grip of wood, although at least one example has an ivory grip. A most interesting example of the type, dated 1629 on the blade and 1654 on the sheath, is inscribed with the name of the owner, Sir John Hotham, about whom a certain amount is known. The historian Edward Hyde, Earl of Clarendon (1608–74) describes him as a rough and rude man, of great covetousness, pride and ambition. In 1642, when he was Governor of Hull, he refused to allow Charles I to enter the city. Later he later went over to the Royalists, but was arrested at Beverley by the Parliamentarians and executed on 2 January 1645 at the instance of Cromwell and the majority of the Commons. The dagger was kept by the family as a memento.

Quillon daggers fitted with comparatively simple guards and massive saw-edged blades – known to collectors as 'sword breakers' – are rather rare. The edge of the blade is cut with a series of huge pointed teeth which would certainly have caught an opponent's sword blade and allowed an undefended thrust to be made, but it is most unlikely that they would have broken a well-tempered blade. Only a few of these extraordinary weapons survive, the majority being of French or Italian origin, made around 1600.

In several collections there are daggers with blades which divide into three separate sections at the push of a button which operates a powerful spring set in the blade. These have been described as duelling daggers – the advantages of being able to catch an opponent's rapier blade and hold it away from the body when lunging are certainly obvious. The shape of the pommels and guards on these interesting weapons suggests that most of them were made in the first quarter of the seventeenth century.

The best-known Italian dagger of the seventeenth century is the stiletto. The tapering blade was of triangular section, the quillons generally short and straight, the grip narrow, and the pommel small. Unlike the blade, which remained virtually the same from the 1650s until the end of the century, the hilt took many forms, although most were made of cut steel. The art of cutting steel was brought to a very high standard in Italy and stiletto hilts provide exceptionally good examples of it. Wrythen grips, grips and quillons pierced and chiselled to represent helmeted warriors, and hilts cut with diamond-shaped facets are all found. The blades of one group of stilettos made for gunners are engraved with a numerical table or ready-reckoner for calculating the weight of shot to be used in cannon. Some stilettos are very short and plain and were probably designed for self-protection. Italian stilettos usually date from about 1650 but there are some very deadly-

Above Gunner's stiletto, Italian, second half of seventeenth century. The grip is of horn with blued steel mounts, and the blade is incised with a scale which enabled the gunner to calculate the weight of shot required in guns of diffferent bore.

Opposite page Two Scottish dirks (left), a dagger and sheath said to have belonged to François Ravaillac (1578–1610). the assassin of Henri IV of France (right), and a rare silver-hilted 'Godfrey dagger' (below).

Both dirks have carved wooden hilts and date from the the second half of the seventeenth century; the weapon on the right has the words 'Thy king and countries cause defend though on the spot your life should end' incised on the blade.

The Ravaillac weapon is Scottish, c.1610, and has an etched and gilt blade.

The blade of the Godfrey dagger is inscribed 'Memento Godfrey' and 'Anno Do 1678'. Godfrey daggers were made to commemorate the murder of Sir Edmund Berry Godfrey, a distinguished London magistrate, at the time of the Popish Plot.

looking thrusting daggers with long narrow pommels in the fashion of the 1600s which may have been their prototypes. These are usually described as French.

In the arsenal of the Saxon Electors at Dresden there are a number of daggers of similar style, also made around 1600. These seem to have been made as part of the equipment of the Saxon Electoral Guard, and like most of the weapons from the electoral arsenal are in exceptionally fine condition. The pommels are large and fluted, the quillons short, and the blades plain and double-edged. Most of the hilts are artificially patinated to a dark blue colour and some are mounted with engraved silver plates. Most of the grips are covered in fish skin, with a reinforcing strip running the length of the grip.

A type of dagger not unlike the stiletto was used by Dalmatian troops in the service of Venice, and continued to be produced until well into the eighteenth century. The blade was of tapering triangular section, with the quillons turning sharply down towards it. Both the pommel and quillon ends were often cut in spiral flutes. The finest examples have scabbards and fittings of silver.

The first bayonets

The earliest mention of the word 'bayonet', clearly meaning a kind of dagger to be used with a gun, occurs in the memoirs of the French Maréchal Jacques de Puysegur published in 1642. He describes his musketeers as being armed with bayonets so that they could defend themselves 'if anyone wished to come at them after they had fired'. The bayonet owes its name to the French city of Bayonne, in the sixteenth century a celebrated centre for the manufacture of daggers. The type of bayonet the Maréchal was describing is known as a plug bayonet, designed to fit into the barrel of a gun. The grip was tapered and the blade was about 12 ins/30 cms long. Plain military versions were made, but also, from 1680 onwards, more elaborate versions with silver quillons and grips decorated with silver inlay (piqué work), or gilt brass quillons cast in the shape of figures. Versions were also made for hunting. These often have a pronounced swelling near the guard or are mounted with an ivory ball.

The socket bayonet, designed to be fixed into a socket on the side of a gun barrel, first appeared in about 1678, a development attributed to the great French military engineer Sebastien Le Prestre de Vauban (1633–1707). A bayonet with a sleeve which fitted over the muzzle of a gun was issued to the French infantry in 1688. A few English bayonets of the 1680s bear patriotic inscriptions, but most are entirely plain except for a stamped cutler's mark. Socket bayonets made for the chase are often decorated, especially those made in Italy and Spain; in Italy silver-mounted socket bayonets engraved with naive animal scenes were popular.

The sword trade

The manufacture of swords and daggers during the seventeenth century was a well regulated and thriving industry. For reasons which have not yet been adequately explained, the blademakers of Toledo in Spain enjoyed a very high reputation during the period, but the genuine Spanish product is virtually impossible to identify since German and Italian cutlers astutely copied the the signatures of well-known Spanish makers and put them on their own blades. Even place names on blades often give no true idea of where a blade was made. The name 'Mailandt', for example, which appears on many seventeenth-century blades, is the old German spelling of Milan, which rather undermines the fiction of Italian manufacture. There is also confusion with makers' marks. The writer has seen a number of 'English' swords inscribed as having been made at Hounslow marked with the name of the celebrated Solingen maker Clemens Horn, but as far as is known Clemens Horn never worked in England.

There is no doubt that the most prolific centre of blade manufacture during the seventeenth century was Solingen in the Ruhr. Solingen blades were highly regarded for their quality and widely exported, the famous 'running wolf' mark appearing on the blades of swords made as far afield as Africa and India.

There was also a considerable trade in Eastern weapons, most of it conducted through ports such as Genoa and Venice. These centres have been somewhat neglected by weapons historians, but in recent years large numbers of seventeenth-century Indian swords from recently dispersed princely armouries have provided an interesting insight into the trade. A large proportion of these weapons are mounted with fine European blades, many preserved in virtually unused condition. All the marks and inscriptions can, for once, be clearly read, and a surprising number are of Italian origin.

There was of course a certain amount of interchange between the different centres of blade production. The Hounslow factory, for example, was initially staffed by cutlers from Solingen, and the sword mills established at Shotley Bridge in County Durham later in the century were also staffed by German cutlers, some of whose descendants are still listed in the current telephone book for the area.

There was also a lively trade in unmounted blades between France and the Indians of North America. A French document dated 14 August 1613 refers to 'three dozen sword blades with their scabbards, but without pommel and guard' destined to be sent as trade goods from Rouen to the Indians of French Canada. Unmounted blades and completely finished swords are recorded as having been distributed to 'savage nations drawn from the colony' by French merchants in 1693. The types of blade exported have been identified as long diamond-section rapier blades and double-edged straight blades with twin fullers and a strong ricasso. However, the trade seems to have declined in the eighteenth century, probably because the North American Indians, as discerning clients, began to want firearms instead.

Seventeenth-century blades were manufactured from billets of steel, cut to the required length, and then forged into shape. The swordsmith had access to water power to drive his hammers and grinding wheel, and these were very efficient. Blades were ground on large wheels, the craftsman usually lying in front of the wheel holding the blade against it. The tang was either drawn out from the blade or welded to it, many blades showing a lap weld near the guard. The blade was then tempered to relieve stresses within the metal. This involved heating it to a high temperature, usually above red heat, then plunging it into a bath of oil or molten lead, which reduced the temperature quickly and evenly along the length of the blade. Final grinding and polishing was followed by any necessary decoration. It is difficult to imagine, looking at a pitted and blunt seventeenth-century blade, how sharp and highly polished it must once have been.

From an account of sword and dagger manufacture in Brescia written in 1610, one gains a very clear idea of the entirely separate crafts involved – some craftsmen made nothing but pommels, others specialized in grips, others were specialist polishers, and so on. A fine sword was the work of a number of skilled craftsmen. The division of labour also meant that many swords could be produced within a very short time.

Opposite page Two late seventeenth-century English plug bayonets with wooden handles and mounts of gilt brass (left), a Saxon dagger and by-knife with chiselled and blued steel 'wave pattern' hilts (right), and a socket bayonet for use with a sporting gun (below).

The dagger and by-knife are from the armoury of the Electors of Saxony and were made in Dresden in about 1590. The sporting bayonet, which has a chiselled steel blade and a brass socket overlaid with engraved silver, is a Sardinian weapon, made in the second half of the eighteenth century. The cutlers of Sardinia specialized in hunting knives and bayonets decorated in this fashion.

Left A swordsmith's shop, as depicted by the Italian artist Bernardino Pocchetti (c. 1542–1612). Craftsmen are grinding and polishing blades. A variety of swords, daggers and pole-arms are displayed for sale in racks around the shop.

7 EIGHTEENTH- AND NINETEENTH-CENTURY EUROPE

Anthony North

By 1700 the rapier had become the smallsword, the short and very convenient hunting sword or hanger was widely worn, and special types of cavalry hilt had been developed. The increasing use of brass for hilts had also initiated major changes in design and manufacture. As early as the 1630s hilt-makers were complaining that their trade was being undermined by what were in fact mass-production methods. The elements of the hilt were cast in brass – knucklebows were usually a separate casting, and pommels were cast in two-piece moulds – and then brazed together. Once a pattern and mould had been made, a maker could turn out hundreds of identical hilts in brass in the time it took a craftsman working in steel to produce half a dozen, and provided the castings were substantial enough, they made very plain, serviceable and cheap weapons. The eighteenth century therefore saw the introduction of brass sword hilts of a fairly uniform pattern for most of the ordinary troops of European armies.

Eighteenth-century military patterns

The evolution of the smallsword was discussed in Chapter 5 but its use as a military weapon deserves comment, particularly as some European cavalry swords were, in effect, merely weightier versions of the smallsword. In the eighteenth century mounted troops still formed a very important component of all European armies. Many of the battles won by Marlborough and Frederick the Great were decided by a cavalry charge with sword in hand. At the battle of Zorndorf in 1758, rightly described by one historian as 'the last great and glorious deed of the Prussian cavalry', thirty-six squadrons of horse led by General Seydlitz charged the Russian infantry and decided the victory.

A form of hilt developed for use by English cavalry in the last quarter of the seventeenth century had a substantial shell-shaped guard linked to a thick knuckleguard by twin bars, a large globular pommel, and a blade which was straight and fairly broad, usually with a double edge and a pronounced central ridge. The majority of these weapons had plain brass hilts, but cast designs with classical motifs on them were also common. Swords like this were certainly being produced by the 1680s and were still in use in the first quarter of the eighteenth century.

Throughout the eighteenth century there was a close relationship between the civilian smallsword and smallswords designed for military use. A pattern of sword used by the French cavalry in 1730, for example, was simply a plainer version of a type of light rapier used by civilians in the second half of the previous century. It had a large pear-shaped pommel, a half-shell guard and a plain knucklebow, all cast in brass. When a design was found to be practical, it was often retained for many years with only minor changes. The pattern just described is basically the same as a French regulation pattern introduced in 1695, except that the grip of the earlier weapon was of wood bound with wire rather than cast. Both patterns had a straight double-edged blade.

Other military smallsword hilts with facetted pear-shaped pommels and plain shells made in brass have also been identified as French. The blades on these are usually of the narrow rapier type, with a channel near the hilt. French hilt-makers, like their English brethren, favoured the use of brass and also seem to have preferred a very simple style for military weapons. There were exceptions of course. A group of smallsword-type hilts in brass with cast relief figures set in scrolls has been identified as French.

The twin-shell guard was used all over Europe, with regional variations of course. Many German and Dutch cavalry swords had a substantial thumb ring attached to the inside of the shell, which was linked to the pommel by a curved bar attached to both knucklebow and pommel. On many examples the shells were also perforated. Usually such hilts are of wrought steel rather than brass, presumably because the extra bars demanded a very complicated mould. The antecedents of the German form were probably the 'Walloon' hilts of the 1650s and 1660s. Another feature found on German cavalry swords in the early part of the eighteenth century is the lion-headed pommel, an echo of the animal-headed pommels popular in the previous century. Except in Germany, animal heads seldom appear on pommels of the period.

The short curved hanger was widely adopted for military use by infantry in the early part of the century, with many regional variations. One English type, made around 1700, has the usual half-shell guard and knucklebow, but the grip and pommel are cast in one. The pommel is in the form of an exotic lion remarkably similar to the beast found on some carved wood and ivory Sinhalese hilts imported into Europe by the Dutch in the 1700s. The short hanger with a brass hilt was also used in Germany, France and Scandinavia, although German hangers retained the large thumb ring and side bar typical of the Walloon sword referred to above.

The incorporation of a small side plate into hanger hilts became standard in the eighteenth century, especially in Germany and Scandinavia. The Danish Grenadier pattern of 1705, for example, has a brass hilt with a small side plate. This feature provided an ideal surface for a regimental or national device, and most Northern European hilts of this kind bear a cast badge.

The basket-hilted sword, in which the entire hand was protected by a leather-lined cage of bars, was made in many variations throughout the eighteenth century. In the late 1600s the plates set into the hilts of Scottish types were customarily pierced with openwork designs, usually hearts and circles, but after about 1710 the plates of the hilt assume a rectangular shape, linked together by bars, and are not only pierced but filed into serrations along their edges. Much of the decoration on Scottish hilts of the eighteenth century was done with saws or files, giving them a very distinctive appearance. Several very fine examples made in the first half of the century carry the initials or names of makers such as John Simpson, Thomas Gemmill of Glasgow, and John and Walter Allan of Stirling, usually on the scrolling projection on the guard. The Allans are noted for their exceptional inlaid brass and silver work. Many of the blades on these weapons date from the previous century, although some bear distinctly Jacobite sentiments, appropriate to the era which saw the Rebellions of 1715 and 1745. One bears the words: 'Property to Schotland and No Union' on one side and 'For God my Country and King James the 8' on the other. The German spelling of Scotland reveals the German origin of the blade. Another fine basket-hilted blade in the Royal Scottish Museum carries the verse: 'With this good

Left Sword with cast brass hilt, English, *c.*1700. The blade bears the mark of Thomas Hollier. This was probably one of the seventeenth-century hangers fitted by Hollier when he worked for the Board of Ordnance after 1715.

Opposite page General The Hon. William Gordon of Fyvie by Pompeo Batoni (1708–87) pictured in the uniform of the 105th The Queen's Own Royal Regiment of Highlanders. His sword is a basket-hilted backsword of about 1766. Swords of this pattern were fashionable for officers in the last quarter of the eighteenth century.

Right Basket-hilted broadsword, Scottish, *c.*1740. The hilt is of steel and the blade is engraved with Jacobite mottoes.

Below Cavalry officer's sword with a gilt brass basket hilt, English. The blade, engraved with the cypher 'GR', is eighteenth-century, but the hilt was made in about 1690.

Bottom Basket-hilted broadsword, Scottish (Glasgow), *c.*1720. Unusually, this sword has never been cleaned and is preserved in fine condition. The hilt is of pierced steel and the blade bears the Solingen 'running wolf' mark.

sword thy cause I will maintain and for they sake O James will breath each vein'. These were swords of very high quality, made for special clients. The less wealthy had to be content with plainer accoutrements.

A large number of plain military hilts of Scottish type were produced throughout the century, many outside Scotland in centres such as Birmingham. In construction they are similar to their more ornate fellows, but they tend to be made of thin-gauge plate, which was cheaper and easier to work.

The variety of basket hilts found on eighteenth-century military swords is in fact enormous, ranging from simple S-shaped scrolling bars set side by side to complete cages formed of solid plates linked together, with square piercings. The quantity of metal needed for such hilts positively invited decoration. Some very beautiful hilts of basket construction with lion-head pommels and plates pierced with trophy designs were produced for cavalry officers in the middle of the century, for example. The distinctive *schiavona* hilt used by Dalmatian troops continued to be carried throughout the century, although late versions can be recognized by their superior finish and ornate mounting. Specimens dating from the second half of the century, for example, often have cast silver pommels and hilts set with applied silver studs.

The cavalry sabre

Contact between Turkish and Eastern European forces in the late seventeenth century brought the curved single-edged sword very much into favour, especially with cavalry regiments. The ancestor of the traditional cavalry sabre – the word 'sabre' probably comes from the Eastern European *sablya*, meaning 'sword' – is to be found in the light stirrup-hilted curved swords used in Poland and Hungary in the seventeenth century. The inspiration for these was undoubtedly Turkish and Persian, since the blade shape and the long langets and crossguard on the hilt are all found on Near Eastern weapons. The knucklebow, extending the crossguard up to the pommel, and a strengthening plate along the back edge of the grip were European contributions. Thus the standard cavalry sabre which remained in use until well into the nineteenth century was already in existence by the second quarter of the eighteenth.

The blades found on early cavalry sabres are usually flat, curved and single-edged, with a series of channels at the back of the blade, but by the middle of the century it was realised that both strength and lightness could be achieved with a single broad channel, and increasingly this became the standard pattern.

The simple design of the stirrup hilt meant that large numbers could be cast in brass or made in steel, and so stirrup-hilted weapons were widely adopted, especially in France and Germany, although in many cases the workmanship was very rough. Swords used by European mercenaries fighting in America had stirrup hilts and considerably influenced the design of hilts in the United States.

Stirrup-hilted swords were mounted with long, heavy blades for cavalry use or with shorter, lighter blades for infantry use. A French regulation of 1767 describes a pattern of short sword for infantry with a broad curved blade and a hilt of standard stirrup form with a small langet and cast brass grip. This particular pattern continued to be made until just after the Revolution. Although German troops also adopted the stirrup hilt to some extent, they preferred a form which incorporated heart-shaped shells extending back along the knucklebow, which gave better protection for the hand.

The French cavalry were among the first to adopt the Eastern European sabre. Cardinal Richelieu, the all-powerful minister of Louis XIII, used companies of Hungarian *houzards* or light cavalry in the 1630s, but the first regiment of hussars in the service of the French king, the Cornberg regiment, was not established until 1692. The regiment had its own distinctive uniform and adopted a very effective curved sword with a short, wide blade. In 1752 the pattern was changed to a longer, narrower weapon with a stirrup hilt, long langets, and a wooden scabbard with brass mounts. The grip was also of wood, bound with wire. With their exotic uniform and weapons, the French hussars saw service in most of the campaigns in which France was involved in the eighteenth century, and created their own traditions, one of which required the officer in charge to consult all his troops before they charged the enemy!

The swords of the rank and file of Europe's various armies in the eighteenth century are seldom shown in paintings in any detail or with any accuracy. Only very occasionally it is possible to recognize a specific pattern from a picture. However a painting in the Bibliothèque Nationale in Paris shows dragoons of Maréchal Schomberg's 17th regiment carrying light curved sabres with hilts constructed of rivetted bars, a pattern introduced in 1767, which proved ideal for fighting on horseback as well as on foot.

Regulation hilts from the second half of the eighteenth century survive in enormous numbers, and most have been studied in minute detail by military historians and other specialists. Many bear regimental devices on the guard and the title of the regiment engraved on the blade. Military reformers such as the Maréchal de Saxe (1696–1750) issued extremely detailed specifications for cavalry and infantry equipment, meticulously describing the length and design of the 'ideal' cavalry sword. Frederick the Great of Prussia (1712–86) also reformed the equipment and organization of the Prussian army for his campaigns in Silesia. It is often forgotten that Frederick was a great advocate of cavalry if it was correctly used. Before the Seven Years' War (1756–63) he wrote of his mounted troops: 'They were besotted with the idea of firing off their pistols. I finally had to make some straw dummies and I was able to show them that all their pistol shots missed, whereas they cut down every single figure with their swords.'

Prussian cuirassiers carried a very heavy straight-bladed sword with a huge cast brass half-basket hilt bearing the Prussian eagle in relief. That this very impressive-looking weapon was both difficult and tiring to use is suggested by the introduction of a lighter, curved, single-edged sabre in 1732.

Production at Tula

Regulation hilts were usually made of locally available materials. Tula, about 100 miles to the south of Moscow, had been a centre for the iron trade since the sixteenth century, and in the eighteenth became a major centre for supplying weapons to the Russian army. In 1712 Tsar Peter the Great established a new arms factory there to supply both firearms and edged weapons for his campaigns against Charles XII of Sweden in the Great Northern War of 1700–12. Initially only regulation pattern swords were made, but in 1748 a special factory was set up to produce better quality swords and other weapons, such as halberds for ceremonial occasions. At first Tula hilt designs followed the conventional patterns of the period. Smallswords with brass or bronze hilts cast with figures and scrolls, sometimes including the imperial cypher, were made for officers. Some of their blades are marked 'Solingen' in Cyrillic letters. Very large cuirassier's broadswords loosely based on Prussian designs were also made. These had large half-basket hilts, a pommel in the shape of an eagle, and a broad double-edged blade engraved with the imperial cypher and the name 'Tula'. Many of these regulation patterns were dated.

However Tula very quickly developed its own style of design and decoration. In the 1750s, for example, a number of large

However, towards the end of the century other centres of sword production became prominent. Zlatoust in the Urals, for example, was noted for its fine blades, in particular for those made by a craftsman named Ivan Bushuyev who specialized in decorating blades along their entire length with scenes inlaid in gold against a blued ground.

Other eighteenth-century hilts

A large number of silver hilts were made throughout the eighteenth century for both officers and civilians. Officers must often have worn a plain smallsword but occasionally swords with silver hilts are found which seem to have been made specifically for military use, judging by the military trophies depicted on them. The wrythen pommels fashionable in the last quarter of the century also appear on military-style silver hilts. In general the blades are of the heavy double-edged regulation form.

A military hilt which was very popular with English officers in the second half of the century was made in steel and silver, with the knucklebow split to form an outside loop on the guard. Both guard and pommel were cut with swirling flutes. This simple and attractive design owed much to the rococo metalwork of the 1750s, and remained fashionable in England until 1800.

Another style of hilt much affected by officers was the boat-shaped hilt, the guard of which was a heart-shaped shell with one side extending up towards the knucklebow. Although based on a seventeenth-century hilt, the wrythen flutes on the pommel and knucklebow gave it a very striking rococo flavour. Boat-shaped hilts were made in silver, gilt, copper, brass and steel, and the design lasted well into the nineteenth century for military use. One reason for its popularity may have been the extra protection afforded by the large guard.

Many of the hilt designs found on military weapons in the eighteenth century were simply adaptations of earlier styles. A classic example of this was hilt on the *bilbo* used by Spanish troops throughout the eighteenth century and well into the nineteenth. Its huge cup hilt was directly derived from the elegant cup-hilt rapier of the previous century. Although *bilbo* blades are very long and ungainly, they are often of surprisingly good quality, stamped with a date and the name of the reigning monarch. A lighter civilian version, with a shallower cup and a light knucklebow, was introduced in the 1760s and used in both Spain and Portugal. Silver, brass and steel hilts were made, fine quality steel hilts of this type often having a knucklebow pierced with series of circles.

The rise of Bonaparte

The wide introduction of the neo-classical style of ornament into Europe in the latter half of the eighteenth century and the huge demand for weapons during the Revolutionary Wars in France in the 1790s resulted in some very fine officer's swords. In the Revolutionary period the French favoured the large half-basket

infantry pattern swords were made, with a very large half-shell guard, and an officer's pattern dated 1748 has a hilt of gilt bronze cast in relief with a crowned eagle set amidst scrolling foliage, a radical departure from the plainer steel hilts manufactured four decades earlier.

A feature of Tula work is the use of low-relief chiselled decoration in steel, the ground of the design being matted with gold. Scrolls, animals and trophies were all chiselled with great skill. Steel hilts continued to be made into the last quarter of the eighteenth century, although the motifs changed. Some were decorated with small oval panels of multi-coloured gold inlaid with flowers; the steel was coloured to a beautiful peacock blue to contrast with the inlaid work. There was also a vogue towards the end of the century for steel hilts set with polished studs, a fashion almost certainly copied from France.

Tula craftsmen, especially in the latter half of the eighteenth century, excelled in the exacting art of using and decorating steel. Sword hilts were not the only objects made. Seals, chess pieces, and even chairs and fireplaces were produced, and what started as a munitions factory ended up as a major artistic enterprise.

hilt, made in a variety of forms, usually in cast and gilt bronze. Military trophies were the most popular form of decoration, one rare example even showing the towers of the Bastille being toppled by trophies. Another bears the pierced device of two axes, with the inscription 'Je sape les tyrans' ('I bring tyrants low'). Many pommels were made in the form of helmets or Phrygian caps.

The Napoleonic Wars of 1804–15 produced a wide range of interesting edged weapons. By this time neo-classicism had gained a very firm hold on design generally, and it was to Ancient Greece and Rome that artists turned for inspiration. Pommels sprouted Roman eagles and hilts were decorated with altars and classical figures. Some designs were modelled directly on those shown in Greek and Roman sculpture. When asked to design a sword for the French military academy, the Ecole de Mars, the artist David (1748–1825) sought inspiration in the swords shown in reliefs of Greek warriors. The massive proportions of his design, unmistakably neo-classical, betray its sculptural origin. Similar swords were made for ceremonial purposes, with scabbards exuberantly decorated with thunderbolts, acanthus leaves and sphinxes.

The swords made for the members of the Consulat, which briefly ruled France before Bonaparte was proclaimed Emperor in 1803, were also in the neo-classical style, although their long, flimsy blades made them totally impractical as weapons. Classical motifs adorn the hilts, and the scabbards are mounted with panels of mother-of-pearl set in frames of silver gilt. They were supplied by the most celebrated manufacturer of presentation arms of the day, Nicolas-Noel Boutet (1761–1833), better known for his fine firearms. The quality of the silver work on the hilts and the inlaid work on the blades of his Consulat swords is every bit as good as that found on other items from his Versailles factory.

Another master craftsmen who supplied swords to the imperial court in the Napoleonic era was the silversmith Martin-Guillaume Biennais (1764–1843). A gold-hilted sword by Biennais, thought to have been made for Napoleon himself, is in the collection of the Duke of Wellington at Apsley House. It is a masterpiece. The simple cruciform hilt is decorated with the full range of neo-classical motifs, and there are three scabbards, covered with velvet, with leather, and with tortoiseshell filled with tiny gold stars. Biennais also mounted up the sword which Wellington carried at the Battle of Waterloo.

Napoleon's campaign in Egypt in 1798–99 brought French forces directly into contact with those of Ottoman Empire, and as a consequence many Eastern weapons found their way back to Europe. The classic Turkish hilt with pistol grip, cruciform guard and langets became very much the vogue with French and also British officers. The French imperial arms factory at Klingenthal in Alsace also made daggers in the Turkish style, with fluted ebony grips, for the Mamelukes of the Imperial Guard. This was originally a mounted company of janissaries founded by General

Right, top to bottom

Gilt bronze hilt cast with a representation of the toppling Bastille and trophies, French, c.1790. The parcel gilt blade is inscribed 'La Vigilance et la force'

Cavalry officer's sabre with gilt brass hilt, French, c.1795. The blade is inscribed 'Les 9me Regt de Chasseur des Armée françoise'.

Sword for a boy, Russian (Tula), c.1780. Hilt and blade are of steel overlaid with gold decoration, probably by the Tula craftsman I. Krapivensov. The monogram on the hilt is that of Grand-Duke Alexander Pavlovich.

Fine quality silver-hilted officer's broadsword, English, c.1760. The blade is inscribed 'ANDRIA FERARA' and stamped with maker's marks, and the leather scabbard is mounted in silver.

Opposite page French recruiting poster of 1757 for the regiment of dragoons of the Duc d'Orléans (left) and the etched blued and gilt blade of a French royalist sword of about 1795 (below). The words on the blade read 'Vangeons le père, sauvons la mère, et couronnons le fils'.

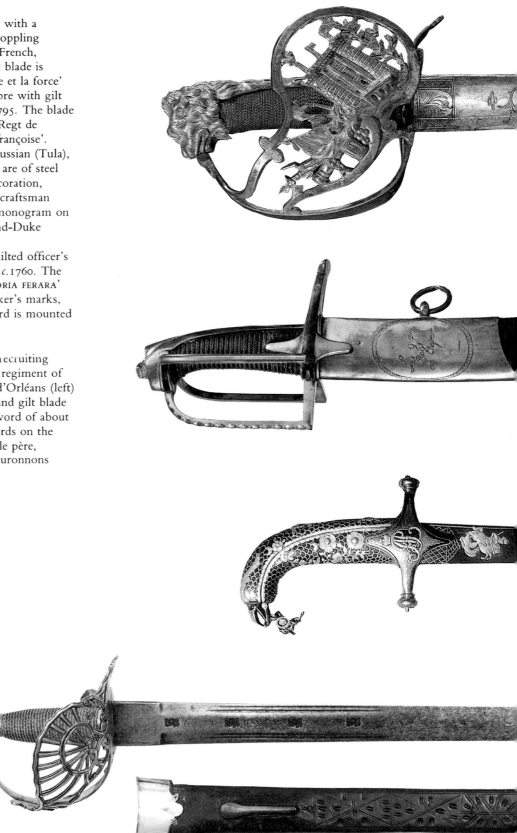

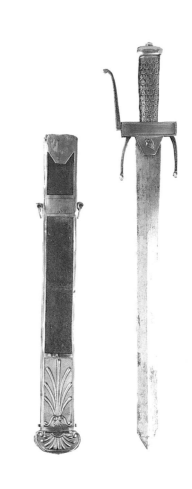

Above Napoleon, as First Consul of the French Republic, presides over a meeting with representatives of the Cisalpine Republic at Lyon in 1802, painting by Nicolas-André Monsiaux (1754–1837). Napoleon's sword, in neo-classical style, is purely ceremonial.

Above right Sword of a member of the Ecole de Mars, French, c.1795, designed by the painter David. The hilt is of brass, with a steel guard, and the scabbard is mounted in brass.

Kleber in 1799 from Turks who had taken part in the seige of Acre. In 1803 the company became attached to the Imperial Guard and saw service throughout the Napoleonic Wars. Several of the most devoted followed the Emperor to Elba. The company wore oriental costume based on Turkish dress and also carried a Turkish scimitar and a dagger virtually indistinguishable from the *khanjar* described in Chapter 11.

The huge variety in the design of swords used by European forces in the late eighteenth and early nineteenth century, in which Ottoman influences are sometimes discernable, bears witness to the skill and ingenuity of hilt-makers of the period. Beautifully pierced half-basket hilts of highly polished steel were produced for English officers in the last quarter of the eighteenth century; these were masterpieces of design, as practical as they were attractive. For everyday wear, however, most officers preferred a light hanger with a comparatively short blade, curved or straight, and a grip made of ivory cut in a swirling design. The plain stirrup hilt was made more elegant by widening the guard and piercing it with slots or chequerboard designs. A loop guard, with additional scrolling side bars, was also fashionable. If these

weapons appear rather too light to have been very effective, it should be remembered that their sharpness has been removed by two centuries of wear and cleaning. When, very rarely, one comes across a weapon preserved in pristine condition, its functional qualities can be readily appreciated.

Makers' marks

In most Europen countries, sword hilts of precious metal, silver and gold, usually but not invariably carry hallmarks. These usually include the initials of the maker, a date letter, and sometimes a quality mark and the mark of the city where the hilt was assayed. However the marking of hilts was not as strictly controlled as the the marking of plate. Hilts could be marked in several places – on the pommel, sometimes on the side of the quillons or on the part of the knucklebow adjacent to the pommel, or on the shell guard – but the fashion for pierced work on hilts in the second half of the eighteenth century meant that there were very few flat surfaces free from ornament on which marks could be stamped, and so marks tended to be badly struck or partly obliterated, making them very difficult to decipher.

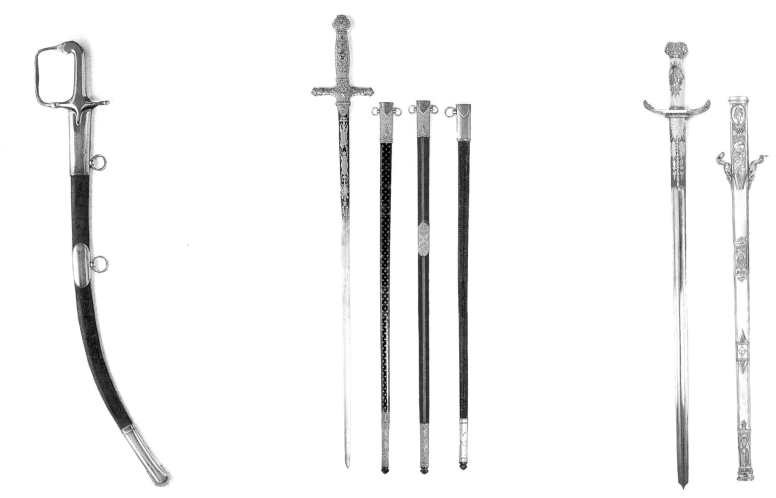

Left to right
Sabre signed 'Biennais à Paris' on the scabbard, French *c.*1800. The hilt and scabbard mounts are of silver gilt. This is the sword which the Duke of Wellington carried at the Battle of Waterloo on 18 June 1815. He probably acquired it from a French officer during the Peninsular War of 1808–14.
Napoleon's court sword, French, *c.*1809. The hilt is of chased gold and the three scabbards, of tortoiseshell, red velvet and leather, are signed by Biennais, Napoleon's goldsmith. The sword was captured from Napoleon's travelling coach after Waterloo.
Ceremonial sword by Nicolas-Noel Boutet, French (Versailles), *c.*1802–3. The mounts are of silver gilt and the blade is overlaid with gold. This was one of three such swords worn by members of the French Consulat in 1802–3.

Certain French and German makers' marks, struck with very small stamps, are easy to overlook, especially if they are struck on the knucklebow or quillons.

Most scabbards have a maker's name and address engraved or punched on the top mount. The scabbard, hilt and blade were the work of different craftsmen of course, the sword supplier usually buying them in and mounting them up to meet customers' requirements.

It is not easy to identify precisely the maker of a silver hilt. Some initials are common to a number of makers, frequently the mark indicating the town where the hilt was made is missing, and the marks are usually very worn. Only a few of the craftsmen who worked exclusively on sword hilts have been identified. A considerable amount of research still has to be done on hilt makers in nearly all countries, so collectors should not expect to be able to attribute a hilt to a particular maker without a great deal of work. An added pitfall with English marks on sword hilts is that false marks were sometimes used, no doubt by provincial makers seeking to sell their wares at metropolitan prices. There is often confusion between American and English marks and many prov-incial English silver hilts have been wrongly identified as American and sold as such. Specialists and collectors are referred to the standard works on hallmarks, some of which have special sections dealing with hilt-makers.

Presentation swords

The practice of making swords exclusively for presentation continued in the eighteenth and nineteenth centuries – a fine sword was considered an ideal reward for bravery in the field. Many were standard weapons 'personalized' by adding an inscription or a coat-of-arms. Some of the fine chiselled small-swords of the 1770s for example bear the lilies of France and the silver medallions of King Louis XV. Occasionally presentation hilts would be commissioned from jewellers rather than sword-smiths. A smallsword with a hilt set with precious stones and presented to Vice-Admiral Charles Middleton by the Assembly of the Island of Barbados in 1757 is clearly the work of a jeweller, being of too clumsy a construction to have been made by a craftsman used to making swords. The recipient had captured a French privateer which had been threatening the island's trade.

Right French infantry uniforms of the First Empire, painted by Pierre and Hippolyte Lecomte.

Below Sword presented to Rear-Admiral Lord Nelson in 1799 by the City of London for his victory at the Battle of the Nile, August 1798. The enamelled gold hilt is set with diamonds and bears the London hallmarks for 1798–9 and the maker's mark of James Morisset.

Below right Three bandsman's swords with hilts of cast brass and steel, English, second half of the nineteenth century. These swords were worn by military band musicians. Their design owes much to the Gothic revival style popular in the latter half of the century.

The Napoleonic Wars saw a positive flood of presentation swords for naval and military personnel, but only a few of these very interesting weapons can be mentioned here. From 1803 to 1809 the members of Lloyds in the City of London presented Patriotic Fund swords for outstanding bravery. There were three grades of sword: the £100 sword for commanders and captains, the £50 sword for naval lieutenants, Royal Marine officers and captains of civilian vessels, and a £30 sword for the lower ranks of officer and master's mates. The general design was based on the standard stirrup hilt of the period, and hilt and scabbard were covered with classical motifs, figures of Britannia and other patriotic emblems. The blades were blued and gilded, and inscribed with details of the event which ocasioned the presentation and the name of the recipient. Many were supplied by a London maker named Teed, whose address is given as Lancaster Court, Strand. Individual actions as well as participation in major engagements were rewarded.

In France, in the Directoire and Consulat periods, French officers were presented with simple gilt brass stirrup-hilted swords, inscribed on the scabbard with details of the campaign in which they were won. A number of scabbards are inscribed 'Armée d'Italie', for example, commemorating Napoleon's campaign against the Austrians in 1796. Boutet's Versailles factory made silver-hilted sabres for presentation. One such sword, which bears the inscription 'Le 1er Consul au Cen Beau chef de Bat.on à la 68e 1/2 Bde de ligne', is plain compared with the Lloyds Patriotic Fund swords but is accompanied by a certificate signed by Berthier, the Minister for War, Secretary of State Maret, and Bonaparte himself, a document which more than makes up for its sobre design.

The age of industry

In the nineteenth century of course the role of the sword on the field of battle was largely superseded by long-range tactics which relied on artillery and firearms. By the 1820s swords had been more or less abandoned as adjuncts to civilian dress, although they were retained for formal court ceremonies.

In 1822 the half-basket Gothic hilt was introduced into the British Army for use by infantry officers. A similar hilt, consisting of a series of bars forming a Gothic-style tracery, is still used on ceremonial occasions by officers today. The French retained their heavy cast brass half-basket hilt for certain patterns, such as the cavalry pattern of 1882, but reverted back to prototypes used in 1816 for the cavalry pattern introduced in 1854.

Some extraordinary short swords were produced for military use in the nineteenth century. Apart from the cross-hilted swords made for bandsmen, pioneers were supplied with short single-edged cutting swords not unlike the Roman *gladius*, although they had a saw edge on the back. Similar swords, with hilts of cast brass, were also used in France and Russia. This reflected a tendency in the first half of the century for the same type of sword

to be used by different European forces. The Spanish infantry sword of 1818, for example, was virtually identical to the French pattern of 1816.

In Russia a sabre without a guard, known as a *shashqa*, was fashionable throughout the century. Regulation *shashqas* are usually mounted in plain brass, but some very fine versions mounted in silver and decorated with niello were made for Russian officers by the craftsmen of Daghestan in the Caucasus.

Ottoman styles of hilt, with their distinctive pistol grip, were widely used on officer's swords throughout the century. In Britain these were known as 'levée' swords, but attractive as they are, with their light single-edged blades decorated with etched designs, they were never intended for use in the field.

Sword-makers frequently exhibited their more extravagent wares at the great international exhibitions which were such an important feature of artistic and industrial life in the nineteenth century. Most of the swords and daggers shown in catalogues of period, however, were never intended for use. They were made solely to demonstrate the skill of the manufacturer, and often their design was medieval or Renaissance in inspiration. Extraordinary swords in the Gothic style, with figures faithfully portrayed in architectural settings, were made in silver for exhibition purposes. Presentation swords decorated with gold and silver inlaid work were also made.

Probably the most skilful artist-craftsman working in the revived Renaissance style was Eusebio Zuloaga (1808–98). A dagger and sheath by him, made for the Great Exhibition of 1851 in London, are illustrated in Matthew Digby-Wyatt's book *Industrial Arts of the XIXth Century*. In 1848 Zuloaga made a copy of the famous sword of Francois I in the Real Armeria, Madrid. He also made some fine hunting bayonets damascened in gold and decorated with ornate chiselling and pierced work. In the Philadelphia Museum of Art there is a large sabre by him, originally part of a garniture of weapons, with an iron hilt chiselled in relief with warriors and scrolling foliage. Zuloaga was not only exceptionally skilful at chiselled work but also a master of gold and silver damascening. As has been observed elsewhere, his skill at surface decoration was unsurpassed in his own century, although the general design of his swords lacks the elegance of the genuine Renaissance article.

The Franco-Prussian War of 1870–71 saw a number of cavalry charges using the sword. Prussian cuirassiers from the Bredow Brigade charged the French infantry and artillery at Vionville in 1870 with some initial success, only to be repulsed by the French cuirassiers of the Forton Brigade, swords being used to great effect by both sides. As the century drew to a close firearms and artillery became the dominant weapons in the field, and the sword was more or less relegated to the role of a parade weapon. Fine presentation swords, with blued blades etched with the recipient's name, were produced for German officers during World War I, and during the Third Reich (1933–45) vast quanti-

Left Two Lloyds Patriotic Fund presentation swords: a £100 sabre (above) presented to George Younghusband, commander of HMS *Osprey*, for engaging with the French ship *L'Egyptienne* in 1804, and a £50 sword (below) presented to Lt George Beatty of the Royal Marines for gallant action in Martinique in 1803.

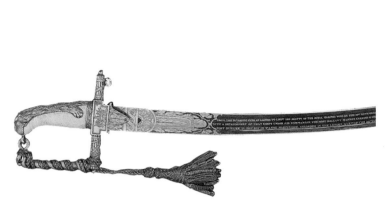

Below Sword presented by William IV to the Duke of Wellington and subsequently worn by him as Colonel-in-Chief of the Grenadier Guards. The hilt, of silver gilt, bears the London hallmarks for 1831–2 and the maker's mark 'IP' for John Prosser. The blade is etched in imitation of watered steel, overlaid in gold, and inscribed 'Prosser Maker to the King and Royal family, London'.

Bottom Silver-hilted *shashqa* with silver-mounted scabbard, Russian (Caucasus), *c*.1830. Latin patriotic mottoes are engraved on the blade.

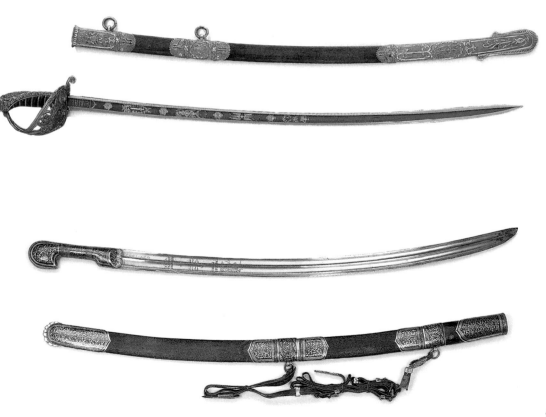

ties of edged weapons, some of very archaic inspiration, were manufactured by the cutlers of Solingen. These are discussed in Chapter 10.

Not all forces kept their swords solely for parade, however. The Russian cavalry used swords in the campaign against Germany in 1945 and Turkish cavalry are said to have charged, sword in hand, in Korea in 1950. Swords are still produced by old established firms such as Wilkinson-Match in London, which in spite of various amalgamations has a full order book to supply weapons to countries all over the world.

Naval swords

The development of naval edged weapons was touched on in Chapter 6 in connection with hangers. From the evidence of portraits we know that the short hanger was, from the seventeenth century onwards, the chosen weapon on board ship. However some fine silver-hilted rapiers produced in the 1630s and engraved with scenes of sea battles are known to have been presented to Dutch commanders by the States General.

With the introduction of regulation hilts towards the end of the eighteenth century, the development of naval swords can be followed fairly precisely. A very popular form for British naval officers at the time of Trafalgar (1805) had a square-sectioned reeded grip, an outer guard, and a series of five balls on the knucklebow. The extremely elegant and light swords carried by French naval officers were based on a light cavalry design and had neo-classical hilts. The grip is of square section, usually of wood, and the guard is a very formalized stirrup hilt with a long pommel. As one would expect, many naval swords have an anchor incorporated in their design.

Naval officers of junior rank in most navies often carried a short dirk, with a simple short quillon and an ivory grip. The familiar naval cutlass, with its heavy single-edged blade and plain iron hilt, probably owes its origin to the cheap munition hilts of the seventeenth century. This sturdy cutting weapon remained in use for a surprisingly long period, even into the present century. The parade sword issued to officers of most European navies today is based on the half-basket Gothic hilt introduced in the 1820s.

Knives and daggers

Daggers made in the eighteenth and nineteenth centuries tended to be made for specific purposes, such as hunting. Countries like Italy and Spain developed their own forms; a heavy-bladed knife with chiselled relief decoration and a wooden handle was used in Italy, and in Spain a type of clasp-knife with a long single-edged blade, called the *navaja*, was fashionable. There were also survivals of earlier types. In Dalmatia a form of stiletto with distinctive down-turned quillons was used. Scottish dirks were made throughout the period, later examples having large stones set into the pommel for use with highland dress. In the 1800s some London sword makers who specialized in cut-steel hilts supplied plain, businesslike daggers with facetted steel mounts. Other English firms, such as George Wolstenholm of Sheffield, produced knives of exceptional quality, exporting many to the United States.

In the century that followed German and French cutlers almost always showed hunting knives at international exhibitions. In 1851 and 1862, for example, various hunting weapons produced by the French goldsmith F.-D. Froment-Meurice (1802–55) were shown. Indeed the fine engraved illustrations which appear in the catalogues to such exhibitions show extraordinary weapons made in the most elaborate Gothic style. One hunting dagger designed by Marrel Frères, Parisian makers, has a hilt in the form of a figure of St Michael spearing a prostrate archangel, with figures of Adam and Eve set within a tasteful Gothic niche on the scabbard.

In recent years there has been a considerable revival in the art of forging knives, much of the stimulus coming from collectors in the United States.

The fake business

The nineteenth and twentieth century have seen the production of a large number of fakes in the field of edged weapons. The esthetic and artistic qualities of swords and daggers have always been appreciated by collectors, by artists in search of props for their more illustrious sitters, and by sword manufacturers themselves.

During the nineteenth century interest in highly decorated metalwork of medieval and Renaissance times could not be met by the few genuine pieces that had survived, and so enterprising antique dealers began to supply replicas of the highly decorated rapiers and daggers so much in demand, deliberately ageing them and selling them as antiques. Naturally the skills needed to chisel and gild a fine steel hilt were still extant in the later part of the century – fine, intricately worked steel caskets and cabinets figure in most nineteenth-century exhibition catalogues. An artist who could produce a fine dagger in the Renaissance style could be persuaded to 'age' it and pass it off as a sixteenth-century piece. Many fakers started off as restorers – it is but a short step from supplying a missing quillon on a rapier to making an entire hilt. Collectors themselves stimulated the trade by insisting on highly decorated weapons in mint condition.

One collector, a partner in a shipping firm around 1900, became so fascinated with very ornate arms, especially those decorated with chiselling and gold and silver damascening, that he spent large sums of money on pieces which had been made only months before. Rapiers with chiselled figures set in niches, huge broadswords with ornate Renaissance-style hilts, and swept-hilt rapiers with gold and silver decoration were all sold to him at very considerable prices. Some of them were sold with provenances, always a trap for the unwary. Most were fitted with

perfectly genuine old blades and grips, which compounded the difficulty of identification. The ornament on some of the hilts was indeed similar to genuine sixteenth-century designs by artists such as Etienne Delaune, and it is likely that the craftsmen who made them had access both to genuine weapons and to sixteenth-century pattern books.

Mention should also be made of the Dresden locksmith Anton Konrad (d. 1938), who made a series of rapiers and daggers which appeared on the market in the 1920s. He had access to the armoury of the Electors of Saxony in Dresden and was able to copy many of the fine quality edged weapons in that collection. He was also advised by a prominent Berlin antique dealer named Willi Kahlert. Quite the deadliest combination for deception in the art world is a skilled craftsman and a knowledgeable dealer.

Fakes will always be made when demand exceeds supply. Daggers and swords of the Nazi era – especially those with dedications – are being faked today to meet a thriving demand. Modern copies of nineteenth-century French cuirassier's swords and plain brass regulation hilts are also being made and sold today. The student and collector can only avoid counterfeit goods by carefully examining the real thing. The Latin tag 'Caveat emptor' has never been more relevant.

Opposite page, above and below
Wilhelm I of Prussia is proclaimed Emperor in the Hall of Mirrors, Versailles, on 18 January 1871. The painting is by Anton von Werner.

Sabre with chiselled iron hilt engraved and damascened in gold, Spanish, dated 1849, from a garniture including some firearms. The blade is signed Eusebio Zuloaga. Zuloaga worked in the Renaissance style and produced some extraordinary metalwork, including cabinets as well as weapons.

Below left Silver-hilted hunting dagger made for the Great Exhibition of 1851 by Marrel Frères of Paris to a design by Marcet (above) and a German naval officer's sword of about 1890, with a pipe-back blade and Gothic-style guard (below). The figure on the hilt of the Marrel dagger is St Hubert, patron saint of the hunt.

Below Broadsword in the style of 1570, German, c.1920. Although the grip is antique, the blade and hilt are by the Dresden forger Anton Konrad. The hilt is of steel, and the blade, which is stamped with marks and incised with letters, has been sprayed with acid to imitate corrosion.

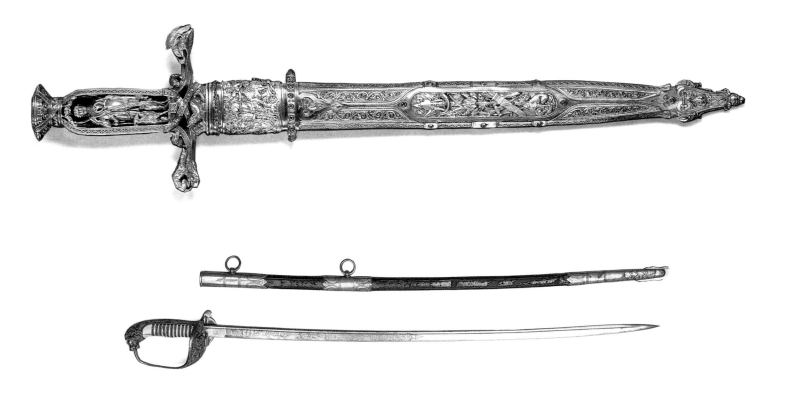

8 COMBINATION WEAPONS

Anthony North

Grouped together in the following pages are a number of weapons which do not comfortably fit into other categories, namely swords and daggers combined with firearms, concealed weapons, and weapons used primarily for hunting. Most of them were civilian weapons and, except for those in the hunting category, made in small numbers. Many were curiosities even in their heyday, and this curiosity value ensures a high price in salerooms today.

Most combination weapons, especially those dating from the sixteenth and seventeenth centuries, are luxuriously decorated with engraving, gold damascening or fine chiselled work. They appealed to the wealthy and gadget-minded, and were often kept in princely *Wunderkammer* simply to be admired.

Blade and firearm combinations

The development of the wheel-lock system of ignition for firearms in the early sixteenth century presented armourers with an ideal opportunity for making combination weapons. Swords and daggers, and even lances and axes, were fitted with missile-firing capabilities, and were popular throughout the sixteenth century and into the eighteenth. Perhaps it was because early firearms were unreliable that this 'belt and braces' approach was adopted. However, nearly all the combination weapons that survive from before 1600 are very elaborately decorated and often have connections with the chase. From their excellent state of preservation it seems probable that most of them were designed as sophisticated toys, curiosities to be kept in the *Kunstkammer* rather than brandished on the battlefield.

The earliest hybrids almost invariably incorporate a wheel-lock mechanism. In fact some of the earliest dateable wheel locks are mounted on crossbows. On daggers and swords the locks are usually mounted next to the hilt and attached to the blade by screws. The barrel is generally fitted to the flat of the blade and the trigger is near the guard.

On some combination daggers and swords the barrel is actually contained within the centre of the blade. A combined dagger and wheel-lock formerly in the Astor Collection has a removable point which fits inside the barrel by means of a spring-loaded rod. The surfaces of the lock and blade are elaborately etched and gilded, as is the hilt, and below the hilt are dummy by-knives, possibly indicating that it was designed as a hunting weapon. The lock and blade are German but the hilt is Italian, so it seems reasonable to conclude that it was made by a German craftsman working at an Italian court. Its date is around 1550.

Sword-and-firearm combinations seem to have been less common than combination daggers during the sixteenth century. However, some of the finest combination swords of the period repose in the collections of the Electors of Saxony in Dresden. These include a swept-hilt rapier presented to the Elector August of Saxony by Archduke Ferdinand of the Tyrol in 1575. Mounted near the engraved and chiselled brass hilt are two catch-operated springs which cause the blade to extend by nearly 12 ins/30 cms, but the capacity of this weapon to spring nasty surprises does not end there. Within the hollow grip and pommel there is a concealed dagger, a rather rare feature. Another rapier from the same collection has quillons shaped like miniature cannons, with touch-holes, and a pommel in the shape of a miniature mortar, with a detachable lid. It was given to Elector Johann Georg I in 1612, as a great novelty no doubt, and was probably made in about 1610. Also in Dresden are several early seventeenth-century swept-hilt rapiers and riding swords with narrow wheel-lock mechanisms mounted on their blades. In some cases the barrel actually forms the back edge of the blade. Judging from the pristine state of the etching which covers the entire surface of these weapons, they were never used.

Less decorative specimens were no doubt intended for serious use. Also in the Dresden armoury is a no-nonsense Turkish sabre with a plain curved blade which has a serviceable wheel-lock and short barrel attached to it. Made around 1600, the whole weapon presents a very businesslike appearance.

Firearms were not the only missile weapons fitted to swords and daggers. In the collection of the Castel San Angelo in Rome there is a dagger dating from about 1600 which converts into a crossbow. When used as a sword the arc of the crossbow folds

Opposite page Combined dagger and wheel-lock pistol (right) and detail of a rapier presented to Augustus Elector of Saxony in 1575 by Archduke Ferdinand of the Tyrol (left).

The pommel and grip of the rapier contain a dagger, and the blade is held by springs and can be extended by nearly 12 ins/30 cm when a catch is operated. The hilt is of engraved and chiselled brass and the blade is etched.

The dagger-pistol is Italian, made in about 1550. The hilt is of steel, chiselled and gilt, and the blade is etched. The dagger is fitted with a dummy scabbard locket showing the tops of three by-knives.

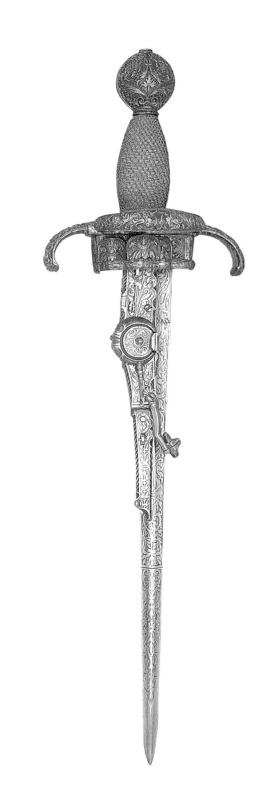

Below Detail of the lock and barrel of a German wheel-lock pistol mounted on the blade of a Turkish-made sabre. The weapon was probably produced in about 1600. The wheel-lock was fired by means of a small knob under the lock.

Right Two knife-pistols and scabbards by Dumonthier of Paris (top) and a knife pistol made in Liege, Belgium (below right). Both Dumonthier weapons were made in about 1860; the larger of the two is a hunting weapon and has a stag and hounds etched on the blade. The Belgian weapon was made in 1840–50.

The other weapons are a fob pistol and a 'palm protector' revolver (left), both made in 1880–90; an unusual eighteenth-century Persian pistol (centre); and a seventeenth-century German arquebus (bottom).

down either side of the blade, and when used as a crossbow the point of the sword becomes a short and unfriendly projection for stabbing opponents at close quarters.

Edged weapons combined with the snaphance and flintlock mechanisms introduced in the seventeenth century are very rare, perhaps because firearms had become extremely reliable by then, but a few survive, including a long dish-hilt rapier dating from about 1640 with a slightly later flintlock fitted to it. This too can be seen in the Castel San Angelo collection. However, from the paucity of similar weapons in European collections the inevitable conclusion is that combined weapons were simply not fashionable in the seventeenth century.

It was in the eighteenth and nineteenth centuries that the largest number of combination weapons was made. The short hanger or hunting sword, fashionable at the time, was an ideal weapon on which to mount a flintlock, and because it was short it was easy to aim. It was also comparatively easy to fit the mechanism and the short barrel along the forte of the blade. Most hunting swords also had simple recurved quillons or single shell guards which allowed the steel and cock of the flintlock mechanism to be fitted close to the guard, protected from accidental discharge. The barrels are often of the 'Queen Anne cannon barrel' type, and the triggers are simple levers set near the grip. One English example of late eighteenth-century manufacture has four barrels, two on each side of the blade, and a box-lock mechanism housed within the grip.

It has been suggested that hanger-and-flintlock combinations were made for hunting, for giving the *coup de grace* to wounded animals. However hangers were very widely carried during the eighteenth century for self-protection, and an extra means of defence would have been welcome, especially when travelling.

With the development of the percussion system in the nineteenth century, various patent combination arms were produced, including the famous Elgin Bowie-knife pistol, much prized by collectors today. In 1837 George Elgin of Georgia, USA, took out a patent for a percussion pistol combined with a sword. The pistol was an ordinary single-shot percussion weapon, and the blade to which it was attached was long, broad and single-edged. The trigger guard was recessed at the back to make the weapon easier to wield. Some versions even have a knuckleguard linked to the butt. The blades were supplied by well-known American sword manufacturers such as the Ames Manufacturing Company and Morril, Mossman and Blair, and most of the assembling was done by C. B. Allen of Springfield, Massachusetts. The Elgin weapon enjoyed brief popularity – several hundred were made, and even the US Navy placed orders – but production ceased in 1839.

In that same year an English cutlery firm, Unwin and Rodgers of Sheffield, were advertising their 'Life and Property Preserver' in the Sheffield Commercial Directory. This was a large penknife with a pistol barrel attached to the side. It has a folding gimlet-

shaped trigger, and a long hook does duty as both handle and ramrod. Unlike Elgin's invention it remained on the market until the 1860s, a cartridge model being patented in 1861.

At about the same date a number of combination hunting knives were produced by the French maker Dumonthier. The quillons formed the hammers, which were released by a folding trigger set in the grip. The blades were elaborately etched and gilded. An example which came up for sale recently was inscribed 'Dumonthier et Chartron 194 R. ST. Martin Paris'. Also produced in France and Belgium in the latter part of the century were a number of pin-fire revolvers fitted with short dagger blades. These were known as 'Apaches' and were designed for gentlemen

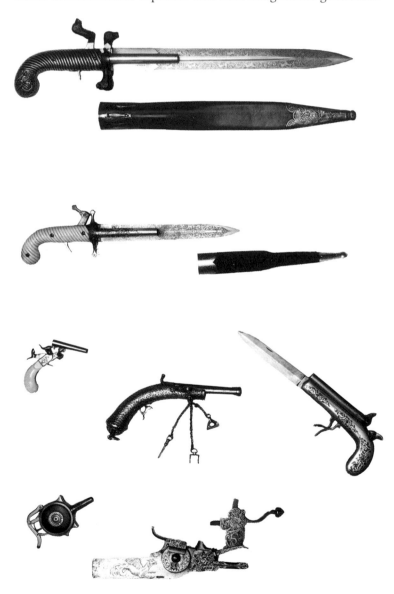

handy with their fists – the grip took the form of a steel knuckleduster.

Concealed weapons

Swords and daggers which masquerade as something else have been made since medieval times. Naturally, it takes more ingenuity to disguise a sword than a dagger. The sinister sword-stick, for example, has a long history, some specimens surviving from the sixteenth century. Very early examples are, to all appearances, long walking staffs but they conceal full-length rapier blades. A memorable swordstick in the Wallace Collection in London combines a long doubled-edged rapier blade with a wheel-lock pistol. The top of the stick is ornamented with a gilt bronze head in the Mannerist style and the shaft is of wood, covered with ebony and ivory. It is thought to be German and dates from around 1600. Another fine early swordstick, probably English and of similar date, belongs to Stratford-upon-Avon town council in Warwickshire; the long wooden staff, which has an ivory cap and staghorn and mother-of-pearl inlay, is the work of a gunstock maker and conceals a long blade.

Colonel Blood's attempt to steal the British Crown Jewels from the Jewel House at the Tower of London in 1671 involved swordsticks. Thomas Blood, born in or about 1618, was a colourful character of Irish extraction who succeeded in ingratiating himself with Talbot Edwards, the keeper of the royal regalia, and also with Mrs Edwards. He and a female accomplice made regular visits to the Edwards family, bringing presents such as pairs of gloves to lull any suspicion. On 9 May 1971, at about 7.30 in the morning, Blood and three accomplices 'all armed with rapier blades in their canes' persuaded Edwards to let them see the Crown Jewels. Edwards admitted them to the jewel room, whereupon they threw a cloak over his head and gagged him, and seized the crown, orb and sceptre. Blood himself took the crown and one of the accomplices, named Parrot, stuffed the orb into his breeches. Edwards succeeded in raising the alarm, however, and the thieves were captured, still with the crown jewels, on Tower Wharf. Blood, a man of spirit and personality, is said to have declared: 'It was a gallant attempt, however unsuccessful, it was for the crown'. He was later interviewed, in private, by Charles II at Whitehall. The king was clearly charmed by him, for Blood not only received a pardon but also an allowance of £500 a year! He died, according to one historian, peacefully in his bed on 29 August 1680, 'fearlessly and without any signs of penitence, totally hardened and forsaken by heaven'.

Most surviving swordsticks date from the latter part of the eighteenth or early nineteenth century. To obtain a close fit the lower section containing the blade was usually fitted with a ferrule at the top. On early examples the blade was simply pulled out of the shaft, but by the nineteenth century complicated thumb-operated catches were introduced which meant that the blade had to be twisted to be drawn out. Various kinds of blade were used,

Left Unwin & Rodgers knife-pistol, made in Sheffield between 1845 and 1862. The barrel bears Birmingham proof marks. Knife-pistols were probably more useful in theory than in practice; they cannot have been very accurate as firearms and must have been difficult to use as knives.

Below left Combined swordstick and wheel-lock pistol, German, late sixteenth century.

Below Swordstick made in India in about 1840, a heavy weapon with a plain and practical blade. The shaft is mounted in engraved brass and iron. Its owner was a surgeon who served in the Indian Army and died at Balaclava in 1856.

including diamond-section rapier blades, hollow-ground small-sword blades and square-section foil-type blades. Early blades were the same as those of contemporary swords, but cut down. Many bear the Solingen or Klingenthal mark, but those with the Toledo mark are probably spurious. The emphasis was always on the point rather than the edge, the intention being to thrust at one's assailant. The narrower, flimsier blades on later sword-sticks, sometimes blued and gilded, were almost certainly designed for play-acting rather than self-defence. As with edged weapon and firearm combinations, the degree of adornment on swordsticks is a good guide to their usefulness. In general only comparatively short, strong and exceedingly sharp blades with little or no decoration on them would have successfully beaten off footpads and other undesirables.

Some of the most extraordinary swordsticks in existence are of nineteenth-century manufacture. Some were disguised as umbrellas. One type patented in France in 1882 and aptly named 'La Diabolique' had a blade which blossomed into several steel spikes. The author has also seen a late nineteenth-century sword-stick designed to be cast javelin-fashion at an assailant. Sword-stick manufacture continued into this century. Indeed a celebrated London umbrella supplier was still producing swordsticks as late as 1980. Until recently, bone-topped specimens could still be bought in souvenir shops in Britain, but their workmanship is very rough and the blades are not intended for use. New legislation has now made the sale of swordsticks illegal.

Daggers can be concealed in ways which swords cannot. The triangular-bladed Italian stiletto of the seventeenth century must have been particularly lethal – even today the word stiletto has connotations of stealth and deadliness. Some Italian smallswords of the 1650s have grips which conceal a small dagger. Daggers disguised as crucifixes, with the lower section of the crucifix forming the blade, are a rarity much coveted by collectors; there is a seventeenth-century crucifix dagger in the Royal Armoury in Madrid and there are other examples, of nineteenth-century manufacture, in private collections. These far from holy curiosities were supposed to have been carried by priests when travelling.

Daggers were also fitted into canes and walking sticks. One nineteenth century dagger-cane even incorporated a patent vitriol squirter. Decorative cloak pins concealing narrow stiletto blades were also made. A few seventeenth-century finger rings have small curved blades which fit into slots set in the hoop, forming a useful small knife-cum-knuckleduster. Our own century has produced a multiplicity of concealed knives, from innocuous-looking ballpoint pens containing spring-loaded blades, to ingenious flick knives, belt-clasp knives, and of course James Bond's throwing knife, neatly concealed within the lining of his attaché case.

Arms of the chase

Hunting swords and daggers have always been of very distinctive design and construction. To kill a boar or stag required a weapon of considerable size and sturdiness. According to fourteenth- and fifteenth-century treatises on venery the ideal blade length for a hunting sword was 48 ins/122 cm. Of course the etiquette of the chase demanded not only special swords with which to deliver the *coup de grâce* but also implements to cut up the quarry once it had been killed. And so a variety of knives, saws and cleavers were made en suite with hunting swords, forming complete 'garnitures' or *trousses de chasse*. The elaborate rituals of the chase have always been accompanied by a vast paraphernalia of uniforms and equipment, these being just as important as the hunt itself.

Part of a garniture made in 1496 for the Emperor Maximilian I (1459–1519) by Hans Sumersperger of Solbad Hall in the Tyrol consists of two large cross-hilted swords and a broad cleaver used, among other things, to serve meats. The hilts are chiselled and engraved in the Gothic manner and the blades, which are in a marvellous state of preservation, are decorated in gold against a blued ground, again in the Gothic style. Both swords were designed to be used with two hands, essential when dealing with a large aggressive animal.

By the sixteenth century the mounts and grips of hunting swords were often made of staghorn. A large two-handed single-edged sword in the Hunting Museum in Munich has an antler grip. It was made in 1520 and follows the fashion of early sixteenth-century swords in having straight quillons terminating in large knobs and a ring guard for the index finger.

Wild boar hunts were very popular in the later Middle Ages – to kill a boar on foot was reckoned a supreme test of courage and skill. A special form of blade was developed for the purpose, based on the long triangular tuck. The hilt was of the usual cross-hilted hand-and-a-half type but the long narrow blade suddenly widened and thickened near the point and was often slotted near the flare to take a short bar. This was designed to keep a safe distance between the huntsman and the scything tusks of the transfixed quarry.

Left Woodknife of Henry VIII, made by Diego de Çaias in about 1544. The hilt and blade are damascened in gold. On the blade is a representation of the Siege of Boulogne and a poem in Latin. The by-knife fits into a separate sheath on the scabbard.

Far left below Hunting sword of Emperor Maximilian I, made by Hans Sumersperger in 1496. The hilt is mounted in silver, and the blade is blued and decorated in gold.

Left Two items carried by ladies for self-protection: a cloak pin containing a small stiletto and a finger ring with twin blades concealed in the hoop. Italian, eighteenth century.

Opposite page, left to right
Steel-hilted boar sword, German, early sixteenth century. The horizontal bar near the flare prevented the transfixed quarry from running up the blade.

Walking cane with 32 spring-loaded spikes fitted to the blade. The spikes spring up when the blade is drawn from the shaft. French, c.1880.

Woodcut by Jost Amman (1539–1591) showing a bear hunt.

Fifteenth- and sixteenth-century hunting scenes depict huntsmen wearing short curved swords clearly based on the cleaver-like medieval falchion. The rear quillon is extended to form a short knuckleguard and the grip is usually made of two plaques of bone or wood rivetted through the tang. A selection of bodkins and small knives fit snugly into pockets at the top of the scabbard. Unfortunately scabbards tend to disintegrate with age and very few hunting swords survive with their matching accoutrements.

However one very famous sixteenth century hunting sword has survived with its original scabbard and by-knife, and that is the sword made for Henry VIII of England by a craftsman named Diego de Çaias in about 1544. We know the date from the blade, which depicts scenes from the Siege of Boulogne. Henry VIII arrived at Boulogne on 19 July 1544 with 40,000 men and personally commanded the siege, which had the desired effect. The port surrendered on 19 September and Henry returned to England, leaving Lord Lisle to hold the town with 4,000 men. Although the French made several attempts to wrest it back, it remained in English hands until the reign of Edward VI. The hilt of Henry's famous sword has simple quillons, and a knucklegard and pommel of flat section extending slightly at the back, a feature found on many hunting swords. At some time before 1550 it became customary to add a small shell guard to hunting swords. This became much larger as the century progressed, offering more scope for decoration. The blade also became ornate, often engraved with scenes of the chase.

Hunting swords became increasingly fashionable for everyday wear by gentlemen during the seventeenth century. If one was riding or travelling by coach they offered protection against highwaymen. In England they were known as 'cuttoes' (from the French *couteau de chasse*) or 'hangers', a term used to describe any sword which hung from the belt. In *The London Gazette* for 14–18 March 1677 there is an intriguing advertisement for a lost sword of this kind: 'A Cuttoe Sword, with a hollow ground back blade, with a single shell, plate Hilt . . . with a strong silver wyer handle found in the possession of a High-way Robber Richard Lunt alias Woodgate'. Seventeenth- and early eighteenth-century portraits suggest that hangers were especially popular with naval officers, presumably because shipboard conditions made longer weapons somewhat unwieldy.

From the seventeenth century onwards hunting swords began to show distinctive national characteristics. A type manufactured in England in the early years of the century had a grip in the form of a bird of prey; several examples are shown in portraits of the period. By the 1630s a firm of swordmakers in Hounslow, near London, was making a hanger with a large shell guard and a cap-shaped pommel, and using cast brass for some of the elements of the hilt. This considerably annoyed those hilt-makers who worked in iron, since once a mould had been made dozens of brass hilts could be turned out in the time it took to forge one iron hilt.

Hunting swords can usually be recognized by the staghorn used to form the grip and by the hunting motifs on the hilt and blade. Hounds pursuing a stag, accompanied by huntsmen bearing hunting spears, were a very popular blade design. Sixteenth- and seventeenth-century blades often have the maker's name incorporated within such designs and are therefore easy to date. Despite the gilding often found on such blades, the engraving or etching tends to be rather crude, although some of the animals have a naive vigour about them. The etched designs of the Munich master Ambrosius Gemlick are a pleasing exception. Gemlick, who was active in the 1530s, is usually associated with 'calendar blades', blades etched with a perpetual calendar, but he also etched blades for hunting swords. One of these, dated 1536 and now in the Bavarian National Museum, is etched with a boar hunt.

Recent research has shown a number of very fine cast brass hunting hilts to be the work of the Zurich goldsmith Hans Peter Oeri (1637–92). These were probably made around 1680, and echo the baroque flavour of the period. The animals and huntsmen which form these hilts are executed in a markedly sculptural style, with scenes from mythology in low relief on the half-shell guards. The impression given is of a mass of figures and animals rushing through foliage – one can only marvel at the ingenuity required to meld huntsmen and animals together in such an attractive, lively fashion. Oeri modelled his hilts in wax first, then cast them in a mould. He also produced fine cast buckles to accompany them.

Towards the end of the seventeenth century a number of precious metal hilts were made for hunting swords. Many of these are hallmarked, so their dates are known and often their makers as well. Some are even of gold, mounted with diamonds. Because hangers were worn almost as costume jewellery, hilts mounted with precious stones were not uncommon. Agate was especially favoured. What was obviously a splendid and useful weapon is described as having been lost in an advertisement in *The Post Man* of 30 August 1715: 'A Saw hanger with a large Agget [agate] handle, and an Agget Handle knife, and silver ink case and silver pen case in the scabbard'. Obviously the owner combined the might of the pen with the might of the sword.

Some very exotic hanger hilts were made by Japanese craftsmen for export to Europe, notably in a soft alloy known as *shakudo* which could be coloured and gilded. Carved ivory hilts from India and Ceylon were also mounted up by European cutlers.

The blades of most early to mid-seventeeth-century hunting swords are quite broad, often with a curve to them and a saw edge down the back, but by the end of the century narrower and shorter blades became the fashion, usually with a single shell guard turned down towards the blade – the large double shell guard caused the hilt to stick out an awkward angle on the thigh and also rubbed the wearer's clothes. In the eighteenth century hilt tastes tended towards the decorative rather than the practical – some marvellous hilts, made entirely of porcelain or of tortoiseshell inlaid with gold, survive from the 1730s and 1740s. However steel hilts did not go out of fashion. Russian craftsmen based at Tula near Moscow turned out excellent work in steel throughout the eighteenth century, specializing in low-relief chiselled work with a gold ground.

During the American War of Independence officers on both the English and American sides wore a type of hanger with a narrow curved blade and a grip of wrythen ivory, usually stained green. The guard consisted of simple recurved quillons and the pommel was a lion's head. Most of the examples which survive have silver mounts. In the last years of the century, Napoleon's campaigns in Austria and Italy and the taste for exotic Polish and Hungarian military uniforms brought an Eastern flavour to hanger hilts. The grip was slightly flattened and often fluted vertically, the guard was small, and a small chain linked the top of the grip to the end of the rear quillon.

Hunting knives are still widely used today. The ancestors of the modern hunting knife were the short *scramasax* of Saxon times and a North European knife known as the *hauswehr*, common in the Middle Ages. The latter was single-edged, good for chopping and stabbing, and had a single small quillon and a grip made of two plates of wood or bone rivetted through the tang. A larger version was made in the later Middle Ages, equipped with various smaller knives, bodkins and other implements sheathed in extra pockets on the leather scabbard. Several such hunting trousses survive, dating from the sixteenth century.

Although any convenient knife can been carried when hunting, knives fitted with staghorn grips are usually thought of as having been made specifically for hunting. Blades with a strong back and a cutlass point are also thought of as hunting knives, some fine chiselled knives of this type having been produced in Southern Italy during the eighteenth century. Perhaps the best known of all hunting knives is the Bowie knife. Frontiersman James Bowie, who died at the Alamo in 1836, is said to have carried a straight single-edged knife about 9 ins/23 cm long and 1½ ins/4 cm wide given to him by his brother Rezin. Under Bowie's direction an improved design was made, with a clipped point and a simple wooden grip. Whatever the truth of this story, English cutlers such as George Wolstenholm of Sheffield and others exported large numbers of Bowie-type knives to the United States, many bearing inscriptions such as 'The Genuine Arkansas Toothpick'. The Bowie knife continues to be made today in Europe and the United States, where the custom-made hunting knife has seen something of a revival.

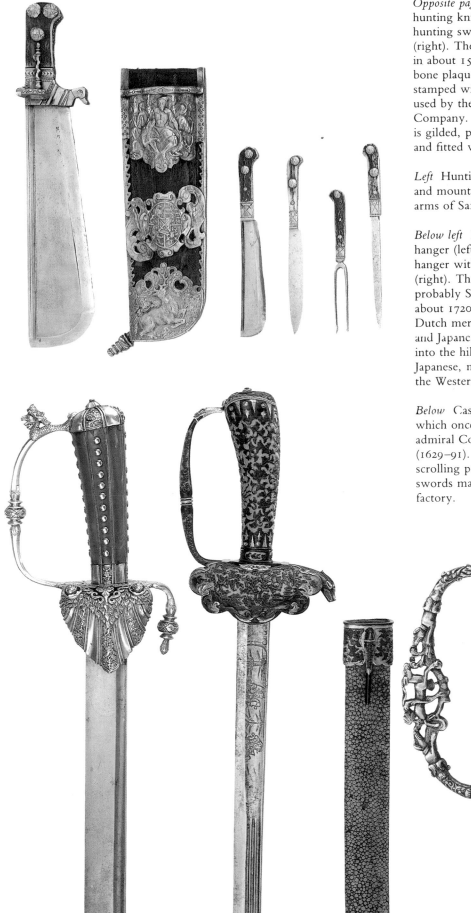

Opposite page Hauswehr-type hunting knife (left) and a German hunting sword made in about 1820 (right). The knife is English, made in about 1560; the grip is formed of bone plaques and the blade is stamped with the the dagger mark used by the London Cutlers' Company. The blade of the sword is gilded, pierced with scrollwork, and fitted with dials.

Left Hunting trousse with scabbard and mounts decorated with the arms of Saxony, German *c*.1630.

Below left Exotic silver-hilted hanger (left) and a *shakudo*-hilted hanger with rayskin scabbard (right). The silver-hilted weapon is probably Southeast Asian, made in about 1720, almost certainly for a Dutch merchant. Motifs from Asian and Japanese art are incorporated into the hilt. The other weapon is Japanese, made in about 1700 for the Western market.

Below Cast silver hilt of a sword which once belonged to the Dutch admiral Cornelis Van Tromp (1629–91). Made in about 1655, the scrolling pommel is typical of swords made at the Hounslow factory.

9 AMERICAN SWORDS AND KNIVES

Frederick Wilkinson

Some of the native cultures of North America, but by no means all, were copper-using, as Michael Coe relates in his chapter on Pre-Conquest America. Copper was indigenous, along the Coppermine River in the Northwest, but iron was not. Even so, copper knives were far from common and were used primarily as tools rather than weapons. Knives fashioned from reeds and animals' teeth were also used, according to accounts from seventeenth-century colonists. Nevertheless it is recorded that by 1623 the Indians were boasting of killing French and English with their daggers. Miles Standish, one of the Pilgrim Fathers, killed an Indian named Pecksout with his own knife. Deerfield in Massachusetts possesses the earliest known knife that can, with certainty, be said to have been used by an Indian. When the Indians raided the town in 1675 one of the dead Indians was found to be carrying a European plug bayonet, presumably for use as a dagger.

During the eighteenth century more and more Indians acquired European blades either by inter-tribal barter or at trading stations such as those set up by the Hudson Bay Company. One buffalo skin was considered to be worth three knives. One of the knives most favoured by the Indians was the 'beaver tail' or 'stabber', which had a broad, straight, double-edged blade with a taper at the point. Most trade blades, if they were of Hudson Bay Company provenance, came from Sheffield. Others came from Rouen in France. It was customary to supply them without hilts, a fact attested by the large number of surviving examples with native-made hilts. The Indians also made their own knives from discarded or broken metal implements, grinding them into shape and wrapping the tang with strips of animal hide.

Later, as American and Canadian industry began to develop, fewer blades were imported. One of the earliest indigenous blade manufacturers was the John Russell Company of Massachusetts, with a factory by the Green River at Greenfield. The knives produced there are still described as Green River knives from the name stamped on the blade. The commonest type seems to have been a type of broad-bladed butcher's knife popular with both trappers and Indians.

Apparently the Indians did not consider the dagger a quick response weapon, for nearly all surviving Indian sheaths envelope the entire knife, including most of the hilt, sensible if one is going to engage in violent physical activity, but impractical if the knife is needed in a hurry. Two distinctive types of sheath were made: plain leather with brass stud decoration and, for ceremonial purposes, leather decorated with elaborate beadwork.

Some Indian knives, such as the Bear knife used by the Bear Cult popular among the Blackfoot and other tribes, had deep spiritual significance. The hilt of the Bear knife was fashioned from the jawbone of a bear. Passing it on to a new guardian was a somewhat hazardous business, for at one stage of the complicated rituals the new trustee had to catch the knife when it was thrown suddenly and unexpectedly at him. Failure to do so barred him from guardianship of the sacred knife.

The colonial period

Whatever the feelings of the Indians towards the early colonists, they were very impressed by the array of weapons which they brought with them. Swords, and of course firearms, were weapons outside their experience. Early records from some of the colonies in Virginia show that the settlers held substantial reserves of swords. Rapiers, swept- and cup-hilt, seem to have been widely owned, as excavations at Jamestown have confirmed, for archaeologists have unearthed complete rapiers as well as hilts and other fragments. In addition to rapiers, popular in the late sixteenth century and throughout much of the seventeenth, the most common sword was probably the all-purpose hanger, which had a short, slightly curved, single-edged blade. The hilt, often of brass, usually had a side shell, a simple knucklebow and a horn grip. Many surviving hangers are known to have been carried by New England colonists. A number of basket hilts have also been excavated, almost certainly belonging to the longer-bladed weapons carried on horseback. Daggers are less well represented, but those carried by the early colonists would certainly have been those popular in contemporary Europe, the quillon and ballock type, and probably a few left-hand daggers too.

An interesting incident involving swordplay with the left-hand dagger and sword together took place in Plymouth, Massachusetts, in 1621. The two participants, who were servants of the same master, succeeded in wounding each other, not too seriously, using these weapons. They were punished on two counts, for duelling and for using gentleman's weapons, and were condemned to be tied up without food or water for twenty-four hours. So great was their suffering that they were pardoned after one hour on the promise of good behaviour in the future. Although it was a punishable offence, the practice of duelling persisted in the state, making it necessary to pass another law depriving anyone found guilty of duelling of his political rights for 20 years. Although the sword rather lost favour as a duellist's weapon and was replaced by the pistol, duels remained a feature of life in the southern colonies and states, especially among the military.

In the seventeenth and eighteenth centuries the main military forces in North America were either French or British, both armed and equipped in the manner detailed by their military regulations. British troops were armed with a matchlock or flintlock musket, a bayonet and a brass-hilted hanger, although the latter was officially withdrawn in 1768 except for sergeants. The French infantry were similarly armed, although their swords were of different design and at first very similar to the brass-hilted smallsword of the period, but in 1764 they too had their swords withdrawn. French grenadiers of the period carried a 1747 pattern sword with a straight blade 32 ins/81 cm long, and after 1767 a sword with a slightly curved single-edged blade and a cast brass hilt known as a *briquet*. On the eve of the American War of Indepence, therefore, both French and English infantry were armed only with muskets and bayonets, a tradition which continued into the present century.

The Continental Army and independence

With the first clashes between the Massachussetts Militia and the British army at Lexington and Concord early in 1775, Congress realised that it had more of a rabble than an army at its disposal,

Left Another example of the workmanlike swords favoured by the early colonists, with double shell guard and simple recurved quillons, English, *c.*1630. The grip is of horn.

Far left Sword carried by John Thompson, one of the early colonists of Plymouth, Massachusetts. This is almost certainly an English weapon. The blade, straight and single-edged, was mainly intended for cutting; the hilt is of typical seventeenth-century basket type with a heavy pommel.

Right Two of George Washington's swords, both from the Mount Vernon Ladies' Association collection.

The dress sword on the left, silver-hilted, was worn by Washington at his inauguration as President of the new nation in 1789. The hilt is of late form with small arms and a pierced pommel. The blade is hollow-ground.

The weapon on the right, now lacking the silver wire which once bound the grip, was worn by Washington when he served as aide-de-camp on General Braddock's expedition in 1775. The hilt is of earlier form, with large side arms and a twin shellguard. Hallmarks indicate a French origin and later importation into England.

for each militia and volunteer unit had its own rules and idea of discipline. Contemporary accounts give details of mutinies and desertions on quite a large scale, not from any lack of fighting spirit but from an overwhelming sense of independence and a reluctance to accept orders. On 15 June the Second Continental Congress, sitting in Philadelphia, appointed George Washington as Commander-in-Chief and he began the enormous task of welding the colonists into the Continental Army. Even so, not all local militias and volunteer units became part of the Continental Army. From this fact stems the great variety of weapons used on the American side.

The colonists had had little practice in the use of the bayonet, previous battles on American soil having been fought by professional soldiers. They had never been involved in set 'line' battles with volleys of musket fire followed by forward pushes with fixed bayonets. Congress therefore ordered the various states to equip and train their troops to meet such conditions. All troops were to be armed with an axe or sword and a bayonet with a blade length of 18 ins/46 cm, although some States varied the regulation and supplied blades between 14 and 18 ins/38 and 46 cm. Sources of supply were limited and at first the colonists had to rely on captured stores and French material which began to trickle through to them.

American-manufactured bayonets were, by and large, rough and rather crude, but the pressures of the war allowed little time for luxury. In the early days of the war many bayonets were the work of the local smith, who aimed at quantity rather that quality. With minor differences in construction, the American bayonet was basically the same as the European socket bayonet of the period. On a few surviving Colonial muskets the bayonet is housed in a hollowed section of the butt, a feature found on some European sporting weapons. In April 1777 George Washington ordered that all American arms should be stamped with the letters 'U.S.' and this mark therefore appears on many surviving Colonial bayonets together with other letters which identify the State of origin. Normally the bayonet was carried in a leather scabbard suspended from a cross or waist belt, but with the chronic dearth of materials during the war even belts were in short supply. In any case Washington issued an order that all troops were to keep their bayonet fixed at all times.

The supply of swords was not such a problem, since at the time most American civilians with any claim to social standing owned a sword. This was less true in Europe where the fashion was already on the decline. Many of the leading figures of the Revolution carried their European swords into battle. Washington is said to have worn his English silver-hilted smallsword with its rather old-fashioned colichemarde blade on state occasions. Another Colonist General, Benjamin Lincoln, also had a colichemarde-type smallsword, although his had a brass hilt.

Many officers would have carried a hanger, a somewhat shorter weapon than the smallsword, with a reasonably substantial,

slightly curved, single-edged blade. Numerous hangers were produced locally, rather crudely at first, then with increasing skill and assurance. When the national coat-of-arms was formally adopted in 1782, eagle-head pommels became very popular, although lion-head pommels were also fashionable. By then, many local cutlers were producing hunting swords equally as good as contemporary European examples.

The Colonies boasted a number of skilled silversmiths who, from the early part of the century, had been mounting blades with silver hilts. William Moulton of Newburyport, Massachusetts, must have been a fairly busy man for there are several surviving swords which bear his initials. The maker of one of George Washington's swords was the famous John Bailey of Fishkill, New York. The hilt of this sword is certainly by him and he is also recorded as the cutler. In form the sword is typically European, with a green-stained, spirally fluted grip of ivory with a silver cap and slightly recurved silver quillons. The gently curved blade has twin fullers and at the forte has a cap which would have fitted snugly over the mouth of the scabbard to keep out moisture.

Most British cavalrymen of the period were armed with a fairly substantial basket-hilted sword, but the swords used by their Colonist counterparts tended to be much simpler, with either a stirrup knucklebow or a slotted guard. With both styles it was a case of utility rather than quality. Numbers of cavalry in the Continental Army were small and, on the whole, they played little part in the war, serving rather as dragoons, riding into the fray, dismounting and fighting on foot.

Swords were carried in scabbards attached to a waist or shoulder belt, mounted troops generally preferring the latter. If the weapon was a smallsword, it was usually hung by two chains attached to a hook-like fitting which slipped over a waist belt. Alternatively, rings on the scabbard clipped onto two short straps hanging from the waist belt.

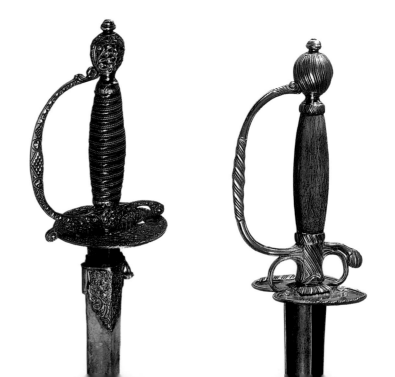

Above The Prussian Baron
Friedrich von Steuben, Inspector
General to the rebel army, drills
colonists at Valley Forge in 1777/8.
The colonists were ill-equipped and
ill-trained for any form of organized
warfare, and sought and received
help from many sources.

Opposite page The death of Dr Joseph Warren, major-general of the American militia, at the Battle of Bunker Hill on 17 June 1775, as depicted by John Trumbull (1756–1843) in 1786. The British attempted to clear the rebels from their strong defensive position by a direct frontal attack with musket and bayonet, and suffered 40 per cent casualties in the process.

Below Cross-hilted militia NCO's sword, *c.*1850–70, with the pommel in the form of a helmeted head (left) and a sabre of similar date with a lion-head pommel (right).

Another item almost universal on the Colonist side was some form of knife, but this was more of a tool than a weapon. Such knives were usually sturdy and devoid of trimmings. Most were ground down from old files or forged by the local blacksmith. Since they were intended as general purpose knives, the blades were fairly long, with a serviceable wooden or antler grip. They were usually worn hanging from the belt in a leather scabbard, but the smaller versions carried by riflemen were attached to the waist bag in which ammunition was carried.

The famed accuracy of the long flintlock rifles carried by some of the Colonists was due to several factors, not least to the long, small bore, rifled barrel which helped to build up the speed of the bullet and also imparted a spin to it. The lead bullets had to fit tightly into the barrel and were therefore wrapped in pieces of greased cloth or similar material before being loaded into the muzzle and pushed down with the ramrod. The short-bladed but very sharp knife carried on the waist bag was used to cut fresh supplies of patches.

The early nineteenth century

When hostilities ceased in 1783, with the British conceding defeat, the Continental Army was disbanded, not without much debate concerning the military future of the new nation. Should there be a standing army or was this a dangerous return to European ideas? Eventually it was decided that the army should be reduced to 80 men, sufficient to guard military stores. However, Indian frontier attacks and imagined threats from the British forced a more realistic approach and the size of the army was gradually increased. In May 1792 the Militia Act became law, requiring every man aged between 18 and 40 to enrol in his State Militia; he could be called on active service at any time, and to this

end was required to keep ready a good musket, a bayonet and twenty rounds of ammunition, with some in reserve.

At the time the supply of arms was still in the hands of private contractors, but in 1798 the government placed a contract, the first since the cessation of hostilities with the British, for the supply of 2,000 sabres. Nathan Starr of Middletown, Connecticut, was the contractor and the weapons supplied had a 33-in/84-cm curved, single-edged blade with a false edge, a hilt with an iron stirrup guard, and a leather-bound grip. They were to be carried on shoulder belts in black leather scabbards with iron mounts. The State Armoury established at Springfield, Virginia, in 1798 did not begin production until 1802. The first cavalry and artillery sabres produced here were similar to those of the Starr contract.

In 1812 another contract was placed, this time with William Rose of Philadelphia. The sword supplied closely resembled the British 1796 Light Dragoon pattern, with a curved cutting blade with a clipped point and a hilt with a simple stirrup knucklebow. The scabbard, like the British one, was of iron with a reinforced chape or drag, and was suspended from a waist belt by two rings.

In that same year Congress voted to go to war with England over what it considered to be the high-handed attitude of the British towards American shipping. Fighting was spasmodic and indecisive, and a peace treaty had already been signed when the Americans administered a definitive rebuff to the British at New Orleans in January 1815. News of the peace treaty signed in Ghent, Belgium, in late December 1814 arrived after the event!

Throughout the 1820s and 1830s American settlers had been pushing west into Texas. In 1845 they demanded that the territory be annexed to the Union. The Union obliged, Mexico objected, and the result was the Mexican War of 1846–48. The cavalry of this war were armed with swords based on European designs. The 1833 Light Dragoon sword, for example, was modelled on the British sword of 1822 which had a pipe-backed blade and a three-bar hilt with a short down-curved rear quillon. The supplier was the Ames Manufacturing Company in Chelmsford, Massachussetts, set up by Nathan Ames in 1832. Ames also supplied the Heavy Dragoon sabre Model 1840. This was based on the French Light Cavalry sword of 1822 and had a three-bar brass hilt and pommel cap and a slightly curved, single-edged blade. Nicknamed the 'old wrist breaker' because of its weight and shape, it saw long and honorable service.

Bowie and his knife

In the popular imagination the American campaign against Mexico is best remembered for an incident that was, in itself, of minor importance, the siege and capture of the Alamo in 1836. The Alamo was a small mission building in San Antonio, Texas, and in it 188 Texan settlers decided to make a stand, having declared Texas an independent republic. The Mexican army, led by General Antonio Lopez de Santa Anna, called on them to

Below, left to right
A group of mid-nineteenth century Bowie knives, showing the variety of sizes, hilts and shapes available. The knife on the far right is unusual in that it was made in France.

An 'Arkansas Toothpick' Bowie by the Sheffield maker W. A. Wooley, flanked by an embossed powder flask (left) and a powder flask for a Colt percussion revolver (right).

A 'Hunter's Companion' Bowie (left) and a large clip-point Bowie, both by Jos. Rodgers and Sons (right). The 'Hunter's Companion' has a spear point and an ivory grip with nickel silver mounts; the other knife has a staghorn grip with gold chased mounts.

surrender, but they refused. After a two-week siege, from 23 February to 6 March 1836, the Mexicans launched their final assault and took the mission, suffering 1,500 casualties in the process. All those inside were killed.

Among those who fought to the finish were Davy Crockett and James Bowie. Crocket was Tennessee-born and had been a colonel in the State Militia and a Congressman before emigrating to Texas. Bowie was born in Tennessee in 1795, moved to Louisiana as a boy and in 1818 set up as a sugar planter with his brother Rezin. In 1830 he too moved to Texas, which was still Mexican territory despite the influx of American settlers, and devoted himself to the Texan cause.

The knife that was to bear the family name probably came into being after an incident in 1827 when Rezin Bowie was attacked by a young bull. His rifle jammed and in desperation he stabbed at the bull's head with the knife he was carrying, but the blade failed to pierce the skull. Instead, the impetus of the animal's charge pushed the knife up through his hand, nearly severing the thumb. Clearly he needed a different kind of knife. The blacksmith he consulted, one Jesse Cliff, took an old file and ground it down to a single-edged blade just over 9 ins/23 cm inches long and 1½ ins/4 cm wide and fitted it with a guard. This description matches a knife currently on display in the Alamo. In fact Rezin commissioned several such knives as gifts, giving one to his brother James as a personal protection weapon.

This was the knife which James used in August of the same year in a fracas on the Vidalia sand bar in the Mississippi River. Although Rezin, writing in 1838, describes it as a 'chance medley or rough fight', there does seem to have been a duelling connection, although James was probably acting as a second rather than a

principal. At all events, a fight developed in which he was shot in the hip and stabbed with a sword cane; even so, he managed to kill one assailant, wound another, and force a third to flee. News of the unequal fight soon spread, giving James Bowie and his knife a notoriety he seems not to have sought, for contemporary accounts speak of him as modest man, unlike his Alamo companion Crockett.

His reputation rose a further notch or two in 1829 when it was reported that he had won a duel fought in the old Spanish manner, in which the left wrists of the duellers were tied together to limit their room for manoeuvre. Bowie wounded his opponent, who was a gambler, but spared his life, which proved to be a mistake, for not long afterwards he was set upon by three thugs eager to avenge the gambler's sullied honour. The facts of the case are not too certain, but tradition has it that Bowie killed two of them, striking the head off one and disembowelling the other. Not surprisingly, the third took to his heels.

The knife he used on this occasion was one that he had commissioned himself, from an Arkansas blacksmith named James Black. He apparently asked Black to make a version of his brother's knife, but Black later stated that he had considerably improved on the design and was therefore the true inventor of the Bowie knife (or should it be the Black knife?) The new knife was certainly more like the 'traditional' Bowie, with a longer, heavier blade, a clipped point and a false edge.

Bowie fought in several battles against the Mexicans before finding himself at the Alamo. Although he was ill and lying on his sickbed when the final assault came, he put up a ferocious fight, laying about him with a broken rifle and his famous knife. His death was avenged at the battle of San Jacinto in April 1836.

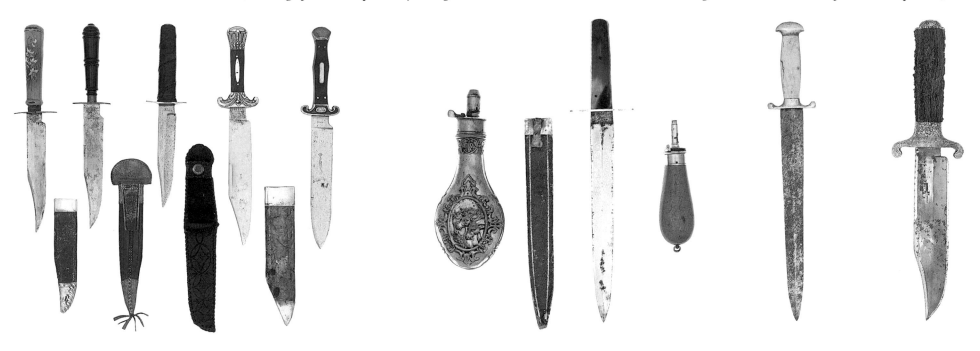

Left Elgin knife-pistol, a combination of large blade and small percussion pistol, designed by George Elgin. The U.S. Navy ordered 150 of these weapons for an expedition to the South Seas in 1833 but, like other combination weapons, they were probably ineffective in both of their intended roles.

The colourful beginnings of the Bowie knife, its well reported use and the heroic death of its inventor were the kind of publicity that market builders dream of. Even the banning of the Bowie knife in some of the southern states did nothing to hinder its general acceptance and soaring popularity. Nevertheless, the exact definition of a Bowie knife is open to debate. The accepted idea of the knife today is certainly not what it looked like when it was first made. Today the name is taken to refer to a fairly substantial knife with a straight blade, single-edged, with a clipped point and possibly a false edge, a hilt with two fairly short quillons forming a simple crossguard, and a plain grip. This was the typical frontier Bowie, although many early examples had a brass strip along the back edge of the blade, the theory being that as brass is relatively soft it would catch an opponent's blade and prevent it sliding up towards the grip. Today, however, many other types of large hunting knives are also classed as Bowie knives.

The majority of early Bowie knives appear to be of American construction but in actual fact a large number of them were made in England. At a very early date English cutlers realised that the Bowie was going to become a favourite with hunters, miners, explorers and frontiersmen, and began to produce Bowies in large numbers and in styles which ranged from the simple and practical to the elaborate and purely decorative. Some were etched with heroic sentiments such as 'Death to Traitors', or with legends of more innocuous appeal such as 'The Hunter's Companion' and 'Self Defender'. The Civil War brought forth such slogans as 'Death to Abolition' and 'Equal Rights and Justice for All'.

The Bowie export trade was more or less the monopoly of two firms, George Wostenholm and Joseph Rodgers and Sons,

both of Sheffield. George Wolstenholm, who entered the market as early as 1830, was by far the more important however. His factory, coincidentally called the Washington Works, probably produced more Bowie knives for the American market than any other, although his very simple trade mark 'I★XL' attracted a number of imitators. Joseph Rodgers and Sons specialized in combination knife pistols, single or multiple-bladed pocket knives fitted with short pistols available in percussion or cartridge versions.

As the century progressed, the functional simplicity of the early Bowie became less and less common. German silver grips, often copied from table cutlery, replaced grips of plain wood or staghorn. Mother-of-pearl was also used on grips and there was also a vogue for pommels in the form of horse's heads. Some sheaths were made purely for effect, consisting of a pressed card body covered with flimsy gold-tooled leather. The ultimate pretension was the folding Bowie knife made towards the end of the century; this had a long blade that could be unlocked and folded back into the hilt.

Despite the dominance of British suppliers, various American manufacturers, many of them in and around San Francisco, specialized in quality knives. San Francisco was, by all accounts, a violent place in the middle of the nineteenth century, but not all the violence was committed by miners and immigrants. There is at least one written report of a law officer being stabbed by a judge! The first recorded San Francisco knife maker, a Mr A. McConnell of Pacific Street, appears in a directory of 1854. Michael Price, an immigrant Irish cutler, also worked in San Francisco. He made Bowie knives mounted in silver and, so it is said, never sold one for less than $50. According to one writer, some of his knives were decorated with gold and diamonds and

Right Satirical sketch published in New York at the time of the California Gold Rush of 1849. The hopeful prospector is girt with every item of equipment he is likely to need on the opposite side of the continent, including a pocketful of knives and a pistol.

Below, left and right
Three silver-hilted cutlery-style Bowies by Limgard, Wragg and Wolstenholm. Two of the blades are etched with scrolls and mottoes — 'Liberty', 'Land of the Free' and 'I dig gold from quartz'.

Early agricultural/plantation knife by Jos. Rodgers, struck with the initials 'GR' and 'Cutlers to His Majesty', and a large rowel spur of the kind commonly used in Mexico.

A GOLD HUNTER ON HIS WAY TO CALIFORNIA, VIA, ST. LOUIS.
Published by H.R.Robinson, 31 Park-Row, N.York

fetched up to $250 each, a very large sum in those days. Several examples of Price's work survive and they are certainly of excellent quality both decoratively and in the forging of the blade.

Many 'Chinese' knives were also produced in San Francisco for the Chinese immigrants brought to work in the mines and on the railways. These were hybrid weapons, with conventional American blades and Chinese hilts. The reeded grip was black, with a central swelling. The same narrow vertical ridges appear on the hilts of many nineteenth-century Chinese swords.

The *navaja* was another typically Californian implement, a legacy of Spanish rule. Used as tool, weapon and table knife, it had a large, single-edged folding blade with a clipped back which looked very similar to the Bowie when open. A catch at the back of the blade released it from the grip and engaged with a lug to lock it open. The grip was often decorated with staghorn. *Navaja* blades come in all sizes, the longest being 12 ins/30 cm.

Union and Confederacy

The American Civil War of 1861–65 has been called the first of the modern wars, for it made use of railways, telegraphs, electricity, photography and other new technologies. The basic needs of war were, however, as old as war itself, weapons, munitions and men, and in all these departments the Unionist North was superior to the Confederate South. Nevertheless it took the North four years to overcome the dogged resistance of the South.

The North was fortunate in that both official arsenals, at Harpers Ferry and Springfield, were in its hands. The South had to rely for much of its material on makeshift suppliers and running the coastal blockade with stocks from Europe.

The Ames Manufacturing Company, at Chicopee near Springfield, had been supplying swords to the government since 1832, so was well able to meet the demands of the war. One of the first swords produced by the company had been the Foot Artillery sword, which bore a strong resemblance to French swords in the Classical style – indeed French influence on weapon design in the United States was always very strong, a legacy of French support during the War of Independence. Some 24,000 Foot Artillery swords were delivered before production ceased in 1862.

European swords were often purchased by the United States War Department and tested with a view to adopting or adapting them for army use. The Non-Commissioned Officer's sword produced by Ames from 1840 to 1865, for example, was very similar to the Prussian equivalent, with a cast brass hilt with knucklebow and twin side shells. In 1850 Ames received two orders for officers' swords based on French patterns, with brass hilts incorporating the initials 'U.S.' and blades etched with the national motto and badge. These swords were used by Union officers throughout the war, some 80,000 being delivered between 1858 and 1865.

The Confederacy was not as fortunate in the matter of edged weapons for, if statistics are to be believed, Union hospitals treated less than 1,000 sword and bayonet wounds throughout the war. This suggests that the Southerners either used their cavalry less or preferred their firearms in action. Many Confederate men and officers were of course still armed with official United States weapons. At the beginning of the war, for example, the Southern cavalry would have carried either the 1840 Heavy Cavalry (Dragoon) Sabre or the 1860 Light Cavalry sword, but as supplies from the North ceased they had to rely on weapons of local manufacture and on imports.

The bulk of Confederate edged weapons were made by small private manufacturers scattered across the length and breadth of the Southern States. Not surprisingly, the quality of such weapons was variable, and as the war progressed stocks of steel and other materials decreased rapidly. Confederate weapons are difficult to identify, a fact which has encouraged the production of a large number of fakes. The Bowie knife frequently appears on lists of weapons supplied – 1,000 from A. McKinstry in Alabama, 136 from J. Ford of Georgia, 296 from George Baker of Georgia, 1,294 from R. Hughes of Georgia. In fact Georgia was one of the largest Confederate supply centres.

The most prolific Georgia manufacturer was Louis Haiman of Columbus. The firm advertised a wide range of weapons, includ-

ing swords, cutlasses and bayonets. One of the Haiman brothers went to Europe in search of supplies which had to be brought in through the blockaded southern ports. His enterprise was rewarded, for the company continued production throughout the war, turning out some 100 swords a week. An officer's plain sword cost $25, a decorated one $35–50, and a cavalry sabre with brass guard, scabbard, sword belt and knot $23. Towards the end of the war Columbus was captured by Federal troops and the factory confiscated. It was offered back to the Haimans on condition that they swore allegiance to the North, but they refused and the factory was razed to the ground.

Another thriving Southern firm was Thomas Griswold & Co. of New Orleans, but as New Orleans was captured quite early in the war, in April 1862, its success was short-lived. Many examples of its output still survive today. The company produced a whole range of edged weapons, including some very elaborate presentation swords.

The South also had several large arsenals. The State Penitentiary of Georgia at Milledgeville, for example, was converted into the State Arsenal. Although set up mainly as a repair and refurbishment centre, it also manufactured some weapons.

By and large Confederate swords were copies of Northern

Below Fine quality cutlery-hilted Bowie produced by Edward Barnes and Sons of Sheffield in about 1860. The blade is etched with sentiments thought likely to appeal to the American market.

Bottom Two small metal-hilted knives of a type in general use around 1850, one with the letters 'NY' etched on the blade.

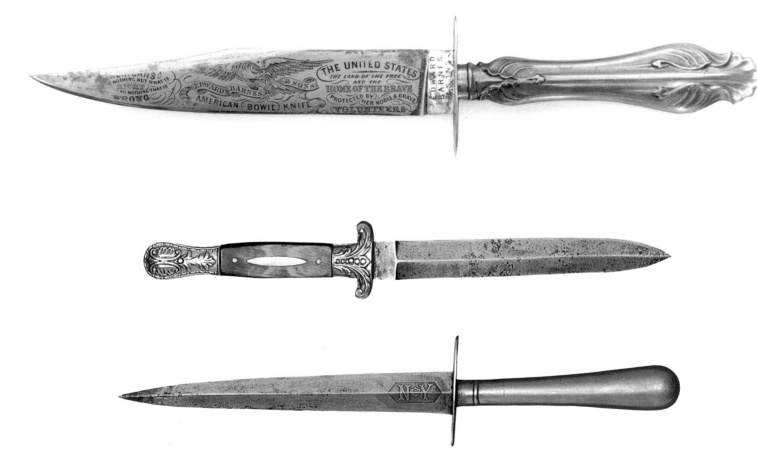

Right S. E. Hollister, the famous hunter and trapper, fights off a she-bear in the wilds of California in 1853.

Below Two swords made by the Ames Sword Company: an enlisted man's Pattern 1840 sword of the Union cavalry dated 1864 (right) and another sword of the Civil War period (left) with hilt and blade decoration indicating that it was a Union officer's sword. The Southern forces also carried the Pattern 1840 sword in the early days of the conflict.

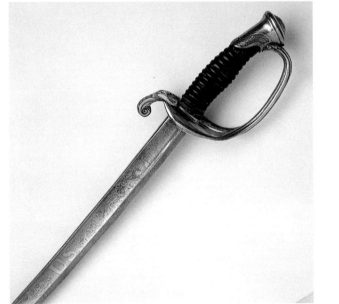

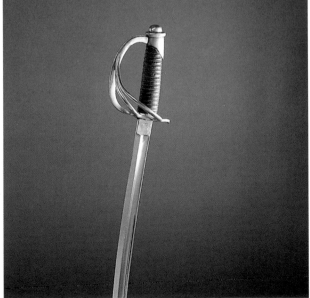

Right The blue and the grey, a contemporary illustration of the uniforms of the opposing sides in the Civil War. The edged weapons of both sides were very similar, with socket bayonets for percussion rifles and swords for officers. As the war progressed the South found it more and more difficult to maintain their arms supplies.

Below Three engravings from *A New System of Sword Exercise with a Manual of the Sword for Officers* by Matthew O'Rourke, published in New York in 1872. Illustrated left to right are: Draw swords, Salute, and Carry.

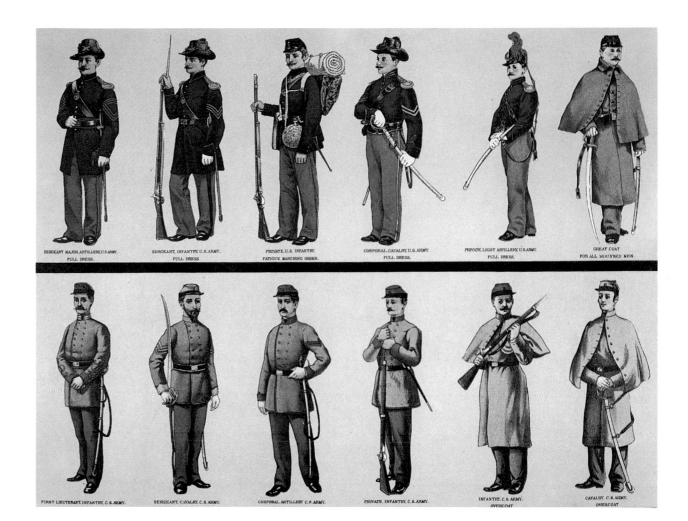

Left Plate from a military uniform catalogue. During the early part of the Civil War there was a vogue for somewhat exotic uniforms; here the French 'Zouave' influence is strong, a heritage from Revolutionary and Napoleonic times when the colonies received a great deal of arms and equipment from France. The designer comments: 'The introduction of the long range rifles has rendered it peculiarly dangerous to wear conspicuous colors or ornaments which, in action, only serve as a mark for the sharpshooters . . .'.

Opposite page Four Union Gettysburg generals photographed in 1863: seated is Major-General Winfield Scott Hancock, and standing left to right are Generals Francis Barlow, John Gibbon and David B. Birney. Hancock took command of the Union forces following the death of Major General J. F. Reynolds from a sharpshooter bullet on the first day of the battle. Army regulations of the period specified that general officers should wear a 'straight sword, gilt hilt, silver grip, brass or steel scabbard', but Barlow appears to have favoured a curved cavalry-type sabre.

weapons, with numerous variations in detail of course. Many bore the letters 'C.S.A.' (Confederate States of America), but not all swords thus marked were made in America. Some were imported, ready-made, from England. In one instance, men from New York purchased a London firm of military outfitters and then supplied the South with swords bearing the London name and appropriate Rebel decoration.

The North probably made more use of the sword than the South, but in a cavalry context the sword had already become a less important weapon than the percussion carbine, in particular the Spencer percussion carbine. As far as is known, only one Northern cavalry unit was ever armed with lances. In post-Napoleonic Europe, by contrast, most armies included regiments of lancers and even increased them.

Cavalry and presentation swords

The Civil War gave fresh impetus to westward migration, which put increasing pressure on the Indians, who fought back in the only way that they knew – guerilla warfare. They were, as one of their European enemies put it, 'the best light cavalry in the world', masters of the hit-and-run, wearing down type of attack. It fell to the army, in particular the cavalry, to defend the routes and settlements west of the Mississippi, a task which stretched their resources to the full. Some 943 Indian engagements are mentioned in army records between 1865 and 1898.

Many of these encounters, and many during the previous century, were notable for the savagery of some actions by both sides. However, although much has been made of the Indian practice of scalping dead enemies, it seems that the practice was

A Scene on the FRONTIERS *as Practiced by the* HUMANE BRITISH *and their* WORTHY ALLIES —

Bring me the Scalps
and the King our master
will reward you —

Reward for
Sixteen
Scalps

Arise Columbia's Sons and forward press,
Your country's wrongs call loudly for redress;
The Savage Indian with his Scalping knife,
Or Tomahawk may seek to take your life,

By bravery aw'd they'll in a dreadful Fright,
Shrink back for Refuge to the Woods in Flight;
Their British leaders then will quickly shake,
And for those wrongs shall restitution make.

Above Eighteenth-century cartoon deploring the British practice of offering rewards for scalps. The musket of the Indian in the centre is hung with the notice 'Reward for sixteen scalps'.

Right Tomahawk and stone club or *i-wata-jinga*. The tomahawk was used by many Indian tribes and varied greatly in design, often doubling as a tobacco pipe. Large numbers were made in England and exported to America via the trading companies.

not widespread before the arrival of the Europeans. In the Northeast, scalping was introduced by the government when a bounty was offered for scalps of unfriendly Indians, male, female or child. Later the French introduced the same system of payment for British scalps who, in turn, offered bounties for French scalps. Scalping seems to have spread slowly from this area and it is thought that many of the Plains Indians did not adopt the practice until well into the nineteenth century.

The Indian Wars provided scant opportunity for the use of swords or bayonets – the Indians were far too shrewd to wait to be charged by cavalry or infantry. In engagements which involved hand-to-hand fighting, the weapons used were the knife and the tomahawk. Despite the stirring productions of Hollywood, battles such as that fought, and lost, by General Custer on the Little Big Horn in June 1876 did not involve swords. Custer's 7th Cavalry did not even have their sabres with them at the time. Nor, shortly afterwards, did 'Buffalo' Bill Cody and an Indian named Yellowhand duel to the death with knife and tomahawk. It seems that the duel was fought with rifles, with Cody shooting his opponent from a distance of 50 feet! One graphic detail that seems to be authentic, however, is that Cody scalped the Indian and waved his gory trophy in the air, shouting 'First scalp for Custer'.

Despite the sword's declining usefulness, the armed forces persisted in keeping it, and in 1902 a standard pattern sword was introduced for all U.S. Army officers. It differed from most previous army swords in that it had a black contoured horn grip with a dull nickel guard and a slightly curved blade etched with floral designs, the national coat-of-arms and the initials 'U.S.'

In 1913 the cavalry, arriving at the same conclusion as the British five years earlier, decided that their sword should be a thrusting rather than a cutting weapon. Designed by the future World War II general, George Patton, then a lieutenant, the new sword had a straight and rather rigid narrow blade and a guard of sheet steel strengthened by three corrugations. The guard was slightly less globose than the British one and the grip was not as well contoured as its European counterpart. It was with this sword that the U.S. cavalry entered World War I, only to find that cavalry action was, for the most part, neither appropriate nor necessary. Nevertheless the horse was not retired from active army service until 1943.

Presentation swords were as popular in the United States as they were in Europe. Congress voted that presentation swords should be awarded for outstanding service during the Revolutionary War of 1776–83. Ten swords were ordered from France, with silver hilts decorated on one side with the coat-of-arms of the new American nation and on the other with details of the valiant deeds of the recipients. The blades were blued and gilt, and of triangular hollow-ground form. Swords presented by the State of New York after the war of 1812–14 had gold hilts decorated with floral sprays and rosettes, pommels in the form of an eagle's head, side shells decorated with classical motifs, and rear quillons with ram's head finials. The blued and gilt blades bore heraldic devices and the figure of Liberty resplendent in an Indian feather headdress.

Many other presentation swords, decorated in styles dictated by contemporary taste, were made to mark other campaigns, however those of the post-Civil War period tend to be rather ostentatious. Most were loosely modelled on the general officer's pattern sword, but with serpents, helmets, eagles, rubies and sundry other embellishments incorporated into the hilt. Although such swords were usually presented by a State, or in some cases a city, they were also freely available from firms such as Schuyler, Hartley & Graham of New York, whose 1864 catalogue offers a range of weapons, including some with solid silver scabbards, scabbard fittings in the form of military trophies or floral ornaments, and hilts fashioned into figures of Victory, Neptune, armoured knights and cavalrymen.

Another purely decorative sword popular in the nineteenth century was the society sword. This usually had a cruciform hilt, recalling the hilts of ceremonial swords since the Middle Ages, and a grip embellished by a cross or similar emblem. The blade was usually etched with sundry Classical themes, and frequently with the owner's name, and the scabbard was similarly embellished. Members of the Masonic Order and various other American societies affected such swords.

A bayonet designed in 1861 by Charles Borum also has every appearance of being decorative rather than practical. Indeed its nearest relative is the medieval staff weapon known as a guisarme, of which it seems to be a miniature version. This very strange weapon has a tapering blade $13\frac{1}{2}$ in/34 cm long fitted with a large spike on one edge and a crescent-shaped projection on the other, and a bulky, squarish hilt with a large pommel grooved on one side. Parallel to the blade are two recurved quillons and on either side of the grip, at right angles to the quillons, are mirror-image shamrock-shaped bars. This very exotic implement was presumably designed to slip onto a double-barrelled gun, with either the spike or the 'axe' blade uppermost but, so far, no one has been able to identify the gun that it was intended to fit.

Into the twentieth century

In 1898, as the Indian Wars drew to a close, the Americans found themselves facing a new enemy, Spain. The war was a short one, however, beginning in April and ending in December, with Spain ceding some territory and selling the Philippines to the United States for $20 million. A strong independence movement in the Philippines objected to this arrangement, and in the six years of guerilla fighting which followed some 116,000 Filipinos died, many from starvation. American casualties were 7,000.

The Spanish War of 1898 was fought by the regular U.S. Army and volunteers. The rifle carried by the U.S. infantry was the Krag Jorgenson magazine repeating rifle introduced in the same

Above Detail from a painting by Charles Schreyvogel (1861–1912) showing U.S. cavalry surrounding a lone Indian. Despite the emotional appeal of paintings such as this, the sabre saw little use in the Indian campaigns, the cavalry seldom having the opportunity to charge.

year. This was fitted either with the short, straight-bladed sword-bayonet typical of the period or with the much more exotic Bowie-type bayonet, which had a slightly curved broad blade with a clipped edge. This unusual form of bayonet was in the tradition of the M1873 bayonet issued for the Springfield rifle, and was known appropriately as the 'trowel' bayonet. Its triangular shape may have been excellent for digging in, but it was not much use as a weapon. Also known as the Rice bayonet after its originator, Colonel E.Rice, it was a singular failure.

The U.S. Army was always rather adventurous in the field of bayonet design, and for the 1903 Springfield rifle decided to experiment with an idea already tried in Denmark and the United States, namely a combined ramrod and bayonet. One simply reversed the ramrod and locked it in position when one wanted to use it as a bayonet. The same rifle could also be fitted with a bolo bayonet. This had a typical sword-bayonet hilt, but the blade had a straight back edge and widened slowly from the hilt to the middle and tapered again towards the point. *Bolo* is Spanish for 'knife', but a bolo knife is also a jungle knife used in the Philippines.

During World War I American troops used the M1917 bayonet, which was virtually the same as the 1907 British bayonet, with a straight blade and simple cruciform hilt. As World War II loomed, however, the blade was shortened to 10 ins/25 cm. A plastic scabbard had already replaced the earlier wood and leather or plain leather article. In 1943 the new shortened bayonet was officially classified as the M1 bayonet.

At the close of World War I three official trench knives were in use: Model 1917, Model 1918 and Model 1918 Mk 1. The first two had a narrow, triangular section stiletto-style blade fitted into a hilt with a knuckleduster-type guard and a wooden grip. The 1918 Mk 1 had a flat, double-edged blade fitted to a cast brass hilt with the same knuckleduster guard. Models 1917 and 1918 were declared obsolete in 1922 and the third was re-designated as Trench Knife Mk 1.

The Infantry Board of the U.S. Army felt that all combatants should carry a knife in case of hand-to-hand fighting and recommended to the Ordnance Department that a weapon with a 7- or 8-in blade designed primarily for cutting but also for stabbing when necessary would be appropriate. Six designs were produced to the Board's detailed specifications and the samples tested. The knife selected was rather like the old Model 1918 Mk 1, but further tests showed that the knuckleguard made it rather clumsy to fit onto a rifle as a bayonet, which was one of the original requirements. Modifications were carried out and in 1945 the Knife, Trench, M 3 was approved. It had a straight blade of 6¾ ins/ 17 cm and a ridged grip composed of leather washers of wide and narrow diameter. The leather scabbard had a securing strip which latched across the hilt and a long bottom thong so that it could be tied to the thigh, preventing snagging as the knife was drawn.

When Japan entered the war in 1941 the American Marines

began setting up groups similar to the British Commandos, the first Marine Raiders group being formed, with four battalions, in February 1942. This was a volunteer force, selected from eight times the number of men required, and their first raid was in August 1942. The knife they carried was a stiletto designed by Lieutenant-Colonel Shuey, who had trained with the British Commandos in Scotland. It was a close cousin of the Fairbairn-Sykes knife, although it had a bigger sheath to fit the American webbing belt. Some 15,000 were manufactured by a New York firm. The Marine Raiders also carried a Bowie-type knife with a grip similar to that of the Knife, Trench, Mk 3; this was known by the name of the trade mark stamped on the blade, Ka-Bar. A few Bowie-type bolo bayonets were also fitted with a knife grip for raiding purposes.

In the summer of 1942 another group of American and Canadian Commando-type units, the First Special Force, was recruited. The knife they carried was also closely based on the Fairbairn-Sykes knife, although the grip was fatter and widened at the centre and the pommel was a conoidal spike intended as a skull cracker. The blued blade had a feature found on some seventeenth-century left-hand daggers, namely a slight depression to accommodate the top of the thumb when the knife was held in the traditional knife-fighter's grip with the blade pointing upwards. The design sketches were passed to three notable American cutlery firms, all of whom submitted sample knives. That submitted by Case was chosen and 1,750 knives designated as V 42 Fighting Knives were forwarded to the group in Montana in December 1942. These knives were all hand-finished and so varied slightly in detail, as did the sheaths, although most were of leather with a tie-down thong at the base. Since the First Special Force was earmarked for Arctic operations, and would therefore be swathed in furs or other protective clothing, the sheath was made long enough – 20 ins/51cm – to allow the knife to be worn well down the thigh. In the event, the Force never saw Arctic service, serving instead in Italy and France before being disbanded in 1944.

One other unusual American knife of World War II was the parachutists' flick knife, designed so that a parachutist could open it with one hand if he was in difficulty with a snagged parachute on landing. It served much the same purpose as the gravity knife used by his British and German counterparts.

In recent years there has been a remarkable growth of interest in custom-made knives in the United States. This has stimulated a revival of the cutler's craft, with numerous American craftsmen producing a wide range of blades for many purposes, most of them of very high quality.

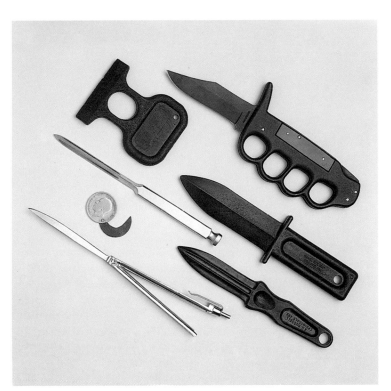

Far left above Knives for covert operations: cigarette lighter with base-mounted knife (top left), two buckle knives (right), a credit card knife and a pen housing a blade (centre), and a conventional flick knife (bottom).

Far left below Two American World War I fighting knives with knuckleduster grips: the spike-bladed Model 1917 (left) and the broad-bladed Model 1918 Mk 1 with a small spike at the top of the grip (right).

Left above Three modern plastic knives (right), a slender knife based on an OSS knife (centre), a coin adapted to house a crude but effective hooked blade (below) and a pen concealing a slender blade (bottom). Plastic knives are extremely strong and capable of piercing wooden planks without breaking.

Left below M 3 Trench Knife introduced in 1943 (left) and a U.S. Navy Utility Knife with a grip of compressed leather washers (right). The M 3 was made by the Case Cutlery Company and was a little unusual in having a metal sheath.

10 WORLD WARS I AND II

Frederick Wilkinson

Death and injury on the battlefields of Europe were, from the fourteenth century onwards, increasingly a consequence of the Devil's powder, gunpowder. Armour heavy enough to withstand musket balls and other missiles could not be marched and fought in for very long, and by the late seventeenth century most European infantry forces had discarded it. A century later, even hangers ceased to be issued for infantry use, and battles were mainly fought with matchlock or flintlock muskets.

The modern bayonet

Muskets suffered from several drawbacks, but one of the greatest was that they were a single-shot weapon. Once fired, they were largely useless until they could be reloaded, and this was a slow business. While he was reloading the infantryman was defenceless and particularly vulnerable to cavalry attack. In the seventeenth century the problem had been solved by using pikemen to deter any attacks, but this was a rather wasteful use of manpower.

Another answer was to convert the musket into a short pike and this was easily achieved by pushing the hilt of a knife into the muzzle. As already mentioned in Chapter 6, the name 'bayonet' was first used in the middle of the seventeenth century. However this simple system had one obvious drawback in that with the bayonet in place the musket could not be loaded or fired. If the musket was fired with the bayonet in place the result could be disastrous. In 1660 Louis XIV of France forbade the use of bayonets because there had been so many accidents. The British army soon adopted the bayonet and it was certainly in use by 1672, for the 'great knife or bayonet' is mentioned in orders.

The majority of plug bayonets of the period had a slightly tapered wooden grip with a bulbous section which engaged with the muzzle. The short crossguard was usually of brass, with finials often in the form of helmeted heads. The blade of some 8–10 ins/20–25 cm was broad at the hilt and tapered to a point, and the great majority were straight although some were serpentine or flamboyant. Many were engraved with patriotic sentiments or martial scenes.

The obvious alternative to the restrictive and rather dangerous plug concept was to fit the bayonet to the outside of the barrel. Initially this was done by fitting rings to the bayonet hilt and slipping them over the barrel, but there was nothing to prevent the bayonet slipping off or being pulled off. In the last decade of the seventeenth century, certainly as early as 1697, a new style of bayonet, known as a socket bayonet, was developed. This had a metal collar with a Z-shaped slot which slipped over the barrel and engaged with a small square lug. Some later bayonets were fitted with a locking ring to make the union of bayonet and barrel even more secure. The blade was also set to one side at the end of a short curved neck so as not to upset the flight of the bullet near the muzzle or interfere with loading.

The socket bayonet remained in use until well into the nineteenth century, and during that time various methods of locking the bayonet to the barrel were developed, some involving socket slots with spring catches. One disadvantage of the socket bayonet, however, was that the design of the hilt made it difficult to use as knife or dagger; the hilt was simply not the right shape to be held comfortably. Numerous bayonets were therefore designed with sockets that allowed them to be used as hand weapons, a practice which became common in the nineteenth century and continues today.

Some bayonets, such as the British Elcho bayonet, were designed for a specific purpose. Produced in the early 1870s and named after its designer Lord Elcho, this bayonet had a saw-tooth back edge and a blade which widened towards the point; it was therefore ideal for slashing and chopping. At the time a small colonial war was brewing on the Ashanti coast of Africa and the Elcho bayonet was recommended as an invaluable weapon for hacking a way through the jungle. Many bayonets of the nineteenth century had a saw-tooth back edge, permitting their use as a tool as well as a weapon.

The major wars of the nineteenth century – the American Civil War, the Crimean War, the Franco-Prussian War – demonstrated the increasing role of technology in warfare, at least to those willing to to see it. The Boer War of 1899–1902 was a severe shock

Opposite page French *poilus* present arms in honour of the flag. Their Lebel rifles are fitted with the stiff metal-hilted bayonet. The scene is set in 1915, **before the introduction** of the Adrian steel helmet.

to the British Army, for a comparatively small number of ill-trained but resourceful irregulars held it at bay, inflicting serious casualties and humiliating defeats. Gone were the days of the British square, bayonet charges through breaches in city walls, and similar dashing events.

At the beginning of the present century the infantry of most nations were armed with some form of bolt-action magazine rifle using metallic cartridges. Bayonets were standard issue. Cavalry units still carried a lance or sword in addition to a revolver or short rifle/carbine, while officers of all branches of the armed forces carried a regulation pattern sword of some kind.

When the great nations entered World War I, their armies were, with the exception of Russia, generally well equipped. There was little to choose between them as far as small arms were concerned. The forces of Austro-Hungary were armed with an 8mm Mannlicher rifle, introduced in 1895, which had a five-shot magazine and a sword-bayonet which latched onto the left side of the barrel. The Austro-Hungarian cavalry carried a carbine version and used the same bayonet, which had a straight blade and one down-curved quillon. Germany armed her troops with the 7.9mm Mauser Gewehr 98, a rifle of sound construction and reliability. Belgium and Turkey used the same rifle but of 7.65mm calibre. Whereas the Turks fitted their rifle with a long-bladed bayonet with a strongly down-curved quillon, the Germans fitted theirs with a comparatively short weapon with only a small upturned guard. France used a Lebel rifle Pattern 1886, firing an 8mm cartridge. This was issued with a rather unusual bayonet which had a metal grip, a down-turned quillon, a blade of cruciform cross-section, and a metal sheath – the majority of bayonets of the period had leather sheaths. Quite early in the war, however, it was decided that the curved quillon on the Lebel bayonet was superfluous and it was removed.

Britain was changing rifles early in the century but most of her troops were armed with the .303-in SMLE (Short Magazine Lee Enfield) or 'Smelly' rifle, fitted with a Pattern 1907 bayonet. This bayonet was available in two versions, one with a down-turned curved quillon, the other with a short straight crossguard. When

the United States joined the Allies in 1917, her troops were equipped with a version of the Mauser-action rifle with a calibre of .300 in; its bayonet was very similar to the SMLE British bayonet.

Italy had the Mannlicher Carcano 6.5mm rifle with a bayonet similar to the British Pattern 1907, attached below the barrel. The bayonet on the Italian carbine was permanently attached to the weapon, spring-operated so that as a small catch was pressed the blade swung forwards to lock in position. Japan equipped its troops with the 6.5mm 1907 Year 38th Pattern rifle; this was fitted with the Arisaka bayonet which, in general outline, was similar to the British 1907 pattern, with a down-turned quillon.

The Russians, or to be accurate some of the Russians, since many had no weapon at all, were armed with Moisin Nagant 7.62mm rifles. The bayonet was of the old socket type, with a tubular fitting which slipped over the muzzle, and the blade was cruciform in section. For the infantry, there was no issue scabbard, but the cavalry were supplied with a sheath for their sword, the *shashqa*, which incorporated a fitting to hold the bayonet.

The armies of all the belligerents in World War I spent many hours training their troops to use the bayonet. Various dummy rifles and bayonets were produced to make practice safer, most of which had a spring-operated simulated bayonet so that thrusts could be made without unduly endangering life, and competitions were devised to encourage proficiency. However the number of bayonet wounds inflicted during the war was minimal compared to those caused by other weapons. Of a sample selection of 200,000 British war wounds, only 600 or so were reckoned to have been caused by bayonets. Likewise, the Americans estimated that only .024 per cent of their casualties were due to bayonets. Personal accounts by those who took part in the fighting suggest that enthusiasm for cold steel was higher among the Allies than among the Germans. One British officer who kept a diary noted that he never saw a German soldier with a fixed bayonet throughout the whole of the war, and a general even went so far as to suggest that the only men who were killed with the bayonet were those who were surrendering!

The bayonet played some part in trench raids when, after lobbing grenades into a section of enemy trench, soldiers with fixed bayonets would scramble across to deal with any survivors. Indeed the British had a colonel who did nothing else but visit front-line trenches and lecture on the subject of bayonet fighting. Dedication to the idea that cold steel was a great frightener continued throughout the war and into World War II.

Germany started the war with an issue Mauser bayonet which, unusually, had no ring on the guard to engage with the muzzle of the rifle. It was attached to it by means of a long slot in the back of the grip which engaged with a long bar on the rifle barrel. The lack of a muzzle ring made for easier manufacture. Even so, by 1916 demand began to outrun supply and all manner of captured weaponry was pressed into service. The bayonets from Belgian

Above, left to right
Belgian Mauser bayonet Pattern 1889.
Pattern 1891 Russian socket bayonet with cruciform blade for the Moisin Nagant rifle. This was carried fitted onto the *shashqa* sheath.
British Pritchard Greener bayonet patented in 1916, designed for the Webley Mark VI revolver.
French Lebel Pattern 1886 bayonet, with downcurved quillon.
American M1917 bayonet for the M1917 30-in Enfield rifle.

Far left German soldier with Mauser rifle and bayonet, *c*.1911. The Mauser bayonet was also available with a sawback edge.

Left British soldier (Devonshire Regiment) of the pre-war period. He is armed with the long Lee Enfield rifle, the precursor of the SMLE, fitted with the 1888 bayonet.

Below Japanese soldier with 1907 Year 38th Pattern rifle fitted with the Arisaka bayonet, *c*.1911.

Mauser, Russian Moisin Nagant and French Gras rifles were fitted with German-type mounts so that they would fit the German Mauser rifle, and many *ersatz* bayonets were made, sometimes from old sword blades.

After the war, there was a general reluctance to accept that the bayonet was outmoded and troops still spend hours bayonetting straw-stuffed dummies and screaming horrible threats, it was nevertheless recognized that the bayonet of World War I had been too long. The trend was towards shorter bayonets. By the late 1930s the British 1907 long-bladed bayonet had been replaced by a mere 8-in/20-cm spike of cruciform section; in place of a hilt there was a short fitting which locked the bayonet to the rifle.

Spring-operated bayonets, popular in the eighteenth and early nineteenth centuries when they were fitted to pistols and blunder-busses, were also experimented with and even considered for use on submachine guns, but very few weapons were fitted up in this way. The spring-operated bayonet was abandoned by the British but adopted for rifle bayonets by, among others, the Russians.

The new British spike bayonet had no hilt and was intended solely for fitting to a rifle, although needless to say it was put to other uses, such as opening tin cans. In 1945 a new hilted bayonet was introduced, designed to fit the British Sten gun. It had an 8-in/20-cm blade with a clipped end like a Bowie knife, a hilt with a contoured plastic grip, and a pommel which rotated to fit onto

the barrel of the gun but afforded a firm grip if the weapon was used as a knife. This type of bayonet was retained after the war and fitted to various types of self-loading rifle.

Trench knives

In 1914, in the opening opening stages of the war on the Western Front, the Germans pushed quickly into Belgium and Northern France. Although partially repulsed by the Allies, there were no decisive victories on either side and by late 1914 there was a general paralysis of the battle lines. A system of trenches sprawled across the fields of France and Belgium, and attempts to break through enemy lines were costly and largely futile, as at Verdun, Argonne, the Somme, Vimy and Passchendaele, but both sides continued to mount such attacks.

Before such pushes, it was vital to know what was happening in the enemy lines, and so small raiding parties would be send by night across the cratered, mined, barbed-wire tangle that was 'no man's land' to take prisoners and acquire information. Such raids were an unpopular part of front-line duty and were often felt by the troops to be unnecessary and only dreamed up **by the** High Command in order to show that something was happening on their sector of the front. The return trip was often more hazardous than the outward one, for by then the enemy was probably alerted, some of the raiding party might be wounded and prisoners had to be kept silent and alive.

Hand-held bayonets with blades 15-20 ins/38-51 cm long proved too clumsy for stealthy, close-quarters fighting, and soon troops on both sides were busy grinding them down, and shortening or removing their quillons. The result was a trench fighting knife. If spare bayonets were unavailable, the metal posts used to secure barbed wire were used instead, with the sharpened end serving as the blade and the other end folded over to form a simple grip. With typical soldiers' irony, this extempore weapon was called the 'French Nail'. More ambitious infantrymen not only shortened their bayonets but also fitted knuckleduster hand guards.

In 1916 a Captain A. Pritchard patented a bayonet for the Webley Mark VI.45 revolver carried by most British officers. Although it was never an official issue weapon, the famous Birmingham gunmaking firm of W. W. Greener thought it worth manufacturing, probably producing several hundred in all. The blade, 7-8 ins/18-29 cm long, was made from the cut-down French Gras bayonet. The hilt, of brass or steel, was machined to fit around the frame of the revolver and locked into position by means of a spring catch. It did not affect the use of the revolver, and when not required was carried in a metal sheath of modified Gras bayonet type secured to the Sam Browne belt by a leather loop.

The Germans had a slight advantage in their search for a trench knife in that a claspknife or *Taschenmesser* was standard issue. This was a general purpose knife, with a locking blade. However, once the demand for trench knives became clear, a number of firms began to produce them. The majority conformed to the same basic design, having a double-edged blade about 6 ins/15 cm long and a diagonally grooved wooden grip. Most were supplied with a leather sheath, with a retaining strap around the grip.

In Britain, Robbins of Dudley, Worcestershire, produced a variety of fighting knives, including some with light alloy hilts and a plain knuckleguard. They also copied the old American push dagger, which has a short blade mounted at right angles to the grip so that the blade projects between the fingers at right angles to the clenched fist. Another firm, Clements of London, produced a fighting knife with a knuckleduster as an integral part of the grip. This style of knife was not seen in action on a large scale until the United States entered the war.

Cavalry in retreat

In the early years of this century many military commanders still believed that the rifle and machine-gun were no match for a charging cavalryman with outstretched sword. Nevertheless

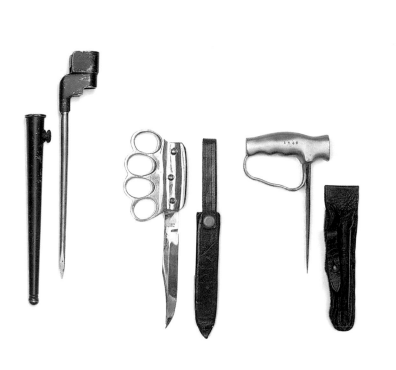

Left The British Mark II skewer bayonet or 'pig sticker' (left) issued in 1940, only half the length of the 1907 bayonet used in World War I; a commerically produced World War I British knuckleduster trench knife and sheath (centre); and a World War I punch dagger and sheath made by Robbins (right). Robbins of Dudley were one of the main British manufacturers of fighting knives during the First War.

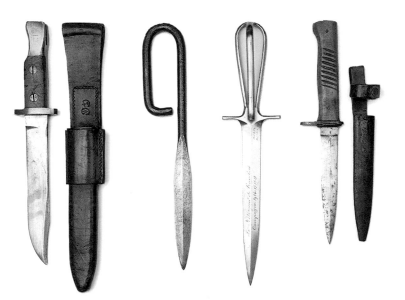

Below More World War I fighting knives: Canadian Ross rifle bayonet (left), shortened and modified to from a Bowie-type trench knife; a 'French Nail' and Trench Cleaner (centre), both with looped grips to fit the belt; and a German trench knife (right) with a wooden grip.

Opposite page Bayonet drill for the crew of a British trawler during World War II (top left). Their weapons are the out-of-date long Lee Enfield and Pattern 1888 bayonet.

American World War I poster (top right) depicting the Doughboy with his P14 rifle and bayonet.

Trench warfare led to some novel uses of the bayonet (bottom left). Here a trench periscope is mounted on a Pattern 1907 bayonet fitted to a SMLE rifle.

World War I saw the end of cavalry as a serious fighting arm. In the early stages of the war there were a few cavalry skirmishes between British and German units, but as the war became more and more static and the system of trenches expanded, there was no place for the horse except as a beast of burden. There was no real opportunity for the massed cavalry charge, although the French, still in uniforms largely unchanged in design since Napoleon I, did attempt a few early in the war, with disastrous results. It was intended that cavalry should follow up the break-through achieved by Allied tanks at Cambrai in November 1917, but despite the unexpected success of the attack the cavalry did not fan out and exploit the gap. In the German counter-attack the cavalry suffered heavy casualties.

It was ironic that when the British cavalry acquired its finest sword, it was no longer needed. The ideal cavalry sword had long been a matter of debate. Should it be primarily for slashing and cutting or primarily for thrusting, or was something in between more desirable? A cutting blade needs to be broad and reasonably flexible, with a good cutting edge, but a thrusting blade needs to be narrow and stiff, with a good point. These are, of course, diametrically opposed demands.

The matter was finally resolved in 1903 by a committee which decided that a thrusting sword was more serviceable than a cutting one. An experimental sword was produced, but it did not satisfy all its critics. More experimental swords were produced and tested and the results studied by another committee which sat in 1906. In 1908 the committee submitted its proposals to the king, Edward VII, who expressed the opinion that the new sword was 'hideous' and wanted to know why a new sword was necessary. A group of senior officers was sent to him to explain, soothe and convince. Eventually he gave his approval and the new sword became official issue.

It had a narrow, stiff, T-section blade, a large steel bowl guard, and a carefully designed grip which automatically put the point in the ideal position for a thrust once the palm was fitted round it and the thumb placed in the thumb recess. It was carried in a steel sheath with two suspension rings near the mouth. In 1912 an officer's version was authorized. This was, in effect, a decorated version of the trooper's sword and was carried in the same type of scabbard or one covered with leather when worn on the service Sam Browne belt.

The ineffectual and anachronistic nature of cavalry on the modern battlefield was experienced by all forces during the Great War, although on the Eastern Front, where there was far more movement, there was more scope for cavalry action. The Russian Cossacks, well known for their magnificent horsemanship, used their slightly curved *shashqa* against Germans, Revolutionaries and Counter-Revolutionaries with equal skill and enthusiasm. In Eastern Europe cavalry traditions lingered longer than in the West, and it is reported that during the early stages of World War II Polish cavalry heroically but futilely charged German tanks.

Top French light cavalry attack German infantry at Lassigny early in the war. This was the war as the card sellers thought it should be, with gallant cavalry charges and flashing swords. In reality there were few such actions.

Above Russian *shashqa* (top), showing the sheath fitting which housed the Moisin Nagant bayonet; Russian post-revolutionary *shashqa* and sheath (centre), virtually the same as the 1881 Imperial pattern for officers; and an officer's *shashqa* (bottom) of the reign of Nicholas II (1894–1917).

Left The *shashqa* grip on the left bears the hammer and sickle emblem of the USSR, while that on the right bears the official cypher of Nicholas II.

Left Henri-Philippe Pétain is presented with the baton of a Maréchal of France, Metz, 8 December 1918. Standing behind him are, left to right, Maréchals Joffre and Foch, Field Marshal Sir Douglas Haig, and Generals Pershing (USA), Gillain (Belgium), Albricei (Italy) and Haller (Poland). Only Generals Haig and Albricei are without a sword.

Below British 1908 cavalry trooper's sword (left), with large steel bowl guard and angled grip; British 1912 cavalry officer's pattern (centre), with decorated guard and wire-bound grip; and a standard British infantry officer's sword Pattern 1897, with the inner edge of guard turned down.

The swords issued to infantry officers in World War I were no less of an anachronism than the horse, and were often one of the first items discarded after a short spell in the trenches. The sword carried by British officers in 1914 had been adopted in 1895. It had a steel three-quarter basket guard decorated with scroll work and the royal cipher, but in 1897 the inside edge of the guard had been turned over to lessen the discomfort caused by the hilt banging against the thigh.

The resurgence of Solingen

The ending of the Great War in 1918 dealt a body blow to the German arms industry. Particularly hard hit was Solingen, the town which had enjoyed a reputation for fine quality swords and daggers since the Middle Ages. The famous 'running wolf' mark and the name Solingen had been guarantees of quality for centuries. Now its craftsmen were unemployed and its factories were idle or trying to adapt to the production of household necessities.

With the advent of the Nazis in 1933 it occurred to the craftsmen of Solingen that if the Party could be persuaded that swords and daggers would enhance the status of its members, a whole new and very large market could be created. First they had to convince the Party leadership of the need for such weapons and the benefit of such a market to the German economy. Steel would be needed, ancillary industries would once again flourish, and polishers, dyers, engravers and designers would return to work. Accordingly, in April 1933, a group of officials from Solingen went to Berlin to present their idea to the new leader Adolf Hitler. He accepted their gift of a letter opener and approved the scheme.

First consideration was given to the SA or Brownshirts, formed in 1921 as a kind of security force for the Party. By 1930 the SA had more than 100,000 members, a sizeable market

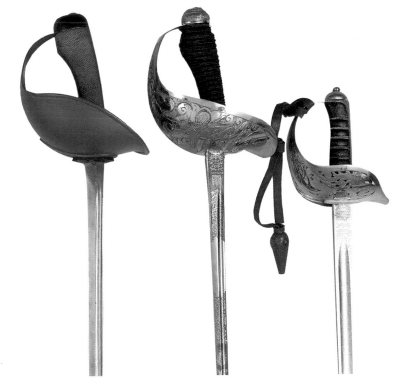

Above Nazi Labour Corps (Reicharbeitsdienst) dagger and sheath. The broad, heavy blade was intended for use as a tool rather than a weapon. A more elaborate officer's version was available.

Above right Hitler Jungend dagger and sheath, sold in millions to the young people of Germany for the benefit of Party funds.

Right Second Model Italian MSVN (Milizia Voluntaria Sicurezza Nazionale) dagger, designed to be worn for parades but also intended as a serious weapon. The scabbard carries the fasces symbol.

indeed. A member of the Solingen Trade School, a Professor Woenne, was commissioned to design a suitable dagger for them and came up with a weapon which was a simplified version of the 'Swiss' or 'Holbein' dagger popular in the sixteenth century. The blade of the proposed SA dagger was leaf-shaped and engraved with the motto 'Alles für Deutschland'. The brown wooden hilt was rather like a capital I, swelling gracefully at the centre and decorated with the Party symbol. It was to be worn in a plain brown painted metal sheath worn on a belt. Hitler approved the design and the first batch of SA daggers was ordered in February 1934.

Hitler then ordered that the SS should have a similar dagger, but with a black grip and sheath to match the feared black uniform. The SS had been founded in 1925 as a personal body-guard and under the command of Heinrich Himmler it grew rapidly in power and numbers, reaching a total of 221,000 members by 1934. The blade of the SS dagger was engraved with the motto 'Meine Ehre heißt Treue' ('My Honour is Loyalty'). The design of the SS daggers underwent minor changes and different grades evolved for officers and for presentation.

A dagger with a mixed combination of colours, a brown hilt and a black painted scabbard, was worn by members of the Nationalsozialistisches Kraftfahrkorps (Party Motor Transport Corps). Another variant was worn by students of the National Political Education Institute, youngsters selected for indoctrination in the politics of Nazism at special schools. Their dagger was like the SA dagger but had a plain wooden grip, a blade with a different motto, and a sheath similar to the standard bayonet scabbard.

In Italy, Mussolini's Blackshirts were also issued with daggers, but the daggers of Italian Fascism lack the variety and panache of those of Hitler's Germany; the dagger made for the Milizia Voluntaria Sicurezza Nazionale (MVSN), for example, was a rather nondescript weapon with a Latin motto etched on the blade and a scabbard embossed with the bundle of rods and axe of the fasces, the old Roman device representing solidarity and the strength that comes through unity.

As the fashion gathered pace, organization after organization in Germany demanded and got their official daggers. These under-went minor changes, and were often available with optional extras, such as specially forged Damascus blades. There were also different grades for officers and versions for presentation.

Solingen was the prime but not the only beneficiary of this avid demand. Nazi Party funds also benefited, not least because the knife worn by the Hitler Youth was not official issue but available by purchase. Officially created as a separate body in 1935, the Hitler Youth was, at first, a voluntary organization, but in 1939 membership became compulsory for all young people between the ages of ten and eighteen unless prohibited by the Party race regulations. Towards the end of World War II membership was about 12 million. Since the Hitler Youth knife was authorized in

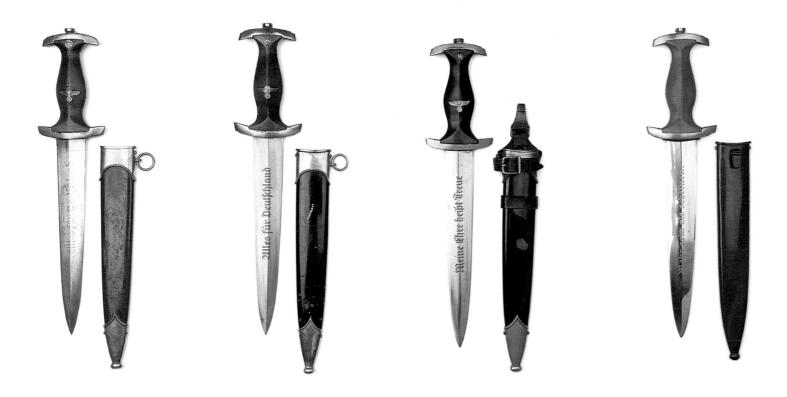

1933, it is not surprising that it was one of the commonest of all Third Reich hilted weapons. In shape the Hitler Youth knife resembled a small dress bayonet of a type commonly worn by troops when in uniform but off duty.

In 1934 the Labour Service was given a dagger with a broad chopper-like blade and the motto 'Arbeit adelt' ('Labour enobles'). This had a simple crossguard and a staghorn grip, and was carried in a big black, nickel-plated scabbard, and unlike most Nazi daggers, it was strong and intended to be used as a tool. Among the very last organizations granted the right to wear their own dagger was the Postal Protection Service. When war broke out in 1939, there were very few official bodies in Germany that did not have an official dagger, including some rather surprising groups such as the Red Cross and the Diplomatic Service.

A variety of other edged weapons were also made during the Nazi period, for bodies such as the German Rifle Association and the German National Hunting Association. These bodies favoured shortened versions of the traditional hunting hanger, with antler grips and small shell guards. Members of the National Forestry Service preferred a short sword with a knucklebow.

The armed forces of the Third Reich

In the German Navy (Kriegsmarine), as in most other European navies, officers traditionally wore a dagger or dirk. The post-war 1919 German naval dagger was straight-bladed, with a simple crossguard incorporating the fouled anchor device, a wire-bound black grip – changed to white in 1921 – and a flambeau pommel,

but in 1938 the authorities felt that the swastika should be part of the design. To minimize the inconvenience and expense to NCOs and officers it was decided that only the pommel need be altered, and so the old globe-and-flame pommel was changed for an eagle and swastika. The dagger was held in the scabbard by a spring catch which engaged with the lip of the locket.

The German Army (Heer) acquired the right to a dagger of its own in 1935. This was not greatly different from that of the Navy in general style, but the guard was in the form of an eagle with outspread wings grasping a swastika and the pommel had a rim of oak leaves. The grip was supplied in a variety of colours ranging from white to orange.

The German Air Force (Luftwaffe), under the command of World War I fighter ace Hermann Goering, was to play a crucial role in World War II and received special attention from the Nazis. The German Air Sports Formation had been set up after World War I to encourage everyone to take an interest in flying, and when it was dissolved in 1937 the National Socialist Flying Corps took its place. This body was, in effect, a training body for the Luftwaffe and as such had its own special dagger, rather similar to that authorized for the Luftwaffe in 1934.

The First Model Luftwaffe dagger, worn by officers and NCOs, had a longer blade than most other Nazi daggers, down-curved and flaring quillons, and a large circular pommel featuring a swastika. The scabbard was covered in blue leather and suspended from the belt by twin chains. Flying personnel were allowed to have an aluminium cord and tassel looped around the

Above, left to right
SA (Sturmabteilung) dagger with brown hilt and scabbard.
NSKK (Nationalsozialistisches Kraftkorps) dagger with brown hilt and black scabbard.
SS (Shutzstaffel) dagger with black hilt and scabbard.
NPEA (National-Politische Erziehungsanstalten) dagger, very similar to the SA dagger but with a different motto.

131

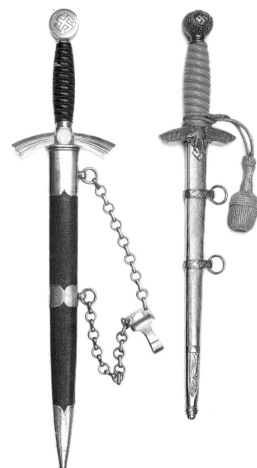

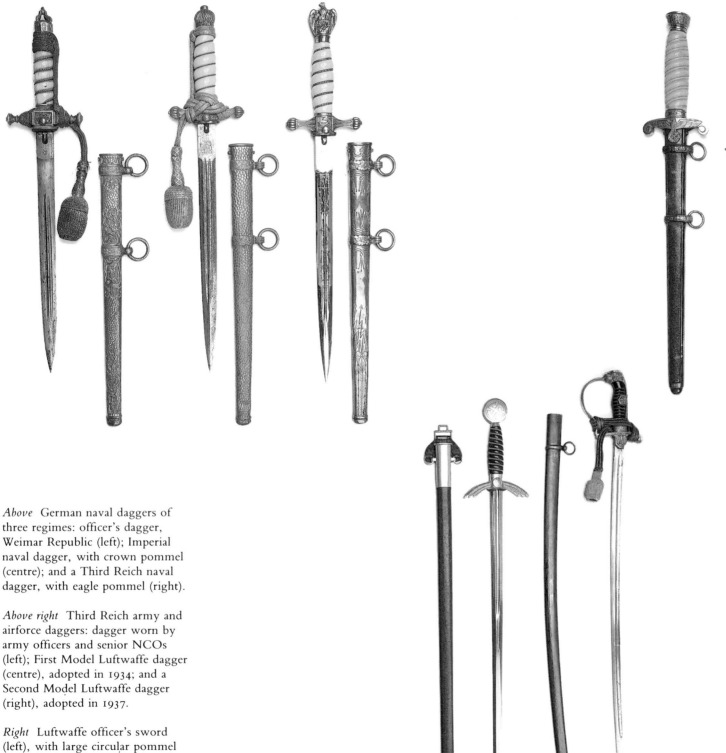

Above German naval daggers of three regimes: officer's dagger, Weimar Republic (left); Imperial naval dagger, with crown pommel (centre); and a Third Reich naval dagger, with eagle pommel (right).

Above right Third Reich army and airforce daggers: dagger worn by army officers and senior NCOs (left); First Model Luftwaffe dagger (centre), adopted in 1934; and a Second Model Luftwaffe dagger (right), adopted in 1937.

Right Luftwaffe officer's sword (left), with large circular pommel and flared quillons, and a Third Reich army officer's sword (right); with metal scabbard painted black.

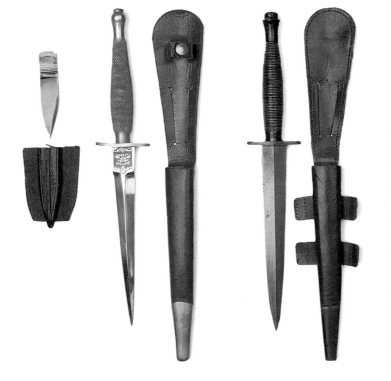

Left SOE lapel knife and sheath (left); First Pattern Fairbairn Sykes fighting knife (centre), with its distinctive slightly curved crossguard and blade etched with the maker's name; and a Third Pattern FS knife (right), with a straight guard and a scabbard designed to be worn in a variety of ways.

Above The FS knife used to attack from behind and worn concealed in a low leg position. Although great play was made of the knife and it was carried by many troops, it saw comparatively little service.

Below right The Smatchet was designed and made as a substantial and effective cutting weapon, although its use for thrusting was limited. It was produced in quantity in Britain and the United States during World War II.

grip. In 1937 a Second Model Luftwaffe dagger was introduced, this time for officers only. In place of the flared quillons of the first model it had an eagle with outstretched wings, grasping a swastika. It was also suspended from the belt by a double strap rather than a double chain.

The Solingen scheme was a resounding success, but the market for hilted weapons did not end with daggers for civilian and military bodies; there were also dress swords to be made for the various armed services. The sword most commonly worn by German army officers on formal occasions had a fairly narrow blade with a stirrup-shaped knucklebow, a lion-headed pommel, and langets, the latter usually bearing a device indicating the arm of the service, crossed swords for cavalry, crossed cannon for artillery, and so on. Naval dress swords were a little more elaborate, with a larger lion head, shell guards decorated with the fouled anchor motif and, most unusually, no swastika. The Luftwaffe dress sword was totally different, having a hilt similar to that of the First Model Luftwaffe dagger, with flared, down-turned quillons and a large circular pommel bearing the swastika. It was carried in a scabbard covered with blue leather, very different from the metal scabbards used by the army and the navy.

World War II and Special Services

In September 1939 the newly modernized German army struck against Poland. England and France declared war on Germany but could do little to assist the heroic resistance of the Poles. The combined might of the German army and the Luftwaffe, and the invasion of the Russians from the east, smashed Poland in less than four weeks. In April 1940 German forces occupied Norway and Denmark and an Allied expeditionary force to Norway was defeated. In May German troops pushed into neutral Holland and Belgium, and soon the Dutch surrendered, followed shortly afterwards by the Belgians. By June the Germans had won the battle of France and were the masters of most of Europe. Britain and the Commonwealth stood alone and the prospects looked grim.

But even as the fleet of small ships and boats evacuated the British and French from Dunkirk, a British officer, Lieutenant-Colonel Dudley Clarke, was starting a train of events that was to have a significant effect on the outcome of the war. He conceived the idea of fighting the enemy with small forces of highly trained men, working on their own with a minimum of support and back-up, who would strike suddenly and silently at special targets. His idea was put to the General Staff and in the incredibly short period of a few days the scheme was approved and Clarke was ordered to mount a raid as soon as possible.

Volunteers were called for 'special services'. The newly formed units were to be called Commandos, a back-handed compliment to the Boers who had given the British Army such a hard time in South Africa 40 years earlier. On 23–24 June Clarke's elite force, hastily trained and briefed, raided the French coast. Ironically, the

first man to be wounded on this raid was Clarke himself, but the raid was a success and many more were to follow.

Equipping the Commandos was not easy in June 1940, and items such as the Thompson submachine gun, the Tommy gun, could only be issued just before they were required. On the first raid half the country's entire supply was issued to the raiders – all 20! Training for this style of combat was tough and to a large extent was in the hands of two experts, Captain William Fairbairn and Captain Eric Sykes. Both had served in the Shanghai police and were well versed in street fighting and close combat. Their combat philosophy was simple: kill or be killed.

Initially the knife used by the Commandos was a knuckleduster knife known as the BC 41, very similar in design to some knives used in the World War I, with a shortish blade fitted with a brass knuckle hilt. It was adequate, but the knuckle section made it rather difficult to hold comfortably for certain blows. It was also felt to be rather limited for general use, for the Commandos had to be self-sufficient and able to butcher any animal they might catch for food. Various other knives were tried, but none seemed quite right, and so Sykes and Fairbairn approached the best-known British firm, the Wilkinson Sword Company, with their special requirements, and as a result of the collaboration the Fairbairn Sykes (FS) fighting knife was developed. The first consignment was delivered in January 1941.

The FS fighting knife had a tapering 7-in/18-cm double-edged blade with a simple oval, slightly S-shaped crossguard and a metal chequered grip with a bowling pin outline and a spherical nut at the pommel. It was carried in a brown leather sheath which could be attached to a belt by the usual loops or sewn to the uniform by means of tabs attached to the sides. There were variations on this

basic pattern, but they were insignificant, the knife being out-standingly well designed for its purpose. The FS fighting knife was issued to many different Special Forces in addition to the British Commandos and was copied by many manufacturers.

In 1943 another British fighting knife was produced which was a direct copy of the gravity knife used by German parachutists. This had a blade which retracted into the handle and was released by means of a catch on the side of it. The advantage of this arrangement was that the blade could be released with one hand, dropping into position under its own weight when the catch was operated and locking into place. It also had a versatile pivotted spike, useful as a tool and as a killing weapon. The British version was produced in quantity by the Sheffield firm of Ibberson. Another British fighting knife of the time was the menacing-looking Smatchet, which had a long elliptical double-edged blade with a simple grip and small crossguard. This was one design that Fairbairn and Sykes thoroughly approved of.

The quiet war

A weapon which, fortunately, was never put to the test was the emergency pike produced for the British Home Guard. During the worst period of the war, in 1940–42, Home Guard volunteers were often desperately short of weapons, and one stop-gap invention was the pike constructed of a metal tube with a 1907 Pattern bayonet welded into one end of it. With this primitive weapon the British Isles prepared to face the victorious German army. Fortunately they never came.

Although the Germans and Italians occupied most of Europe, there were many who opposed them, and a few extremely brave men and women actively fought them on their own ground. Various resistance movements, backed by the secret operations run by the British and Americans, the Special Operations Executive and the Office of Strategic Services, did much to harass the occupiers. SOE and OSS agents trained in sabotage, explosives, self-defence and similar skills were sent into Europe to work with the local underground. Various concealed and disguised weapons were used in this nasty war. Some were traditional hilted weapons with short triangular blades and small sheaths which could be fastened to the arm or leg; others were simply spikes with crude handles. Pens and pencils were a favourite means of concealment. One combination weapon even had a fine wire garotte in the hilt.

But war did not end with the German and Japanese surrender of 1945, and the numerous conflicts which have since blazed out across the world have stimulated new designs of weapon. Newer knives and bayonets continue to be made, and the only real difference between them and the weapons of the Middle Ages is their method of production. Human nature does not alter very much.

Below left Two British World War II Home Guard pikes fashioned from blades welded into lengths of gaspipe or tubing.

Bottom left German Flight Utility or gravity knife (below); the heavy blade dropped into place when the side catch was operated. The Ibberson knife (above) was the British equivalent.

11 SWORDS OF ISLAM

Anthony North

In those lands governed by the concepts of Islam, the sword and dagger have represented not only the wealth and authority of their owners but also the spirit of Islam. The banners carried by Islamic warriors bore the device of 'Dhu'l-Faqar' ('Zulfiqar'), the famous cloven blade used by the Prophet Mohammed, and the leaders of the Arab world today wear gold daggers with traditional dress as a symbol of status.

The study of early Islamic swords and daggers, that is to say of weapons from the seventh to the tenth centuries AD, is made especially frustrating by an almost complete lack of early dated or datable specimens. Very few early swords and daggers have been excavated under acceptable archaeological conditions, and the lack of representation on early miniatures and sculpture only compounds the problem. It is also a fallacy to assume that the advent of Islam and the *jihads* of Mohammed and his followers produced a sudden standardization of weaponry. The Islamic faith eventually spread across a huge geographical area, from Spain to India and the Mongolian steppes, and many regions retained their traditional weapon forms, some of them reaching back to the Bronze Age.

The metalworkers of Islam have always had a strong tradition of thrift, ruthlessly stripping gold and silver inlays from old or damaged weapons to make new. At the end of their useful life, therefore, edged weapons were reworked or cut down. Exceptionally, a sword or dagger associated with a special event or with a particular leader was preserved as a relic - the earliest surviving Arab and Persian swords come into this category.

The hilt construction of Arab swords differs from that of Western weapons. The pommel, for example, is not a weight to counterbalance the blade but merely a cap terminal for the grip; the tang of the blade is comparatively short and broad, and sometimes set at a slight angle to the blade; the grip is either glued to the tang or rivetted to it.

This seemingly fragile method of hilt construction, at least to Western eyes, was in fact extremely effective. Anyone who has tried to dismount the blade of an Indian or Arab sword from its hilt will quickly appreciate how adamantine the adhesives

Right Page from a late sixteenth-century Turkish manuscript showing Ali, Mohammed's son-in-law, wielding the sword 'Dhu'l Faqar'. The blade has been split in two.

employed were. This simple but effective method of hilt construction was certainly in use by the ninth century, for it is shown on swords depicted on frescoes of that date and also appears on swords of the same period excavated from Patzinakh graves near Kiev and Kursk in the Ukraine, and remained the standard mode of attaching hilts to tangs until the modern era. It has the great advantage of simplicity – a grip could be very easily replaced with simple materials such as horn or wood – and as Islamic swords were almost invariably designed for cutting, especially from horseback, the lack of a large defensive guard for the hand was not a serious disadvantage.

The reputation of Damascus as a manufacturing centre for fine quality blades has tended to overshadow other equally important centres of production. Early Arab writers on metallurgy, such as Al-Kindi (c.801–870), state that the finest swords came from the Yemen, Qal'a in the desert, and India. Damascus, as the capital of Syria, undoubtedly produced good blades, but its chief claim to fame was as a centre of distribution for fine weapons produced elsewhere. Much of this trade was with the West, which probably explains the reputation of 'Damascus' blades in the West.

Pre-Islamic and early Islamic weapons

The antecedents of many Arab and Ottoman swords and daggers are to found in the swords of the Sassanians, who ruled Persia from the third to the eighth century AD, and also in those of Bronze Age Luristan. The long straight-bladed broad swords of medieval times almost certainly have links with Byzantine and Sassanian cavalry swords. A Sassanian silver dish in the British Museum dating from 500 AD shows a mounted king wielding a long straight-bladed sword not unlike early Arab weapons. The well-known Turkish short sword, the *yataghan*, can also be traced back to prototypes used in Luristan in the tenth century BC. The very long curved narrow battle axe of Middle Kingdom Egypt (1990–1798 BC) may have been the prototype for the curved swords which the popular imagination always associates with Islam. Curved bronze swords had been in use for at least two millennia before Islam burst upon the world.

Above Bronze matrix for a sword guard, Seljuk, twelfth–thirteenth century. Matrices such as this appear to have been used to cast parts of sword hilts in silver or gold.

Left Cast silver dagger hilt with lions and flowers, Luristan, c.750 BC. This form of hilt was the prototype for the ear dagger and *yataghan*.

Above Bas relief of David and Goliath from the Armenian church of Gacık on Ağtamar Island, Lake Van, Turkey, c.920. Goliath is wearing lamellar armour and carries a sword, spear and shield.

Above right Straight single-edged sword excavated from a site in Nishapur, Central Asian (Avar?), ninth century. The sword, in the fragments of a wooden scabbard, was found beneath some tenth-century pottery. The quillons and scabbard mounts are of bronze.

Opposite page Parade sword with hilt and mounts of gold filigree with panels of cloisonné enamel, Hispano-Moresque, c.1500.

Although the early centuries of Islam lack material, the picture improves somewhat after the eighth century, with frescoes and sculptures providing useful information. A fresco dating from the tenth century, now in the Museum of Islamic Art in Teheran, depicts a mounted Persian warrior carrying a sword at his saddle-bow; the short quillons, cap-shaped pommel and scabbard mounts are clearly shown. There is also a wealth of material, some of which may well be early, preserved in the armoury of the Sultans in the Topkapı Palace in Istanbul. This includes swords and other weapons associated with the Prophet Mohammed (570–632) and his followers. Two of the swords in the Topkapı are said to have belonged to the Prophet himself; the hilts and scabbards of these have been enriched with precious stones and gold at a later date, as a courtesy to such a precious relic, but the blades have been left quite plain. One is broad, straight and double-edged, and the other is comparatively narrow, slightly curved and clearly of some antiquity. Various accounts are given of the famous sword 'Dhu'l Faqar' wielded by the Prophet at the battle of Badr in 624. Tradition has it that the blade was cloven in two near its point, and this is how it has been shown in manuscripts and on banners ever since. 'Dhu'l Faqar' was bequeathed to Ali, son-in-law to Mohammed, who was Caliph from 656 to 661.

Also in the Topkapı collection are swords associated with two Arab commanders, Khalid ibn al-Walid (d. 641) and Zayn al-Abidin (d. 712). Significantly, these swords are straight, double-edged and broad, as are many old weapons, that associated with Zayn al-Abidin being particularly broad and massive. Unfortunately the date of these blades cannot be established, although the hilts and scabbards could well date from the fourteenth century, being similar to those shown in manuscripts of that period.

The grips of early medieval Islamic swords were usually of wood covered with skin or leather. The guard consisted of a simple cross with extensions known as langets projecting down the front of the grip and down the face of the blade; these gave a firm seating to the grip and also ensured a snug fit on the scabbard. We know this from the fine early scabbards preserved with the Topkapı swords described above. These are of wood, with metal mounts at top and bottom and two metal metal reinforcing collars half way down from which scabbard and sword were suspended.

Judging from the early swords in the Topkapı collection, several styles of crossguard seem to have been current in the thirteenth and fourteenth centuries. The sword of Zayn al-Abidin, for example, is fitted with a guard with arms of rounded section. A crossguard formed as a pointed spatula is also found on some of the swords associated with the Prophet's followers. During the thirteenth century a type of guard was introduced with arms which curved sharply down towards the blade and terminated in animal heads with gaping jaws. This type is found as late as the fifteenth century and was produced in jade as well as metal.

As the reader may have gathered, the early swords in the Topkapı cannot be dated with any precision. While the scabbards and hilts are unlikely to be earlier than the thirteenth century, the blades, especially the narrow, slightly curved blade on one of the swords attributed to the Prophet, may well be of very early date.

The introduction of the curved single-edged sword seems to have occurred in the eighth or ninth century. A single-edged sword with a distinctive curve is shown on a ninth-century fresco from Avolokitesvaru in eastern Turkestan, for example, and by the thirteenth century the standard 'scimitar' blade profile, with a distinct broadening towards the point, was being depicted in manuscripts. It should be noted that curved blades only gradually became more widely used than straight-bladed weapons, and until the fourteenth century both straight and curved blades seem to have been equally common.

Various interesting early Islamic swords have been excavated, albeit in fragmentary condition. One of the most significant, because it retained its blade, gilt bronze hilt and the remains of a scabbard, was found at Nishapur in northeastern Iran. The blade is fairly narrow and may have been slightly curved since the hilt appears to have been set at an angle to it, and the guard is cast with palmette terminals. The scabbard has a series of reinforcing bronze mounts fitted to it, including a flap of bronze set at the top, a feature found on some Sassanian weapons. This interesting sword was retrieved from a level which indicated a date in the ninth century, and shares many of the characteristics of the second of the Prophet's swords mentioned above. The Patzinakh grave swords referred to above, which may also date from the ninth century, have straight, narrow, single-edged blades, stubby cruci-form guards, cap-like pommels, and very angular tangs. The scabbards had metal mounts, the bottom one cut off square, as on the Nishapur sword.

Few daggers survive from early Islamic times, but a silver-hilted dagger in the British Museum dating from 750 BC may be a guide to at least one early form. In shape it is virtually identical to those made in the Maghrebi countries of North Africa until this century. The pommel consists of an oval plate divided vertically, with projections towards the hand. There are few illustrations of daggers in early sources and any attempts at reconstruction must be purely speculative.

Medieval Islamic swords

Developments from the eleventh century onwards are easier to trace because one is assisted by extant weapons, contemporary manuscripts and sculpture. A type of hilt which clearly owed a debt to the swords of Rome and Byzantium had a short, straight grip with a small pommel, and a guard with short quillons folded down the blade, forming a sleeve into which the short, straight, double-edged blade was set. Swords of this type are shown on carved ivory boxes from eleventh-century Moorish Spain, and an even earlier representation appears on a tenth-century relief of Goliath from the church of Gacık on Ağtamar Island in Lake Van in Turkey. An actual hilt of this type, made in bronze, was discovered in a shipwreck at Serce Liman in Turkey in 1977.

The fragmentary hilts of several Seljuk-period swords (mid-eleventh to mid-fourteenth centuries) seem to be related to the type just described, in that the guard is constructed as a sleeve, with cast reliefs of animals or geometric designs. The pommel takes the form of a simple cap. One of the guards is of silver gilt decorated with niello, although bronze guards have also been discovered. These may have been matrices from which versions in precious metal were cast, but there is no reason why hilts should not also have been made of bronze.

In the Askeri Museum in Istanbul are a number of swords with hilts of steel which seem to be related to those of the Seljuk period. These have short quillons, bronze grips and cap pommels, the blades being long, straight and broad. On the basis of inscriptions on the blades, which record their deposition in the arsenal at Alexandria, these were probably manufactured in the fourteenth and fifteenth centuries. Another related hilt form, said to be Omani and of fifteenth-century date, has a cap pommel and short quillons with short projections which turn down towards the blade.

The civilization of Moorish Spain, which endured for seven centuries, has left surprisingly few examples of the armourer's art. The only swords known are a handful of parade weapons decorated in the most ornate style, the work of jewellers rather than armourers. The best known of these is the sword associated with Boabdil, the last emir of the last corner of Moorish Spain, Granada, who was deposed in 1492. It is preserved in the Cabinet des Médailles in Paris. The hilts of these highly decorated weapons are of cast gold, with filigree work set with panels of cloisonné enamel bearing inscriptions in Arabic. One of the gilt copper sheath mounts from the group is in the Victoria and Albert Museum; another sheath has mounts of gilded and pierced iron. In fact the whole group poses problems for scholars: it is not certain where they were made and they do not seem to replicate any other known hilt form. Current opinion is that they were produced as regalia swords, their hilts being deliberately archaic.

The Ottoman period

Curved single-edged blades became increasingly fashionable after 1400, especially in Persia and in those areas under Ottoman influence (by 1341 the Ottoman Turks had ousted the Seljuk Turks from Asia Minor and by 1444 they were masters of the Balkans). As early as the twelfth century, blades had been engraved with titles and names. This tradition had become firmly established by the mid-fifteenth century, enabling many surviving blades to be dated within precise time brackets. In a few instances details of the maker and place of manufacture are also given. The inscriptions are usually inlaid in gold along the length of the blade. A sword made for the Mamluk Sultan Tumanbay I, who reigned for three months only in 1501, gives the very formal, resonant flavour of such inscriptions: 'The Sultan, the Royal al-Malik al-Adil Abu'l Nasir Tumanbay, Sultan of Islam and all Muslims, Father of the Poor and the Miserable, Killer of the Unbelievers and the Polytheists, Reviver of Justice among All, may God prolong his kingdom and may his victory be glorious'. In 1517 the Mamluks, who had ruled Egypt, Palestine and part of Libya since 1250, were destined to succumb to the Ottomans.

The blade of Tumanbay's sword is curved, with a broad channel in which the inscription is inlaid and a pronounced back. A short section near the point has been sharpened on the back. This comparatively simple, light blade seems to have been very fashionable around 1500, especially in Mamluk lands. The Ottomans, however, preferred a heavier, broader blade. In Topkapı collections are the swords of Mehmet the Conqueror (1451–81), who captured Constantinople, and Bayczid II (1481–1512). These are massive broad-bladed weapons. One of the swords of Mehmet is clearly a two-handed weapon; the long grip is composed of ivory plaques and the heavy, single-edged blade has a long point. Swords of this form are in fact shown in contemporary miniatures.

An interesting blade in the Victoria and Albert Museum bears the genealogy of Shah Tamasp, ruler of Persia from 1524 to 1576. This too is of massive proportions, although it has been cut down at some period to fit a change of hilt. In the process some elements of the long inscription on the blade have been lost. As on the sword of Mehmet II, the inscription appears in a widish channel which runs the length of the blade.

In the early part of the sixteenth century the heavy Ottoman blade gave way to a much lighter, more strongly curved type, usually forged with a ridge at the back for strength. These blades have a pronounced widening at the section near the point and a broad channel running some way down the centre of the blade. The general effect is very elegant and the style remained fashionable, with minor adaptations, until the nineteenth century. The

tradition of inlaid work in gold and silver continued, but the prayers, genealogies, poems and formalized titulatures which are such an enjoyable part of the study of Islamic blades are unfortunately rare. The poems especially, found on swords and daggers, often contain powerful images of love or war. A late sixteenth-century Ottoman blade in Dresden bears the verses: 'May your blade be as prosperous as the Palace of Knowledge,/O you whose aspirations are those of Faridun, the courage that of Rostam, the glory that of Jamshid./May your blade be victorious over the necks of your foes.' On a sixteenth-century Persian dagger, also in Dresden, there is the verse: 'A dream about thy dagger appears in my eye like a tear,/Like the moon which whirls hither and thither in the water'.

Characteristic of Turkish hilts of the first half of the sixteenth century is the skilful use of ivory, silver and niello. The cruciform guard, small pommel cap and short grip were retained until the seventeenth century. A rare form which derived from medieval prototypes consisted of a bulbous grip formed in one with the sleeve guard and pommel; hilts like this are usually of silver gilt, embossed and worked in the wrythen style fashionable in the 1550s. The sword said to be that of the last Emperor of Byzantium, Constantine XI Dragazes Palaeologus (1448–53), is of this type and is unusual in that it is made entirely of steel. The silver gilt form was certainly still in use in the late seventeenth century and some examples with enamelled floral decoration may be of early eighteenth-century date. The blades fitted to them are almost invariably straight broadsword blades of German origin.

In the seventeenth and eighteenth centuries there was a tendency for the Ottoman sword to become shorter, even more strongly curved, and broader, with a very thick ridged back. The cap pommel was replaced with the characteristic pistol-shaped grip made of horn or ivory. The scabbard was of wood, mounted in embossed silver. Swords of this type seem to have been used over a very wide geographical area and are often found in European collections, taken as trophies in sea fights. An interesting example can be seen in the National Maritime Museum at Greenwich, London. On the blade is the maker's name, Mustafa, the name of the owner, Haj Mahmud Bey, and its date of manufacture, 1768/9. It belonged to a Lieutenant William Tottenham, who fought in the Greek War of Independence (1822–29) and took part in the attack on Morea Castle in the Peloponnese.

Many Ottoman blades are decorated with engraved and chiselled decoration in addition to gold inlay work. From the sixteenth century it became fashionable to chisel out areas of the blade near the hilt in arabesques. In the finest work the blade is cut away in closely interwoven floral designs and the gold set flush with the surface, giving a very rich effect. One group of straight Ottoman blades, identified as dating from the second half of the sixteenth century, is damascened in gold and silver with dragons and simorghs (monstrous birds which, according to Persian myth, had the power of speech and reason) and also with Persian verses. Most of these exotic blades are mounted in fine early seventeenth-century European hilts, suggesting that they were either captured during Turkish advances into Eastern Europe or sent as gifts to leaders whom the Turks hoped to influence. The workshop which produced them seems to have been a court workshop in Istanbul. The very elaborate decoration found on sixteenth- and seventeenth-century Ottoman metalwork also appears on swords and daggers. Some have hilts and scabbards mounted with jade plaques, large turquoises and other precious stones. Many of these luscious weapons, which were intended solely for parade, appear in the collections of Eastern Europe (Vienna, Budapest, Cracow) where Turkish arms and dress were much admired.

Regional variations

The short cap-like extension set at an angle at the top of the grip is one of the characteristic features of Islamic swords. In North Africa, however, and possibly as early as the fifteenth century, a form of hilt evolved in which the cap pommel became simply a large angular extension protecting the back of the hand, both cap and pommel being made in one. Swords with this type of hilt were known as *nimchas* and were used from the late sixteenth century onwards. In the more complex forms the guard consists of two downward-curving quillons, a knuckleguard and a prominent wide ring. Another feature found on many early examples is the cusp-like projection where the hilt joints the blade. This feature appears on a large number of late fourteenth- and fifteenth-century Italian hilts and the ring and knuckleguard construction clearly derives from Western European prototypes. It is significant that the region where these swords are found was one where trade and conflict between Islam and the West were very frequent.

The earliest *nimchas* were mounted with straight European blades, many from Venice and Genoa, but by the seventeenth century a short broad curved blade became fashionable, usually made by local blacksmiths. This type was especially popular for use at sea. Like the European curved hanger, it was a convenient size for use in the confines of a deck. There are several fine weapons of this type in Western European armouries which were taken at sea. One in the Rijksmuseum in Amsterdam is included in the trophies of the Dutch admiral Cornelis Van Tromp, who

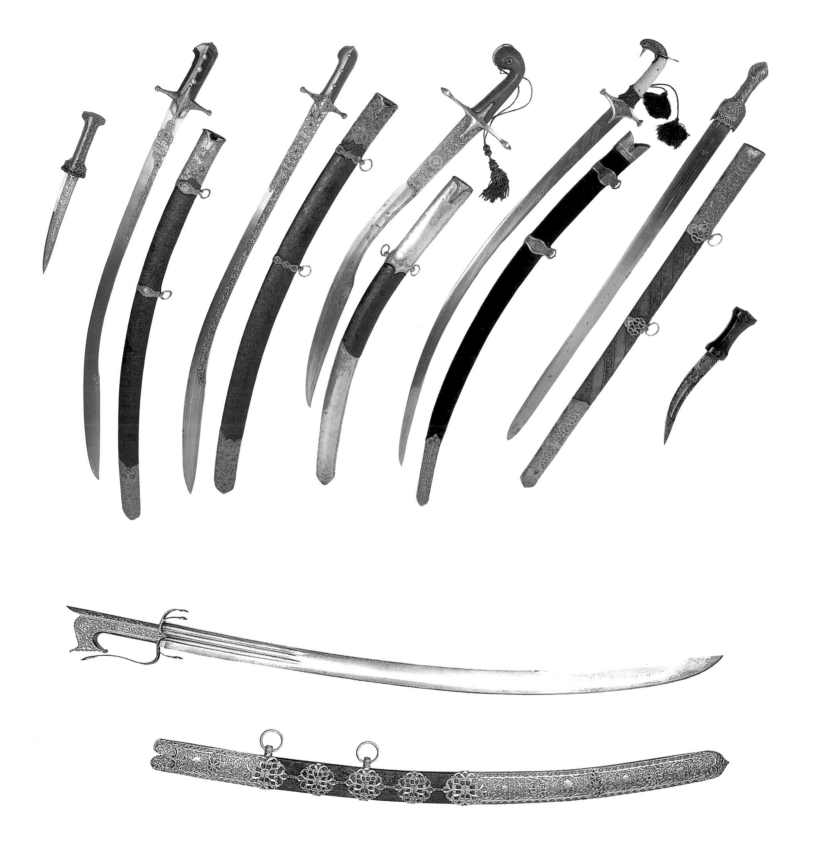

Above Copper gilt sword grip set with silver panels decorated with niello, Arab, seventeenth century.

Above left Group of Turkish and Persian swords and daggers with silver mounts and blades inlaid with gold, sixteenth–eighteenth century.

Below left Sword with silver hilt and scabbard mounts, North African (Morocco), seventeenth–eighteenth century.

Opposite page Sword of Mehmet the Conqueror (1451–1481), with the genealogy of the Sultan inlaid in gold along the blade (top), and the sword of Shah Tamasp, ruler of Persia from 1524–1576 (left and below left). Both are rare survivals of heavy fighting swords.

The gold inscriptions on the sword of Shah Tamasp stop abruptly at the guard, indicating that the blade has been shortened at some period.

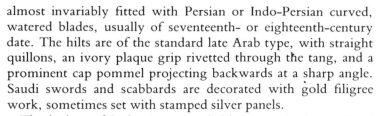

Below, left to right

Sword and scabbard of the Sultan of Darfur, Sudanese, nineteenth–twentieth century. The hilt is mounted in gold and the blade is incised with genealogies and invocations.

damascened in gold with the maker's name 'Abdallah ib. Ibrahim', Sudanese, *c.*1610. The hilt is mounted in embossed silver. Some of the swords used by the Mahdi's forces in the 1880s were mounted with heirloom blades.

Yataghan with silver scabbard and blade damascened in gold with verses, Turkish, *c.*1800. The blade has been etched to imitate watered steel.

captured it from an Algerian pirate in 1648. Another in the National Maritime Museum at Greenwich belonged to the English admiral Sir Thomas Hopsonn, a lieutenant on HMS *Dragon*, which boarded an Algerian corsair in 1676. This hilt is mounted in pierced and engraved silver. The convenient size and excellent grip made such swords fashionable in Europe in the first half of the seventeenth century and a number of contemporary European portraits show them being worn with fashionable clothes. Without external evidence, they are hard to date accurately but in general the earlier forms, that is to say those made before 1700, tend to have rather narrow grips, often mounted with silver plaques. Some late parade versions were made in the nineteenth century, probably for presentation, but the guards tend to be clumsy, being constructed of one large ivory block, and the blades are very narrow and weak.

A variation on the *nimcha* hilt, the *saif*, was used in Arabia, probably from the seventeenth century. The term *saif* is rather loosely used and true Arab *saifs* are comparatively rare. The authentic article has a hilt which is usually made entirely of silver, the short projection at the top of the grip lacking the elegant curve of the Mediterranean forms. These hilts are often cast with raised plaques and decorated with floral scrolls filled with niello. Inscriptions are usually invocations to Allah and a prayer for victory, and occasionally a date and a maker's name are found engraved in panels on the hilt. As with the *nimcha*, the blades of better quality *saifs* are of European origin, single-edged and curved.

In Saudi Arabia the very angular cap pommel seems to have been adopted during the eighteenth century. Saudi swords are almost invariably fitted with Persian or Indo-Persian curved, watered blades, usually of seventeenth- or eighteenth-century date. The hilts are of the standard late Arab type, with straight quillons, an ivory plaque grip rivetted through the tang, and a prominent cap pommel projecting backwards at a sharp angle. Saudi swords and scabbards are decorated with gold filigree work, sometimes set with stamped silver panels.

The *kaskara* of Sudan is a remarkable survival of a medieval Arab weapon. It has the hilt and blade of the straight-bladed broadswords used in the late medieval period, the only significant difference being that the pommel is a circular disc. The majority of *kaskaras* date from the nineteenth century, although some are mounted with heirloom blades. The best known are those from the personal armoury of the Sultan of Darfur in Eastern Sudan who was killed by the British in 1916 for intriguing with the Turks. The hilts are mounted in silver and gold, and the Sultan's name usually appears inscribed on the blades and crossguards.

A weapon which can be traced back in an almost unbroken line to the Bronze Age in Luristan is the *yataghan*. Its ancestor was the short bronze sword with ear-like projections at the top of the hilt, a type already well established by the tenth century BC. Similar weapons were still being made in the early part of this century.

The *yataghan* was extensively used in Turkey and in those areas under Turkish influence, such as the Balkans, but its history and appearance in medieval times is not known since the earliest recorded examples, made of iron, date from the sixteenth century.

The *yataghan* was really a short sword and consisted of a single-edged blade with a marked forward curve and a hilt formed of plaques attached through the tang, the end of the hilt being shaped like large ears. What are clearly the detached blades of *yataghans* have been found in sixteenth-century archaeological contexts in Yugoslavia, mostly from forts occupied by the Turks.

Undoubtedly the finest and one of the earliest examples of the type was the weapon made for Suleyman the Magnificent, who ruled over the still expanding Ottoman empire from 1522 to 1566. This sword now lies in the treasury of the Topkapı Palace in Istanbul and is of particular interest in that it is not only dated, 1526/7, but also has the name of the artist who made it, Ahmed Tekelü, on the back of the blade. It is a weapon of unparalleled richness and one of the great works of art of the Ottoman period. The hilt is of ivory overlaid with gold delicately carved with cloudbands and scrolls. The blade is set with applied figures of a simorgh and a dragon amid applied gold floral scrolls. Near the hilt, the blade is inlaid with gold verses in praise of Sultan Suleyman, and the date quoted above.

The majority of *yataghans* date from the period 1750–1860, and from the number of plain, wooden-hilted weapons that survive in areas such as Vienna, unsuccessfully besieged by the Turks in 1683, they were honest fighting weapons as well as parade weapons. Occasionally blades were cut down from broadswords or cavalry swords, but in general the forward-curving single-

edged blade was used. Verses in gold or silver are often laid along the blade, together with details of the owner and maker. Various hilt materials were employed – wood, bone, ivory, silver – and sometimes the hilt style betrays a particular place of origin, especially on examples made in the late eighteenth century and the first half of the nineteenth. Silver hilts mounted with filigree and coral, for example, are associated with Bosnia; many of these are dated 1800 or thereabouts. The scabbards of the richest examples are of wood, entirely mounted with silver embossed in the flamboyant late Ottoman style. Having no guard, the *yataghan* fitted closely into the top of the scabbard; this was customarily worn thrust into a waist sash, retained by a hook. Many *yataghan* blades bear clearly stamped armourer's marks and many silver-mounted examples carry a *tughra* or Turkish reign mark. Sometimes the date and name of the owner are set into nielloed plaques on the hilt.

The area of Daghestan in the Caucasus was an important centre for the manufacture of fine arms in pre-Islamic times. The favourite weapon of the region was the short sword known as the *kindjal*. This had a two-edged blade with a long point and a waisted grip without a guard, and was mounted in silver decorated with niello or with ivory inlaid with gold. The blades were made by craftsmen in Amuzgi and Kharbuk, then sent for mounting and finishing to the metalworkers of Kubachi. Most surviving *kindjals* date from the first half of the nineteenth century, many being made for Russian clients.

Persian weapons

Swords made by the armourers of Persia had a high reputation throughout the Near and Middle East from the earliest times, but so few examples survive that it is difficult to distinguish early Persian weapons from those of other regions. The ninth-century Nishapur sword mentioned near at the beginning of this chapter is possibly one of the earliest surviving examples, but a definite Persian style did not really emerge until the fourteenth century. Contemporary manuscripts such as the 'Demotte' *Shah-Nameh* ('Book of Kings') of 1340–50 show both straight and curved single-edged blades being worn. The crossguard is usually of spatulate form, with projections down the hilt and blade; the grips taper slightly towards cap pommels and are made of plaques rivetted through the tang, with the rivet heads forming a decorative feature. The scabbards are cut off square at the end and reinforced with metal bands. Since the grips are often shown as white, one assumes they were of ivory or bone, but the mounts are gilt. Several swords of this general pattern are preserved in the Topkapı and may well date from the first half of the fourteenth century. Although the pommels are of engraved gold, the quillons are usually of steel.

Below left Detail from a sixteenth-century Turkish manuscript depicting Suleyman the Magnificent (1496–1566) at the Battle of Mohács in 1526, when the forces of Islam triumphed over King Louis II of Hungary and captured Buda. Three years later Suleyman besieged Vienna.

Below *Yataghan* of Suleyman I, Turkish, dated 1526/7. The grip is of carved ivory, and the blade is decorated in relief with dragons and monsters and a gold inscription in praise of Suleyman. On the back edge of the blade is the name of the goldsmith Ahmed Tekelü.

Bottom Silver-hilted *yataghan* and scabbard, Turkish, dated 1777. Hilt and scabbard are decorated with filigree and set with coral, and the blade is damascened in silver with the maker's name, 'Umar', and the name of an owner, 'Mustafa'.

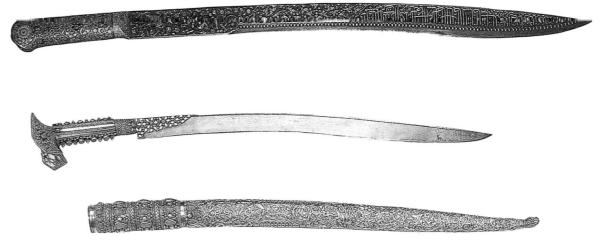

Persian swords were renowned for the quality of their blades, which used 'watered' steel, the surface of which appears like moiré silk, with alternating bands of light and dark wavy lines. This effect was created by forging the blade from steel ingots containing a very high proportion of carbon. The dense, dark areas on a blade are the carbon whereas the light-coloured areas are formed by particles of iron carbide. The contrast was enhanced by etching the surface with acid. Surface colour could also be altered by using different chemicals and by repeatedly etching the surface, which tended to darken it.

Persia had large resources of iron, probably exploited since the second millenium, in the Elburz Mountains and around Fars, Qutruh, Masula and Tabriz. Islamic scientists studied and wrote treatises upon the different methods of manufacturing steel, and their texts would have been available to swordsmiths. Watered steel was especially good for the manufacture of cutting weapons because it combined hardness with elasticity and could be sharpened to a very fine, tough edge. Watered steel as a raw material was supplied in the form of flat cakes known as *wootz*, which were then forged by specialist craftsmen into the required shape. By skilful forging, the smith was able to arrange the watering of the blade into particular patterns. The highly prized Mohammed's Ladder pattern, which has a series of transverse 'rungs' down the length of the blade, was produced by cutting horizontal grooves across the plane of the blade, then forging these flat.

Although most Persian hilts are of steel, a few surviving specimens are of jade. The first of these date from the early part of the fifteenth century and are preserved in the Topkapı. Jade is used for the grips and the crossguards, which are most beautifully carved as dragons' heads, and the mounts are of silver and gold. These have been attributed to the workshop of Ulugh Beg, working in Samarkand in 1417–79.

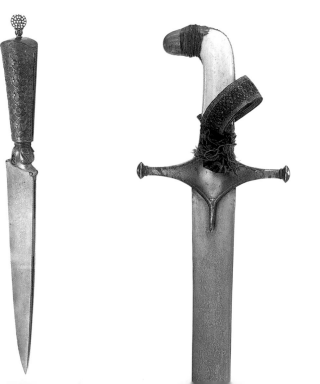

The form of the Persian blade – flat, long, elegantly curved and tapering gradually to a point – changed little from the sixteenth to the eighteenth century. Some early seventeenth-century blades have a series of channels cut towards the back of the blade, possibly to remove imperfections revealed by sharpening – the same technique is used on Japanese blades. The maker's signature and details of ownership are usually engraved, then inlaid with gold, the owner's name often being inscribed on the back of the blade. The names that occur most often are those of Asad Allah (or Assadullah) of Isfahan and Kalb Ali. These are arranged in cartouches in a set formula and should be interpreted as quality marks rather than as indications of the actual maker. Both Asad Allah and Kalb Ali are generally accepted as having worked during the reign of Shah Abbas (*c.*1557–1628), probably at Isfahan. However, their names appear with a variety of dates and it must reluctantly be accepted that very few of the blades bearing their names are likely to have been their personal work.

Although the majority of Persian blades are curved, at least one straight blade of early date has been identified. This blade, lacking its hilt, is double-edged, surface-chiselled in relief palmette design and damascened, and has been attributed to a workshop in Tabriz operating about 1500.

Because Persian blades changed so little, especially between 1500 and 1700, they pose considerable dating problems. In general, however, broad heavy blades with linear watering can be dated to the period before 1700. After that there was a trend towards lighter, more strongly curved blades. The watering also becomes much denser. Being relatively fragile, grips and pommels would have been replaced quite often, so are of little use in establishing dates. The crossguards of swords made before 1600 often terminate in spatulate quillons, whereas those of a later date are usually simple turned knobs. A large crossguard with long quillons may also be taken as an indication of an early date.

It is often very difficult to distinguish between Persian blades and those of India. There is no doubt that Indian blades were imported into Persia from the earliest times, and many Persian blades may in fact be Indian blades imported in an unfinished state, then completed and furnished with the marks of well-known Persian makers.

Decorative techniques

For the decoration of fine quality arms, every skill of the armourer and metalworker was employed. The tradition of inlaid work in gold and silver was very strong, especially in Egypt and Syria, from which very fine metalwares of bronze inlaid with gold and silver survive, dating from the thirteenth century. The weapons of certain areas such as Arabia have traditionally been mounted in gold because it was readily available. Silver is very commonly used for scabbard and hilt mounts all over the Islamic world.

Other techniques such as enamelling and the use of lacquer are also found, especially in Persia, which had a strong tradition in

these crafts. Finely pierced steel work was also a speciality of Persian craftsmen, who often combined it with the use of so-called damascening in gold and silver. This is a form of inlay produced by tapping thin ribbons of gold and silver wire into a surface which has been cross-hatched with a sharp engraving tool. The surface is usually darkened and blued with the aid of chemicals to provide a vivid contrast with the gold and silver. Scrollwork arabesques, floral decoration and inscriptions were all put on swords and daggers using this technique. Superficially, damascened work, when it is well done, can look impressive, but the ribbons of precious metal were easily removed by cleaning and any rust tended to lift them away from the surface. The best inlaid work involved cutting away the surface of the steel with a chisel, leaving a dovetail recess into which gold or silver wire was then hammered. Not only did this give a very firm seating for the inlays, it also permitted comparatively large pieces of gold and silver to be used. These could then be engraved or modelled to the required profile. Inlaid work of this quality is comparatively rare, since it required a trained engraver and entailed considerable

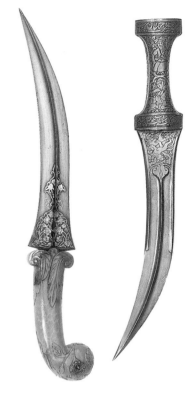

Above Dagger with carved jade hilt and watered steel blade inlaid with gold, Indo-Persian, eighteenth century (left), and a Persian dagger of about 1840 with hilt and blade of chiselled watered steel (right).

Left 'Jamshid and the Artisans', detail from a sixteenth-century Persian manuscript showing armourers forging and filing blades and repairing armour.

Opposite page, left to right
Page from the manuscript *Khusrau and Shirin* by Nizami, showing the battle between Bahram Chubina and Khusrau Parviz. Persian, *c.*1540.
Dagger with watered steel blade and steel grip chiselled in relief with floral scrolls, Persian *c.*1600.
Sword with watered steel blade inlaid with the name of the swordsmith Assadullah of Isfahan, Persian, seventeenth century. The grip is of ivory and the steel guard is damascened in gold.

Above Ivory-handled dagger with watered steel blade chiselled with inscriptions, Persian, dated 1824.

Right Seventeenth-century Turkish parade sword with silver hilt and scabbard mounts set with turquoises and panels of jade (left) and a twentieth-century Omani dagger, made for a member of the Saidi family (right). The dagger hilt is of rhinoceros horn mounted in gold. By tradition, such daggers may only be worn by an Omani ruler or his family.

expense, large quantities of gold and silver being used in the process. This technique was often used for inlaying maker's or owner's names into the flat of the blade near the hilt or along the back edge of the blade. In the fifteenth and sixteenth centuries it was used to decorate fine quality Persian daggers and swords with verses and arabesques.

Other metalworking techniques such as chiselling and engraving were extensively used on swords and daggers. The fine interwoven arabesque scrolls found on seventeenth- and eighteenth-century Persian weapons necessitated the removal of all the steel surrounding the design before any attempt was made to work on the area of ornament itself. Pierced work in steel was usually reserved for guard ornamentation and lockets on scabbards.

In the late Ottoman period, that is in the eighteenth and nineteenth centuries, scabbard mounts and the scabbards themselves were decorated with embossed work, where the required design is punched out from the back using a punch and hammer. This technique was widely used on the scabbards of *yataghans*.

Persian and Turkish daggers often have hilts carved from hardstones such as jade, rock crystal and occasionally onyx. A typical form from Turkey has a strongly waisted grip which is facetted and inlaid with engraved arabesques in gold. The type most often found, however, is the pistol-grip hilt, echoing the design of sword hilts. Semi-precious stones mounted in gold flowers were often inlaid into the surface. The majority of carved hardstone hilts, however, come from Moghul India.

Mention should also be made of the skilful use of base metals such as brass and copper for sword and dagger hilts. The craftsmen of the Maghreb in North Africa were able to produce great variety in their daggers by using very simple materials such as brass, often combined with silver. These were engraved in 'wriggle work', in which a narrow engraving tool is used to produce a zig-zag line across the surface, the ground of the design being filled with coloured compositions. The Ottomans used gilt copper (*tombak*) for many of their finer metalwares, including daggers, in the sixteenth and seventeenth centuries, although gilt copper appears less frequently on sword mounts. The finer examples seem to have been cast, then worked up afterwards with chisels and engraving tools.

Dagger forms

It is nonsense really to talk about 'Islamic daggers' since the huge geographical region covered by Islam meant that the varieties of design were legion. The *jambiya* used in the Maghreb and Arabia, for example, can be directly related to types used in Luristan in the eighth century BC.

One of the earliest types of dagger to be identified as 'Islamic' comes from Persia. This and others like it have been dated, on the basis of inscriptions, to the last quarter of the fifteenth century. Made entirely of steel, the hilt is chiselled in relief, with panels showing dragons, birds and kylins (fabulous animals) set amidst

foliage. The blade is short, double-edged and slightly curved, decorated with multiple grooves. The scabbard is mounted with ray skin, with long chiselled steel chapes at top and bottom.

Some very beautiful Ottoman ivory-hilted daggers dating from the first half of the sixteenth century have been preserved in armouries and treasuries. These are made without a guard and are carved in high relief with interwoven palmettes and flowers. The blades are comparatively short, often damascened in gold and pierced with slots. The scabbards, where they survive, are of ivory carved in a similar manner to the hilt.

Hardstone hilts are a characteristic of many Islamic daggers. Rock crystal, jade and agate are all found, sometimes set with other stones mounted in gold.

A very elegant single-edged knife used extensively in Persia was the *kard*. This has a blade of watered steel, often chiselled with palmette scroll reliefs near the hilt. The grip consisted of bone or ivory plaques but had no guard, simply slotting into the top of the scabbard. It is not known when the *kard* was first introduced in Persia but there are examples bearing dates in the early years of the seventeenth century. However it seem to have been especially fashionable in the second half of the eighteenth and early nineteenth centuries.

The dagger has always been an important feature of ceremonial dress in Arabia. The formal dress dagger is the *jambiya*, which usually has a strongly waisted grip with a flat-topped pommel and a broad curved blade; the scabbard has a very strong curve, often curving back towards the grip. Weapons like these really come into the category of jewellery and the most lavish decoration is used on the mounts and scabbards – gold filigree work, silver set

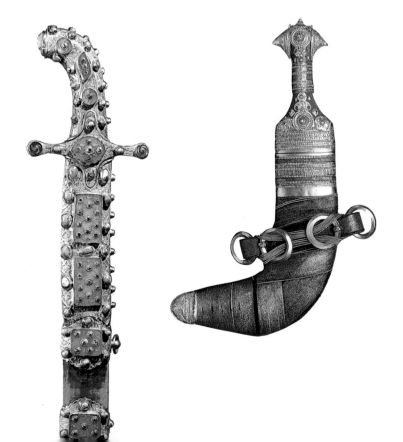

with coral, precious stones, amber, coins and so on. Regional and tribal differences are denoted by different hilt designs and by the different colours of the cords used to attach the dagger to the sash.

The use of ivory for dagger hilts was very fashionable in Persia, especially in the nineteenth century, when carved relief techniques were widely used. The usual form had a waisted grip, carved in low relief with figures, flowers and inscriptions – maker, owner and date – and was fitted with a good-quality watered blade. The scabbard was usually of laquered wood. Moghul India also adopted a similar form, known to collectors as a *khanjar*.

Also in Persia in the eighteenth and nineteenth century there was a revival of the fine steel daggers first produced in the sixteenth. The hilts and scabbards are made entirely of steel, chiselled and engraved with cartouches containing verses and scenes from Persian epics. Less expensive daggers in this style were decorated with crudely etched designs. These were widely copied all over the Near East and formed the models for the crude souvenir daggers sold today.

Historical bias

The majority of Islamic weapons that have come into Western collections by purchase or by war are items of luxury – the *Turkenbeute* ('Turkish booty') to be seen in many of the castles of Eastern Europe and Germany were the possessions of rich pashas, not of ordinary troops. Except for a few examples in the military museums in Vienna and in the Askeri Museum in Istanbul, humbler 'munition' weapons have not survived. This has led students to draw wrong conclusions about the arms of Islam. A hint of the equipment worn by the ordinary Turkish soldier is provided by the large number of plain swords and cheaply produced armour to be seen in the Askeri Museum in Istanbul, but in many areas, such as Persia, Islamic India and Arabia, only the most finely wrought and luxurious arms have been preserved. In all likelihood, the common soldier whose courage and endurance provided Islam with its earliest conquests was comparatively lightly armed, with sword, spear and shield, only his leaders having the wealth to buy fine weapons.

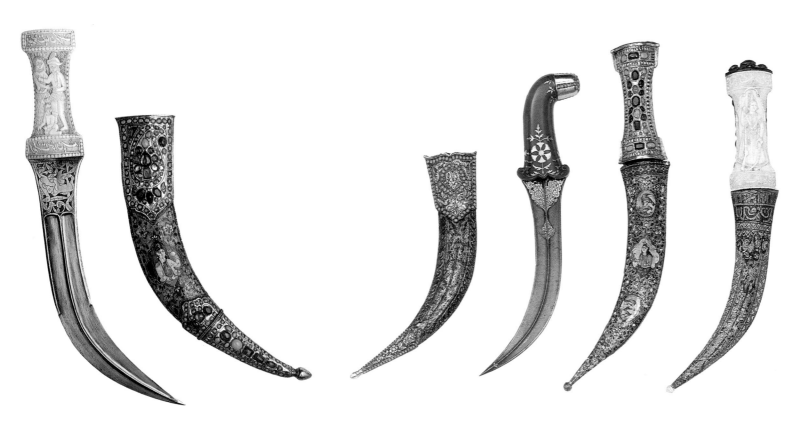

Far left Ivory-hilted dagger and scabbard, Persian, nineteenth century. The scabbard is of lacquered wood mounted in silver set with semi-precious stones.

Left Indo-Persian dagger with jade hilt and turquoise-set scabbard (left) and two nineteenth-century Persian daggers (centre and right). The blade and scabbard of the Indo-Persian weapon are eighteenth century, but the jade hilt is probably Moghul, about 1700.

147

12 JAPANESE SWORDS

Victor Harris

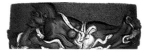

Above Hilt fittings, *fuchi* and *kashira* of the Late Edo period. These luxurious pieces were made of alloys such as *shakudo* (copper and gold) and *shibuichi* (copper and silver).

Opposite page Swordsmiths at work. Detail from a sixteenth-century screen, Kita-In, Saitama province.

The Japanese sword is many things. Functionally, its deadliness is attested by countless episodes in which it has cut through iron armour to kill, and also by inscriptions on tangs certifying terrible testing procedures in which whole bodies have been cut in two at a stroke.

In all countries with a martial tradition the sword has been elevated to a symbol of temporal power and justice, and in many it has acquired a spiritual status. But in Japan it is more than this. It has been described as the very soul of the samurai. The samurai's spiritual development was by means of Kendo ('The Way of the Sword'), or traditional swordsmanship. The sword was inseparate from the samurai, part of his very character.

The Sword, the Jewel and the Mirror constitute the three articles of the Japanese imperial regalia – they are divine objects according the the Shinto religion. Any one of them might be established in a Shinto shrine as the *shintai* or object in which the earthly presence of a god resides. So in Japan one finds swords more than a thousand years old venerated as gods in their own right. One example is the splendid *chokuto* or straight-bladed sword known as 'Futsu no Mitama Oken', the resident deity of Kashima shrine in Ibaraki prefecture. The importance of such a tradition is demonstrated by the fact that many such old swords are designated National Treasures, or Important Cultural assets, by the Japanese Government today.

But the Japanese sword possesses a further property which is immediately evident even to those who know nothing of its history, and even to those who have no love for weapons. It is an object of great beauty. As an art object it is unmatched – its finely polished steel surface has an intrinsic beauty unique among objects made of steel. The deep lustre and the bewitching variations in the crystalline structure of the surface steel have been likened to the beauty of the glaze on ceramics. As in ceramic art, elegance of shape is intimately related to function. Further, the robustness of both ceramics and swords depends on the treatment of the material of which they are made, and the manufacture of both depends upon a high level of skill in furnace technology.

The Japanese regard the beauty of the sword as close to that of *sumie* (ink painting) and calligraphy, widely felt to be the highest forms of art. The line of the brush stroke and the variations in the texture of the ink are reminiscent of the shape of the curved sword blade and the subtle lights and shadows on its surface. Indeed, sword connoisseurs and master swordsmen in Japan today are often very proficient with the brush, and an understanding of the one art implies an understanding of the other.

The history of the Japanese sword spans one and a half millennia. It is the story of the perfection of steel, and the development of a unique artefact which is at once Holy, Dreadful and Beautiful.

The manufacture of the blade

The beauty and the efficacy of the Japanese sword both derive from its sophisticated method of manufacture, and the unique and painstaking way in which it is polished. Swordsmith and polisher are different craftsman, and the art of each takes many years to perfect. The smith first prepares his steels by repeatedly heating, quenching, breaking up, and re-fusing the pieces together in order to obtain the required degree of purity and adjust the carbon content. Next, a prepared billet is heated in a charcoal furnace, beaten out and folded, and then welded back onto itself using a flux of ashes. This process is repeated several times until the billet is composed of a large number of intimately welded layers. The *shingane*, or core steel, is folded just a few times, and is of relatively low carbon content for final toughness. The *hadagane*, or skin steel, may be folded as many as fifteen times, although more foldings than that will cause carbon dispersal across the boundaries of the layers and break up the layer structure. The *hadagane* will have a higher carbon content than the *shingane*.

Finally, both *shingane* and *hadagane* are beaten out into long bars, and the *hadagane* folded around the *shingane* and welded to it throughout its length. Then the welded length is beaten into its final shape in preparation for the heat treatment. This involves covering the blade with a mixture of ingredients, including clays and ashes, leaving only a thin layer along the cutting edge and a thicker layer on the body of the blade, and heating the whole to 'the colour of the moon in February or August', and then quenching it in a trough of water.

The sword now has a central core of tough steel which gives the resilience required to resist the violent shocks of combat, a hard surface to deflect the cuts of enemy swords, and a yet harder edge which will retain its sharpness even when used to cut through hard objects such as iron armour.

After the sword has been polished, the full effect of the complex manufacturing process becomes evident. The hard *hadagane* will have a fine visible grain due to the thousands of layers resulting from the folding process – there are several types of grain pattern, by which different schools of swordmaking can be identified. The heat treatment will have produced different metallurgical structures on the surface, visible as shadows, depths, and both dark and bright lines and clusters of crystals. And the extreme hardness of the cutting edge will be revealed in a continuous line of bright crystalline steel reaching from the tang to the point, where it usually turns slightly over the back of the blade. This is called the *hamon* or 'badge' of the blade, since the maker can be identified from its characteristic shape. The *hamon* turns back at the *kissaki* or point of the blade to form the *boshi* or 'cap'.

The quality of the *hamon* is categorized as *nioi* ('visible fragrance') or *nie* ('boiling'). *Nioi* crystals are not discretely visible to the naked eye, but have the appearance of mist, or the Milky Way on a clear night. *Nie* crystals are visible, like a coarse frost or a cluster of stars. The formations expressed along the *hamon* are usually based on natural phenomena – clouds, the waves of the sea, the line of a mountain range, flowers, or the profile of a forest. These patterns enable the maker to be identified, and have been the subject of recorded study for at least a thousand years.

Since the *raison d'être* and the soul of the Japanese sword is the blade, this chapter is largely about blades and the smiths who made them. The exquisite sensibilities awakened by the form and appearance of a good blade are of course reflected in a large specialized vocabulary, of which a taste has just been given. A Japanese–English glossary appears on p. 170-171 , as repeated translations would have made very tedious reading.

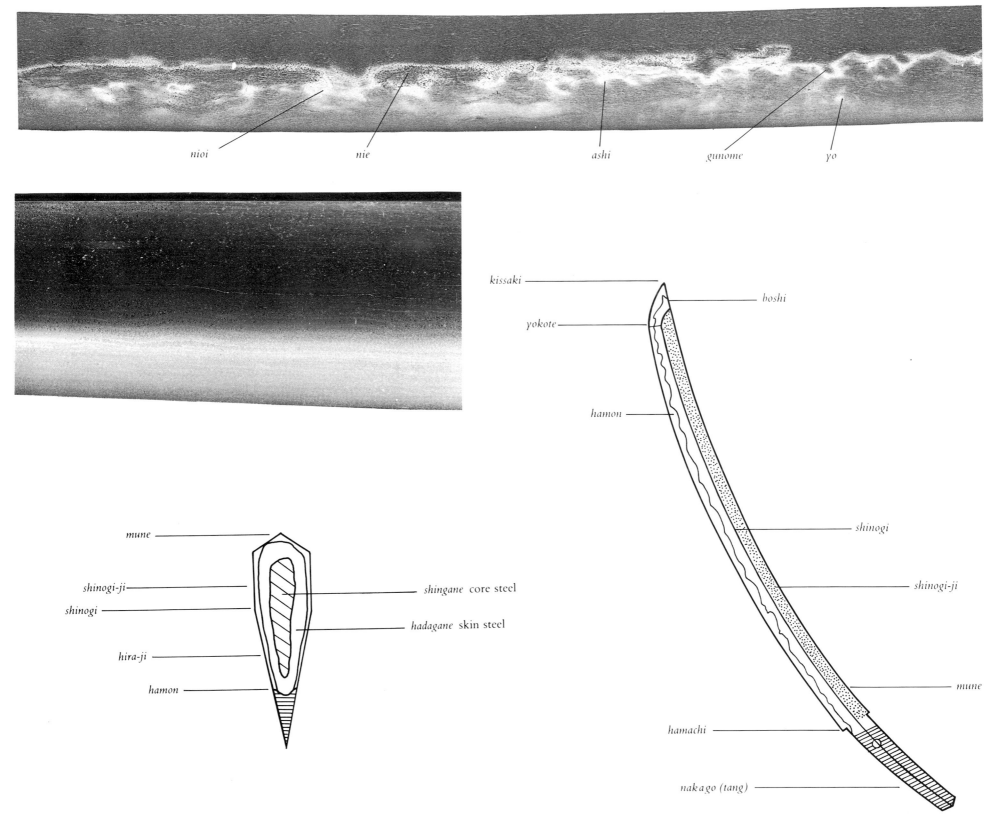

nioi   *nie*   *ashi*   *gunome*   *yo*

kissaki

boshi

yokote

hamon

shinogi

mune

shinogi-ji

shingane core steel

shinogi

hadagane skin steel

hira-ji

shinogi-ji

hamon

mune

hamachi

nakago (tang)

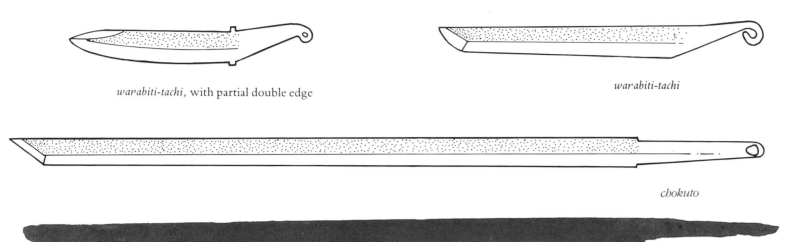

warabiti-tachi, with partial double edge

warabiti-tachi

chokuto

Left Sketch of two *warabite-tachi* or 'young fern hilt swords' (above) and a *chokuto* (below). The *warabite-tachi* on the left has a semi-double edge.

Below left *Chokuto*-type single-edged straight sword blade excavated by Professor William Gowland from a sixth-century burial mound in Higo province.

Opposite page Metallurgical characteristics of a Japanese sword blade (top) emphasized by the use of special photography (photograph by permission of the sword polisher Mr Okisato Fujishiro).
  Masame hada or 'straight grain' on the blade of a nineteenth-century dagger (below).
  Cross-section and profile of a typical Japanese sword blade (bottom and right).

Sword furnishings, most importantly the *tsuba* or guard, are an art in their own right and have considerable appeal to collectors today. However, to do them even rough justice would require a chapter of equal length to this. The illustrations on p. 159 are therefore intended only to whet the appetite.

The Kofun and Nara periods (c.300–794)

The Kofun or 'Ancient Mounds' era describes the time between the third and the sixth century AD when the warlike clans of Japan, under the strong influence of the countries which then made up Korea and China, grew in power. These clans were sword-wielding horsemen, and the burial mounds of their chieftains have yielded goods including rich gilt bronze and iron horse trappings, armour and swords. The excavated long swords are *chokuto*, straight and single-edged, with several distinctive types of *tsuba* or mountings. Shorter, broader swords known as *warabite-tachi* and the remains of daggers have also been found.

Contemporary Japanese technology owed much to continental skills, and many swords of the period were imported. Some *chokuto* were massive indeed, and blades with a cutting edge of 31 ins/80 cm are not uncommon. *Chokuto* blades are of even width throughout their length, and have various cross-sectional shapes. Some are triangular with flat sides, a shape known as *hirazukuri*. Some have a longitudinal ridge or *shinogi* on one side, dividing the flat of the blade from the slanting cutting portion.

Some excavated *chokuto* have a tang with a shaped butt, with the hilt attached by binding, but others have holes in the tang for the attachment of the hilt. This became the standard method of fixing the hilt, and remains so today. Some blades have a further hole above the tang which may have been used, together with a peg, to secure the blade in its scabbard, but insufficient archaeological evidence remains for us to be sure of this.

The hilts of these early swords were, until about the fifth century, of plain wood wrapped with textile, although stag antler

pieces have been found. But mountings from the latter part of the period include rich iron and gilt bronze components, dressed with gold and silver wire and sheet. Study remains to be done, but there is a weight of evidence to suggest considerable influence from Sassanian Persia both in the size and shape of Kofun era blades and in the style of their mountings and decoration.

Early *warabite-tachi* have a semi-double edge, extending a little along the back. *Warabite-tachi* literally means 'young fern hilt sword', the sloped back and turned-over tang being in the shape of a young fern shoot. It is tempting to say that the longer *chokuto* was mainly used for thrusting and that the shorter, broader *warabite-tachi* was used for cutting at close quarters. It is also tempting to say that the curved samurai sword of historic times developed from a combination of both.

Examples of both *chokuto* and *warabite-tachi* have been preserved since the Nara period (eighth century) in temple collections. In the Shosoin repository of the Todaiji Temple in Nara there are 55 *chokuto*, 38 *hoko* (a kind of glaive, a staff weapon with a long single-edged blade) and 70 small knives called *tosu*. The Shosoin was built by the Empress Komyo to house the personal effects of the Emperor Shomu, who died in 756. Both it and its contents were dedicated in 758 to the huge image of the Buddha Vairocana, which can be seen at the temple today.

The Shosoin contains many great treasures and for centuries was rarely opened, and then usually at the behest of the Emperor. Its contents have therefore remained almost intact. The swords were taken out briefly in the eighth century for use in battle against the Ainu, the bearded race of hunters who occupied Japan before the arrival of the continental horsemen. A *chokuto* in the Kurama Temple is said to have belonged to Sakanoue Tamura Maro (758-811), who finally subjugated the Ainu after an intensive campaign, so we can be certain that the weapon was in common use at least until the eighth century; after that it became a ceremonial weapon.

Right Sword-polishers at work, detail from a sixteenth-century screen, Kita-In, Saitama province. The presence of a woman in the doorway is interesting as women are traditionally excluded from all swordmaking operations.

Below, Tenth-century *kenuki gata tachi* or 'tweezer-shaped sword' with a long slit in the tang (left) and a typical Heian period *tachi* (right), with a blade which abruptly widens above the tang and straightens as it approaches the small *kissaki*. Note the deep *koshi zori* or waist curve.

The transition to curved blades

The first curved long swords were curved at the tang only, and later just above the tang, so that the upper part of the blade remained perfectly straight like a *chokuto*. In fact the first suggestion of a curve seems to have been the sloping tang of the short *warabite-tachi*.

It is not clear exactly when the fully curved sword first appeared, but a number of transitional blades exist from around the middle of the Heian period, that is from the middle of the tenth century. A long sword in the Imperial Collection known as 'Kogarasu Maru' ('Little Crow') seems to owe something of its shape to the *warabite-tachi*. It has a broad blade with a cutting edge extending half way along the back, and is deeply curved at the tang, yet only slightly curved in the blade. The sword is said to have been given to the Emperor Kammu (781–806) by a holy princess of Ise Shrine, and was later given to Taira Sadamori in reward for his victory over Fujiwara Sadatomo in the tenth century. Some more obviously transitional long swords are known as *kenuki gata tachi* ('tweezer-shaped swords'), since the tang is split to resemble tweezers. One such sword preserved in the Ise Shrine belonged to Tawara Toda who was appointed governor of Shimotsuke province in the Engi era (901–922) and a similar *kenuki gata tachi* is shown in a portrait of Fujiwara Yoritomo who became Shogun in 1198.

At all events, by the end of the tenth century many smiths, including Yasutsuna of Hoki (active around 980), were making fully curved swords.

The Heian Period (794–1185)

The Heian period saw the emergence of a pure Japanese classical culture. Female aristocrats wore their hair long, blackened their teeth seductively, and wore layer after layer of beautifully fashioned silk kimono. Cursive calligraphy was developed, along with a purely Japanese literature, and temporal poetry came to replace religious dogma as the pursuit of the aristocracy. One of the literary jewels of the period, *The Tale of Genji*, written by the Lady Murasaki Shichibu and read aloud to the emperor in 1008, paints a perfect picture of court life.

During the Heian period Japan gradually abandoned cultural exchange with China and society stabilized into class divisions. The military guards of the capital and the armed gentlemen of the provinces came to form the samurai class. And the priesthood, now that Buddhism was a political as well as a religious force, formed large armies of Sohei or Warrior Monks, who worked for the government on hire and protected their own vast land interests.

Beauty and elegance are the hallmarks of the Heian period, and both were sought in the making of swords. In the *Engishiki Chronicle*, a record of events between 901 and 922, reference to the several stages of polishing a sword over many days confirms that beauty in the steel was a subject of considered study.

Typically, Heian period blades are of *shinogi zukuri* form, with a ridge, and narrow to about half their width towards the point. The *kissaki* is small. The top part of the blade has a shallow curve, becoming almost straight as it approaches the point, but the bottom part or *koshi* (waist) is deeply curved, together with the tang – this bottom curve is called the *koshi-zori*. The blade broadens out acutely near the hilt, a characteristic known as *fumbari*, meaning 'tenacity' or 'bottom'. The tangs are long, tapering and curved.

From the Heian period onwards the name and province of the smith, and sometimes the date of manufacture, are engraved on the tang, so it has been possible to accumulate accurate information about schools of swordmaking to an extent which has not been possible with any other art or craft form. Whereas *hamon* of the *chokuto* era were straight, although rich in activity, from the Heian period onward *hamon* became varied and expressive.

The mounted samurai carried a *tachi* slung edge downwards from his belt, and a variety of shorter swords and daggers. But although the sword was the most revered of his weapons, tactically the bow was more important. The Japanese bow is long, taller than a man, composite, lacquered and bound with strips of bamboo and leather, and the grip is about one third of the way up from the bottom, which makes it easier to aim when bringing it right or left over the horse's head. The Japanese samurai's stirrups were large platforms which enabled him to stand up firmly above his saddle while shooting with his bow or reaching out to cut with his sword.

The armour of the Heian samurai was composed of a robust iron helmet, a cuirass, and a split apron, or *tare*, of loosely laced horizontal plates. The latter rode up forwards to protect the lower abdomen and thighs once the wearer was mounted. The sleeves were made of fabric to which chain mail with small armour plates was attached. Strung at the shoulders were rectangular *o-sode* ('great sleeves'), also made of horizontal plates laced together. A number of plates rivetted together composed the bowl of the helmet, to which was attached a hanging neck guard, or *shikoro*. The *shikoro* was composed of a number of bands of iron or other hard material laced together so that it did not catch on the shoulders when the head was moved; it also folded easily, dropping back into place when lifted, so that both hands could be raised above the head to deliver a large downward cut with the sword. Above the temples two large ear-like flaps called *fukigaeshi* swept forward and back. The *o-sode* and the helmet, with its *shikoro* and *fukigaeshi*, were arranged so that when the head was turned and lowered to aim the bow, only the bow hand and the aiming eye were exposed to the enemy. A poem extols the virtue of the archer who waits until he can shoot into the *tehen*, the hole in the crown of his opponent's helmet. Two hanging plates, the *sendan ita* on the right and the *muna ita* on the left of the breast, fell across the exposed trunk when the arms were raised in combat. The whole armour, light and mobile, provided considerable protection against arrows and glancing sword blows.

Since the bow was held in the left hand, the reins were held with the right, or *mete* ('horse hand'). So a dagger carried on the right side with the cutting edge facing forward was called a *mete zashi* ('horse-hand dagger'). When closing with the enemy the *mete zashi* could be drawn swiftly to cut upwards under the hanging pieces of armour, under the armpits, or under the throat from behind. The tang of such daggers is sometimes turned deeply upward to facilitate the awful thrust. This mode of use of the dagger has been favoured by assassins up to the present day, and the penalty at law for a person found guilty of assault with a dagger held edge upwards has been more severe than in other circumstances.

The *tachi* type sword was carried slung by cords or chains from the belt, with the cutting edge downmost, so that when drawn on horseback, the scabbard could be turned across the body to avoid touching the violently moving horse's head. As we have seen, the blade of the Heian period *tachi* narrows considerably towards the small point, making it light and easy to manipulate when held in

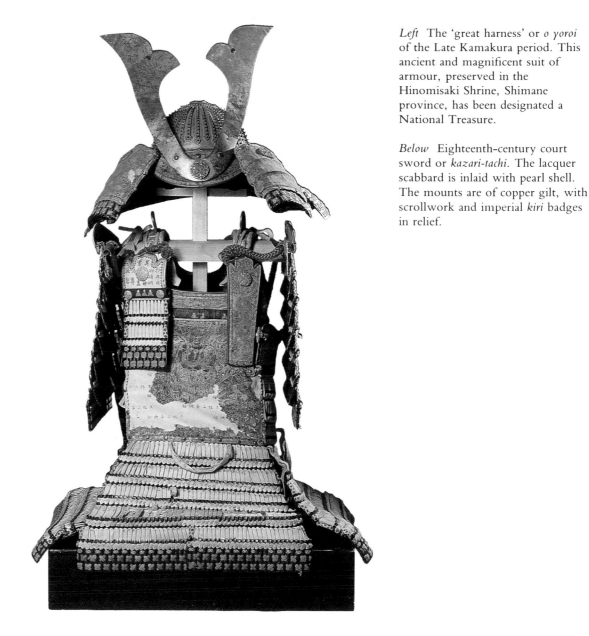

Left The 'great harness' or *o yoroi* of the Late Kamakura period. This ancient and magnificent suit of armour, preserved in the Hinomisaki Shrine, Shimane province, has been designated a National Treasure.

Below Eighteenth-century court sword or *kazari-tachi*. The lacquer scabbard is inlaid with pearl shell. The mounts are of copper gilt, with scrollwork and imperial *kiri* badges in relief.

Characteristics of Kofun and Nara period blades

Hamon on blades of the Kofun period are often absent, and ill-defined where present. However, Nara period *chokuto* and other swords in the Shosoin, and also those preserved in the Shitennoji Temple and elsewhere, have distinct *hamon*, usually straight, with some patches and irregularities. The blades have a fine grain called *itame* ('wood plank'), which may be *nagare* ('flowing') or *masame* ('straight'). The steel appears moist and white.

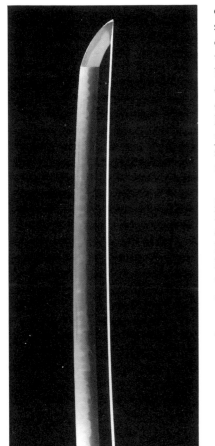

Above Choji-ba or 'clove flower' *hamon* on a blade by the Edo-period smith Tadatsuna.

Below right Various types of *jihada* or grain patterns in the steel of the cutting surface of a blade.

Opposite page Three details from a seventeenth-century folding screen depicting the twelfth-century wars between the Keike and Minamoto clans. On the left a rider uses the *mete zashi* to inflict a backward cut intended to behead his opponent. On the right a mounted samurai delivers a two-handed cut with the *tachi*, striking forwards and down in a natural arc. In the scene below two groups of samurai armed with sword and *naginata* meet in combat.

one hand. The small point could be used rather like a rapier, to seek out the chinks in an opponent's armour, and strong cuts could be made with the lower, broader part of the blade. The weight distribution was also such that a single-handed cut could be made at speed and the sword quickly raised again for another cut. When necessary it could be gripped with both hands to deliver a cut powerful enough to split open an enemy's iron helmet. The *kashira*, or butt of the hilt, of many *tachi* is provided with a hole or a metal band to take a loop of cord which could be slipped over the wrist to prevent the sword being dropped after the impact of a cut or thrust.

In keeping with the refined manners of the age, etiquette was of prime importance even during the heat of battle. The samurai's hair was tied up into a cloth scarf, which developed into the court cap known as the *eboshi*. Using scarf or cap, the hair could even be bunched up and pushed through the *tehen* in order to seat the helmet more firmly on the head. Since Japanese military strategy was largely based on Chinese practices, the Chinese habit of counting the heads of fallen enemies in order to decide the outcome of battles became adopted. A special sword, or *koshi-gatana* ('waist sword'), shorter than the *tachi*, was carried to behead the slain on the field. Etiquette decreed that the samurai should prepare himself for the worst outcome of battle by bathing carefully, rouging the cheeks, and keeping perfumed herbs inside the helmet so that his head should remain presentable if taken.

Before combat commenced, introductions were shouted, followed by an exchange of arrows and then swordplay at close quarters. Grappling and throwing techniques which involved grasping the helmet, sleeves and belt gave rise to various schools of close combat. *Kito ryu* jujitsu was one such form which Dr Jigoro Kano, the founder of modern judo, loved and which he included in his curriculum as *koshiki kata* ('the form of ancient style'). This form of judo is conducted with stiff and ponderous movements as if the protagonists were wearing armour.

Some Heian period swordsmiths who lived in regions where there was a good supply of ore refined their own iron, and were known as O Kaji. Munechika of Sanjo Street in Kyoto is recorded as Munechika Ko Kaji, since he used steel from elsewhere. One of the richest areas in iron ore was Kibi on the Sanyodo road linking

Kyushu with central Japan. 'Nakayama in Kibi, where the iron comes from' is mentioned in *Kokin Wakashu*, an anthology of classical poems compiled in 905. Kibi contained the provinces of Bitchu, Bingo, Bizen and Mimasaka. Important smiths from these provinces included Tomonari and Masatsune of Bizen, and the Ko-Aoe school of Bitchu. Yasutsuna, working in the tenth century, excelled among the smiths of Hoki, which lies in the Chugoku region together with the provinces of Kibi.

There were also many smiths in Kyushu, the southern island of Japan, where steel technology had been first introduced from the continent. Yukiyasu of Satsuma founded the Namihira school, which continued well into the fifteenth century. Tenta Mitsuyo of Chikugo made the National Treasure sword known as 'O Tenta', a perfect and robust blade of elegant proportions. Yukihira of Bungo made many swords with small carvings of deities on the blade just a few centimetres above the hilt. Yukiyasu, Tenta Mitsuyo and Yukihira were active during the tenth and eleventh centuries.

Swords of the Heian period are regarded as the most refined ever made. In later days centuries samurai lords spoke with longing of the 'Tenka Goken' ('The Five Swords under the Heavens') made in the Heian era, and today they are treasures almost beyond price. The great Five were 'Doji-kiri' (Boy Cutter) by Yasutsuna of Hoki, 'Onimaru' (The Demon) by Kunitsuna, 'Mikazuki' (The Quarter Moon) by Munechika, 'Juzumaru' (The Rosary) once owned by the priest Nichiren, and 'O Tenta' (Great Tenta) by Tenta Mitsuyo. 'Doji-kiri' was used in the Heian period by Yorimitsu, a captain of the Genji clan, to kill a monstrous creature known as the Shuten Doji. Strange stories abound relating to this event, but the truth is probably that Yorimitsu subdued a band of brigands operating in Oniyama of Tango province, for lawlessness abounded outside the cities.

Dissatisfaction with the government by the samurai clans who held provincial lands resulted many times in rebellion and war. In 1185 the Minamoto clan resoundingly defeated their old rivals the Taira in a sea battle at Dan-no-Ura, and Minamoto Yoritomo had himself proclaimed Shogun, taking the centre of power away from the nobility in Kyoto and establishing the first samurai government at Kamakura.

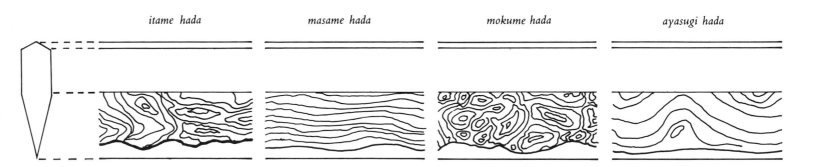

| *itame hada* | *masame hada* | *mokume hada* | *ayasugi hada* |

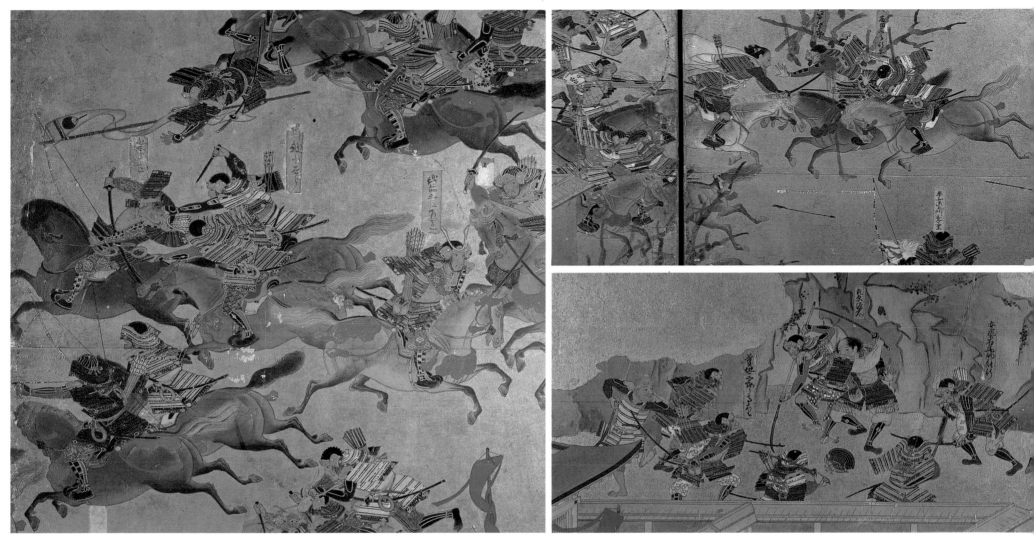

Characteristics of Heian period blades

The *hamon* of the Heian smiths are fine and continuous throughout their length, and rich in activity. The *ko-nie* (fine *nie*) of the *hamon* is of even texture, and *jinie* (*nie* in patches on the *ji* or 'ground' of the blade) is also found. *Ashi* ('legs') are short lines of fine *nie* or *nioi* running from the *hamon* towards the cutting edge. Small patches of *nioi* within the boundary of the *hamon* are called *yo* ('leaves'). Short lines of *nie* running haphazardly through and around the *hamon* are called *kinsuji*. Longer lines of *kinsuji* are called *inazuma* ('lightning').

In overall form, Heian *hamon* may be straight, *suguha*, or irregular, *midare-ba*, and in parts may exhibit a pattern known as *choji-ba* ('clove flower pattern'), like a row of petals clustered together. A faint shadow called *utsuri* ('reflection') is found along parts of the *hira-ji*, the sides of the blade.

Generally the *hada* or skin steel of Heian blades is of *itame* form, but if the sword has been polished many times over the years the core steel may have become visible, in which case the blade is said to be 'tired'. The core is usually folded fewer times than the *hadagane* during the manufacture of the blade; being of softer steel, the exposed patches look watery and have a larger grain. Sometimes the grain of the core steel is *masame*, while that of the *hada* is *itame*.

The *boshi* or 'cap' of the blade is most important in showing the quality of a sword at a glance. Early *boshi* turn back along the *mune*, the back or blunt edge of the blade, in a small graceful curve. Some are delicately rounded, *ko-maru*, some are of irregular wavy form, *midare-komi*, and others are flame-like at the tip, *ka-en*.

Active at around the same time as Yasutsuna was Munechika of Sanjo in Kyoto. His swords, of which four splendid examples survive, are slender and elegantly shaped. The *hada* known as *nashiji hada* ('pear skin' *hada*) is particularly fine. Munechika's *hamon* sometimes forms a double line, or *niju-ba*, and there are small crescent-shaped *nie* called *uchi-no-ke* whose tips rise into the *hira-ji* or flat of the blade. Lines of *nie* spots known as *yubashiri* ('hot water run') lie along the *hira-ji* against the *hamon*. These are also found on later swords of the Yamashiro school. The Bizen school, founded by the smiths Tomonari and Masatsune, flourished from this period onwards, and came to specialize in *choji-ba*.

In Bitchu province smiths of the Ko-Aoe school made swords with exceptionally fine *hada* patterned with minute *nie* called *chirimen-hada* ('silk crêpe' *hada*). In Satsuma, Yukiyasu and the Namihira school made *hada* which included parallel wavy lines known as *ayasugi-hada*. Yukihira, the first of a long tradition of prolific makers in Bungo province, used to start his *hamon* a few centimetres above the tang. He also carved small figures of deities like Fudo-Myo-O and Jizo-Sama on his blades.

The Kamakura period (1185–1392)

The Minamoto clan remained in power only from 1185 until 1219, when Hojo Yoshitoki became Shogun. In 1221 the Hojos defeated the forces of Emperor Gotobain, and installed Emperor Gotakakurain in his place. Under the strong government of the Hojos a century of uneasy peace was imposed upon the country's feuding clans and monasteries.

Gotobain, exiled to Oki Island, where he lived for a further twenty years, was intrigued with the sword as an art object and devoted the years of his exile to the study of swords, summoning smiths from the main schools to instruct him in sword-making. He even instituted a rotational system so that they should each stay with him for a month at a time. Swords made by Gotobain, or at least heat-treated by him, are found with the mark of the imperial chrysanthemum on the tang. These *kiku gosaku* ('noble chrysanthemum make') swords were given as presents to nobles and important samurai, considerably adding to the prestige of the swordsmith's profession and particularly to the reputation of the Bitchu, Bizen and Yamashiro schools of the smiths who made the journey to Oki Island. Surviving lists of Gotobain's attendant smiths differ somewhat due to deaths and replacements over the long period of the his retirement, but the fourteenth-century book *Kanchiinbon* mentions Norimune, Nobufusa, Muneyoshi, Sukemune and Yukikuni of Bizen, Sadatsugu, Tsunetsugu, Tsuguie and Sukenobu of Bitchu, and Kuniyasu and Kunitomo of the Awataguchi school in Tokyo as having attended during the same year. Two polishers are also listed, Kunihiro and Tamesada, each of whom attended together with an assistant.

The swords of the early decades of the Kamakura period were slender and refined, similar to those of the late Heian period. But by the middle of the thirteenth century, in keeping with the more military atmosphere of the times, blades had become sturdier, with less decrease in breadth towards the point. In 1232 the Hojo government published an extensive legal code, part of which confirmed the duty of the samurai to train in the martial arts, particularly in the arts of horsemanship and archery. People other than samurai were prohibited from carrying the *tachi*.

Whereas the blades of the early Kamakura period were only slightly curved in the upper part, by the middle of the thirteenth century the curve had become deeper throughout the length in order to increase cutting efficiency. Curiously, the *kissaki* on many blades of the middle Kamakura period remained the same length as before although the blades were broader. They appear 'stunted' in consequence and are known as *ikubi-zaki* ('bull-neck' points). The *hira-ji*, the flat surfaces containing the cutting edge, were also made slightly convex in order to split armour plate more efficiently. Such blades are sometimes described as *hamaguri-ba* ('clam-shaped').

In the eleventh year of the Bunei era, 1274, an event occurred which had a far-reaching effect on Japanese swords and on Japanese methods of war. Following the failure of several envoys

to Japan, Kubilai Khan, grandson of Genghiz Khan and first emperor of the Yuan Dynasty, attempted an invasion with a fleet of 900 ships. As news of the landing spread, the Japanese sped to meet the enemy, eager for battle and glory, each man intent on acquiring heads. But instead of opponents willing to stand and exchange greetings as a prelude to single combat they met an army highly trained in group tactics. The Mongol foot soldiers, using short, powerful bows, blanketed the field with arrows. They also advanced and retreated to the sound of drums, encircled the Japanese cavalry, and terrified and confused the horses with the sound of cymbals and explosives, which the Japanese had never seen before. The enemy spearmen played havoc with the Japanese from outside the reach of their swords. The Japanese also

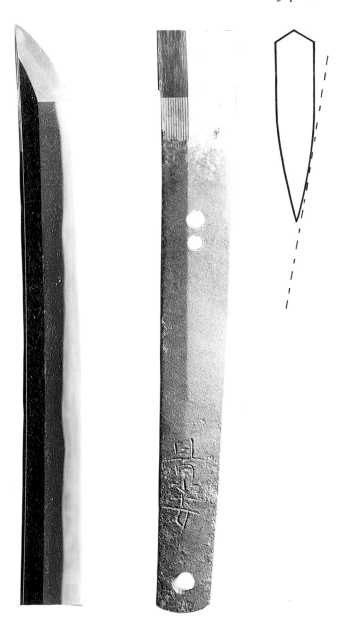

found that although their swords were suitable for cutting through iron, they made little impression on the tough leather coats of the Mongols. Fortunately, the invaders retreated to their ships overnight, allowing the Japanese to regroup ashore, and the next day a typhoon destroyed the greater part of the Khan's fleet. The immediate threat of invasion was over.

Seven years later the Khan came again, with a larger army of 140,000 men, only to be met with determined resistance by a samurai army under the leadership of Hojo Tokimune. But again fate intervened: another great storm blew up and destroyed the Khan's armada. The Shinto shrines, the aristocracy and the Buddhists all claimed the credit for having summoned the *Shimpu* or *Kamikaze* ('The Wind of The Gods') to the aid of Tokimune's army. Though elated by their victory, the Japanese remained in a state of permanent readiness throughout the remaining half a century of Hojo supremacy. And in the spirit of preparedness for war, further great changes were made in sword design and in fighting methods.

The Mongols taught the Japanese the value of longer weapons. Accordingly, swordsmiths began to turn out large numbers of long-bladed spears and *naginata*, the glaive-like weapons pre-ferred by the Sohei. Fighting on foot rather than on horseback gradually became the established form of combat, and a lighter form of armour known as *domaru* replaced the *o yoroi* previously worn by cavalrymen, with a gain in mobility and speed of action. At the same time, the sword rather than the bow became the main weapon.

Swordsmiths from all over the Japan went to Kamakura in Soshu province, the seat of government and the centre of demand for weapons, and the school which grew up in Kamakura developed a means of intimately mixing hard and soft steels together to produce a much tougher cutting edge without sacrificing any sharpness. One defect of the *ikubi tachi* or 'bull-neck' sword was that the point was not acute enough for thrusting deeply into armour; also if the point became chipped there was often insufficient hardened edge left to reshape. It is said that during the Mongol affair many sword points were broken, and rudely reshaped and re-hardened on the battlefield. Afterwards, swords became much longer, with extended points and an even curve throughout their length. *Hamon* were predominantly of *nie*, and the *jigane* became rich in *nie* and the varying hues of different quality steels.

Opposite page Three views of a *tachi*-type sword signed Kageyasu, Bizen School, Kamakura period (early thirteenth century). Although the blade has been cut down a few centimetres, it retains the elegant shape of late Heian and early Kamakura swords, with the deepest curve just above the tang. The *hamon* is in *ko-choji* style and there is a discontinuous pale *utsuri* along the blade.

The 'clam shape' or *hamaguri-ba* cross-section on the right was introduced during the Kamakura period in order to split armour more effectively.

Characteristics of Kamakura period blades

In the early Kamakura period the schools of Yamashiro centred around Kyoto and Bizen (Okayama province today) came to the fore. One group of smiths in Fukuoka of Bizen, among whom the name of Norimune is prominent, called themselves the 'Ichimonji', meaning 'the character one', signifying that they were the 'first in the world'. *Hamon* of the period became more grandiose, and the blades more strikingly beautiful and deadly-looking as a result. The *choji* ('clove flower pattern') *hamon* of the Bizen and Bitchu schools became more vivid and contrived, and was used by other schools, notably by the Rai school of Yamashiro. This was the golden age for Bizen swords, and the Ichimonji school spread to Yoshioka and Katayama in neighbouring Bitchu province.

In Osafune of Bizen, the 'village of swordsmiths', Mitsutada, Nagamitsu and others formed a school which was to survive for several hundred years. The *choji* of the Osafune school soften out at the *mono-uchi* ('striking place'), that part of the portion of the blade about one quarter back from the point where the classic cut is made. Nagamitsu, Mitsutada and some of the Ichimonji and Rai school smiths made exaggerated clove-flower patterns called *juka-choji* ('layers of choji'). These characteristically rise and fall in undulations, with the larger petals on the crests and the smaller, more tightly packed petals in the valleys of the undulations. Some smiths, notably Ichimonji Yoshifusa, made *choji* with high, rounded petals known as *kawazu-ko-choji* ('tadpole choji'). The *choji* of the Rai school differ from those of other schools in that the heads of the petals are roughly in a straight line, while the *ashi* are of differing lengths. Some Bizen and Bitchu smiths used a backward-sloping form of *choji* called *saka-choji*.

The Awataguchi school of Yamashiro, under Kuniie and his sons and pupils, flourished during the Kamakura period. Among the smiths of the Awataguchi school in Tokyo was the genius of the *tanto* or dagger, Toshiro Yoshimitsu, active around 1260. Kuniyuki of Awataguchi made grand swords, signing his name 'Rai Kuniyuki' ('Rai' means 'come', possibly because he had come to the capital to work). In Ayanokoji Street, a flourishing thoroughfare in Kyoto today, Sadatoshi made sound Yamashiro-style blades with a whitish *hada*. The Yamashiro style of fine *hada* and *ko-nie* contrasted strikingly with the exuberant patterns of *choji* in *nioi* found on Bizen swords. *Choji* flower patterns became popular all over the country in the middle Kamakura period, especially with the Rai school, who made *choji hamon* in *nie* whereas the Bizen school specialized in *nioi*. The *utsuri* on Bizen swords of the period is vivid, and is sometimes wavy as if it were a true 'reflection' of the *hamon*.

The Yamato schools, originally those which made swords for the priests of the great temples around Nara, had a very different style. The grain of their swords is generally of flowing *nagare* type or, in the case of the Taema Temple school, absolutely straight. The *hamon* is rich in small activity in *nie*, and often has *hotsure* (fraying, wispy lines of *nie* around the *hamon* rather like frayed textile).

In the late Kamakura period, in addition to *choji* of the Bizen school, a new kind of *hamon* developed called *gunome*, consisting of a distinct rising and falling line. The Yamato smiths continued to make swords with straight *hada* in their own special style.

The advent of the Soshu school at Kamakura marked a turning point in the history of the sword in Japan. Shintogo Kunimitsu, Kunimune, Yukimitsu and Masamune forged strong swords using mixtures of different strengths of steel. This is visible in their *jigane*, which have whirls of *jinie* and *chikei*; the latter are like dark pools of water which become deeper and more serene the more one looks at them.

Masamune, active in the fourteenth century, is generally held to have been the mainstay of the Soshu school. Masamune's *jihada* is finely forged, and rich in *jinie* and *chikei*. His *hamon*, which rises and falls in abrupt and lively style, is richer in *nie* than that of any other smith; characteristially, his *nie* are large, bright and punctuated with long formations of *inazuma* ('lightning') and thicker lines known as *sunagashi* ('floating sands'). Smiths came from far and wide to study at Masamune's forge, but after the fall of the government at Kamakura in 1333 his pupils scattered throughout Japan.

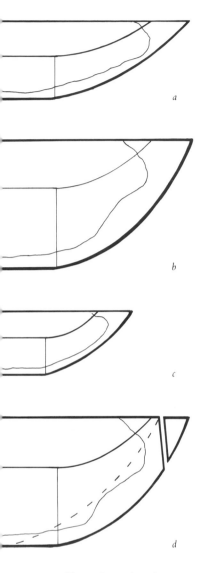

The Yoshino or Namboku Cho (Northern and Southern Courts) period (1333–1393)

It had always been the custom for the government to reward military service with the spoils of war, usually in the form of enemy land. But nothing had been gained with which to recompense the losses suffered during the abortive Mongol invasion. This was a major source of dissatisfaction among various factions of samurai, and in 1333, with the backing of the Emperor Godaigo, a samurai army stormed and laid waste Kamakura. But the resulting government was not strong enough to control the whole country, and a rival emperor, Emperor Komyo, was set up in the northern part of Kyoto by the warlord Ashikaga Takeuji. Sixty years of continuous warfare followed, culminating in victory for the North and the establishment of the Ashikaga as Shoguns in the Muromachi area of Kyoto.

This period marked the peak of the Soshu sword-making tradition and the supremacy of the branch schools of Masamune's Ten Pupils. Much of the fighting was in the hills and moors around Kyoto and Nara, using the new-style long *tachi*. The longer *tachi* had a blade length of about 40 ins/100 cm, although longer examples survive as votive objects in shrines and temples. Daggers of the periods were correspondingly broad and long. Long *tachi* were most suitable for fighting on foot against cavalry, and also advantageous in the dark. They were often carried slung across the back, and were drawn diagonally over the shoulder. Known as *no tachi* ('moor swords') or *seoi tachi* ('swords carried on the back'), they were sometimes carried into battle drawn, the blade resting on one shoulder, the disposable scabbard having been abandoned – there are records of such weapons being carried wrapped in paper or straw.

Sadly few of these great swords have survived in their original length. Later generations cut them down for everyday wear and in the process discarded the original tangs and their inscriptions. No *tachi* by Masamune have survived in their original length, and his signature is found only on daggers. The slight indentation remaining from a *mekugi ana* (a peg hole in the tang) at the very tip of the tang of a fourteenth-century *tachi* by Motoshige of Bizen indicates that the original sword must have been considerably longer, as must the sword attributed to Sa, one of Masamune's pupils.

Above Long *kissaki* on Late Kamakura and Namboku Cho blades (a). *Ikubi-zaki* or 'bull neck point' on blades of the Middle Kamakura period (b). *Ko-kissaki* or small point on Heian and Early Kamakura blades (c).

The defect of the *ikubi-zaki* was that if the point broke and had to be reshaped, the new edge exposed the core steel above the *hamon* (d).

Right *Hamon* characteristic of Kamakura blades.

Far right Detail of a blade by Samonji (see caption on opposite page).

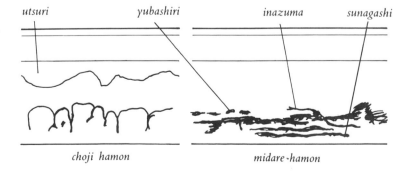

utsuri   yubashiri   inazuma   sunagashi

choji hamon   midare·hamon

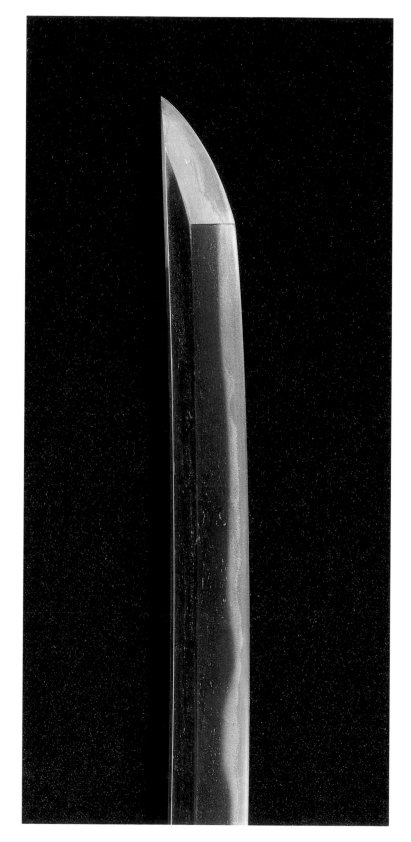

Left Group of *tsuba* or sword guards, showing a range of designs and metalworking techniques, fifteenth–nineteenth century.

Below Two Yoshino period (fourteenth-century) *tachi*, both slightly shorter than their original length. The lower of the two is attributed to Motoshige of Bizen; the *hamon* is *saka-choji* in *nioi*, a characteristic of several smiths of Bizen and of the Aoe school of Bitchu province. The weapon above is attributed to Sa, or Samonji, a pupil of Masamune, Soshu school. As can be seen from the blade detail on the opposite page, the steel is rich in *jinie*, with deep utsuri, and the *hamon* is full of variation, with clusters of *nie* and bright *kinsuji*.

Characteristics of Yoshino period blades

In the Yoshino period the Soshu style was popularized by Masamune's Ju Deishi or Ten Pupils. In Soshu province his best pupil Sadamune, who never signed a blade, made swords considered by some to have a finer *jigane* than those of his mentor.

From Chikuzen there was Samonji, whose name means 'the character left'. Stories abound concerning the origin of this name. According to one source, when the time came for Samonji to return to his home country, Masamune grasped him by the left sleeve with tears in his eyes, unable to bear his departure. Another unlikely story is that Samonji put his hand into the water Masamune used to quench his blades in order to surreptitiously test the temperature, and had his offending arm struck from his body.

Two more of Masamune's pupils, Akihiro and Hiromitsu, also active during the fourteenth century, specialized in *hitatsura* ('full cover'), a style of *hamon* which spreads in patches all over the blade. Yoshihiro, also known as 'Go', made swords similar to Masamune's. Kanemitsu, son of Kagemitsu of Bizen, and Kunimitsu of Bizen are considered to have been the founders of the Soden Bizen style. Shizu Saburo Kaneuji, who had also studied in the Yamato Tegai school made swords in the grandiose Soshu style, with *hamon* that splash up almost to the *shinogi* and down to the cutting edge. Some of the hillocks in his *hamon* are slightly pointed, and this was to be the hallmark of the smiths in Mino, where Kaneuji went to live. Norishige of Etchu province made swords with striking interlinked bands of dark and bright steel in the *jihada*; this has become known as *matsukawa-hada* ('pine bark hada') or *hijiki-hada* (*hijiki* is a seaweed delicacy with slender, entangled stalks). Hasebe Kunishige made swords with *masame hada* near the back edge of the blade, and discontinuous, thick, patchy *nie* along the flat of the blade. Another of Masamune's pupils, Sa, made exceptionally fine daggers.

There are differing versions of the Ten Pupils, some of which include other smiths like Naotsuna of Iwami or neglect the Bizen smiths. But whatever the truth about Masamune and his pupils, the Soshu tradition made a lasting impact on sword-making throughout the Yoshino period. The Soshu school was included by later connoisseurs of the sword as being among the Five Traditions of Koto blades, the other schools being Yamato, Yamashiro, Bizen and Mino.

Below left Long swords of the
Kamakura and Namboku Cho
periods were cut down to a more
convenient length for ease of
carrying and in response to the
changing style of battle. Often this
resulted in the original signature
being lost, although sometimes the
old tang was folded over to
preserve the inscription. On some
o-suriage or cut-down blades the
portion of the blade bearing the
signature was cut out and inlaid
into the new tang.

Below right A *saki-zori* curve on a
blade of the Muromachi period, and
a blade section known as *oroshi-
mune* found on swords of the same
period.

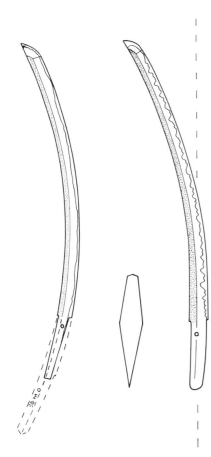

The Muromachi period and the Age of Wars (1392–1477)

After the unification of North and South under Ashikaga Yoshimitsu in 1392, the spirit of the Kamakura once again prevailed in Japan. The Ashikaga rulers re-opened the old lines of communication with China, and the fine arts of the Ming dynasty were enthusiastically pursued. Noh theatre, the Way of Tea, flower arrangement, artistic landscape gardening, and other arts inspired by Zen all became popular. The samurai devoted themselves to the study of Zen. Indeed the teachings of the schools of Kendo founded in the Muromachi period are all steeped in Zen philosophy; the ultimate aim of the swordsman is not to vanquish an opponent but to achieve spiritual enlightenment.

But while the samurai lords devoted themselves to spiritual studies, the country gradually went to ruin. For a decade from 1467, in the Onin period, there was continuous civil war in and around Kyoto. For the next century, known as the Sengoku Jidai, or Age of Wars, the government lost control and the provinces were in a state of turmoil.

Warfare during this time was between vast provincial armies of samurai and a newer kind of conscripted man, the *ashigaru* or light infantryman. Faced with masses of spear-wielding *ashigaru*, the horse became impractical. The demand for swords increased, and many poor quality weapons were produced. In Bizen and Mino provinces blades were mass-produced and sold in bundles. In Bizen many smiths signed their work with well-known signatures, sometimes in response to a commission. The *Kaketsuki Chronicle*, an account of wars between 1441 and 1444, for example, records that Akamatsu Mitsuke, a lord of Bizen, ordered three hundred swords by Yasumitsu, one of the great fifteenth-century smiths of Osafune village in Bizen. Other records indicate that several hundred thousand swords were made for export to Ming China. Naturally the quality of these swords was inferior. The eighteenth-century book *Bankin Sangyo Bukuro* ('A Bag of Metal Industries') tells us that the metalworkers of Nara could transform an 'iron bar' [sic] into a number of swords in a single day, whereas previously the making of a blade required several weeks. We also read in an early Edo-period training manual for *ashigaru*, the *Zohyo Monogatari*, an exhortation to the common soldier to 'cut at the enemy's arms and legs with large sweeping cuts. Do not try to cut the man in two with a straight cut down on his head as we [the samurai] do, for you have not the necessary skill, and the swords you have would break on a helmet.'

The *tachi* of the early part of the fifteenth century were similar in shape to those of the middle Kamakura period. But in the middle and later part of the Muromachi period swords acquired a characteristically deep *saki-zori* or curve in the upper part of the blade. This improved cutting efficiency and appears on swords of all lengths. The *uchigatana* ('hitting sword'), a weapon about 24 ins/60 cm long and wielded with one hand, also became popular. This was carried edge uppermost, thrust through the belt. In addition to the standard *shinogi-zukuri* section blade, a new blade section known as *oroshe-mune* was developed. This echoed, in exaggerated form, the high *shinogi* of the old Yamato style and was specially designed for cutting through flesh and bones, its sloping shape offering less friction during the cutting. A new type of dagger with a slight curve, and sharp on both edges, was also made.

The wearing of a pair of swords, or *daisho*, became fashionable during the Muromachi period. The *katana*, or long sword, and the *wakizashi*, or shorter companion sword, were worn out of doors. Indoors, the *wakizashi* was worn at all times and kept by the bed at night. The samurai lived inseparable from his sword, his most valued possession. He walked armed every day of his life, sat armed at the table, and went armed to bed.

In 1543 a singular event occurred. Three matchlock guns were found on board a Portuguese ship which had aground on Tanegashima Island. In no time at all, Japanese swordsmiths were producing exact copies of them, with better and more accurate barrels, and in battles such as Nagashino, in which Oda Nobunaga succeeded in bringing the country under control, firepower decided the day. After the advent of the gun, and the new tactics of using musketeers backed up by groups of spearmen, the old type of armour fell into disuse, and for a few decades heavy plate cuirasses imported from Europe, or modelled on European styles, replaced the light laced plate of old. The *fukigaeshi* on the helmet and the *o-sode* shoulder pieces became irrelevant and merely decorative.

Nobunaga made his headquarters at Momoyama in Kyoto in 1568, and in the relative stability of the remaining decades of the sixteenth century the samurai lords built huge stone castles in their provinces. Life became relatively luxurious and commerce thrived in the larger cities. The greatest luxury for a samurai was to possess a fine old sword, and in this period many blades of the Kamakura and Yoshino periods were cut down into *uchigatana*.

In 1603, after the death of Nobunaga and then Hideyoshi, Tokugawa Ieyasu became Shogun and made his capital at Edo, present-day Tokyo. Opposition from the family of Hideyoshi and their supporters was crushed in the siege of Osaka Castle in 1615, after which the Tokugawa family imposed peace on the nation, a peace which was to last for more than 250 years.

Left Detail from 'The Battle at Ozaki', an eighteenth-century handscroll depicting sixteenth-century warfare. The horsemen are wearing armour in ancient style and carry *tachi* suspended by cords. The foot soldiers wear *harumaki*-type corselets or no body armour, and carry *katana* worn through the belt with the cutting edge up. In the foreground a warrior leaves the field with the head of an enemy.

Below Seventeenth-century *katana* and scabbard (left), a *wakizashi* by Tadayoshi of Hizen, also seventeenth-century (centre), and a nineteenth-century *tanto* or dagger with a maple leaf design on the scabbard (right).

Right Some typical *hamon* of the Muromachi period. *Kani-no-tsume choji* were characteristic of Sukesada of Bizen, *gunome* of Kanefusa of Mino, *sambon sugi* of Kanemoto of Mino and *suguha* with thickets of Kanetsune of Mino.

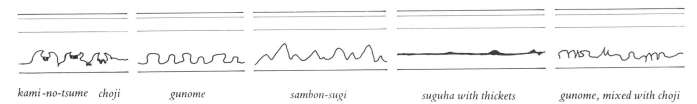

| *kami-no-tsume choji* | *gunome* | *sambon-sugi* | *suguha with thickets* | *gunome, mixed with choji* |

Right and below *Katana* blade by Gassan, Dewa province, late fifteenth–early sixteenth century. The steel is forged in the vivid undulating grain known as *ayasugi*, common to many generations of the Gassan tradition. The Gassan family were inspired by the Shugendo religion, whose deities inhabited the 'Three Mountains' of Dewa province.

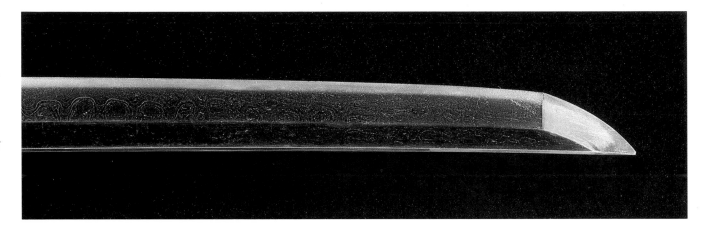

Characteristics of Muromachi period blades

Smiths still made swords at Soshu during the Muromachi period, but the capital had moved back to Kyoto and so Soshu declined as a centre of supply. Bizen, however, whose rulers had always put trade before political considerations, remained a major sword-producing province.

The smiths of the early fourteenth century still worked in *choji*, but usually with a mixture of *gunome*. One often finds *suguha* work at one end of a blade blossoming into deep *gunome* or *choji* at the other. Various exotically contrived hamon abound, such as the *kani-no-tsume* ('crab's claws') style introduced by 'Sukesada', with the rise in the *hamon* broken into a shape reminiscent of a crab's pincers. Yosozaemon Sukesada was the greatest of a large number of smiths, some say as many as 60, who used the name Sukesada. Morimitsu, Yasumitsu, Katsumitsu and the Omiya Bizen smiths, notably Morokage, made excellent swords, but they lacked the deep *utsuri* of their predecessors of the middle Kamakura period.

Later poorer quality Bizen work is characterized by rough and broken *nie* and coarse *jigane*. In Bungo, the Takada school produced large numbers of serviceable blades, many in Bizen-style *choji*, but many in *midare-ba* with whitish, inelegant *utsuri*.

Mino, more central in Japan, was better placed to supply the armies which battled around the central regions. Smiths came from Yamato to Mino in the footsteps of Shizu Kaneuji, which explains the strong Yamato feel about the Mino swords of this period. The *shinogi-gi* (the parallel sides of the blade above the ridge line) of Mino blades, for example, has the classic Yamato style straight *hada*. But the *hamon* of the period are characterized by styles of *notare* and *gunome* in addition to the pure *suguha*.

Smiths in the town of Seki, including Kanemoto and Kanesada, both active during the sixteenth century, made robust and practical blades. Generations of Kanemotos made *hamon* in the form known as *sambon-sugi*, rows of three cryptomeria treetops linked together. Kanefusa, also working in the sixteenth century, made 'priest's head' style *hamon* in *nioi* and fine *nie* of *gunome* (sharply undulating) form, with rounded heads and valleys. Many of the Seki swords, however, are in *nioi*, with *shirake*, a white shadow rather like *utsuri*, on the ground. The Mino smiths, through their ancient connections with the temples and shrines linked by the Kasuga Shrine, found travel around the country easy, and the Mino tradition therefore exerted considerable influence on smiths of the *Shinto* ('New Swords') period.

Next to Masamune, the name of Muramasa of Ise is perhaps better known than that of any other smith in Japan, for his blades had a reputation for bloodthirstiness. Muramasa was active during the sixteenth century and worked in a mixture of Soshu and Mino styles, with fine *itame hada*, and hamon of *o-notare* ('great swelling') and *gunome*. He was held to be unlucky by the Tokugawa family, since Tokugawa Ieyasu's grandfather was killed by mistake by one of his own retainers with a *naginata* made by Muramasa. Since that episode, several instances involving accidents, suicides and battle injuries suffered by the Tokugawas have been linked with the name Muramasa.

Kanesada of Seki, a contemporary of Muramasa, made swords in a similar style. His swords were also considered deadly, and later described as *owaza-mono* ('great technique swords') by sword appraisers.

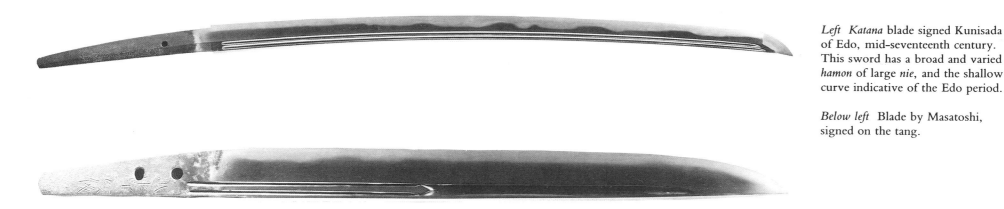

Left Katana blade signed Kunisada of Edo, mid-seventeenth century. This sword has a broad and varied *hamon* of large *nie*, and the shallow curve indicative of the Edo period.

Below left Blade by Masatoshi, signed on the tang.

Characteristics of Momoyama (*Shinto* or 'New Swords') period blades

At the end of the sixteenth century the smiths of the traditional schools, predominantly those of the Mino tradition, dispersed to the towns which grew up around the castles of the provincial lords or *daimyos*, and the stage was set for a new era of swords.

The style of swords made by these early Edo period smiths was very much based on the current idea of perfection, namely the *tachi* style of the Kamakura and Yoshino periods. This style was generally characterized by *nie* in the *hamon* and on the *ji* of the blade.

Notable among the early seventeenth-century smiths was Yasutsugu of Echizen. Some of his early Echizen work he signed Shimosaka, as he originally came from Shimosaka in Omi province. He also had links with the school of carvers signing their work 'Kinai', who often carved dragons on Echizen-school sword blades. Yasutsugu obtained the first character of his name from the 'yasu' in 'Ieyasu', for the Shogun employed him and his school for several generations. Both Yasutsugu I and Yasutsugu II lived for alternate years in Edo and Echizen, but the family split into two groups after the third generation. Ieyasu gave Yasutsugu I the right to carve the Tokugawa family *mon* ('emblem') of three hollyhock leaves. Many of Yasutsugu's swords are inscribed 'made with Namban iron', 'Namban' meaning 'Southern Barbarian', thus foreign steel. He also made copies of famous old blades, including the 'Hocho' ('kitchen knife') Masamune, and re-tempered valuable old blades which had been damaged in castle fires.

Kanewaka of Kaga made blades in Soshu and Mino styles, his Soshu-style blades often being similar to those of Sadamune. In Sendai, the smith Kunikane was retained by the *daimyo* Daté Masamune, and made swords in the Yamato Hoshu style, as did his sons and descendants.

In Wakayama, Nanki Shigekuni also followed the Yamato tradition, and in Saga of Hizen province the line of Tadayoshi continued through until the twentieth century. Mino no Kami Ujifusa made splendid broadswords culminating in fully tempered points, with *hamon* of rolling clouds in large *nie*.

Umetada Myoju in Kyoto claimed twenty-fifth generation ancestry from Munechika, he who made the great treasure sword 'Mikazuki' in the Heian period. Myoju made swords with exceptionally fine *koitame* (fine 'wood grain') and broad, undulating *hamon* in bright even *nie*. He also made beautiful carvings on his own blades and on the blades of others. The words 'carved by Umetada' are found on the tangs of many swords, including those made by his pupils. Myoju died in the eighth year of Kinei (1631) aged 74. His name is taken as the borderline between the 'Old Swords' and 'New Swords' periods, perhaps because of his many pupils from provinces throughout the country, including Tadayoshi of Hizen, and Yamato Daijo Yoshinobu and his son Shigeyoshi.

Tadayoshi of Hizen went as a young man to study under Myoju, adopting the name Tadayoshi in 1596, the year he went to Kyoto. Tadayoshi and his school made fine swords throughout the Edo period, with bright fine-grained *hada* rich in *jinie*. His *hamon* include *suguha* in *nie*, more defined than those of the old Yamashiro style - this is the type of *hamon* found on about 60 per cent of all Hizen province blades - and sometimes *gunome* or, more typically, *o-choji* (large 'clove flower' patterns). The *ashi* on Hizen swords are long, and characteristically reach down almost to the edge of the blade. The unfailing quality of the work of generation after generation of smiths in Hizen, particularly those of the direct line of Tadayoshi, has made Hizen swords as highly prized by collectors today as they were by the samurai of the past. Like Nabeshima porcelain ware, Hizen swords were used by high-ranking men of the province and given as presents to the *daimyos* of other provinces.

Horigawa Kunihiro made swords in the Soshu style, with blades rich in *nie* and resembling the cut-down blades of the Yoshino period. Indeed his work is so good that some of his swords were, in the past, ascribed to Masamune. A samurai of Furuya in Higo Province, Kunihiro, was employed as an armourer at the time of Hideyoshi's expeditions to Korea in the closing years of the sixteenth century. Kunihiro's *hada* is speckled with *nie* and has a 'rough' appearance, and his *hamon* is like that of Masamune, in *nie* with a continuous *gunome* and *chikei* and *kinsen* (bright lines of *nie* crystals). He also carved skilfully. Among his eminent successors were Dewa Daijo Fujiwara Kunimichi, Kunisada and Kunisuke, who were still young men at the time of their master's death.

The Sampin brothers, active in the early seventeenth century, were the sons of Kanemichi from Seki, ninth generation in descent from Kaneuji, the pupil of Masamune. Their swords have a fine grain, with Mino style *hamon* in *nie*. Izumi no Kami Rai Kinmichi was given the prestigious right to carve the imperial chrysanthemum on his sword tangs. Etchu no Kami Masatoshi made many *wakizashi* with *o-gunome* (large, abruptly undulating *hamon*) and *midare-ba* (an irregular pattern on the cutting edge). Tamba no Kami Yoshimichi made Soshu-style swords with *o-itame hada* (coarse 'wood grain' *hada*) quite unlike those of the other Kyoto smiths. His son moved to Osaka, and the line continued for several generations. The third Yoshimichi specialized in picturesque *hamon*, such as *sudare-ba* ('bamboo curtain'), Mount Fuji and chrysanthemums floating on water.

The Edo period (1603–1867)

The Edo period marked the end of the *Koto* or 'Old Swords' period, and the emergence of a number of distinct *Shinto* or 'New Sword' traditions. The centres of commerce and craft were the castle towns which sprang up around the castles of the provincial lords, and the new sword traditions were established by the smiths who worked in these towns, some of whom were accomplished enough to obtain employment with the local lord or *daimyo*.

The Tokugawa government prevented the possibility of insurrection by instituting rigid controls on these provincial lords and their families. Every *daimyo* had to live for six months of the year in Edo, leaving his family in the capital when he returned home to run his estates, and there was an elaborate system of border guards and spies to ensure that the system was obeyed. The guards were instructed to watch for 'guns going in and women going out'. Farmers paid their taxes in rice and samurais' incomes were paid in rice. The merchant classes thrived in the towns, while many samurai lived in poverty.

At the beginning of the seventeenth century there were many unemployed samurai or *ronin* ('wave men') with little means of livelihood in an era of peace. Some gave up their swords and worked; some became tutors; others set up schools of Kendo. Some became ne'er do wells, and set their thumb prints in blood to seal their allegiance to brotherhoods like the Kabukimono (the Swaggerers). Many *ronin* lived violently, enacting duels to the death, and testing their skill at arms in the bloody sport known as *tsuji-giri* ('cutting at the crossroads'), in which unsuspecting travellers would be suddenly set upon and cut to pieces. The Kabukimono in particular were seen as a threat to the government. They dressed and behaved exotically in the spirit of the Momoyama period, with scant regard for authority. But various edicts were published to wipe out the *ronin* as a class. The Kabukimono were proscribed and the practice of *tsuji-giri* was prohibited. Swords over the length of 2 *shaku* 8 or 9 *sun* (about 38 ins/80 cm) were prohibited, as were gold and vermilion scabbards. Swords with large square *tsuba* guards were also prohibited, as they could be used as a step to vault over walls. The employment of *ronin* was forbidden, and so were outlandish clothes and hairstyles. The *chomage* hairstyle, with the hair drawn back and tied up in a short queue and the forehead shaved, became compulsory for samurai, who also had to wear swords with black scabbards in the capital.

Toyotomi Hideyoshi, in his 'Sword Hunt' of 1588, had attempted to disarm the large armies of common soldiers which threatened the peace of the provinces, collecting swords ostensibly in order to obtain the material for a great image of Buddha. The Tokugawas also introduced legislation aimed at limiting the possession of arms. In 1623 commoners were prohibited from wearing swords. In 1640 the attendants of samurai were prohibited from carrying long swords. In 1683 the Shogun

Tsunatoshi ruled that musicians and painters should not carry a long sword, even if they were of samurai class, but that commoners might carry a dagger. In 1798 the wearing of *wakizashi* over 1 *shaku* 8 *sun* (21½ ins/55 cm) in length was prohibited. This regulation, which was later changed to 1 *shaku* 5 *sun*, was aimed at the merchant class, among whom only the *wakizashi* was legal. As a result it is common to find *wakizashi* which have been shortened to comply with the regulation.

In the first few decades of the Edo period swords were modelled on the shape of the *suriage* or cut-down blades of the Kamakura and Yoshino periods, although the blades were generally thicker. But from the middle of the seventeenth century onwards a new type of shallow curved blade about 28 ins/70 cm long and narrowing towards the point, and known as *Kambun-Shinto* after the Kambun era (1661–73), became popular. This seems to have resulted from the development of indoor schools of Kendo, which emphasized the large circling downward cut holding the sword in both hands.

Since the samurai class had by now become relatively impoverished and could not afford to commission swords from the better smiths, many fine quality *wakizashi* of the period were made for wealthy merchants. The *hamon* of such blades are characteristically picturesque, and fine carvings of auspicious subjects appear on many of them.

Since the early seventeenth century Japan had been isolated from foreign intercourse save for a Dutch and a Chinese trading post in Nagasaki harbour, but in the eighteenth century people began to question the wisdom of this policy. Movements in opposition to the establishment and favouring a revival of the past gathered momentum. This was partly dissatisfaction with the rigid social system imposed by the Tokugawa, and partly a rising feeling of nationalism and respect for the Emperor, for the imperial line continued even though the Shogun held power. People were increasingly aware of the might of the Western powers, and while some were for continued isolation backed up by military power, many wanted Japan to establish herself internationally.

The revivalist movement found its echo in sword-making. One smith in particular, Suishinshi Masahide (1750–1825), devoted himself to the study of the old schools and made swords in the styles of the Kamakura and Yoshino periods. Other smiths followed suit, and many swords were made in both Kambun shape and in the shapes of the Kamakura and Yoshino periods throughout the eighteenth and the nineteenth centuries. The forging and tempering methods of the ancient schools were revived, so that at first sight such swords have the appearance of early weapons. These swords are known as *Shin-Shinto* ('New New Swords').

When the Emperor Meiji was restored to power in 1867 the wearing of swords in public was prohibited, and the number of active swordsmiths dwindled to a handful. There was a revival in

Oppostite page, above and below
Part of a two-fold screen showing samurai youths dressed in the height of fashion, school of Matabei, seventeenth century.
Wakizashi by Masatoshi (see caption below).

Left Portrait thought to be of a lord of the Nabeshima clan, nineteenth century.

Below Component parts of a sword, in this case a *wakizashi* signed on the blade by Etchu no Kami Masatoshi, one of the Sampin brothers of Osaka. The fittings, of *shakudo* (an alloy of copper and gold patinated black) with gold inlay, are seventeenth-century Mino school work.

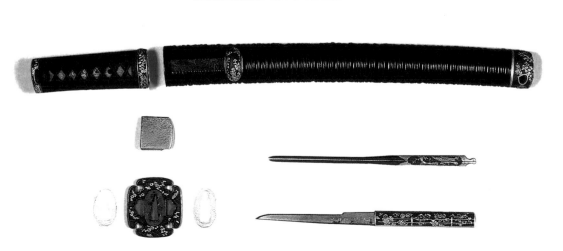

Far right The blade on the right is signed by the seventeenth-century smith Echizen no Kami Sukenao and has the typical *Kambun-Shinto* shape of the Middle Edo period, narrowing somewhat towards the point and with a shallow curve. The *toranba* or 'billowing wave' pattern of the *hamon* is executed in bright *nie*, and the *hada* is so fine as to appear almost grainless. Sukenao was the son of Sukehiro of Osaka.

The weapon on the left is a *Shin-Shinto* blade by the nineteenth-century smith Enju Nobukatsu. This long 'Restoration sword' is made with *hamon* in the Bizen style and the deep curve of the Kamakura-Namboku Cho periods.

Right An Aizu samurai in winter dress, late nineteenth century.

Opposite page Some *hamon* typical of Edo period blades. Sukehiro of Osaka specialized in *toranba*. *Yakidashi*, where the *hamon* slopes away gradually down towards the tang, were also characteristic of Osaka blades. *Juzuba* were characteristic of Kotetsu, *sudare* of the third Yoshimichi, *kobushi gata choji* of Kawachi no Kami Kunisuke, and broad *suguha* of Tadayoshi of Hizen.

sword-making during the Showa era (1926–1989), which suffered an understandable setback after the World War II, but in recent years the number of active smiths has increased to satisfy the demand for swords as art objects in their own right.

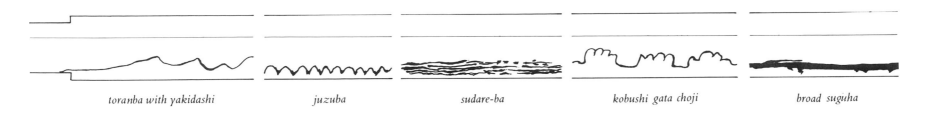

| *toranba with yakidashi* | *juzuba* | *sudare-ba* | *kobushi gata choji* | *broad suguha* |

Characteristics of Middle Edo period blades

Izumi no Kami Kunisada's swords have rough *hada*, but are otherwise in the Osaka style (see below). His *hamon* are usually *suguha* or *o-notare midare*. Kunisada's adopted son, the second Kunisada, made swords with *hamon* in *nie* like his father's, but his *hada* and *hamon* are altogether brighter and more accomplished. At first he signed his swords Inoue Izumi no Kami Kunisada, but upon taking lay orders he changed his name to Shinkai. He was one of the privileged number of smiths who were permitted to inscribe the imperial chrysanthemum on the tangs of their swords.

Noda Hankei began his career as the gunsmith Kiyotaka. His swords are prized as *owaza-mono* ('great technique' swords), and have a uniform blade width and a rather elongated point. His long swords are in Soshu style and closely resemble those of Etchu no Norishige. Like Norishige, his steel is very hard, and the mixture of different quality steels shows as a peculiar open-looking *itame* grain with *jinie* and *chikei*; this is sometimes called *hijiki-hada* and is reminiscent of Norishige's *matsugawa* ('pine bark') *hada*. The *nie* is large and sprawling, making it difficult to follow the shape of the *hamon*. Round-ended grooves were the only carvings Hankei used on his blades.

Eminent smiths of Osaka

After the fall of Osaka castle in 1615, the city grew into a major centre for commerce. Many of the second generation *Shinto* smiths flourished there. Osaka swords are noted for their fine *hada*, which is very close-forged. *Hamon* are generally flamboyant, sloping down towards the *hamachi* (end of the cutting edge) like the side of Mount Fuji; this feature is called *yakidashi*. Kawachi no Kami Kunisuke, Ikkanshi Tadatsuna, Tsuda Sukehiro, Izumi no Kami Kunisada and his adopted son Inoue Shinkai, and several other good smiths worked in Osaka from around the middle of the seventeenth century.

Kawachi no Kami Kunisuke was the pupil of Horigawa Kunihiro, and made swords with *o-gunome hamon* (large, abruptly undulating *hamon*) and thick *nie*. His son, known as Naka Kawachi, forged swords with typically fine Osaka *hada* which appears almost grainless. He made a characteristic *hamon* in fine *nie* known as *kobushi gata choji* ('fist-shaped pattern'), which has the appearance of rows of clenched knuckles.

Ikkanshi Tadatsuna, active around 1690, studied in the Awataguchi school of Kyoto and made blades with the elegant *kyo-zori* curve, with bright *hamon* of broadly rounded *choji-midare* (irregular clove flower pattern). His son Ikkanshi Tadatsuna used a large *gunome* resembling billowing waves, *toranba*, and clean and bright *jigane*. He was a notable carver, especially of dragons, and would often sign proudly on the tangs of his swords that he had made the carving.

Tsuda Sukehiro, active around 1660, also known as Soboro Sukehiro, came from Tsuda in Harima, and studied under the first Kunisuke. He worked in either broad *suguha* or *gunome-midare*. His adopted son was given the title Echizen no Kami in 1664, and signed his blades 'Tsuda Echizen no Kami'. His swords are either in medium *suguha*, or in the characteristic *toranba* ('billowing waves') *hamon*. His *jigane* is bright and the outline of his *hamon* soft. His pupil Sukenao made fine swords with *toranba*-style *hamon*, and the style became so popular in Osaka that many smiths copied it.

Eminent smiths of Edo

In the city of Edo, in addition to the line of Yasutsugu of Echizen, there were several excellent smiths, including Nagasone Kotetsu, Yamato no Kami Yasusada, and the Ishido and Hojoji schools. Generally their work is more sombre than that of the Osaka smiths, reflecting the military air of the capital.

Nagasone Kotetsu (d. 1678) was originally an armour-maker of Nagasone village in Omi province, lived for a while in Fukui of Echizen, and settled in Edo when he was 51. The demand for swords had outstripped the demand for armour, and Kotetsu found more than a ready market for his fine swords. Although his work was modelled on that of Go Yoshihiro, the fourteenth-century pupil of Masamune, his swords are in the typical shape of the Kambun era (1661-72), the shape which became the norm during the second half of the seventeenth century. His *hamon* can be *suguha*, *o-notare midare* or, more characteristically, *juzuba* (a form of *gunome* resembling the beads of a rosary). Wide *ashi* in *nioi* sweep down from the valleys of the *gunome*. Alone among the smiths of Edo, Kotetsu's work sometimes has a Kyoto-style *yakidashi*. He made long swords and daggers, and many *wakizashi*. Many of these are finely decorated with carvings of all kinds. He must have been proud of his sculpture, and probably spent a lot of time over it in order to satisfy his clients, but as he became older and more established his blades became more severe, and he bothered less with cutting tests.

The Ishido Bizen school

The Ishido school followed the Bizen tradition, making *hamon* in *o-choji midare* after the Kamakura-period Ichimonji school. There were branches of the school in Fukuoka, Omi, Kii and Osaka. Musashi Daijo Korekazu (d. 1891) and his descendants worked in Edo.

Characteristics of Late Edo period blades

Starting with Suishinshi Masahide, many smiths reverted to the styles of ancient schools during the late Edo period, and all kinds of *hamon* and grain are found on their work. However, they could not reproduce the finest quality steel of their ancestors' blades, and certain characteristics, such as *utsuri*, are missing from their work. *Shin-Shinto* blades can be excellent copies of the Mino, Soshu, Bizen or Yamato styles, but in nearly all cases the *hamon* and other details appear youthful and contrived.

Cutting tests

Many stories are told of the cutting efficiency of famous old Japanese swords, and indeed many swords are named after an episode which demonstrated their fearfulness. It was natural to test a sword before using it in battle, for one's life depended on it, and cutting practice was a necessary part of the old Kendo schools.

In the Edo period, a particular profession specialized in testing swords and grading them according to their cutting powers. The most active testers were the Yamada family. Yamada Asaemon, for example, was employed to try the swords owned by the Tokugawa family; he would relieve the public executioner of his duties and behead condemned criminals with the swords he was given to test, using the bodies for more cutting tests afterwards. The results of such tests were carefully recorded, and sometimes inlaid in gold on the tangs of the swords concerned. Thus one finds inscriptions like 'cut through an arm and trunk', 'cut through both hip bones', or even 'cut through three bodies'.

The Yamada reputation was great, and many samurai commissioned tests for their swords. In the seventeenth century the swordsmiths of Edo would have their swords tested and inscribed before delivery to the customer, thus considerably enhancing their value. The famous seventeenth-century Edo smith Nagasone Kotetsu seems to have had a long relationship with the official Bakufu government sword-tester Yamano Kayemon Nagahisa, known also as Kanjiro, since many of his swords are inscribed in gold with Yamano's attestations.

The custom of testing swords is of great antiquity, and certainly originated in China. In Japan it was an important part of a samurai's education. The classic book *Hagakure*, about the spirit of the Nabeshima clan, tells of boys just come of the age to wear swords being provided with limbs from the execution grounds to practice on. There are also countless tales of surprising feats both on the field of war and at the execution grounds during the peaceful Edo era.

During Hideyoshi's Korean campaign of 1592 there was ample opportunity to test swords. According to the *Daté Ke Tokenki* ('Sword Records of the Daté Family'), during a meeting of officers to test swords a prisoner was presented who was as big as an ox. Kato Kiyomasa, a skilled swordsman, was to do the testing. The gathered samurai were rather reluctant to offer their swords for fear that the edge might chip on the bones of such a big fellow, but the *daimyo* Daté Masamune lent his own personal blade. Kiyomasa cut through the prisoner and deep into the block with one cut, so that the sword could not immediately be withdrawn. Since the unfortunate prisoner had a swarthy complexion, the sword was on the spot named 'Kurombu-giri' ('Black Chap Cutter'). The same sword was also known as 'Kura-giri' ('Saddle Cutter') according to the book *Wakan Token Dan* ('Tales of Chinese and Japanese Swords'), since with it Daté Masamune cut down a fleeing enemy captain with such vigour that the blade went through to the enemy's saddle. The sword

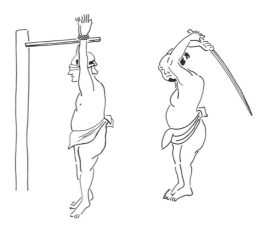

was a *tachi* by Kagehide of Bizen, with a cutting length of about 29 ins/73 cm. It is now an Important Cultural Asset.

The Shogun Tokugawa Ieyasu himself, in his final decline two days before his death, was moved to test a sword known as 'Sohaya no Tsurugi'. The test was perfectly successful and the sword was thereafter deposited in the Kumanozan Toshogu Shrine in whose collection it remains today, as a holy object which ensured the good fortune of the Tokugawa family.

The Yamada family specified cuts across the body at ten different places from the hips up to the shoulders, and two cuts known as *kesa-giri*. The *kesa* is the surplice of a Buddhist monk, and the cuts were made following the drape of the surplice, slanting through the shoulder and also through the shoulder and trunk. Sometimes more than one corpse would be used and the number of bodies cut through at one stroke recorded. Tests with more than three corpses tied together were rare, although a sword made by Yamato no Kami Yasusada was said to have been used to cut through five bodies by Yamano Kaemon when he was 64 years old. There also exists a sixteenth-century sword by Kanefusa of Seki with an inscription claiming that seven bodies were cut through at one stroke. During the later part of the Edo period tests were frequently done on bundles of straw wrapped around bamboo, and against pieces of armour and other hard objects.

Much was required of the *fukko-to* ('restoration swords') with which the feudal lords expected to repel any attempt at invasion by Russia and the Western powers. In Mitto province, for example, an oak pole 2 ins/5 cm in diameter was used in the first of a series of tests, beating the sword from all directions. Another test was to cut rolled straw bundles, and a further test was to cut hard staghorn. Swords were also expected to stand the shock of cutting against other swords, although only the best swords could survive a strong cut on the *mune* or back edge.

Carvings on Japanese sword blades

Many Japanese swords have *horimono* or carvings on their blades, the simplest being the groove, whose primary purpose was to lighten a blade of thick cross-section. But the groove also added to the elegance of a weapon, and many different styles of groove developed, showing regional and period characteristics.

Some Japanese swords are carved with Chinese characters. One of the earliest examples is the Nara period *chokuto* in the Shitennoji Temple; it is known as the 'Heishi Shorin Tsurugi' and the corresponding characters are carved and inlaid with gold on the blade. The meaning of the Chinese inscription is not fully understood, but carvings on later swords clearly indicate the deep religious beliefs of both samurai and swordsmiths. Sometimes the Chinese characters invoke Buddhist or Shinto deities, and sometimes the deities of both religions share the same blade. Occasionally a single Sanskrit character is used to represent the name of a deity.

Many blades from the Heian period onwards are grooved or carved with the figures of deities. Smiths like Yukihira of Bungo province, working in the late Heian period, often carved representations of Bodhisattva Jizo or the Buddhist deity Fudo-Myo-O (Acala in Sanskrit). Fudo-Myo-O, the Immovable, was one of the Five Myo-O or Rajas of Light in the Shingon sect of esoteric Buddhism and is depicted sitting or standing in flames, with a dreadful countenance. He holds two attributes, in his right hand the double-edged *ken*-type sword with a hilt in the form of a *vajra* (ritual weapon of esoteric Buddhism), and in the other a coil of rope. The rope serves to bind illusions, and the sword to cut through the illusionary world, revealing the ultimately real world, or *Kongo-Kai*.

The esoteric Buddhist belief that by contemplation and ritual it is possible to cosubstantiate with Buddha, or that spiritual enlightenment can be achieved by one's own endeavours, found favour with smith and samurai alike. For it is by endeavour that a fine sword is made, and by endeavour that the warrior acquires his fighting skills and makes spiritual progress. The unmoving nature of Fudo-Myo-O represents the spiritual attitude sought by the samurai, calmness and steadiness in the heat of battle and the inner strength not to be provoked by the enemy into unprofitable actions. The ultimately real world, or spiritual enlightenment, as revealed by Fudo's sword, is paralleled by the spiritual nature of the samurai's own sword and devotion to Kendo. In many respects the world as we see it, including life itself, was seen by the samurai as an impediment to understanding.

The ancient Kendo schools developed in Shinto shrines and Buddhist temples. The sons of emperors became monks, and the daughters became nuns or shrine maidens. During the Kamakura period in particular many smiths and samurai ascetics were devotees of the Shugendo cult or 'mountain religion'. These 'mountain men' or Yamabushi sought knowledge from the awesome Shinto deities of the mountains and the uncompromising figures of esoteric Buddhism. The main Buddhist figures were Zao Gongen, a strange meeting of Buddhism and Shinto, who also holds the *vajra*, and Fudo-Myo-O, sometimes depicted beneath a waterfall, illustrating one of the forms of harsh spiritual

training associated with the mountain religion. There are stories of mountain men living alone in the wilds who could communicate with animals or fly with the birds. Minamoto Yoshitsune, hero of the Genji clan, is said to have been taught Kendo by the *tengu* of Mount Kurama. *Tengu* were mythical winged humanoids with beaks or long noses who inhabited wild places, but in reality Yoshitsune was probably the pupil of the Yamabushi of Mount Kurama, centre of the esoteric Tendai sect.

Other carvings on Japanese sword blades were the *ken* sword of Fudo-Myo-O, or sometimes just the rope. Two short parallel grooves represented *gomabashi*, the tongs used in exorcism rites. The lotus, *cintamani* jewel, and other religious paraphernalia are also found in stylized form. Sometimes the *ken* motif is contained within the coils of a dragon who holds the *cintamani* jewel and whose tail is a sword.

Throughout the *Koto* or 'Old Swords' period, which came to an end with the accession of the Tokugawas in the early seventeenth century, *horimono* reflected the religious beliefs of the samurai, but from the Momoyama period onwards, that is from the late sixteenth century, their significance became more that of good luck charms. The austere *horimono* of the past gave way to mere decoration, providing the smith with a further means of showing his style. Whereas during the Muromachi period the principal popular Shinto deities Ebisu and Daikokuten appear clad in armour as gods of war, in the Edo period they become cheery deities of good fortune. Also depicted in later *horimono* are the auspicious plants plum, bamboo and pine, the crane and the tortoise, and Horaizen, the island of immortality. The motif of a dragon ascending one side of the blade and descending the other is found exclusively on *Shinto* blades.

Swordplay and swordsmen

Ancient Japan abounds with tales of daring and feats of combat which are almost unimaginable to the normal person, and often it is the quality of the sword which has enabled the samurai to succeed. There are many recorded instances of one man, or a small group of men, overcoming vastly superior forces in combat. But the greatest admiration has always been for the man who, out of duty, has taken his own life by cutting open his stomach in the form of suicide called *seppuku*, or commonly *hara kiri*. It is not the vulgar profit obtained by combat, not victory for its own sake, but rather the resolute acceptance of death by the sword as part of the warrior's everyday philosophy which is the heart and soul of swordsmanship. And the ultimate aim of a long study of swords and swordplay is an absolute understanding of the nature of life and death. Enlightenment is the true object of swordplay.

In the grounds of the Sengakuji Temple in Tokyo there are forty-eight carefully tended graves, the resting places of the Lord Asano and forty-seven of his loyal retainers. Asano, insulted in the grounds of Edo castle by a government official named Kira,

Above Dragon carving in Kinai style on a seventeenth-century Echizen blade. The tang has been antiqued to substantiate the false signature 'Masamune'. Probably by Yasutsuga, *c*.1600.

Opposite page The deity Fudo-Myo-O (Unmoving King of Light) carved on a late sixteenth-century blade by Kanabo Masazane (left).

A sword tester prepares to cut diagonally through the torso of a prisoner (right).

Opposite page Gold lacquered *ito maki no tachi* mounting, eighteenth century. The *tachi*-style mounting was used when armour was worn in battle, and by *daimyos* and high-ranking samurai on the road to and from Edo during times of peace. The gold 'triple flagstones' badges are those of the Tsujiura clan.

Below A *kozuka* or utility knife, a *kogai*, a kind of bodkin used for cleaning the ears, dressing the hair, and other purposes, and a pair of *menuki* ornaments, all of eighteenth-century date. The *menuki* fit under the binding on either side of the hilt of a sword.

drew his short sword and wounded the man, and for this offence against bureaucracy was sentenced to death by *seppuku*, his estates forfeited and his retainers disbanded. After a period during which his now masterless retainers gave the outward impression of having abandoned thoughts of revenge, Kira became careless. One snowy night in February 1703 a group of forty-seven of the most loyal of Asano's men forced their way into Kira's house and killed him, taking his head to their master's grave. Although public opinion was on their side, and even the Shogun expressed his admiration for their loyal behaviour, they too were eventually sentenced to death by suicide. Since that time the band of forty-seven have been fêted as heroes and made the subject of the most popular of Kabuki dramas, *Chushingura*. There is constantly burning incense at their graves.

Probably the best known of all Japanese swordsmen is Miyamoto Musashi (1584–1645), who became enlightened at the age of 50, having won more than sixty life and death contests between the ages of 13 and 28 or 29. His best remembered contest was with the young swordsman Sasaki Kojiro, a retainer of the Hosokawa family. Kojiro used a long sword and specialized in a fencing technique known as *tsubame gaeshi* ('swallow tail counter'), and everyone expected him to win the fight. The contest was to be held in early morning on an island called Ganryujima. Musashi arrived late by boat and, taking an oar, rushed up the beach to the waiting Kojiro and killed him with one blow of the oar. Some sources say that he then retired several paces and drew both his swords, flourishing them at his fallen enemy with a terrible shout. This was one of many occasions on which Musashi used a wooden implement instead of a steel blade in a contest to the death.

Musashi fought alone with a sword against many men several times during his life, and described in his classic exposition *A Book of Five Rings* how it is done. But the essence of his book, jotted down in the week before his death, is the attainment of spiritual enlightenment through the Way of the Sword. He writes of the sword that 'weapons should be robust rather than decorative' and that 'to become too familiar with a weapon is as bad as not knowing it at all'. On cutting with the sword, Musashi says: 'If you are concerned with the strength of your sword you will try to cut unreasonably strongly, and will not be able to cut at all. It is also bad to try to cut strongly when testing the sword. Whenever you cross swords with an enemy you must not think of cutting him either strongly or weakly; just think of cutting and killing him.'

In more recent years another great swordsman, and also a politician and confidant of the young Emperor Meiji, Yamaoka Tesshu (1836–88), also achieved enlightenment through devotion to swordplay. But although Tesshu's training methods through traditional exercises and fencing with bamboo swords were terribly harsh and almost beyond human endurance, he never killed a man with his sword. After his enlightenment he called his

school the Muto Ryu ('No Sword School'), explaining that there is no real sword outside the heart.

Kondo Isami, hero of the Shinsengumi movement and master of the little-known Tennenrishiryu school of Kendo, only fought with swords twice in his life. Once was in Kyoto in 1864, when he was on night patrol with his companion Sannan Keisuke. Three enemies, supporters of the imperialist cause, appeared, whereupon Sannan killed one and Kondo cut down the others. In the process, Sannan damaged his sword point on the stone wall of the house of a merchant named Konoike. Konoike, a Shinsengumi sympathizer, generously invited the pair to select new swords from his own armoury of about fifty swords. Kondo selected a sword by the seventeenth-century master Kotetsu, a sword which was to serve him well in his second fight.

The Shinsengumi, hearing of the presence in the city of around 300 'Sonjoha' imperialists bent on causing trouble, asked for the aid of certain friendly clans. However, before aid arrived Kondo and his small group of around thirty men split into three to comb the town for the Sonjoha. Kondo and his few Samurai chanced upon thirty or so of the enemy's best men in the upper rooms of the Ikeyada Inn, and a fierce fight commenced. Most of Kondo's companions were quickly disabled: Okita fainted with a brain-storm, Fujido Keisuke lost the metal forehead-protector he wore fixed over his head with a towel and was cut deeply, Nagakura sustained a deep cut between his thumb and forefinger and so could not use his sword, and Ando was grievously hurt. Kondo alone fought on, always beset by several of the enemy. When aid eventually arrived there were nine dead in the Ikeyada Inn, and twenty-three of the enemy made captive.

Although he was not able to see his leader in action, Nagakura was afterwards to tell of Kondo's terrible war cries shaking the bottom of his stomach. Most of the swords used in the affray were found to have been chipped and bent during the combat, but Kondo's Kotetsu was quite undamaged, tribute both to the blade and to Kondo's great skill.

Glossary of technical terms

ashi   'legs' or short lines of *nie* or *nioi*
ayasugi hada   parallel wavy lines on flat of blade
boshi   'cap' or turnback of *hamon* at point of blade
chikei   serene pools of shadow on flat of blade
chirimen hada   silk crêpe effect on flat of blade
choji   'clove flower'
choji-ba   'clove flower' pattern
choji midare   wild or irregular clove flowers
chokuto   long, straight, single-edged sword of Kofun and Nara periods
daisho   pair of swords worn by samurai of Muromachi period onwards
fumbari   'tenacity' or 'bottom', the broadening of a blade near the hilt

gunome   an abruptly undulating *hamon*

gunome midare   an irregular and abruptly undulating *hamon*

hada   skin or surface

hadagane   skin steel, harder than core steel (*shingane*)

hamaguri-ba   'clam-shape' blade, one with slightly convex flat surfaces

hamachi   point where the cutting edge stops and the tang starts

hamon   'badge' of blade, the continuous line of bright steel formed by cutting edge of blade

hijiki-hada   slender, intertwining lines on flat of blade resembling stalks of *hijiki* seaweed

hira-ji   sides of the blade

hira-zukuri   blade of triangular cross-section, with flattened sides

hitatsura   'full cover' *hamon* which spreads in patches over whole blade

hoko   glaive of Nara period

horimono   carvings on blade

hotsure   wispy lines of *nie* rather like fraying textile

ikubi tachi   'bull-neck' point sword

ikubi-zaki   'bull-neck' point

inazuma   long lines of *nie* running haphazardly through and around cutting edge of blade

itame   'wood plank' grain found on flat of blade

ji   ground of blade, that part of flat of blade above hardened edge portion

jigane or *jihada*   the type of grain on the *ji*

jinie   *nie* on ground of blade

juka-choji   layers of *choji* pattern

ka-en   flame-like cap or turnback at point of blade

kani-no-tsume   'crab's claws', a pincer-like rise along edge of cutting surface

kashira   butt of hilt

katana   long sword often worn with *wakizashi*

kawazu-ko-choji   'tadpole-shaped' *choji* pattern

kenuki gata tachi   'tweezer-shaped' sword

kiku gosaku   'noble chrysanthemum make'

kinsen   bright lines of *nie* crystals

kinsuji   short lines of *nie* running haphazardly through and around edge of *hamon*

kissaki   point or tip of blade

kobushi gata choji   'fist-shaped' or clenched knuckle pattern along edge of cutting surface

koitame   fine 'wood grain' effect

ko-maru   delicately rounded cap or turnback at point of blade

ko-nie   fine *nie*

koshi   'waist' of blade nearest the tang

koshigatana   'waist' sword used for beheading fallen enemies on field of battle

koshi-zori   blade which curves near the tang

kyo-zori   blade which curves evenly throughout its length

masame   'straight' grain found on flat of blade

matsukawa hada   'pine bark' grain on flat of blade

mekugi ana   peg hole in tang for attaching hilt

mete zashi   'horse-hand' dagger, held in right hand

midare-ba   irregular pattern on cutting edge

midare-komi   irregular or wavy cap or turnback at point of blade

mon   family or clan emblem

mono-uchi   'striking place' of blade, a quarter of the way back from the point

mune   blunt back edge of blade

nagare   'flowing' grain found on flat of blade

naginata   staff weapon with long single-edged blade

Namban tetsu   'Southern Barbarian' or imported steel

nashiji hada   'pear skin' grain

nie   patches of distinct steel crystals on cutting surface of blade

niju-ba   double line along edge of cutting surface

nioi   'visible fragrance', misty crystalline structures on cutting edge of blade

no tachi   moor swords, very long blades made in fourteenth century

o-choji   large 'clove flower' pattern

o-gunome   large, abruptly undulating *hamon*

o-notare midare   large, irregular, wavy hamon

oroshi-mune   blade cross-section with exaggerated ridge between cutting surface and flat of blade

owaza-mono   'great technique' sword

saka-choji   backward-sloping *choji* pattern

saki zori   curve in upper part of blade

sambon-sugi   *hamon* in form of rows of three interlinked cryptomeria treetops

seoi tachi   sword carried on the back, another name for a *no tachi*

shingane   core steel, softer than skin steel (*hadagane*)

shinogi   longitudinal ridge dividing flat of blade from sloped cutting edge

shinogi-ji   parallel surfaces of the blade above the ridge line

shirake   white shadow on ground of blade, rather like *utsuri*

sudare-ba   'bamboo curtain' effect along edge of cutting surface of blade

suguha   blade with straight-edged cutting surface

sunagushi   a form of *nie* resembling 'floating sands'

suriage katana   cut-down sword

tanto   dagger

toranba   'billowing waves' effect along edge of cutting surface of blade

tosu   small knife

tsuba   sword guard

uchigatana   'hitting' sword

uchi-no-ke   crescent-shaped spots of *nie*

utsuri   faint shadow or reflection along ground or flat of blade

wakizashi   shorter companion sword to *katana*

warabite-tachi   short, broad sword of Kofun and Nara periods

yakidashi   that part of *hamon* which slopes away gently into the *hamon*

yo   single 'leaves' of *nie* or *nioi*

yubashiri   'hot water run' spots of *nie*

13 CHINA AND CENTRAL ASIA

Thom Richardson

The history of the development of edged weapons in China and Central Asia is one of the most obscure areas in the study of arms and armour. Surveys of either subject in English language publications have seldom run to more than a few lines, and have concentrated, in general, either on the types of weapons available on the open market to collectors, or on archaeological material. The only attempts at overall surveys of the subject have been conducted in relatively obscure Chinese publications, and these too have been brief. It is hoped that the following overview will stimulate wider interest and further, more detailed studies.

From legend into history

The origins of the sword in China are enshrined in the legendary past. The single-edged cutting sword, the *dao*, is supposed to have been invented by Sui Renshi, second of the mythical San Huang emperors, who made it by melting gold. Swords were either male, *xiong*, or female, *ci*; names were bestowed upon them, such as 'Insurgent Conquering General'; and many had magical powers, such as the ability to glow in the dark or to utter sounds. The straight two-edged thrusting sword, the *jian*, was likewise first made of gold, according to myth; it too possessed supernatural powers, such as being able to change into a dragon and put evil spirits to flight. Sacrifices, sometimes human, were made in thanks to such swords.

The archaeological record paints a more prosaic picture. Mastery of the use of bronze in China was the achievement of the Shang Dynasty (*c.*1700–*c.*1100 BC). Until their overthrow by their neighbours, the Zhou, the peoples known as the Shang dominated northern China. Warfare in the early and middle Shang period was conducted by infantry, armed with bows and arrows for long-range conflict, and with the dagger-axe or *ge*, a knife-shaped bronze blade mounted at right angles to a long wooden shaft, for hand-to-hand fighting.

The late Shang period, however, saw the introduction of the Central Asian chariot into the Chinese arsenal, and also the bronze knife. The archaeological site of Anyang in Shaanxi province, which seems to have been the capital of the late Shang, contains numerous chariot burials. The deceased were interred, with all their equipment, beneath the small rectangular platforms of their two-horse chariots, and their slaughtered horses were buried with them. The chariot-borne Shang dominated the battlefield by their mobility. Their bows were of the composite type, but for close fighting, and probably for general purposes too, they used small curved animal-headed knives. These were probably introduced at the same time as the chariot – similar bronze knives are found on sites in northwest China and in southern Siberia.

Another type of knife, the *xiao*, also of bronze, with a curved blade and a ring pommel, has been excavated from Shang sites which predate the introduction of the chariot. Unlike the animal-pommelled group, ring-pommelled knives continued in use throughout the Shang and Zhou dynasties, eventually giving rise to the ring-pommelled sword.

Early bronze swords

The sword probably entered the Chinese arsenal at the same time as the use of cavalry – the practice of riding became widespread in Central Asia from the eighth century BC onwards. Encountering this new means of transport, probably among the nomadic tribes of the Ordos region, and perceiving its military potential, the states of northern China equipped themselves with mounted troops.

The earliest Chinese swords come from sites in northwestern China, for example from Zhangjiapo in Shaanxi province. These swords, of cast bronze, are of *jian* type, with straight leaf-shaped blades reinforced by rounded medial ribs. Blade length was very short, about 14 ins/35 cm. The tang was also relatively short and fitted with a large bound and guardless grip. This type persisted in southern and western China, but in the east the blade was cast with a much longer round-sectioned tang and an integral disc pommel. This development, which seems to have taken place by the seventh century, was a distinct improvement, for it reduced the tendency of the hilt to part company with the blade. A small

Opposite page, left, right and bottom right
Sketch (after Yang Hong) of a bronze *jian* sword with a bone hilt and scabbard, Western Zhou Dynasty.
Bronze *ge* dagger-axe from Liangwangshan, Yunnan Province, Eastern Zhou Dynasty, third–second century BC.
Two bronze knives with animal-head pommels, late Shang Dynasty.

Left Two bronze swords of the fully developed solid-hilt type, Eastern Zhou Dynasty, fourth–third century BC. The sword on the right has gold bands on the hilt.

173

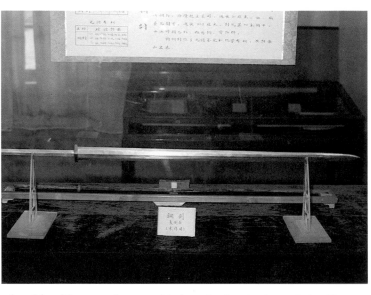

Above Bronze *jian* sword, Eastern Zhou Dynasty, sixth–fifth century BC.

Above right Qin Dynasty bronze sword excavated from Pit 1, Mount Li, Xian.

Opposite page Steel ring-pommel *dao* sword (above), Han Dynasty, and a steel *jian* sword in a lacquered bamboo scabbard (below), Han Dynasty, third–second century BC.

shoulder-like guard was added at the beginning of the Eastern Zhou period in the sixth century.

The increasing importance of the sword at this time – no doubt a reflection of the growing significance of cavalry on the Chinese battlefield – gave impetus to various technical improvements. The 'hollow-hilt' type, with its narrow grip and broad guard and pommel, was given a longer blade (up to 16 ins/40 cm) and also a stronger flaring tubular tang. At the same time, the medial-ribbed blade gave way to one of diamond section. By the fourth and third centuries, the fully fledged bronze *jian* had appeared. This magnificent weapon had a diamond-section blade up to 20 ins/50 cm long, a solid tang reinforced by two integral rings, and a substantial cusped guard. This and the rings on the grip were often decorated with gilding and the late *taotie* ornament found on contemporary bronze vessels. Occasionally the blade would be decorated with inscriptions in bird script, recording a dedication to family ancestors. Provenanced examples of fully developed *jian* all come from the metropolitan area of the Eastern Zhou, particularly around Luoyang in Henan province.

As the bronze *jian* evolved, so did its dagger form, the *bishou* ('hand dagger'). Scaled-down versions of *jian* continued to be made and used alongside the single-edged *xiao* or ring-pommelled dagger mentioned above.

The discovery in 1974 of the extraordinary terracotta army associated with the tomb of Qin Shihuangdi, the First Emperor of Qin, at Mount Li near Xian in Shaanxi province has enabled the last phase of the history of the Chinese bronze sword to be written. The main pit at Mount Li was plundered by rebels at the fall of the Qin Dynasty in 206 BC and most of the life-size figures were stripped of their weapons, but those weapons which remained have given us a reasonably clear picture of sword developments in the third century BC. The *jian* became very long and slender, measuring about 33 ins/83 cm from pommel to blade

tip; the blade, which was straight-edged and of flattened octagonal section, measured about 26 ins/65 cm. More importantly, the technique of chromium-washing the blade during manufacture seems to have been used; this had the effect of enhancing, or at least preserving, the sharpness of the cutting edge. The narrow guard was cast separately, as was the rectangular pommel. The tang, of hexagonal section at the guard and chamfered to a rectangular section towards the pommel, was pierced with a hole for the retaining peg which held the grip.

The vast majority of the Chinese bronze swords in European and American collections were acquired between 1900 and 1930 when Chinese archaeological artefacts were very popular with collectors. At that time Chinese tombs were plundered as never before, without any attempt to record the provenance of the objects removed. The development of Chinese archaeology to the very high level of maturity it has reached today has enabled a satisfactory chronology for Shang, Zhou and Han finds to be established, but it has also made it clear that the early evolution of the sword in China is far more complex than the brief survey above suggests. One of the most important archaeological sites of the Western Han to be excavated in recent years is the tomb of Liu Sheng (half brother of the Emperor Wu, who died in 113 BC) at Man Cheng, Hebei province. This site has yielded a most remarkable assemblage of bronze and iron armour and weapons, some recognizably archaic, others entirely new to arms and armour experts.

Iron and steel

Long before iron was used to produce weapons in China, it was used in the form of cast iron to make agricultural implements and also moulds for bronze weapons. But, as Joseph Needham, author of *Science and Civilisation in China*, has astutely commented: '. . . the transition was not so much from bronze to iron, as from bronze to steel'. Certainly there were experiments with iron cores, probably meteoric, in bronze weapons – a dagger-axe or *ge* in the Freer Gallery, Washington, has a cast iron core – but steel seems to have been used in weapon-making by the end of the Warring States period, for in about 250 BC we find the philosopher Xun Qing writing: '. . . the people of Chu use shark skin and rhinoceros hide for armour, as hard as metal or stone, and spear heads of steel from Wan, as sharp as a bee's sting'.

Although the use of steel for swords inevitably led to an increase in blade length, long blades made of bronze were perfectly serviceable, as the Mount Li excavations have shown. An incident recorded in the *Shi Ji* of Sima Qian is interesting in this respect. In 227 BC, we are told, the scholar-swordsman Jing Ke attempted to assassinate King Zheng of Qin, later the First Emperor: 'On being instructed to do so, Jing Ke took out the map, unrolled it, and exposed the dagger. Seizing the sleeve of the Qin king with his left hand, Jing Ke grasped the dagger in his right and struck at him. In alarm, King Zheng leapt backwards so that his sleeve tore off. Though he tried hard, the king was unable to draw his sword, which was very long . . . Jing Ke pursued the king, who ran around a pillar . . . Then a courtier cried out, "Put your sword behind you, King!" By doing so, he could unsheathe the weapon and wound Jing Ke in the left thigh.' The long bronze swords excavated from Mount Li suggest that the King's sword was of bronze and not steel, as is often assumed.

The Han Empire and the nomad conquests

The steel swords of the Western Han (207 BC – AD 9) were usually of two-edged *jian* type, and very similar in shape and style to the bronze swords of Qin. A superb example in the British Museum retains all its carved wooden fittings and its lacquered bamboo scabbard – the scabbard slide by which the scabbard was attached to its hanger is fitted almost one third of the way down. The overall length of this weapon is 34 ins/85 cm. A number of similar swords were excavated at Man Cheng, along with a very late bronze *jian*, and a variety of iron *xiao* daggers and bronze and iron *bishou*, the latter superbly decorated in gold. Many Han *jian* were ornamented with fittings of carved jade.

In Eastern Han (AD 25 – 220) sites the steel *jian* is joined by a new type of sword, the single-edged *huanshou dao* ('ring-pommelled sword'). Both weapons had a blade about 36 ins/90 cm long, but that of the *huanshou dao* was very narrow and of elongated shield-shaped section. The tang of the *huanshou dao* was very broad, almost wider than the blade, and forged with an integral ring pommel. Tang and grip were held together by a peg slotted through the tang, a feature found on most steel swords and daggers of the period. In fact the *huanshou dao* is so similar in form to the *xiao* daggers produced in bronze and iron in western China that it is tempting to see them as variants on a uniquely Chinese theme until one looks farther afield and sees that they are equally related to Central Asian types. The culture of western China, particularly during the Han period, was inextricably linked to that of the nomad tribes beyond its northern and western frontiers. At its widest extent, the Han empire incorporated as protectorates the Tarim Basin and areas on the Silk Route as far west as Kashgar.

The immensely effective military system of the Han, which combined both infantry and cavalry, was the descendant of that used by the Warring States and by the armies of their eventual conquerors, the Qin. Solid blocks of infantry armed with crossbows could outrange and outshoot the bow-armed cavalry of the northern nomads, preventing them from closing with their mêlée weapons; if close fighting was called for, the Han infantryman had his dagger-axe. The essentially defensive role of the infantry was supported by chariots and cavalry. The chariots were drawn by four horses, and their occupants were equipped with both missile and mêlée weapons. The cavalry were more variously equipped, some with composite bows to match the bows of their nomad foes, some with traditional Chinese dagger-axes, and

some with crossbows; the sword was worn as a side-arm. Officers also wore swords, and there is evidence from tomb reliefs that some foot soldiers wore swords as well.

The unification of China achieved by Qin Shihuangdi in 221 BC lasted until AD 220, when army commanders in the west and south declared independence. Then came reunification under the Western Jin Dynasty (AD 265–317); indeed such was the feeling of complacency under the Jin that in 280 a general disarmament was decreed and weapons were actually sold to China's ancient enemies in the north, the Xiongnu and Xianbi. Mayhem promptly broke loose.

The endless complexities of the nomad conquest of northern China are beyond the scope of this chapter but, to cut a labyrinthine story short, the tribes of the Hu (as the Xiongnu came to be called after 300), in association with the proto-Mongol-led Xianbi tribes, quickly overran northern China and established the Zhao Dynasties (304–52). These were supplanted by the Tibetan Jin Dynasties (265–417), and they in their turn by the Northern Wei Dynasty (384–534) of the Toba, who included the residue of the Hu and Xianbi, by this time primarily proto-Turkish with a considerable proto-Mongol admixture.

These nomadic peoples all relied on cavalry for their conquests. Part of their forces consisted of heavily armed horsemen, equipped with lance, composite bow and sword; both horse and rider were protected by lamellar armour. The larger part of their forces, however, consisted of lightly armed cavalry equipped only with bow and sword. This was the military system used, with minor variations, throughout Central Asia, from Korea to the Balkans. It comes as no surprise, therefore, to find that the single-edged sword with a ring pommel is the dominant type

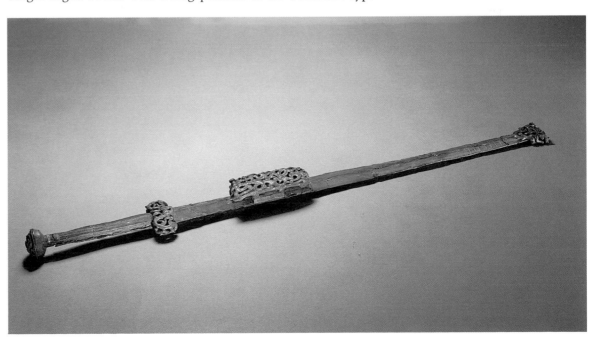

throughout the archaeological sites of this massive area. However, Chinese finds which can be dated to the turbulent centuries of the post-Han period are disappointingly few.

With the second unification of China under the Sui (581–618) and Tang (618–907) Dynasties, the archaeological record becomes richer. Two particularly fine Sui swords, said to have been excavated in 1929 from the Imperial tomb at Beijueshan near Luoyang, Henan province, are now in the Metropolitan Museum of Art, New York. Both have a gilt bronze ring pommel and a straight blade with a single edge, and both retain their scabbard and hilt fittings. The ring pommel of one is decorated with confronted dragons, and the other with a phoenix. The scabbard fittings are of silver. Numerous other examples of Sui *dao* survive, perhaps the most famous being the *tachi* of the Emperor Shomu in the Shosoin at Nara in Japan. In fact, for the period from the dissolution of the Han to the Tang, our best corpus of Chinese swords comes from Japan, where materials of the highest quality were exported and presented.

The sword in Central Asia

From at least the seventh century until the second century BC, the predominant Central and West Asian sword was the *akinakes*, frequently illustrated in Achaemenid Persian and Scythian art. The characteristic P-shaped suspension mount of the *akinakes* scabbard continued to be used on Sarmatian and Sassanian long swords, and is eventually found on Sui and Tang *dao*. One of the finest scabbard covers of the *akinakes* type, made of gold, was excavated at Solokha in southern Russia, along with the celebrated Solokha comb. The short *akinakes* held sway until the second century BC, when it was gradually replaced by the long single-edged iron sword of the Sarmatians. This weapon, closely related to the contemporary Chinese *huanshou dao*, was also used by the eastern neighbours of the Sarmatian tribes, the Scythian Sakas and Kushans. Although no excavated examples of Kushan swords are known, the type is clearly visible in coin portraits, particularly those of King Vasudeva I, and also on the life-size sandstone sculpture of the King of Kings, Kaniska, from Mathura in India.

The same sword type makes its appearance in Sassanian Persia, presumably under Central Asian influence, but here it is found with a quite different type of hilt, a slightly curved 'pistol grip' with a nock for the index finger. Three excellent examples of the type, probably made in northern Persia in the sixth century, can be seen in the British Museum and in the New York Metropolitan. The intriguing suggestion has been made that these swords may be examples of the elusive *urepos* used by the Huns. One of them has a bird-headed hilt and a silver-covered scabbard, and although the scabbard has been decorated with quite inappropriate embossed panels, apparently based on much earlier Scythian work, the rest of the weapon may be our clearest evidence for the Hunnish sword. Was this weapon a Sassanian product made for the Hunnish market? Our only other evidence for the Hunnish sword rests on the fragmentary Altissheim sword found in 1932 and on an agate guard from the Chersonese.

By the fifth century the kingdoms of the Scythian Sakic and Kushan rulers had been overrun by the Huns. The Indian parts of their territories were occupied by the Hephthalite or White Huns, themselves displaced from Central Asia by the Avars, or Ruan Ruan, who simultaneously caused the migration of the Black Huns into Europe. The Avars were driven out of Asia in about AD 550 by the Blue Turks, who occupied the whole of Mongolia. Our knowledge of the sword of the Avars has recently been augmented by a new reconstruction of the Pereshchepina sword, which shows that it had a long straight blade and a ring-pomelled hilt with vestigial quillons.

Ample evidence for the use of the long single-edged cavalry sword in the Tarim Basin in the seventh and eighth centuries is provided by the magnificent frescoes of Kızıl, Piandjikent and Sorcuq, and on the famous shield fragment from the castle at Mug. The curved cavalry sword, however, probably originated in Turkestan. Perhaps the earliest representation of such a weapon appears in a fresco from Sorcuq, usually assumed to date from the eighth century; examples excavated from graves can be dated to the ninth, tenth and eleventh centuries. The curved sword was not diagnostic of a different method of warfare, nor did it oust the straight single-edged sword in Central Asia.

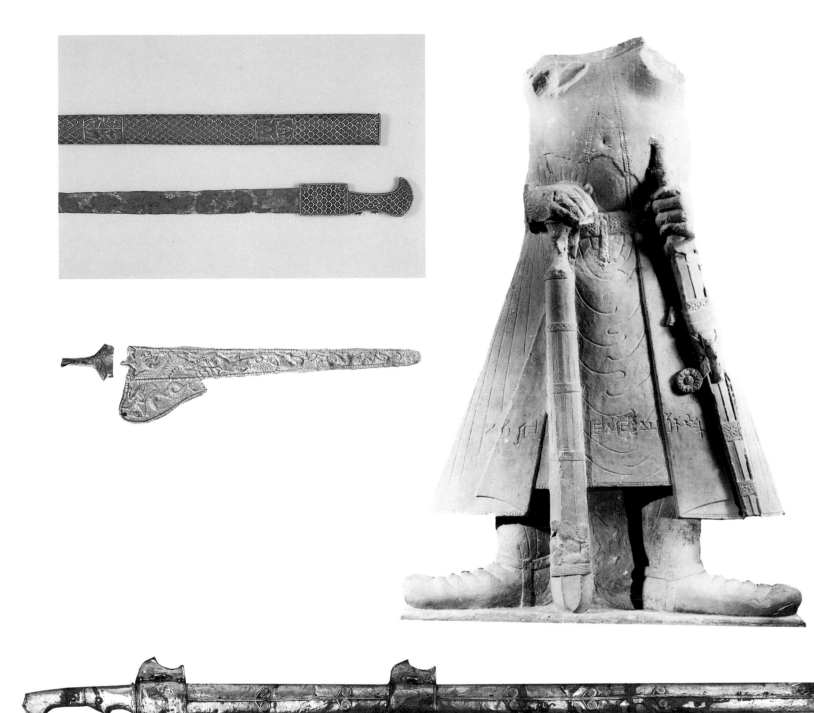

Opposite page Two steel ring-pommel *dao* swords from Beijueshan near Luoyang, Henan Province, Sui Dynasty, *c.*600 AD. The ring pommels are of gilt bronze.

Left Pink sandstone statue of the Kushan king Kaniska (*c.*78–123 or 120–162 AD). The king is depicted with his right hand resting on a cudgel, possibly symbolizing his royal status, and his left hand gripping the hilt of his sword.

Far left above Steel sword with beaked pommel, possibly Hunnish, *c.*500 AD. Both hilt and scabbard are covered in silver, with feather decoration. The figured plaque is probably associated.

Far left below Gilt *akinakes* hilt and scabbard from Kul Oba, Scythian, sixth–fourth century BC.

Bottom Two Sassanian steel swords dating from the sixth–seventh century AD. One has a plain silvered hilt and scabbard, and is possibly from Amlash, and the other has a gilt hilt and feathered scabbard.

Next page 'General Guo Zuyi making peace with the Uighurs', a scene from a handscroll by Li Gonglin (1049–1106), Song Dynasty. Although the events depicted here occurred in 765, it is likely that Li Gonglin represented the Uighurs as he saw them three centuries later.

177

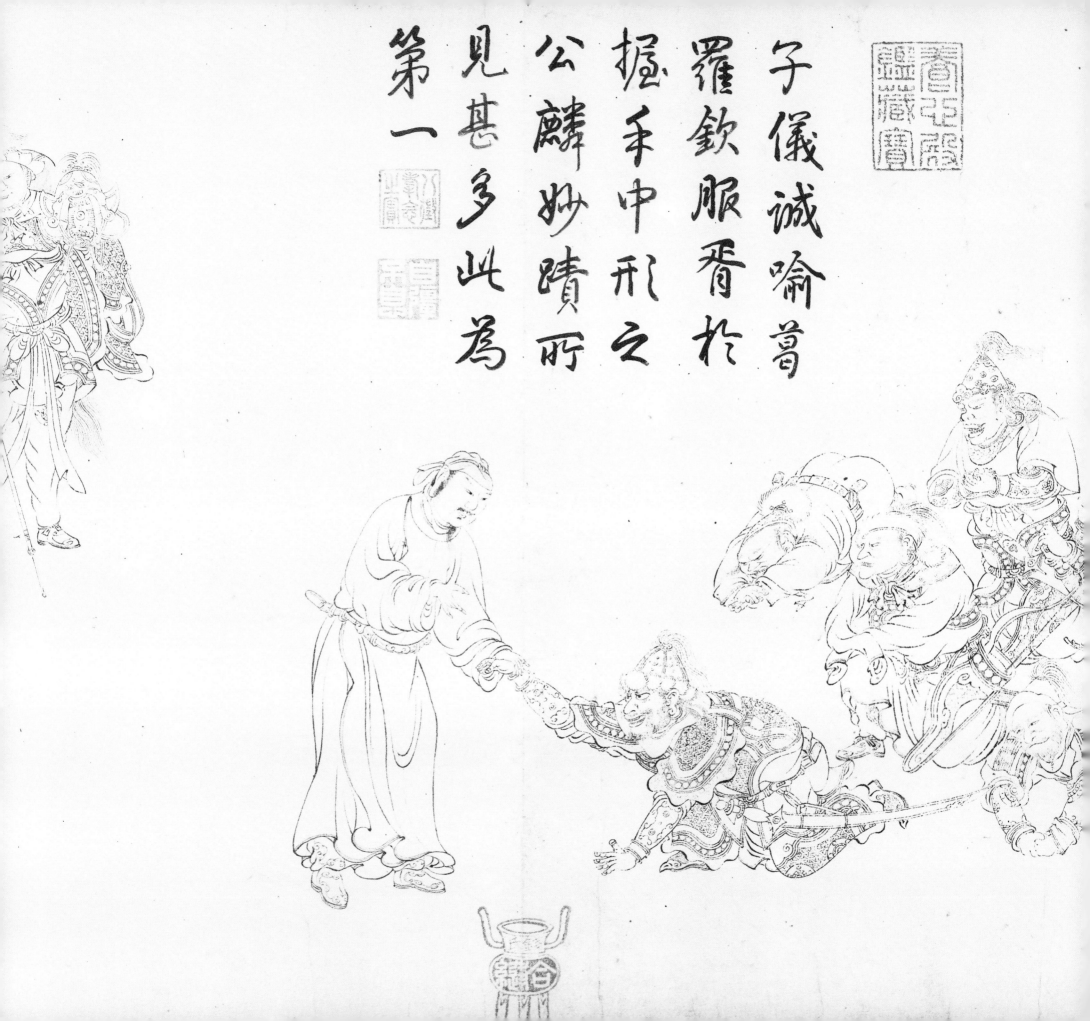

子儀誠喻蜀
羅欽服香於
摑手中形之
公麟妙蹟所
見甚多此為
第一

In all likelihood, the curved sword was introduced by the Uighurs. This Turkish people, originally Manicheans, were converted to Buddhism in the mid-ninth century and established a kingdom in eastern Turkestan centred on Turfan and Kucha. The handscroll by Li Gonglin, now in the National Palace Museum in Taipei, depicting the meeting in 765 of the Tang General Guo Zuyi and the Uighur leaders, illustrates the Uighur sword well. The earliest excavated examples of these curved swords belong, however, to Khirgiz finds of the tenth century.

As Islamic culture spread eastwards, the weapon types of Persia spread among the nomadic people of Central Asia. However, one remarkable non-Islamic survivor deserves mention and that is the *shashqa* of Georgia and Azerbaijan. Although the *shashqa* has a curved blade, frequently of Iranian manufacture, its hilt, guardless, with a recessed grip and beak-like pommel, would seem to be the last descendant of the putative sword of the Huns. The traditional sword of Bukhara bespeaks the same ancestry.

The Tang and the coming of the Mongols

By the late Tang or early Song period, the forms of Chinese sword which were to continue in use until the nineteenth century had become established. The straight double-edged *jian* acquired, instead of the ring pommel, a solid pommel, usually of a triple-lobed form and often decorated with semi-precious stones. Imperial swords were invariably of this form and became symbolic of high military office. The Central Asian curved single-edged sword, in China the *dao*, became the most common military sword, particularly for the Chinese cavalry, which now dominated Chinese military thinking.

The Tang period was a Golden Age in the history of China – the empire was at its greatest extent, cultural activities flourished, and trade across the world was encouraged. Chinese culture, written language and political institutions were adopted by many neighbouring states, notably Japan and the rising Korean kingdoms of Silla and Koryugo, and the techniques and styles of the superb steel swords of the period were transmitted in the same manner.

Tang civilization reached its zenith in about 660, but by 755, with the An Lushan rebellion, it began to decline. The Uighurs and Tibetans won back their territories in the Tarim Basin and Gansu, and in 907 the Tang Dynasty collapsed, to be replaced by the Five Dynasties and Ten Kingdoms. The south was reunited by the Song Dynasty in 960, but the north fell yet again to northern nomads, the Khitan.

The Khitan, a proto-Mongol people who had been raiding the north since about 695, established the Liao Dynasty in the north from 916 to 1125, becoming considerably sinicized in the process, as so many of their predecessors had been. The long straight cutting swords they used are illustrated in numerous Tang and Song paintings. In the official history of the Khitan, the *Liao Shi*, we are given a description of the Khitan cavalryman's equipment:

'Each man has nine pieces of iron armour, along with saddle cloths, bridles, armour of leather or iron for the horses according to their strength, four bows, four hundred arrows, a long and a short spear, a mace, a halberd, a small banner, a hammer and a knife, a flint, a bucket, a quantity of dried food in a bag, a grappling hook, a felt umbrella, and two hundred feet of rope.' This passage emphasizes the relative scarcity of the sword, even among these lavishly equipped troops.

In 1115 the Liao Dynasty was largely displaced by the Manchurian Ruzhen (also Jurchen, Jurched or Nuchen), who formed the Jin Dynasty, which ruled the whole of northern China until 1234. In 1189, Genghiz Khan became the leader of the Mongols, and made them the greatest power in Central Asia. Their campaigns of conquest in China began in 1210. By 1234, they had annexed the Jin empire in northern China, and in 1280 Kubilai Khan, the grandson of Genghiz, established the Yuan Dynasty, ruling the whole of China.

The Mongols were much influenced by the Uighurs, Khitan and Ruzhen, and their military equipment was very similar. Joannes de Plano Carpini, leader of a Papal embassy to the Mongols in 1246–7, described their equipment in his *Liber Tartarorum*: 'They all have to possess the following arms at least: two or three bows, or at least one good one, three large quivers full of arrows, an axe, and ropes for hauling engines of war. As for the wealthy, they have swords pointed at the end but sharp at only one side and somewhat curved, and they have a horse with armour; their legs also are covered and they have helmets and cuirasses . . . some of them have lances which have a hook in the iron neck, and with this, if they can, they will drag a man from his saddle.' The Mongol sword, together with the armour worn by both men and horses, is well illustrated in Rashid al-Din's *Jami' al-Tawarikh* (c.1314).

The Ming and Ching Dynasties

The years from 1355 to 1368 saw the formation of a great popular rising and a rapid military campaign against the Mongols. This was led by the former monk and peasant's son Zhu Yuanzhang, who became the Hongwu Emperor, the first emperor of the Ming Dynasty (1368–1644). The Ming *Wubei Zhi*, or Military Records, contains a survey of all the Chinese weapons available at the time of its composition. Among the vast proliferation of missile weapons, crossbows, composite bows and siege equipment, hand-to-hand weapons appear to have been of minor significance. Swords are simply lumped together with all the other mêlée weapons; indeed, by this time, the term *dao* had come to mean any form of cutting weapon, and the majority of *dao* were halberds, like the *jidao*, or glaives (staff weapons with long single-edged cutting blades), like the *qudao*, *yanyue dao*, or *meijian dao*. The sword types illustrated in the *Wubei Zhi* include the *shoudao* ('hand sword'), with a heavy, curved cutting blade; the long *changdao* and short *duandao*, both of the light curved form used by

بصحراء ذلك المصاف قرب من خنمة الآن حيفة من جيف الكفار وصارت طعمة للكلاب وحفة للذياب وعقر واحدة عشر فيلا

Left Mongol cavalry under Mahmud ibn Sebuktijn invade the Punjab, from Rashid al-Din, *Jami' al-Tawarikh, c.*1314.

Below 'An Imperial Procession departing from and returning to the Palace', a scene from *Chujing Tu*, Ming Dynasty, *c.*1538. The Emperor's *jian* sword is carried in the foreground by a bodyguard.

the Mongols; and the almost identical *yaodao* ('waist sword'). The straight swords, *jian*, are illustrated among the wide variety of cudgels (*bang*), maces and flails. In fact, the form of the *jian* during the Ming period indicates that it had become an archaic weapon, produced in the traditional Tang style, with a pierced, lobed pommel, a swelling grip, and a narrow, pointed quillon block.

Although the sword remained a symbol of office, its relegation in the *Wubei Zhi* to the ends of sections is indicative of its relative unimportance. Ming cavalry are depicted with composite bows, bow cases and quivers, and a variety of pole-arms, but very seldom with swords.

China under Manchu rule

In 1581–83 bitter fighting broke out between the Tungus tribes of Manchuria, the remnants of the Ruzhen. The Chinese stepped in, set out demarcations between the territories of the various tribes, and thus contributed to the formation of a tribal league among the Manchus. Towards the end of the reign of the Emperor Wanli, the Manchus began to attack Chinese cities in Manchuria, and in 1616 their leader Nurhachu assumed the title of Emperor in the dynastic name of Qing. By 1637 the Manchus, assisted by various Mongol princes, had conquered Korea and made incursions into northern China. After the death of Wanli in 1619, the Ming Dynasty's hold on the rest of China weakened; rebel armies sprang up around the country, new dynasties were proclaimed, and in 1644 the last Ming emperor committed suicide as Beijing was captured. One of the rebel generals entered Beijing with the Manchus as allies; he left it as their commander-in chief and with the Manchu emperor Qing Shunzhi on the throne.

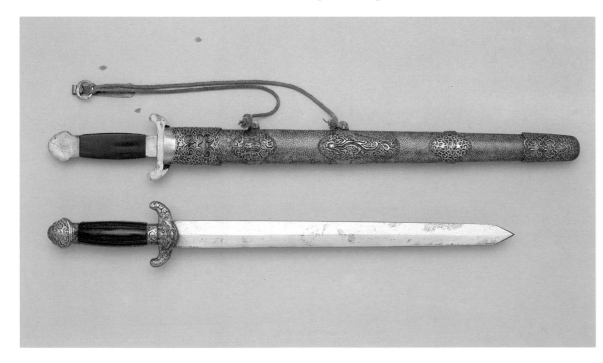

Despite their small numbers and the fact that they imposed Manchurian dress and the wearing of pigtails on the Chinese, the Manchus established a dynasty which was to rule China for nearly three hundred years. Manchu rule finally came to an end in 1912 with the abdication of the last emperor, Pu Yi.

A very large proportion of the Chinese weapons and armour which survive today were manufactured in the Qing period, that is during the seventeenth, eighteenth and nineteenth centuries. Traditional Ming styles continued to be produced and the bejewelled *jian* continued to be made for the Imperial court. A particular type of curved *dao* was also produced in large numbers for Manchu officials, replacing to a great extent the long Ming *dao*. But in addition there arose a great variety of new edged weapons.

Double or paired swords, which seem to have come into use in the late seventeenth century, were one of the most remarkable innovations of the early Qing period. Those most commonly found are *shuangjian* ('paired swords') or *yuanyang jian* ('loving-couple swords'). These fit back-to-back in the same scabbard and were intended to be wielded one in each hand; the blades are short and double-edged and the hilts are half hilts. Sometimes referred to as 'butterfly knives', paired swords are widely used in Chinese martial arts today, along with the *jian* and *dao*. Most of the double swords which survive today were made in the first half of the nineteenth century. Less common and much sought-after are pairs of curved single-edged swords, or *shuangdao*, an example of which can be seen in the British Royal Collection at Windsor Castle. Until drawn, paired swords appear to be quite ordinary single swords.

Other paired weapons of the Qing era include a variety of cudgels and the *dai yueya tieqing ji* ('old moon plain iron halberd'), a halberd with a bound grip behind the blade and a long hooked blade at the top.

The Chinese never had much use for two-handed swords, principally because the vast majority of mêlée weapons were halberds or glaives which had a much greater reach than any sword. Indeed, as we have already seen, the distinction between swords and other types of cutting weapon was simply not as marked in Chinese military thought as it was in Europe. However, the Ming *Wubei Zhi* does have a section on drill exercises for the two-handed sword, the sword illustrated being straight and double-edged. Nevertheless most surviving two-handed swords are *dadao* ('great swords'), with long broad curved blades. These have a ring-type pommel, a simple bound wooden grip, and quillons which angle backwards and forwards to form a knucklebow. Swords of this sort are extremely difficult to date because of their simple form, but the writhing dragon etched on the blade of the specimen in the Royal Armouries' collection suggests that it may have been made in the seventeenth century. Other surviving Chinese two-handed swords were made in conscious imitation of Japanese *no tachi*.

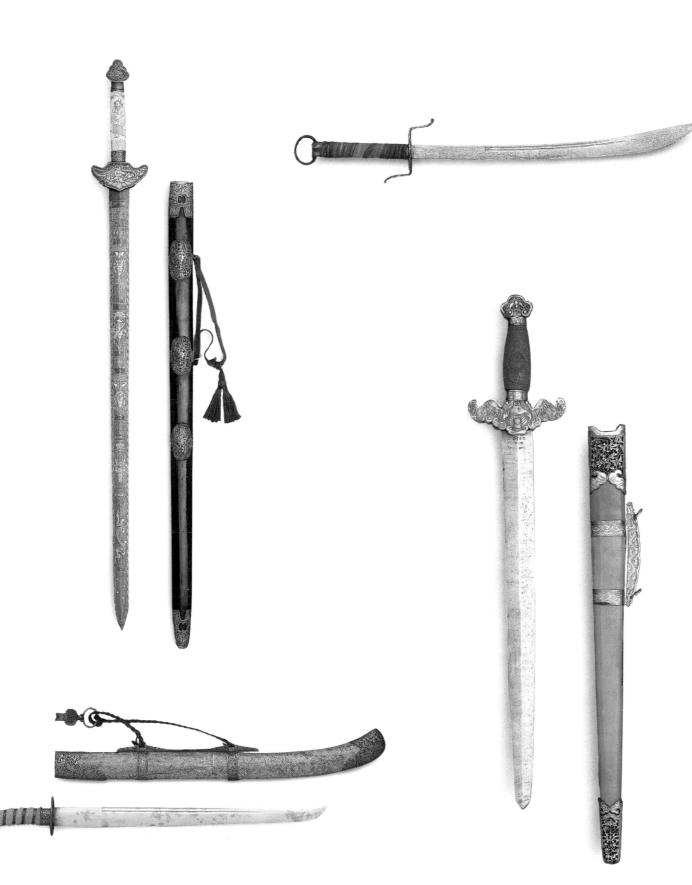

Left Two-handed sword or *dadao* with a ring pommel, probably early Qing Dynasty.

Far left Ivory-hilted *jian* sword and scabbard. The blade of this sword is decorated in silver inlay with constellations and the *nian hao* 'Da Qing Qianlong Nian Zhi' in seal characters. Qing Dynasty, Qianlong period.

Far left below A *dao* sword and scabbard, Qing Dynasty. This was the standard sword used by Manchu troops.

Left below Lacquer-hilted *jian* sword and scabbard, Qing Dynasty. The embossed silver hilt and scabbard fittings suggest western Chinese production, possibly for the Tibetan market, although other examples of this type in the Musée de la Marine in Paris were captured from Hanoi in 1882.

Opposite page Paired swords or *shuangjian*, Ching Dynasty. These are designed to fit back-to-back in the same scabbard.

Below Ornate Tibetan swords and scabbards, possibly eighteenth century. Although the blades are of the characteristic laminating, pattern-welded type, it is by no means clear whether Chinese workmanship was involved in their manufacture.

Below right Sino-Tibetan *dao* sword, possibly nineteenth century. The back of the blade is decorated with gilt tear-drops and a dragon, the ricasso with a gilt, fretted dragon, and the hilt with silver fittings inlaid with coral.

Opposite page Eighteenth-century dagger and scabbard (above), possibly Bhutanese, and a Bhutanese sword and scabbard (below), possibly of eighteenth century date. The latter are decorated in the Tibetan 'plain style'; the Bhutanese attribution is purely conventional.

The vast bulk of Qing swords are of very poor quality indeed, with crude, plain, irregular blades and cast brass hilt and scabbard fittings. However, some of the surviving swords of Imperial quality are extremely good. One blade in the collection of the Musée de l'Armée in Paris, possibly of the Kangxi period (1662–1722), is etched with the cracked-ice pattern associated with Jingdezhen blue and white porcelain of the same period. Its hilt and scabbard fittings are gilt, and its grip is covered in ray skin. Other swords of Imperial quality are mounted with cloisonné enamels, and possibly belong to the Jiaqing period (1796–1821). A series of *jian* with blades decorated with the constellations in silver, and bearing the four-character marks of Emperor Qianlong (1736–95) in seal script, are fitted with superbly decorated ivory grips, while others have red lacquer grips and silver fittings.

Tibetan swords

Some of the very finest Qing swords seem to have been made for the Tibetan market. One example, again in Paris, has the long straight single-edged blade characteristic of Tibetan swords, yet with a gilt saw-back to it. The hilt fittings are gilt and encrusted in the Tibetan taste with semi-precious stones, but the blade is etched next to the hilt with the four-character mark of Qianlong. An even finer example, illustrated opposite, has a gilt fretted dragon overlaid on the ricasso, and a gilt dragon forming the terminal of the saw back. It is not known whether these swords reflect the Tibetan taste prevalent in China during the Qing era, or whether they were intended to be sent to Tibet as gifts.

Tibetan military equipment, seen during the early years of this century by European visitors to Tibet at New Year Festival time, is a remarkable example of survival. Tibetan armour, which is of lamellar construction, represents a continuous armour-making tradition stretching back, in all probability, to pre-Mongol times. Those armours which survive were probably made in the seventeenth and eighteenth centuries, but are extraordinarily similar to the ancient excavated *keiko* of Kofun Japan; they seem to be the last remnants of one of the most universally used armour types in history. Tibetan swords are in the same centuries-old tradition. Their blades, which are single-edged with an angled point, are survivors from the period before the curved sword took over in Central Asia. Two principal styles are found, ornate and plain. 'Ornate' denotes semi-precious stones and *tsuba*-like guards on the hilt, and a scabbard decorated with fretted and possibly silvered mythological creatures. Swords of the 'plain' type have no hilt guards and no decoration, or very simple decoration, on the pommel or scabbard, although these are often silvered overall. The former are sometimes called Tibetan and the latter Bhutanese, but the same distinction does not seem to work when it comes to armour styles. It may be that the two styles stem from two different centres of production, possibly located in western Sichuan and in the Tibetan Autonomous Region. The lack of satisfactorily provenanced examples of swords of either style makes identification and dating extremely difficult at present. The weapons of Nepal and the western Himalayan region are of course more closely related to the arms and armour of India, and to those of Islam.

14 INDIA AND SOUTHEAST ASIA

Frederick Wilkinson

India is an enormous land mass, a subcontinent, with a mix of races and religions, a great variety of climates and terrains, and a profusion of plant and animal life. In past centuries princes with unimaginable wealth and power were as typical of India as peasants living in grinding poverty. Climate, environment and way of life have all influenced the swordsmiths of India, lending their products a variety in size, shape, design and quality that is truly staggering. To the European student of arms and armour, Indian weapons appear very strange, quite unlike those developed by the armourers and weaponsmiths of the West.

India has a long and proud martial history, not least because its mineral, vegetable and animal wealth have been a magnet for invaders, including the Aryans, the Macedonians under Alexander, the Kushans, the Huns, the Arabs, the Mongols, the Turks, and last and not least the French and British. It has, in addition, always been a land divided by religion, tribe and family into large and small rival states, each with its own traditions, values and rulers.

Hindu epics such as the *Mahabharata* and *Ramayana*, composed in the middle of the first millennium BC, refer to a system of castes or social divisions which, in all probability, dates back to the middle of the second millennium. There were four classes, the most exalted being the Brahmins (priests and religious teachers), followed by the Ksatriyas (kings, warriors and aristocrats), Vaisyas (traders, merchants and professional people) and Sudras (servants, peasants and labourers). Members of the Ksatriya caste were pledged to follow the code of the warrior, *kshatram dharma*, the duty of war, with its obligation to fight for community or state. Their role was not entirely defensive and it was their task, and doubtless their pleasure, to organize raids on neighbours to acquire cattle or women. The epics also suggest that, like the Japanese samurai with their code of *bushido*, the Ksatriyas developed a series of laws which regulated their conduct and the waging of war.

The epics tell of battles fought with a variety of weapons, but the bow seems to have played a dominant role and is described as being 'powerful enough to drive an arrow through twenty-four layers of leather'. Unlike the English long bow, the Indian bow was powered by a stave composed of a mixture of sinew, horn and wood, a type favoured for centuries in the Orient, while the arrows were tipped with a variety of points intended for war or hunting. When warriors closed in hand-to-hand combat, weapons such as spiked maces, axes and a form of lasso with a running noose were used. Mention is also made of a *maustika* or fist dagger, a vague description that might well fit a later weapon known as the *katar*.

Nevertheless the composers of the early epics stress the importance of the sword, and its value is emphasized by the variety of names by which it was known – Nistrima (cruel), Tiksnadhara (fiery), Vijaya (giving victory). The sword was an instrument of power, for was it not invented by the god Brahma himself? The sword's beginning was in a sacrificial fire lit by Brahma, and from its flames came a creature so terrible that all the world was afraid. This monster changed in form and became the sword, with Agni, the god of fire, as its presiding deity.

The ideal sword was described as being 'fifty fingers' long, with a blade of metal which was 'the colour of a cuckoo's neck' and gave a good ringing tone when struck. If it was possible to recognize natural shapes in the surface texture of the metal, then the sword was thought to be a very special one. Hilts were made of ivory, horn or wood, and the weapon was carried in a sheath worn on the left side and supported with the left hand.

Early swords are represented on sculptures such as those at Bharhut, which date from about AD 100, as being straight, with a fairly broad blade, and warriors are shown using them with a two-handed grip. Later sculptures also show a scythe-shaped sword in use. By about AD 400 cave paintings such as those at Ajanta depict a short curved sword rather like the modern Nepalese *kukri*. And, unlikely as it may sound to students of European arms and armour, the available evidence does not suggest any major changes in the design of Indian weaponry until the late Middle Ages. From that date, however, Islamic influence spread from the north and the Europeans, following in the wake of the Portuguese explorers, began to arrive by way of the Cape of Good Hope.

The Portuguese, and later the Dutch, French and English, eyed the riches of India, and set about establishing trading centres along her coasts, either by negotiation or by force. Most of these European toe-holds were established during the sixteenth century, at the time when much of the northern part of the continent was falling under the control of the great Moghul rulers, beginning with Babur, the grandson of Timur Lenk or Tamerlane.

Zahir-ud-Din Babur (1483–1530) conquered first Afghanistan (1504) and then, as Tamerlane had done thirty years earlier, moved south into India, capturing the capital Delhi in 1529. After his death in 1530 there were setbacks to Moghul ambitions, but in 1556 the great Jalal-ud-din Akbar, Babur's grandson, succeeded to the throne. Under his firm rule the Moghul Empire flourished, and art and literature thrived.

The *Ain-i-Akbari*, a systematic account of the resources and administration of Akbar's empire written in Persian by Abdul Fazl, actually describes the the contents of an arsenal, but many of

Left A fierce battle rages as Babur captures Fort Chanderi in 1528. This miniature from *Babur-Nameh* by Khaman Sangtarash(?), painted in about 1590, clearly shows the weapons of the period. Mounted archers carry quiverfuls of arrows and make good use of their circular shields (*dahls*), while the foot soldiers ply their *talwars* and daggers.

Opposite page The goddess Durga, mounted on a lion, destroys the demon Mahisha, who is armed with a shield and a *talwar*. Durga, with the advantage of her numerous arms, wields a mace, an *ankus* (elephant goad), a trident, a quoit, a bow and arrow, and a shield.

Above Moghul miniature showing Raja Ajit Singh (1678–1725) of Jodhpur, Rajasthan, with his sons and grandsons. *Talwars* are much in evidence, and all but one have an S-shaped knucklebow.

Below Hilt of a good fighting *talwar*, probably eighteenth century. All the usual features are present – disc pommel with central dome, short stubby quillons, and langets to hold the scabbard firmly.

opponents brave, sometimes to the point of virtual suicide, with a strong sense of honour, but also capable of treachery. And they found themselves opposed with a variety of edged weapons as well as firearms, some acquired from European sources, others locally manufactured.

Indian swords

One of the first swords encountered by the Europeans was the *talwar*, one of the characteristic swords of India. It is difficult to define a *talwar* in precise terms for the name is used to describe a whole range of swords, but the weapon was apparently introduced into India via Persia and was probably a descendant of the Mongol sword.

One feature most evident with Indian edged weapons is the predominance of the curved blade. Curved swords were known in India as early as the fourteenth century but do not seem to have come into general use until the sixteenth. Moghul miniatures show courtiers armed with *talwars*, some of which resemble *talwars* used up to the present day; the other type of sword shown is very similar to the *shamshir* (discussed later) in that it has a single-edged blade, slightly curved, and a pistol grip. Both types of sword are depicted with blades which vary in shape from almost straight to strongly curved, but all seem to be of uniform width except where they taper towards the point.

The most common form of *talwar* hilt is all-metal, with a disc pommel which has a slightly upturned rim and a low central dome. The grip swells at the centre and then sweeps down to finish in two short stubby quillons or guards. From the centre of the quillons two tongue-like extensions, the langets, project down parallel with the blade. Plain hilts were the exception, the majority being decorated with intricate patterns of intertwining foliage and similar designs, commonly inlaid with gold or silver. Hilts made for important rulers and courtiers were sometimes enamelled or set with jewels.

Some hilts were fitted with a knucklebow which sprang from the front quillon and curved up in an elongated S form to touch the disc pommel. The hilt was secured to the blade by embedding the tang or extension of the blade in an extremely strong adhesive compound which filled the inside cavity of the grip.

Decoration was not limited to the hilt, and many blades were embellished with inlay, damascening or chiselling. Persian-made blades were especially valued, particularly those made in the same manner as earlier European blades using the method known as pattern welding. Strips of iron and steel were welded into one bar which was then hammered, twisted, cut and re-welded, and then folded, twisted and hammered again. This produced a sturdy blade with a particularly fine textured and patterned surface. Some smiths were so skilled at combining and working their metals that they could produce specific designs. One pattern known as the Ladder of the Prophet or *kirk nardaban* ('forty steps') was prized above all others, and consisted of a series of chevrons

the weapons illustrated appear strange and are difficult to equate with modern examples. Perhaps the artist allowed himself a little too much licence. But inaccurate illustrations are only one of the problems which face the scholar and collector of Indian arms. The nomenclature of Indian weapons is always a headache. Few authorities, ancient or modern, seem able to agree upon the correct designation for many Indian edged weapons. What is more, similar weapons are known by different names in different parts of India.

Akbar ruled until 1605, but his successors faced rebellions and feuds as well as conflict with the increasingly powerful Marathas in the south. These difficulties were further complicated by the growing strength of the fortune-seeking Europeans. These adventurer–merchant–soldiers were assuming an increasingly important role in Indian affairs as they played off one ruler against another to acquire military or commercial advantage.

After the War of Austrian Succession (1740–48), the French and English came into direct military conflict in India, and after a long struggle the English prevailed. Shortly after the decisive British victory over the French at the Battle of Wandiwash (near Madras) in 1760, the Great Moghul was defeated by an Afghan warlord, and the political and military organization which might have deterred British penetration collapsed. The British were to dominate India until independence in 1947.

During the long period of conquest and pacification the troops of the Honourable East India Company and the British army found themselves fighting many different races. They found their

or stripes running down the blade. Second in estimation was a scatter pattern known as *bidr* or *qum* ('gravel').

Traditionally, blades produced in Damascus were considered superior to all others, although fewer and fewer blades were produced there and after the fifteenth century production virtually ceased. By the late sixteenth century the patterned surface was produced from native Indian steel called *wootz* without the necessity of the tiresome hammering and folding. As *wootz* steel cooled, its crystals formed the volutes so prized by swordsmen, and then polishing and other means were used to enhance the patterning. Like most craftsmen with a pride in their work, Indian swordsmiths often signed their blades but it was not unknown for some to seek reflected glory by using the name of the famous seventeenth-century Persian smith Assadullah. Signatures are usually enclosed in a cartouche inlaid in the section of the blade just below the hilt. Another feature found near the signature at the top of the blade is a square, or *bedouh*, divided in four, each quarter holding one of the Arabic numerals for 2, 4, 6 and 8. These numbers were believed to bring good luck to the user. Some Hindu *talwars* have the blades chiselled with gods and animals but these weapons were primarily intended for ceremonial and temple use.

Talwars were carried in wooden sheaths which were covered with leather or fabric, with a metal chape at the end. The sheath was shaped at the top to accommodate the langets, and slipped into a loop which was part of a belt or baldric slung across the shoulder and chest. The quality of the baldric reflected the wealth of the wearer and ranged from unadorned leather to leather covered with silk, velvet or other decorative materials.

Above Detail of a *talwar* blade showing the watered texture of the metal and applied silver decoration. The two cartouches are invocations to Allah and Ali; the quartered square or *bedouh* is a lucky talisman.

Above left An Indian swordsmith explains a subtle point to a customer.

189

The *talwar* blade, with its curved edge, was primarily intended for cutting, and contemporary accounts indicate that by and large the Indian swordsman seldom used the point of his blade. Local schools of swordsmanship taught the art and skill of using the sword to best advantage, but following the Indian Mutiny in 1857 there was a drive to disarm the Indians and consequently the demand for such institutions declined and the art withered. For a while, schools of swordsmanship called *akharas*, under the direction of a leader or *khalifa*, were allowed, but they were subject to control and the students had to use dummy swords and daggers.

Such schools were still active until at least the end of the century. On one occasion, according to a 1897 issue of *The Cavalry Journal*, the Deputy Inspector-General of the North-Western Provinces and Oudh Police, P. Bramley, gave a lecture to the officers and men of the 5th (Princess Charlotte of Wales's) Dragoon Guards at Meerut which was followed by a demonstration by local 'professors'. The article comments on the Banetti exercises designed to develop supple limbs, the 'five cuts' when using a talwar, and stresses that a good swordsman was expected to be ambidextrous. The author also mentions the use of a variety of articles of clothing – shoes, shawls and handkerchiefs - to avoid blows rather than deflect or meet them. Travellers report that such was the skill of Indian swordsmen that they could face a tree, place their bent knee against the trunk and slash their swords left and right without touching the tree.

Mr Bramley also comments on the hilt of the *talwar*, pointing out that for the average European hand the grip feels cramped and uncomfortable since the average Indian hand is smaller than that of a European. In general this seems to be the case, for the majority of Indian hilts do feel slightly uncomfortable. He also

suggests that the swelling at the centre of the grip helps to ensure that the sword is held in a manner particularly appropriate for cutting strokes. He also praises the two langets – he calls them 'slides' – saying that they hold the sword firmly in the scabbard, preventing the blade from rubbing against the lining and so becoming blunt.

In the same article the writer refers to an Irani sword as being designed for horseman and the Guzerati sword as being primarily for foot soldiers, adding that the Irani sword was Persian and the Guzerati sword Hindu in origin. These comments are accompanied by two sketches, unfortunately too small to show much detail, but apparently the Guzerati weapon was lighter and handier than the Irani, and also had a broader blade with a false edge which could be used for a backhanded cut. Both types are described as razor-sharp and capable of decapitating an enemy with one blow. The writer's use of the terms Irani and Guzerati is interesting since these are not names normally encountered in the literature on Indian weapons and illustrate the problems faced by the scholar in this field. They may well have been local names for the swords he describes.

Although the common *talwar* was hilted in the fashion described above, there were variant styles which have been tentatively classified in regional terms. In the Punjab the pommel disc tends to be wide, while in Lucknow the central dome of the pommel disc has a finial rising from it. Persian *talwar* hilts bear a superficial resemblance to those of the *shamshir*, for the pommel is integral with the grip and rolls forward usually in the form of a real or mythical animal head. The entire hilt is frequently cast as one piece and is often in brass.

Another curved sword of India and the Middle East was the *shamshir*, usually fitted with a heavier blade than the *talwar*. The hilt is normally tubular, with the tip, which forms the pommel, turning forward in an inverted L shape. The quillons are commonly formed by a diamond-shaped plate through which the blade passes; two of the points of the diamond are drawn out to terminate in slightly flared finials, while the bottom tips form the langets. The grip is usually of bone or ivory and secured to the tang by two or three rivets. The blade is strongly curved, normally single-edged, and of a fairly substantial wedge-shaped section. Many *shamshir* blades are finely watered and often bear the *bedouh* quarterings and the maker's signature, sometimes inlaid in gold. *Shamshirs* from Persia, Turkey and Egypt all conform to the basic pattern just described, but on Turkish and Egyptian weapons the hilt often has a horn grip and the pommel section is much more rounded or swollen.

After Napoleon invaded Egypt in 1798 a British force was sent out to thwart his ambitions in the Near East. Eventually the French were defeated and expelled from Egypt, but during their time in Egypt the troops of both forces came to know the Mamelukes. These heavily armed Egyptian warriors carried, among a variety of other weapons, the *shamshir* and its elegant and, to western eyes, rather unusual shape found favour among the French and British officers, many of whom equipped themselves with authentic *shamshirs* while others had them made with Western-style blades. *Shamshirs* were especially popular among cavalry officers and became a well established type of European military sword, so much so that in 1833 a rather formalized version with a metal sheath was adopted as standard issue for general officers of the British Army.

Similar to the *shamshir* was the *kilij*, which had a broader blade, widening towards the point and terminating in a cusp. The *kilij* was most common in eastern parts of the Ottoman Empire, but some examples do occur in India. Such was the curve of some *kilij* and *shamshir* blades that their wooden scabbards had to be adapted in order to allow them to be drawn. A slot was cut along the back edge of the sheath and covered with a thin, sprung metal strip which pushed away from the slot as the blade was drawn but sprang back once the blade was clear.

Although the curved blade has a prominent place among the edged weapons of India, not all Indian swords were curved. However, even those with straight blades were primarily used for cutting rather than thrusting. One type of straight-bladed sword was the *pata*, with a long blade often of European origin. It is not uncommon to find *patas* with blades bearing the names or marks of European makers of the seventeenth or eighteenth century, although this does not necessarily mean that such weapons were made then. Mr Bramley, in his informative talk to the dragoons at Meerut, describes this weapon as the *saif*, which is yet another example of his surprising terminology, for today the term *saif* usually refers to a North African sword.

The unusual feature of the *pata* is its hilt, which is a rigid half-gauntlet with a long cuff which is usually decorated and on some richer examples inlaid and embellished with gold and silver. The blade is attached to the hilt by decorative arms which extend forward on both sides of the blade from the 'knuckle' of the gauntlet. The hand was slipped into the gauntlet to grip a cross bar inside, while the cuff of the gauntlet was held close to the lower part of the forearm by a linked chain or bar. The inside of the gauntlet was padded. The extended grip provided by the forearm would have permitted a very powerful sweeping blow, but would surely have restricted any thrusts. Some miniatures show mounted warriors armed with the *pata*, which is rather surprising considering its limited thrusting capability. The *pata* was apparently popular with the warlike Marathas who so strongly challenged the Moghul empire in the seventeenth and eighteenth centuries, but it also saw service with other races and Bramley says that when some warriors used one on each hand they looked 'much like a windmill'.

Another weapon which favoured European blades was the *firangi*, a name which means 'foreigner'; however, if it was fitted with an Indian-made blade it was called a *sukhela* and in the Deccan a *dhup*. The blade was straight and narrow, with the back

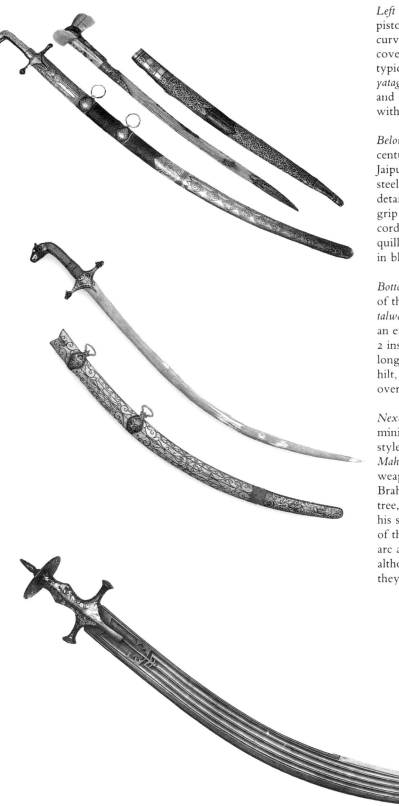

Left An elaborate *shamshir* with pistol grip, short quillons, shallow curved blade, and a black leather-covered sheath. The long chape is typical. The shorter weapon is a *yataghan*, common in the Balkans and Caucasus; it too has a sheath with a long *shamshir*-style chape.

Below left A fine eighteenth-century *shamshir* and scabbard from Jaipur. The blade is of dark watered steel. The hilt (shown in more detail on the opposite page) has a grip of fossil stone bound with gold cord; the bull-head finials on the quillons and pommel are decorated in blue enamel and silver.

Bottom left The overall appearance of this eighteenth-century all-metal *talwar* suggests that it was used as an execution sword. The blade is 2 ins/5 cm wide and 28½ ins/72 cm long, and has several fullers. The hilt, of typical form, is decorated overall with silver foliate patterns.

Next page An eighteenth-century miniature in provincial Moghul style depicting a scene from the epic *Mahabharata*. The artist has shown weapons typical of the period. The Brahmin Drona, seated under a tree, is decapitated with a *talwar* and his soul flies from his body. Three of the attendants in the foreground are armed with *gargaz* (maces), although these are not typical since they lack sword-type hilts.

191

LXXXIII

edge strengthened by a thin fold-over rib, and the hilt was of the form known as the Hindu basket; this consisted of a tubular grip with a domed disc pommel and two wide cusped plates which served as guard, the front plate angling upwards and uniting with the pommel to form a substantial and solid 'basket' for the hand. From the centre of the pommel projected a decorative spike which was slightly angled forward; this was grasped by the warrior if he wished to deliver a two-handed blow. For extra protection and comfort, the inside of the basket was fitted with a padded cushion which was often embroidered. From the base of the basket two metal arms extended to secure the blade firmly in the scabbard.

A sword of very similar construction was the *khanda*, which also had a Hindu basket hilt but differed in the blade, which was broader than that found on the *firangi*. The vast majority of *khanda* blades widen towards the point and have a fretted rib along much of the back edge of the blade. with a corresponding but shorter one along the cutting edge just below the hilt. This type of construction enabled a thinner, lighter blade to be used without losing the rigidity of a thicker and heavier one.

Numerous surviving miniatures which portray Moghul rulers and courtiers from the seventeenth century onwards show them armed with *khandas* or *firangis*. Rather surprisingly, these swords are not carried in a sheath at the belt but appear to have been carried in the hand almost like a walking stick. Perhaps their length – many are much longer than the usual *talwar* – made them too awkward to carry in the conventional manner. The scabbards are normally quite decorative, with a covering of fabric, and some have a small integral sheath at the mouth which houses a knife.

One sword which falls somewhere between the straight-bladed *firangi* and the strongly curved *shamshir* was the Rajput *sosun pata*, which had a recurved or double-curved blade, sharpened on the inside edge of the curve. These weapons are found with Hindu basket hilts and, like the *khanda,* many have a strengthening rib on the back edge of the blade.

Some Indian warriors wielded a weapon known as a *gargaz*, which seems to have no parallel in the West, for it was a mace with a sword hilt. The mace was a popular weapon in Europe and where it usually had a tubular shaft with a shaped grip, often leather-covered, and frequently some form of disc guard, the *gargaz* had a Hindu basket hilt fitted onto a metal shaft which terminated either in a flanged mace head very similar to the European style or in an impressive ball studded with numerous stubby spikes. Despite their lethal intent, these weapons are decorated overall with chiselled ornamentation.

The hilted weapons described above constituted the main, but by no means the entire, armoury of Indian swordsmen, most of whom were experts in their use. Mr Bramley discussed the relative merits of the mounted Indian warrior and the British trooper in his lecture at Meerut, and gave it as his opinion that the lighter, more agile Indian got a better performance from his mount. It was also his belief that the Indian warrior did not like to start a fight but preferred to circle and weary his opponent, waiting for an opportunity to dash in and deliver one devastating cut. Other articles published in *The Cavalry Journal* compared the qualities of British-issue swords with Indian-made blades and the general conclusion seems to have been that Indian blades were sharper and far more lethal than the British.

One of the things Mr Bramley warned troopers to watch out for was 'the Afghan who approaches with leaps and bounds and suddenly unwinds his turban to shake it and so startles the horse and upsets his opponent'. Such an attacker would almost certainly have been armed with the Khyber knife, which had a short simple hilt and a long murderous tapering blade. One slightly unusual feature of the Khyber knife was that it sat very deeply in the scabbard, with only the very tip of the hilt visible above the lip. Bramley also told his audience about the Ghazi, a man determined to die a martyr's death, warning them that his strength was greater than expected and that he would keep coming. His advice to the dragoons was: 'If you want to escape an ugly mauling, kill him dead!'

As was pointed out earlier, it is difficult to equate early drawings of Indian weapons with later types, but swords from southern Indian do resemble some earlier swords. The commonest style of southern sword has a flamboyant or recurved blade similar to that of the *yataghan*, an edged weapon popular in the Balkans. However, the blade of the southern Indian weapon flares out towards the hilt, which has a deep V-shaped guard plate and a large decorative pommel. Another southern Indian group of swords known as Nayar temple swords, this time reminiscent of the medieval European sword, have straight blades with a strange hook or scythe-shaped section at the end of them. The hilts have a plain tubular grip with a rather plain and simple pommel and a slightly dipped plate guard. Some of these swords have a line of small holes along the edge of the blade which held jingles, small metal plates which provided a musical accompaniment as the sword was shaken in dances. From the Madras area came a straight-bladed sword with a large, rather Chinese-looking hilt with a pointed and pinnacled pommel.

Indian knives, daggers and combination weapons

Although swords figured prominently in Indian armouries, smaller weapons were not neglected. Most warriors would have felt naked without some kind of knife or dagger. As with swords, such weapons occur in bewildering variety, but possibly the most familiar to Western eyes is the *kukri*, the honoured weapon of the Gurkhas from Nepal. These men of the Himalayas, who still serve as mercenaries in the British Army, are noted for their loyalty, courage and sense of honour. The *kukri* is rather like a small *sosun pata*, for it has a recurved blade sharpened on the inside edge of the curve. The hilt is usually very simple, normally carved from wood or horn, or occasionally ivory. Just below the hilt the

blade is cut with a small semi-circular depression with a small central pillar, a feature which has given rise to many theories but few facts. Even the proud owners seem unsure as to its real purpose. The most commonly accepted idea is that it represents the female principle, which imparts some magical quality to the weapon. It is reported that during World War II, and later in Borneo, the Gurkhas were delighted to acquire leaf springs from U. S. Jeeps, as they could be fashioned into excellent *kukri* blades!

The *kukri* is carried in a sheath which has a small scabbard at the top for two smaller knives and occasionally for fire-making implements as well. The sheath is normally plain, sometimes with slight moulding on the black leather, but presentation weapons are frequently embellished with silver bands and other decoration. The military version is carried on a belt in the small of the back and tradition has it that the weapon should never be

Below left An eighteenth-century *khanda*-hilted *gargaz* (mace) with a spirally flanged head.

Below centre and right Two examples of the *khanda*, both with the typical Hindu basket hilt. The spike protruding from the pommel allowed the user to take a two-handed grip for a stronger swing. Note the ornate strengthening rib along the back edge of the blade. The scabbard of the weapon on the left is made of wood and covered in velvet. The chape and locket are of thin gold sheet.

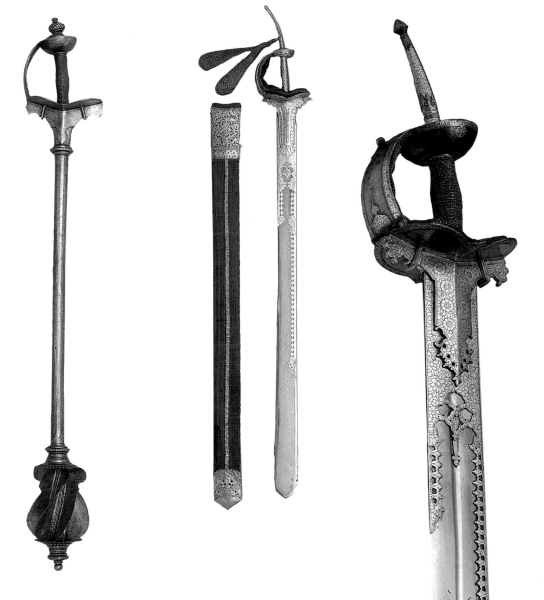

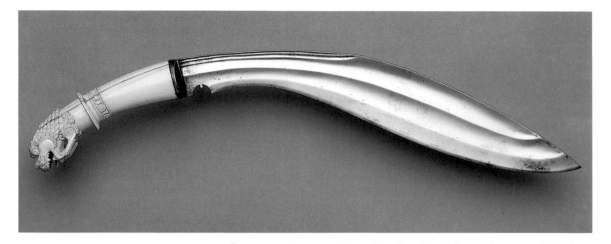

Above A nineteenth-century ivory-hilted *kukri*. Older examples tend to have rather narrow blades with a slightly less acute angle and plain wooden grips. *Kukri* blades are sharpened on the inside edge of the curve.

Opposite page, top row A group of *jambiyas* (left), an Indian or Persian *jambiya* with a green jade hilt (centre) and an eighteenth-century *khanjar* from Lahore (right). *Jambiyas* come in a variety of shapes and sizes, but the blade is always curved and double-edged, and usually has a median ridge.

Opposite page, bottom row, left to right A selection of late eighteenth–early nineteenth-century Near Eastern daggers: an ear dagger, popular in Turkey; two *pesh-kabz*; a *jambiya*, decorated in a style which suggests an Egyptian origin; and a Persian *kard*. The weapon on the far right is a nineteenth-century twin-bladed *katar*. Some *katars* have a blade which opens out, scissor-like, to form a trident-style weapon when the two hand bars are squeezed together.

drawn and returned to its sheath without drawing blood, a superstition which may be satisfied by the owner nicking a finger to draw blood. A very large version of the *kukri* is used in Nepal for the ceremonial beheading of an ox, which is traditionally done with a single blow – no mean task. In the hands of the Gurkha the *kukri* is a fearsome weapon and the Nepalese who serve with the British army have a reputation for courage and devotion to duty. In the recent Falklands War it is reported that some Argentine soldiers fully expected to be slaughtered and eaten by the Gurkhas. In the event, they arrived too late to take an active part in the fighting.

Another weapon peculiar to the mountain kingdom of Nepal is the *kora*, also fitted with a curved blade. The hilt is simple and not unlike that of the medieval European rondel dagger; there are flat discs at either end of the grip, which is usually cylindrical and plain. The blade is only slightly curved, but widens abruptly at the end and has a cusped tip. Most *kora* blades have some simple chiselled decoration along the back edge, and a chiselled disc or eye near the tip. Of necessity, the sheath is broad, with parallel edge, to accommodate the broad end of the blade. The similarity of the *kora* to weapons depicted on early carvings in Nepal and India suggests a long lineage. Also, it may not be too far-fetched to suggest that the warlike reputation of the Gurkhas was partly founded·on this fearsome weapon, for the extra weight at the forward end of the blade made it an extremely efficient cutting instrument. This probably explains why the *kora* was used by executioners, when one swift lethal blow was required.

Many miles to the south of mountainous Nepal, in Coorg, Mysore and Malabar, warriors used a weapon which resembled an overgrown *kukri*, the *ayda katti*. This had a semi-oval blade about 18 ins/45 cm long, tapering in a rounded fashion between hilt and point. Unlike the *kukri*, the cutting edge is straight and the hilt is fitted with a large, flat, comma-shaped pommel. Another unusual feature of this weapon was the way in which it was carried. Instead of slipping into a scabbard, it was hooked onto a brass fitting or *todengah* attached to a belt and carried in the

small of the back. Carried at the front of the same belt was the *pichingatti* (lit. 'broad knife'). This had a wide blade with a slight cusp on the back edge near the point and was carried in a wooden sheath with appliqué metal decoration. Since it was more a tool than a weapon, the *pichingatti* had various domestic items such as tweezers and gimlets attached to it by a short length of chain, rather like the chatelaine of a Victorian matron.

Another weapon with an extremely large blade was the *ram dao*, a sacrificial rather than a fighting weapon, found mostly in the north of India where the worship of Kali Mai, the 'Dark Mother' and wife of Shiva, was strong. The blade is somewhat similar to that of the *kora*, although on some the curve is almost hook-like, but the hilt is an extension of the back edge. Almost all *ram dao* have an engraved eye somewhere near the tip of the blade. These weapons were used to behead the animals offered in sacrifice to the dread goddess, and many are very decorative since they were presented by devout believers anxious to please her.

While many Indian swords can be locally classified with varying degrees of certainty, many daggers are less easy to identify. The *jambiya* is possibly the most widely used of all Indian daggers, but even here there are many regional variations. One thing is fairly certain, however, and that is its Arab origin. In all probability it was taken to India by Arab traders.

The Indian *jambiya* has a slightly curved blade which almost invariably has a central narrow rib and frequently patches of applied silver *koftgari* decoration. This is a style of decoration commonly used by Indian craftsmen and is applied by engraving the pattern directly onto the metal, roughening the area with criss-cross hatching, then covering it with thin silver tape and gently hammering the silver into the roughened surface. Many Indian *jambiyas* are carried in metal sheaths decorated en suite with the hilt.

Hilts of both Indian and Persian *jambiyas* are of two main types, the all-metal type with a waisted grip or the pistol-butt type. The former are elliptical in section, taper from top and bottom to a waist at the centre of the grip, and often have *koftgari* decoration. More common perhaps are the latter, with a grip rather like that of the *shamshir*: the hilt has a wide cusped and flared section where it joins the blade, then sweeps up to the pommel, which gracefully curves over at a right angle. One of the favourite materials for *jambiya* hilts was jade, available in a variety of colours. Jade is extremely difficult to work, and yet Indian craftsman succeeded in fashioning it into animal heads and other graceful shapes. Crystal was also used. Today modern Indian craftsmen are reproducing these attractive weapons, a fact which causes collectors great concern as it becomes increasingly difficult to distinguish old *jambiyas* from new.

Another dagger which looks superficially similar to the *jambiya* is the *khanjar*, the important difference being in the blade, which is normally slightly less curved, lacks a central rib, and curves not away from the pistol pommel but towards it. *Khanjar* hilts are

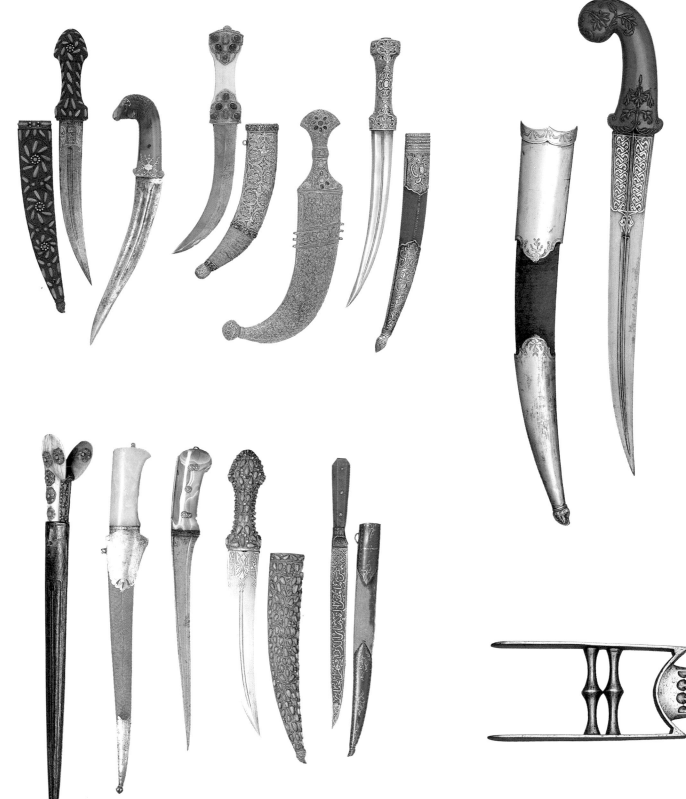

usually decorative, commonly of ivory or jade, and the scabbard is also decorated, often en suite. It must be said, however, that this is a working description only, for even authorities on Indian daggers tend to use the name *khanjar* rather indiscriminately. Another dagger similar in name but different in shape is the *khanjarli*, which has a fairly substantial double-curved blade and a hilt with a large, almost semi-circular pommel.

One weapon which appears to be unique to India is the *katar* or punch dagger which, in some respects, resembles the *pata* for it is gripped in the same fashion, the blade becoming an extension of the arm. The hilt consists of two bars or flattened arms which spring from the base of the blade and join with two parallel bars which are gripped by the hand. The *katar* of northern India has a blade which is wide at the hilt and tapers fairly quickly to the point. In most cases the blade thickens at the point, giving the extra strength need to punch through the metal rings of an enemy's coat of mail. Some *katars* have wide blades engraved with a variety of themes, and some have a central rib, but many are quite plain. Those from the southern part of the country are more frequently found with a longer, straighter blade rather like a short sword blade, and the hilt often has a knucklebow which curves up from the top of the blade; the whole weapon is usually more elaborate and decorative than its northern counterpart. A variant form is the scissors *katar*, which has an outer hollow blade which divides down the centre; this is opened by squeezing together the two central holding bars to expose a third inner blade. The *katar* could well be the descendant of the *maustika* mentioned in the arsenal list of Abdul Fazl.

All the weapons discussed so far have been 'open' weapons, clearly displayed and seen by all, but there was one secret weapon peculiar to India and that was the tiger claw or *bagh nak*. The simplest form comprised a metal bar with a ring at each end, with three or more sharp down-curved blades extending from the bar. If the first and last fingers were placed through the rings, the 'claws' were easily concealed by the curved fingers of the hand. The wearer could approach an enemy, seemingly unarmed, and then strike with a slashing stroke. Another form of tiger claw incorporated a dagger extension at the end of the metal palm bar.

A *bagh nak* was carried by the Maratha hero Sivaji (1627–1680) when he agreed to meet the enemy general Afzal Khan. It was arranged that the two leaders should meet, each accompanied only by a single attendant. Sivaji, taking no chances, wore a mail-shirt beneath his cloak and a metal skull cap beneath his turban. He also armed himself with a *bagh nak* on his left hand and another form of dagger, a *bichwa*, up his right sleeve. On greeting Afzal Khan, Sivaji struck him with the tiger claw and then with his dagger. Afzal Khan had time to strike back with his *talwar*, but to no effect as Sivaji was protected by his mailshirt. The *bichwa* (meaning 'scorpion sting') which Sivaji used was a dagger with a recurved blade attached to one end of a more or less elliptical band which fitted round the hand rather like a knuckleduster. Another dagger, the *chilanum*, was fitted with a similarly shaped blade which, like that of the *bichwa*, was occasionally split into two prongs, but it had a metal hilt with a very narrow waisted grip which flared at top and bottom.

Much more elegant and carried by many as a normal part of their costume was the *kard*, which appears to have originated in Persia. This knife is usually of good quality and has a simple hilt, frequently of jade or ivory, which widens slightly at the pommel. The blade is often of T section and tapers to a point which is commonly strengthened for piercing mail. Like the Khyber knife, the *kard* usually sits deep inside its scabbard. Both blade and scabbard are frequently decorated with *koftgari* work. A few *kard* hilts have a small knife concealed inside them.

A larger knife not dissimilar in shape is the *pesh-kabz*, but on this weapon the blade tapers very abruptly to a narrow point. The hilt is similar to that of the *kard* but much chunkier.

European monks were not supposed to resort to violence or use the sword. However, like Odo, the brother of William the Conqueror, they got round this stricture by using a mace. Indian holy men, fakirs, were similarly barred from using weapons, but they too evaded the prohibition by using a *bairagi* or fakir's crutch instead. This interesting item fitted under the armpit when the owner was seated, and could therefore be construed as a support. It was, in fact, a hollow tube with a T cross-piece in the form of a hand holding a spike, and heavy enough to be used as a mace. If this failed to finish an opponent, there was a steel dagger concealed in the haft.

Early Hindu epics speak of the axe as a weapon of war and it remained so until recent times. The shape of the blade varied, ranging from a great crescent to an unusual L shape; a few are fitted with spearheads or spikes at the end of the shaft. A particularly distinctive form of axe was the *bhuj*, which had a fairly substantial blade fitted in line with the shaft. Since the majority of these weapons have an elephant head moulding at the junction of haft and blade, they are sometimes called elephant knives. The blade usually has a decorative sheath. Like the fakir's crutch, many *bhuj* have a knife concealed in the shaft.

Many Indian weapons combine blades with firearms. *Katars, khandas* and axes were all made with pistols, flintlock and percussion, mounted along the side of the blade. One *pièce de résistance*, probably made for the 1851 Exhibition in London, went one better and combined *khanda, katar* and pistol. Like most combination weapons, it probably emphasized the worst features of each and was not really practical.

Ceylon, Burma and Assam

Although not far in terms of distance, the island of Sri Lanka or Ceylon is strangely distant from India in terms of weapon design. The two 'national' weapons of this tropical island are the *kastane* and the *piha khetta*, neither of which can be directly related to any of the weapons of India. If the epics are to be believed, the island

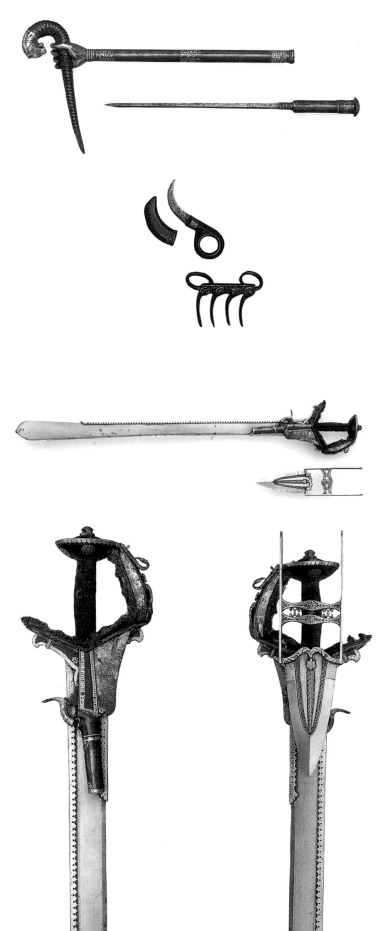

Above *Bhuj* and sheath with gilt decoration, late eighteenth or early nineteenth century. The *bhuj* is midway between an axe and a broad-bladed dagger. The hollow haft frequently houses a dagger.

Above left A *bairagi* or fakir's crutch. The thin-bladed dagger fits inside the hollow shaft. The transverse prop could be used as a vicious club.
Two secret weapons, the *korimba* (above) and the *bagh nak* or tiger claw (below). The short curved blades of the *bagh nak* could be concealed in the clenched fist. The *korimba*, a small curved dagger with a horn hilt and sheath, is typical of Malaya and Burma, and was worn concealed in the hair or clothing.

Bottom Three views of a most unusual combined weapon, a *khanda, katar* and percussion pistol all rolled into one. The powder and caps for the pistol are housed in the hilt of the *khanda*. The *katar* locks onto the other side of the hilt. Rajput, mid-nineteenth century.

Opposite page 'Couple on a terrace', a Deccan School miniature, *c.*1750. Few rulers could afford to be unarmed even in moments of tranquillity, hence the *talwar* and *katar* in the foreground.

197

was first conquered by an army led by the god Rama, aided by the monkey god Hanuman. The first historically recorded king landed in 504 BC, having sailed from the mainland, probably from somewhere in the Bay of Bengal, but over the centuries there were frequent invasions from India. In 1505 the first Portuguese landed on the island and their behaviour aroused a great deal of hatred. In 1602 the first Dutch sailors landed, and by the middle of the century the Dutch had won control of the entire island. There followed a century and a half of reasonably benevolent Dutch rule. This came to an end in 1795 when a British expeditionary force seized the island and ousted them. The island was officially ceded to Britain in 1802 after the Treaty of Amiens, which brought a brief respite from the Napoleonic Wars, and remained under British rule until 1971.

In view of their long occupancy, it is not surprising that the Dutch left their mark on Sinhalese culture, and it is in the supply of blades for the national sword, the *kastane*, that this connection is apparent. Many of the short, slightly curved, heavy blades typical of *kastane* bear the marks of the Dutch East India Company. The hilts, however, are almost invariably of native manufacture and of characteristic form, usually moulded or carved with a dragon-head pommel and an upswept knuckle-guard with the same motif at its tip. Two stubby quillons terminate in finials of the same form and from the junction of blade and quillons two small arms curve down towards the blade. This style of hilt is peculiar to Ceylon (although dragon-head hilts are found on some Persian *talwars*, the resemblance is slight).

The other typically Sinhalese weapon is the *piha khetta* which, if anything, resembles the *seax* of Saxon times. The single-edged blade is sturdy and slopes fairly acutely at the tip. Many have a slightly droopy look, with a very slight curve to the cutting edge. Much of the back edge and forte of the blade is decorated with applied brass or silver sheeting, and the junction of the blade with the hilt has a substantial collar of brass or silver. The bone grip, which is usually carved with a complex and scrolling foliate pattern, is secured to the tang by rivets. The *piha khetta* is carried in a fluted wooden sheath, often decorated with sheet silver or brass en suite with the knife.

Another peculiarly Sinhalese weapon is the *sanger*. This looks like a rather heavy and clumsy dagger but is, in effect, an elaborate processional spearhead with a long ribbed socket.

To the east of Ceylon were fresh fields for conquest and trade, and the demand for spices to stimulate the taste buds of European palates urged Portuguese, Dutch, French and English companies to expand eastward, with inevitable conflicts as their paths crossed. As in India, there was a constant interplay of loyalties and alliances as strong kings and sultans sought to benefit from European help. The story was, to a degree, a repeat of that of Ceylon, with the Portuguese leading the way and being elbowed out by the Dutch and English, although the Dutch retained control of much of the East Indies until after World War II. The English gained control of Malaya and Burma and were a strong influence in parts of the East Indies, fighting several colonial wars there during the nineteenth century.

During the Burmese Wars of 1824–86, British and Indian troops were primarily armed with muskets and rifles, but many of the Burmese carried their national sword, the *dha*. This weapon has a passing affinity in shape with the Japanese sword, although there is no comparison in quality. The blade is slightly curved, single-edged and usually tapers to a point, although some examples have square tips, and along at least part of the back edge there is often a band of silver inlay. Blade length varies from a few inches to full sword length. The hilt is guardless, sometimes with a plain, almost tubular wooden grip and sometimes with an ornate silver-banded grip with a large onion-shaped pommel. The Burmese carried their *dhas* in wooden sheaths, some of which were wrapped in sheet silver; a length of woven cord was bound around the mouth of the sheath, leaving a loop which passed over the shoulder.

To the north of Burma the Nagas of Assam carried a sword somewhat similar to the *dha* known as a *dao*. The blade was straight with a slightly flared end, while the grip was very similar to that of the *dha*. The sheath was unusual, for unlike the vast majority of scabbards it consisted of a board with a slight lip around the edge and a cross-binding of rattan to hold the blade in place.

The Malay archipelago

The Hindu faith spread from India through most of Southeast Asia, including Assam, Burma, the Malay peninsula and out through the numerous islands, large and small, of the Malay archipelago. In some areas it remained the dominant faith, but in others it was overwhelmed by Islam or Buddhism. In some places all these faiths survived side by side, to be influenced later by Christianity. In fact the whole of Southeast Asia is such mosaic of races, ethnic groups and religions that it is not suprising that its weapons display characteristics found in the weapons of India, China and Europe. Many of these features clearly indicate their ancestry, and while some are to be found all across the archipelago, others are local to certain areas.

The variety of hilted weapons, large and small, is legion and most have local, ethnic names. In some cases the differences are only those of detail, the basic pattern being the same; but other weapons are peculiar to certain areas and cultures and immediately identifiable as such. Interestingly, only the Nagas of Assam used a basic all-metal two-handed sword with an unmistakable hilt which had two crossguards.

If there is one weapon which might, with any justification, be said to be common to much of Southeast Asia, it is the *kris* or *keris* – both spellings are found. Both the blade and the hilt are quite unlike those of the majority of swords and daggers. The former gradually flares out from the point towards the hilt, rather like a wedge with a flat top edge, with a small tang projecting from the top. Hilts vary throughout the region, but most are set at an angle to the blade, some at an angle of 90 degrees, so that when the hilt is gripped in the hand the blade projects straight forward, rather like an extension of the forearm.

The origin of the *kris* has long been a matter of dispute among arms historians. One early theory was that it was derived from the sting of the stingray fish. R. Hales, a leading expert on the subject, has advanced the attractive theory that it may have evolved from the *ko*, a Chinese halberd or pronged spear – this weapon had a conventional spear blade and a sharpened arm projecting at right angles from the base, suggesting the L shape of the *kris*. There are further arguments, both historical and archaeological, which certainly seem to support this theory.

Kris blades can be straight or sinuous (wavy) and their surface texture is rough and grainy, for they are made from a mixture of metals. It was said that a blade of reasonable quality required at least two kinds of metal, while a top quality blade demanded seven. The best iron was thought to be that of meteoric origin, but obviously the supply was limited. The manufacturing process was complex and laborious, as the blade was built up sandwich-fashion. The smith started with a central plate of steel as the core; to each side of this he applied a bar of iron which had been folded and hammered several times; he then completed the sandwich with two more outer plates of steel, making five layers in all; the whole compound sandwich was then heated and hammered to weld it into one strip of metal, which was then beaten into shape. If the blade was to be sinuous, it took much longer to make, for each curve had to heated, shaped and beaten individually. When the desired shape was achieved, the blade was ground and polished so that the various layers, folds and patterning gave it the distinctive appearance or texture known by Malay smiths as *pamor*. The pattern was enhanced by soaking the blade for several days in a bath of boiling water containing a mixture of sulphur, rice and salt. Finally the blade was rubbed over with the acid juice of limes. This emphasized the patterning, the acid reacting with different vigour to the various component metals. The final texture was rough and very grey. Ironically many fine *kris* have been ruined by collectors who thought that the blade should be bright.

Each part of a *kris* blade has its own name. The plain band at the edge of the widest part of the blade, for example, is called the

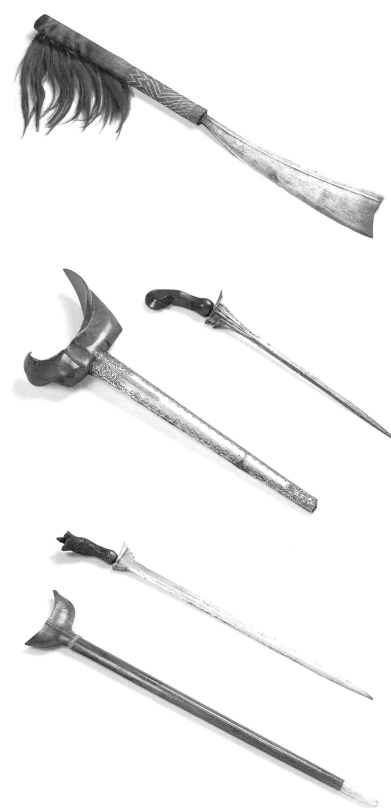

Left A heavy-bladed *dao* from Assam. The quality of the weapon suggests parade or ceremonial use. The coloured tufts of hair on the grip are typical of the weapons and shields of the Naga people.

Below left A Javanese *kris* (above), with a typically upswept *sampir* on the sheath, and a Malayan *kris datoh* (below). The unusually long narrow blade on the Malayan weapon is of a form usually associated with Java.

Opposite page A *piha khetta* and sheath from Sri Lanka (top) and a Burmese *dha* and sheath (below left).

The *piha khetta* has a heavy single-edged blade. Most examples have a bone grip carved with elaborate scroll decoration and a wooden sheath with a long applied sheet-silver chape.

The *dha*, although superficially similar to the Japanese *katana*, lacks the quality of most Japanese weapons. The narrow blade is frequently decorated with scrolling silver bands, while the sheath and tubular hilt are usually plain and made of wood. On this example, however, the grip is carved ivory and the sheath is covered in embossed silver sheet.

Above A pair of Balinese *kris* with exquisitely carved silver grips in the form of demons.

Right A *kris* stand. The *kris* was venerated for its potent powers and when not in use was kept in a decorative stand. Most *kris* stands are of gods, demons or humans carved from wood.
Opposite page The two *kris* on the left are from Bali (top) and Malaya (bottom). The serpentine blade on the Balinese weapon is found on weapons from many of the islands of the East Indian archipelago. The Malayan weapon is a 'Kingfisher' *kris*, with the hilt in the form of a long-nosed demon.

The two weapons on the right are a *sundang* from Malacca or Sulu (top) and a *golok* from Perak (bottom). Although the *sundang* looks like a larger, heavier version of a serpentine *kris*, its blade is quite different – bright and smooth rather than rough and grey.

The term *golok* is used to describe a range of heavy-bladed, single-edged, slightly curved knives used throughout Southeast Asia. The example shown here is relatively short.

ganja, which simply means 'guard', and on many *kris*, again near the widest part of the blade, there is a small hook-like projection known as an 'elephant's trunk'. Although Westerners tend to think of the sinuous blade as being typical of the *kris*, the Malays themselves much preferred the straight blade, which is far more common. Dr S. Gardener, an early writer on the subject, argued that the wavy blade indicated an early Indian influence. He also suggested that wavy-bladed weapons were produced largely for the tourist trade!

A narrow tang was hammered out of the upper section of the *ganja* and then heated, forced into a hole in the hilt and set in place with a gum mixture. Various materials were used for the hilt, wood being the commonest, but horn, ivory, silver, gold and stone were all used. Bejewelled hilts were usually the mark of nobles or courtiers. In Malacca the sultan decreed that only persons of royal blood might own a *kris* with a gold hilt. It was also reported that in some parts of Malacca it was not unknown for a noble to test the sharpness of his new *kris* on the first lowly inhabitant he met after acquiring the weapon.

Perhaps the most striking of all *kris* grips is the type known as the 'Kingfisher', although in fact it is represents Garuda, the eagle who bore the Hindu god Vishnu on his back. It is carved with a long, slightly curved, forward-projecting beak which makes it rather vulnerable – on many examples, the beak is missing. As for the sheath, this was usually fashioned from several pieces of wood glued together and bound with rattan or covered with thin sheet brass or silver. The shape of the *kris* sheath is unmistakable, the wide section of the blade necessitating a correspondingly wide top section known as the *sampir*.

Kris were treated with care and when a really old weapon was being handled it was raised to the forehead as a mark of respect. They were also feared, for it was thought that they had magical force. Many Malays believed that a *kris* should never be pointed at anyone, even when sheathed, but should always be kept with the point either down or up so that the risk of accidental magical harm to bystanders in line with the point was reduced. In Bali, special stands carved in the shape of humans, gods and demons were made to hold the *kris* vertically. To find out if a *kris* would serve its owner well, the weapon was measured while repeating a special rhyme of the 'She loves me, she loves me not' variety. If the last measure was made on the 'not' part of the rhyme, the kris was not going to be the best for the owner.

In Malaya it was common practice to take several *kris*, including the 'family' one, into combat, but the personal one was carried on the left side ready for instant use. For normal wear, it was carried on the right as an indication of peaceful intent. In combat it was not uncommon for two *kris* to be used, one in each hand. In emergencies the sheath was held in the left hand and used as a small shield.

There were variations in blades, hilts and sheaths throughout Southeast Asia and these features can be useful for identification

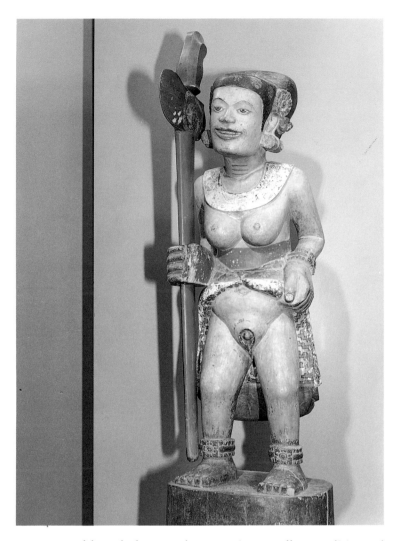

purposes, although there can be exceptions to all generalities and parts from various islands were often united. In Java a *kris* with a long thin blade was frequently used for executions; a wad of fabric was placed on the shoulder and the blade was plunged straight down through it just behind the left clavicle, piercing the heart with minimum effort and bleeding. Malayan *kris* have a very angular grip and a sheath with a rather rectangular *sampir*. Javanese sheaths have a more curved appearance, with a scroll-like tip. Balinese sheaths have a slight resemblance to those of Malaya, but are less angular. The typical Balinese *kris* has a scabbard of wood with a rounded top section to house the wide section of blade; the grip is basically pistol-butt shaped but with facetted sides.

Another Malayan sword which bears a superficial resemblance to the *kris* is the *sundang*. This has a polished blade, either straight or sinuous, but it is larger and broader than that of most *kris*. The hilt has a more or less tubular grip with an S-shaped pommel, and at the junction of blade and hilt there is often a brass band which crosses the front part of the wedge-shaped section of the blade.

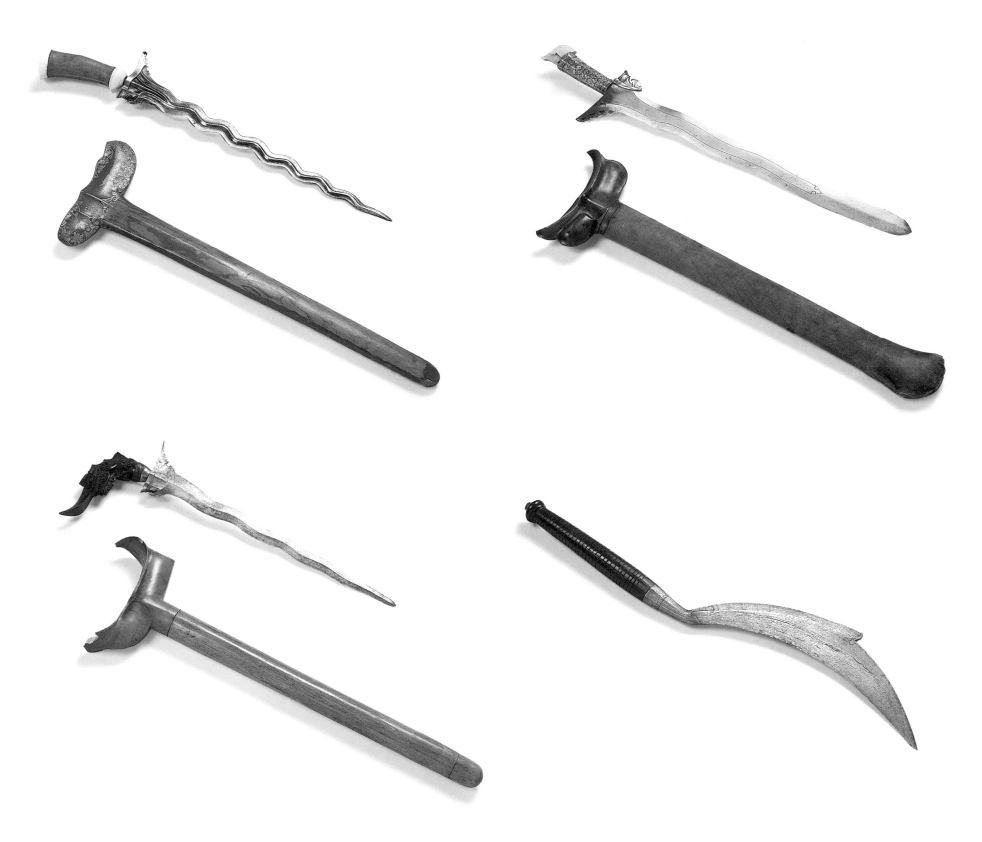

The *sundang* hilt is also found on the *barong*, at one time a popular weapon in parts of Borneo and related areas, but the blade is elliptical in section and much heavier than that of the *sundang*. It must have been a very effective slashing weapon. The Malayan *golok* is similar, but has a straight-backed blade rather than an elliptical one.

Widely spread across the Malay peninsula and neighbouring islands is the *bade bade*, a spidery dagger which often has a very elongated angled grip and a narrow blade. Seen in its sheath, the *bade bade* gives the impression of being rather like a *kris*, for it is often carried in a sheath and has the typical *kris sampir*, but in most cases this is a purely decorative feature.

Tradition has it that the princes of Malaya brought the Ibans, a tribe of sea rovers commonly known as Sea Dyaks, to Borneo. This fierce tribe, together with others such as the Kayans, believed that the head was home to the powerful ghost-soul, the *toh*. To take an enemy's head was an act of bravery, propitiation or revenge, and once taken the head was treated with respect, cared for, and even fed. The weapon of the Dyaks was a very efficient heavy sword known as a *parang ihlang* by the Malays, but to collectors it is a *mandau*. The heavy blade has an unusual profile, with one face slightly convex and the other slightly concave, a design supposed to improve cutting efficiency. The blade is otherwise straight, with the tip cut at an acute angle, and on many there is a line of inset brass dots. The hilt is L-shaped, with the short arm forming the pommel and the grip usually bound with rattan. The pommel section is carved into demonic or dragon heads and decorated with tufts of hair, allegedly human.

The *mandau* is carried in a wooden sheath made of two shaped boards bound together with cane and rattan and almost invariably decorated with beads and hair. Like that of the Burmese *dha*, the binding on the *mandau* sheath often incorporates a loop for carrying the weapon. On the back of the main sheath is another very narrow sheath which, on specimens seen in Europe, is frequently empty. In this sheath the Dyaks carried a short-bladed knife with a very long wooden handle. Strangely, this knife was more treasured than the *mandau* and the Dyaks seldom parted with it. The *mandau* appears to have evolved from an earlier weapon known as a *kampilan*, which has a plainer appearance and a much simpler hilt with a Y-shaped pommel, although the form known as an *opi* used on Wetter Island is probably closer to the *mandau* for it often has locks of hair on the pommel. Differing in its sheath and pommel is the *klewang*, which has a similar blade with an obtuse point, but the hilt is plainer, with a slight backward curve to it; the design of the sheath varies according to the locale.

Another sword common throughout the islands of Southeast Asia is the *parang* or jungle knife. This is produced in a variety of designs, although an angled blade is more or less standard. The *parang nahbur* used in Borneo has a blade which is only slightly curved and also a knucklebow. The most unusual type must surely be the *parang jengok*, reportedly used by thieves among the Malays of Kalentan. The acutely angled blade has a second short blade set at a right angle to it near the point and it was with this that the thief allegedly struck backwards over his shoulder as he walked past an unsuspecting victim, sending him senseless to the ground to be robbed at leisure.

At the other end of the scale was a small hidden knife only a few inches long, the *korimba*. This has a curved blade, a horn grip pierced with a hole, and a sheath of wood or horn. Traditionally the *korimba* was concealed in the bun of hair worn by many Malay and Burmese women; it could be drawn with a sweep of the hand across the hair if the wearer was in danger of dishonour or death.

Persistent traditions and modern reproductions

All of the weapons discussed above were commonplace until well into the twentieth century, when cartridge firearms largely replaced them. In the Philippines campaigns of 1899–1905, the United States Army was forced to adopt a large calibre handgun, the Colt .45, because the Moros kept coming even when hit by smaller calibre bullets and still had the strength to cut down a soldier with their primitive knives. The martial traditions of many Southeast Asian groups were kept in check until World War II, but subsequent campaigns gave them the opportunity to take up old ways – head-hunting was not unknown during the Borneo confrontation of 1962–65. Even today so-called independence groups and freedom fighters such as the Nagas and Karens still arm themselves with traditional weapons in addition to their Kalashnikov rifles.

In the past collectors rather neglected the weapons of the Orient and top quality pieces fetched only a fraction of comparable European pieces. However, since the turn of the century there has been a gradual growth of interest in and appreciation of Islamic and Asiatic art. Inevitably this generated a rising demand, which in turn pushed up prices, and it was not long before the craftsmen of India and Pakistan, encouraged by eager dealers, began to fill the growing gap in the market. Today a considerable number of first-class modern copies of early Moghul daggers and swords are finding their way onto the antique market. So good are these reproductions that it is often difficult to distinguish them from the originals. The wheel has turned full circle.

Left The *parang ihlang*, a weapon favoured by the Dyak peoples of Borneo. The heavy blade has a slightly convex cross–section. The sheath is often decorated with tufts of hair and glass beads, and also accommodates a long–hilted knife.

Left below A wooden–hilted *klewang*, as used by the Lanun people of Borneo.

Bottom left A Malayan *parang* or jungle knife. *Parang* is a Malay word used to describe a wide range of sturdy knives used throughout Southeast Asia. Some, such as the *parang latok*, have an acutely angled blade; others, such as the *parang nahbur*, closely resemble a European cutlass.

Opposite page The Balinese *kris* is worn thrust through the waist band (top). On Bali the *sampir* and grip are rounded, as shown in the hilt and sheath detail at the bottom of the page.

15 AFRICAN HILT WEAPONS

Christopher Spring

The conventional scholarly approach to African weaponry is represented by meticulous studies of the form and function of particular types of weapon, concentrating on their diffusion from theoretical places of origin and their evolution from hypothetical models. This approach was reflected in the way weapons were exhibited at various museums, notably at the Pitt-Rivers Museum in Oxford, England. More recently, however, authors such as Werner Fischer and Manfred Zirngibl have more or less abandoned attempts at classification and simply used fine colour photographs to portray African weapons as works of art in their own right. Exhibitions at Dartmouth College Museum and Hillwood Art Gallery, both in the United States, followed this approach, although the accompanying catalogues by Tamara Northern and Peter Westerdijk contain some of the most interesting essays on the subject to date.

Conventional studies of the distribution of African weapons can only be of limited importance. This is because weapons always tend to be dispersed by warfare – many were dispersed by the *jihads* or holy wars of Sudanic Africa – and because, in Africa, weapons were frequently used as currency. Studies of a particular type of weapon also have their limitations. They may be fascinating for the diversity of form which they reveal, but they can give birth to some highly speculative theories. The assumption, for example, that the evolution of that very African weapon the throwing knife in some way mirrors the migration patterns of the Fang of Gabon and the Kuba of Zaire is very tenuous. It is also becoming increasingly clear that many of the weapons which have for many years been classified as 'throwing knives' were never used as missiles.

More recent studies have tried to demonstrate the esthetic qualities of African weapons. This has helped to contradict the Western notion that if an object is functional it cannot be a work of art, but does not necessarily deepen understanding of the function of weapons within the traditional societies which created them.

It has often been said that no African language possesses a word or group of words meaning 'art' as we in the West understand the word. We must be wary, therefore, of describing African weapons in terms of a Western esthetic. For instance, the *musele*, a knife produced by the Kota people of Gabon, has been described as 'a throwing knife . . . conceived as a bird in profile with a long bill . . . both eyes are shown, giving a Picasso-like effect'. The description is both functionally and artistically misleading, firstly because the *musele* was almost certainly never thrown, and secondly, while it is true to say that Picasso and his con-

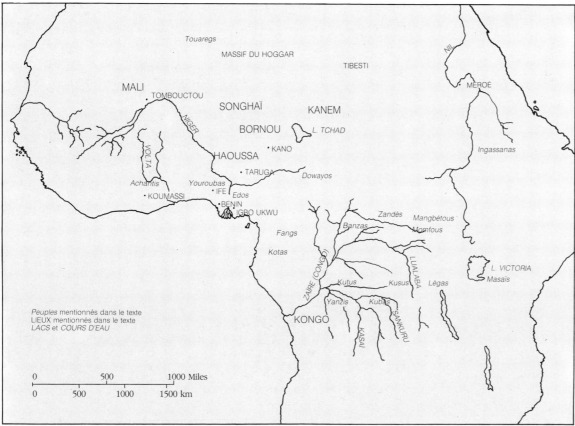

temporaries were strongly influenced by African and other non-Western art, it is dangerous to imply a connection between the creative intention of an African craftsman and a European artist's use of form and motif.

Whatever the approach adopted by scholars and art historians, published literature on African weaponry is undeservedly slight, certainly in comparison with the extensive literature on African masks and sculpture. Yet many African swords and knives incorporate figure sculpture into the design of their hilts and play just as important and integral a part in dance costumes as masks. In this context, it is interesting to turn again to the Kota *musele*, about which relatively little has been written, and compare it with the striking copper and brass-covered reliquary guardian figures also produced by Kota craftsmen. These have inspired a voluminous literature ever since the painter Juan Gris made a cardboard cut-out of one and found that it had a profound effect on him and his contemporaries.

The *musele* and the reliquary guardians of the Kota people are sculpturally very closely allied, both in the materials used (brass, iron, wood and copper) and in the multitude of effects achieved with simple motifs such as lozenges and triangles. Louis Perrois recently described the ritual use of the *musele*. 'The *nganga-mungala*, or dance chief,' he wrote, 'plays the role of *mungunda* monster. He crawls along on the ground, uttering raucous cries, brandishing the *musele* and attempting to hurt the initiates who must jump above him as energetially as possible. The sculptural theme "toucan beak" suggests the form of the blade but is not fully explained.'

Even from this short description it is obvious that the *musele* is an integral part of the dance costumes of preceptors of the Mungala cult, a male secret society similar to the Bwiti cult for which the reliquary guardians were made. The *musele* is therefore a possession which imparts considerable prestige to its owner. Leaving aside the fact that toucans are not found in Africa, it is unlikely that the blade is intended to portray any particular species of bird, just as the Bwiti reliquary figures do not represent any particular ancestor. In the mythology of Bwiti, an evil spirit in the form of a fierce bird constantly seeks to gain access to the human body; it may well be that the *musele* plays this role in the dance drama described above.

Among the Kota and the closely related Fang people, display swords and knives, including the *musele*, were considered to be emblems of status and were left on the tombs of chiefs after their death, along with the family reliquary. It has been suggested that the enigmatic form of the Bwiti reliquary figures may be meant to represent a fusion of man and sword. Kota oral history relates that the reliquary figures were 'danced' by chiefs. In other African societies, swords and knives are also ceremonially 'danced' on occasion.

My purpose in making this detour into the function of the *musele* is to demonstrate that all African swords and knives have a significance beyond the obvious. This theme, which I believe represents a fruitful and largely overlooked approach to the study of African weaponry, will recur many times during the course of this chapter.

Iron technology and the blacksmith

To appreciate the significance of knives, swords and other weapons in African society, the unique position of the blacksmith has to be understood. In European mythology, the blacksmith has been demoted from a thunderbolt-hurling god to a purveyor of demoniacally fast deliveries at village cricket matches. In traditional African societies the blacksmith is still a figure of mystery and magic.

Many writers have observed that in sedentary horticultural societies blacksmiths are, more often than not, highly esteemed; in nomadic, cattle-rearing communities they tend to be feared, despised, ostracized even. This is a very simplistic distinction, and not always true. Blacksmiths do usually constitute an out-group, a socially or ethnically distinct group within the society. They are considered to be 'different', even if they are not. It is commonly believed, for example, that blacksmiths have

Opposite page Map showing the peoples and places mentioned in this chapter.

Below Kota reliquary guardian figure (right) and bird-headed knife, *musele*, with brass-covered wooden sheath, from Gabon. The sculptural similarities between these two objects echo their ritual functions. Both were used by members of the Bwiti secret society.

Bottom Fang knives and a lizard-skin sheath alongside another Kota reliquary guardian figure, also from Gabon.

Right Maasai swords with red leather sheaths and beaded belts, Kenya. Spare and elegant, they make an interesting contrast with the more ornate weapons of forest agriculturalists to the west.

Below right The wooden handle and polished blade of the *ngindza* (left) of the Banda people of the Central African Republic indicate that it is a true knife rather than a currency piece, and probably used for ceremonial purposes. The Kutu *woshele* (right) from Zaire was made specifically for use as currency. The design of both implements is derived from certain types of throwing knife.

Below Stone relief showing Prince Arikankharer striking his enemies, Meroe(?), northern Sudan, first century AD. The decorated leather sheath of the knife in the prince's belt is similar to those produced in the area today.

supernatural powers, that they indulge in all sorts of strange and secret rituals, that they eat the flesh of unclean creatures . . . . Among the Tuareg of the Hoggar region of the Sahara blacksmiths even have their own language, *tenet*.

Esteemed or despised, it is precisely the mythology which surrounds the blacksmith and fences him off from the rest of society which invests the weapons and other objects he makes with special potency. The Maasai, for example, who apparently hold their blacksmiths in particular disdain, nonetheless look upon their swords and spears as their most precious possessions after their cattle.

How did the mythology of the blacksmith arise? Part of the answer lies in the early history of iron technology in Africa. There was no Bronze Age in sub-Saharan Africa. The earliest evidence of metalworking is in iron. By the third or fourth century BC iron was being worked in northwestern Tanzania, at Taruga on the Jos plateau of northern Nigeria, and at Meroe in the Sudan. Whether ironworking skills developed independently in all three places or whether they diffused from Egypt or the North African coast we do not really know. Meroe is often described, incorrectly, as the most likely source of ironworking technology throughout Africa, but it did not become a major smelting centre until the first century AD. Swords have not been found in any of the early graves there, although swords are depicted on various first-century reliefs, such as that of Prince Arikanhkarer striking his enemies.

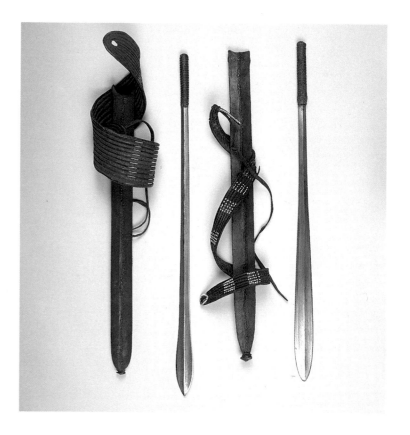

Archaeological and linguistic evidence suggests that during the latter part of the first millennium BC there began a great easterly and southerly expansion of Bantu-speaking peoples from homelands in present-day Cameroon and eastern Nigeria. The ironworking skills of the blacksmiths who went with them must have made an immense impact on societies whose agricultural implements and weapons of war were made of stone and wood. So swift was the migration that by the fourth century AD ironworking communities had established themselves as far south as Natal.

The itinerant blacksmith could set up his forge and, provided a supply of charcoal and of iron-rich rock was available, begin to work within a few hours. He used an anvil of stone, hammers of stone and iron, a split stick or a piece of bent iron as tongs, a pair of animal skin bags or two chambers covered with a loose diaphragm of skin as bellows, and coarse clay tubes or *tuyères* to funnel the air to the fire. With these relatively simple tools the African blacksmith mastered all the techniques of his trade, in some parts of the continent adding the skills of casting and wiredrawing to his repertoire. Many sword and knife hilts are exquisitely bound or inlaid with wire.

As soon as European goods and materials became available in Africa, particularly after the beginning of the colonial period in the late nineteenth century, the African blacksmith began to use imported iron in his work. As firearms and other European weapons replaced bladed weapons of traditional African make, the swords and knives he forged were increasingly used for ritual or ceremonial purposes. Weapons of particular prestige, however, continued to be made of locally smelted iron because of

its higher quality and inherent magical properties. He also began to use imported files to finish his work, although traditionally metal implements were given a final painstaking polish with sand and other natural abrasives. File marks or the lack of them on knife and sword blades are often good dating clues.

In addition to producing ceremonial regalia, weapons of war and agricultural tools, the African blacksmith also made metal currency. This predated by many hundreds of years the minted coinage introduced by colonial authorities in the late nineteenth century. Instead of coins African traders used ingots of various shapes and sizes, hoes, manillas, metal rods, and various currency 'blades'. Into this last category comes the curious *ngindza* of the Central African Republic. It is based on certain types of throwing knife, but its blades are blunt and bulbous, quite unlike the sharp, narrow, pointed blades of its morphological model. Frequently, currency pieces adopted the functional forms of weaponry, but were encrusted with valuable metals such as copper or brass. Knives and swords, whether made specifically for the purpose or not, were favoured items of trade. This poses considerable difficulties when one tries to attribute a particular form of weapon to a specific ethnic group.

In some parts of Africa the blacksmith became closely identified with wealth, kingship and state institutions. On a material level, he made the weapons of war which made the society strong, the agricultural implements which made the earth fruitful, and the metal currency which ensured the acquisition of wealth through trade. On a spiritual level, he made the items of regalia which were the outward and visible signs of 'divine kingship'. In Africa the monarch was the centre and focus of religious and political life.

The empires of the Sahel

The ancient empires of Sudanic west and central Africa – Kanem Bornu, Mali, Songhai, Hausa and others – all rose to power through the might of their armies of horse-borne warriors and their ability to control one or several of the trans-Saharan trade routes and the northerly reaches of the great waterway systems of the Niger and the Volta. These heavily armed horsemen procured vast numbers of slaves from central Africa and traded them across the Sahara, together with gold, ivory and other commodities from the woods and forests to the south. In return they received European goods, including weapons, and from the central Saharan people salt, upon which man and beast depended for survival. Not surprisingly, the horse is to this day a powerful image in the arts of the indigenous peoples of this part of Africa.

In the first half of the second millenium AD the Sudanic empires and kingdoms were one by one converted to Islam, but the roots of the new religion were shallow and in many places the old system of divine kingship and the beliefs that went with it reasserted themselves. It was this constant backsliding towards a pagan or at least a less fundamentally Muslim way of life which

Below left Fulani cavalrymen of northern Nigeria, armed with spears and 'Hausa' swords. Horses and riders are protected by quilted cotton armour.

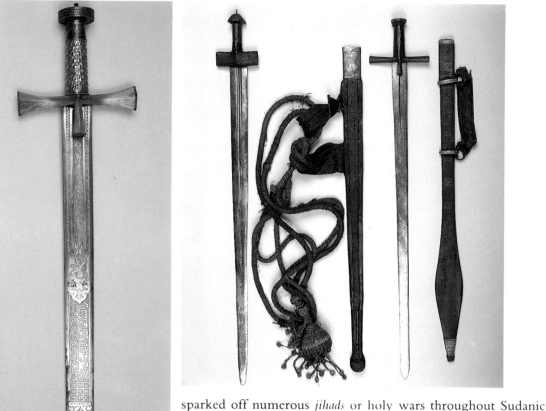

Above Both European decorative engraving and Islamic inscriptions appear on the blade of this *kaskara* taken at the Battle of Omdurman, Sudan.

Above centre Tuareg *takooba* with sheath and baldric (left) and a Hausa sword from northern Nigeria (right). The latter has a characteristic leaf-shaped point to its leather sheath.

Above right Tuareg man wearing a *takooba* on a long tassled baldric slung over his right shoulder.

sparked off numerous *jihads* or holy wars throughout Sudanic Africa. The armies of the faithful, ostensibly intent on maintaining the purity of the original teachings of Mohammed, waged war against the waverers, and in the process many types of weapons were spread from one end of the continent to the other.

In addition to spears and lances, the armoured horsemen of the Sudan were armed with swords and daggers. From the time the Arabs first crossed the Sahara in AD 753 the weaponsmiths of Sudanic Africa must have been influenced by Islamic as well as European weapons technology. However the fascinating hybrid weapons which are so characteristic of the region were probably not produced until the beginning of the sixteenth century, when the supply of European blades increased dramatically.

European blades forged in the smithies of Solingen, Toledo and Belluno were traded across the Sahara from the Mediterranean ports of Tunis and Tripoli and the Atlantic coast of Morocco. From the fifteenth century onwards, European blades may also have come from the new Portuguese trading posts in Mauretania to the west. They were then fitted with locally made hilts and scabbards, and to the various European hallmarks on the blade were added a variety of Koranic and talismanic inscriptions to protect their owners from harm.

Despite the influx of European blades, many fine weapons continued to be forged entirely in the great smithies at Kano, Timbuctoo and other trading towns. It was simply that the demand for weapons far outstripped their capacity and also the

supply of local iron ore. In fact European blades were often copied in such precise detail that it is sometimes difficult to tell where they were originally made. Until recently Sudanese smiths were still turning our accurate copies of seventeenth-century European blades for sale to tourists.

It has often been suggested that the two most vigorous sword forms of Sudanic and Saharan Africa, the Hausa sword and the Tuareg sword, owe their design to an influx of European crusader swords during the thirteenth century, but outside Egypt there is no evidence for the use of European swords earlier than the fifteenth century. There is too much about Hausa and Tuareg swords which is the invention of African craftsmen to support the view that they are intact survivors of archaic Western weapons.

The Hausa sword was not, as its name implies, limited to that area of northern Nigeria known as Hausaland. In fact, from the sixteenth century onwards, it was a standard piece of equipment from the Niger to the Nile. The blade is straight and double-edged. The hilt, with its disc-shaped pommel, cruciform cross-piece and grip, is unembellished. The Tuareg sword or *takooba* is similar in basic form, but the cruciform hilt is ornate, elaborately decorated with a variety of materials, including leather, brass, tin plate and iron nails.

Another weapon habitually used in the Sudanic region of Africa is the arm dagger. Like the throwing knife, there is nothing quite like it anywhere else in the world. It is worn in a sheath attached by a leather loop to the inner side of the left forearm,

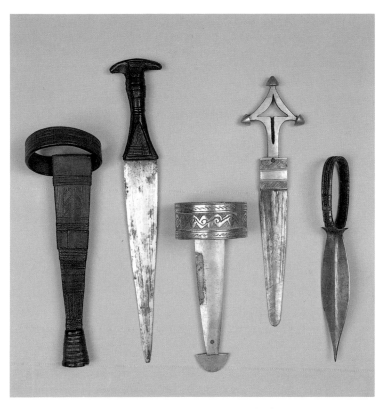

with the blade pointing to the elbow and the hilt resting against the inside of the wrist. From this position it can be quickly drawn. Arm daggers are particularly favoured by the nomadic Tuareg peoples who inhabit the Hoggar massif of the central Sahara, where the weapon is known as the *telek*. On many older examples the blade is European, cut down from a broken or truncated sword.

Environment and lifestyle play a big part in the design of African swords and knives. In general the weapons of cattle-herding or nomadic peoples of the desert or savannah are more severe and functional in their design than those of settled agriculturalists whose habitat is woodland and tropical forest. What greater contrast could there be than that between the spare elegance of Hausa swords and the knives of the forest peoples of Zaire which seem almost to be growing before one's eyes into a variety of swelling and budding organic forms? Ethnographers keen to explain form by function have suggested that the Yanzi knife, because of its broad discus-like blade, might have been thrown, and that the Kusu knife might have been designed to be dropped from a great height on the heads of enemies, the heavy pommel giving added weight and the winged blade acting as a stabilizer rather in the manner of the flights on the tail of a bomb! Both suggestions are equally implausible, especially when one considers how valuable these knives would have been to their owners and how easily they would have been lost if employed in this way. Probably they were used only for show, the width of

the blade and the size of the pommel indicating the wealth and prestige of their owners.

Benin

In the thirteenth and early fourteenth centuries AD when the Sudanic empires of Kanem Bornu and Mali were at the height of their power, the kingdom of Benin began to emerge as a dominant force among the multitude of clans and chiefdoms in the equatorial forest of present-day southern Nigeria. Kingdoms and cultures with highly developed artistic traditions had already been flourishing for at least two centuries at Ife, and possibly from an even earlier period at Igbo Ukwu, but it was the culture and military might of Benin which were to dominate the area for the next five centuries.

According to the oral traditions of the Edo people, the indigenous inhabitants of Benin, the *ada* or ceremonial sword has always held a position of the utmost importance among the items of regalia embodying the social, political and religious beliefs which constitute 'divine kingship', although its symbolic role may have changed somewhat over the centuries.

The early rulers of Benin were known as Ogiso or 'rulers of the sky', and tradition has it that the *ada* represented the ancestors' power over the destiny of the kingdom; this was logical since iron was supposed to possess *ase*, the power to impart prophecy. In Benin mythology the Ogiso dynasty was brought to an end by a popular uprising, after which the people requested the ruler of the

Above left Yanzi knives from central Zaire. The beautiful, organic shapes of the blades are not intended for any particular practical purpose. Their function is probably symbolic, imparting prestige and authority to their owners.

Above far left Two arm daggers with their sheaths (left and centre) and a loop dagger (right). The loop dagger is that used by the Tiv people of northern Nigeria. Arm daggers were worn on the inner side of the forearm, with the blade pointing to the elbow, so that they could be quickly drawn. The example on the left comes from Hausaland (northern Nigeria) and the other is a Tuareg weapon.

neighbouring Yoruba kingdom of Ife to send them a ruler. This was not such a surprising request, for one of the tenets of divine kingship is that the monarch should be seen as different in every way from his subjects. Oranmíyan, one of the sons of the ruler of Ife, duly became Oba or king of Benin. At about this time the *ada* seems to have taken on another symbolic role; it was now carried before the Oba when he appeared in public and symbolized his ability to control events as the Ogiso had done before him. In effect the *ada* legitimized and strengthened the position of the Yoruba dynasty without offending existing tradition.

During the fifteenth and sixteenth centuries the Benin kingdom expanded rapidly through the power of its well-trained armies, whose soldiers are sometimes depicted on brass plaques. The standard soldier's weapon was the *opia*, a short sword of varying form, sometimes double-edged and pointed, sometimes single-edged and blunt-ended, like a smaller version of the *ada*. As more and more neighbouring chiefdoms were conquered it became increasingly necessary to show that their rulers were the deputies of the Oba himself. Certain high-ranking hereditary chiefs of the royal lineage were therefore given the right to have an *ada* carried

before them, symbolizing their power to decide whether men should live or die. The *ada* was the property of the Oba himself and had to be returned to him on the death of the title-holder.

All Benin chiefs had the right to have an *eben,* another type of ceremonial sword, carried before them as a symbol of authority. The looped handles and very thin, broad blades of these swords, often elaborately decorated with openwork and inlays of brass, have intrigued morphologists. It has been suggested, for example, that their inspiration was a large fan, but a more likely prototype may have been the loop dagger, a weapon found in many parts of West Africa and depicted elsewhere in Benin art. At the annual rite of Ugie Erha Oba, said to have been instituted in the mid-fifteenth century by Oba Ewuare, the first of the warrior kings, each chief dances with his *eben* in honour of the Oba's dead father. At the climax of the ceremony the Oba himself 'dances' his *eben* in honour of his father and of the ancestors of Benin, twirling the blade and tossing it high into the air.

The blacksmiths of Benin were divided into four wards, the senior of which were headed by hereditary chiefs. According to oral tradition, the blacksmiths of Benin did not originate among the Edo people but came from other lands, perhaps to assist past Obas in times of war. The truth is that in time of war blacksmiths would have been considered prize captives, unlike their less economically useful countrymen, who would have been executed or sold into slavery.

Asante

By the mid-eighteenth century, when the fortunes of Benin were on the wane and her artistic traditions were in decline, the kingdom of Asante was reaching the peak of its power. Its capital was at Kumase, in the heart of the equatorial forest, and its sphere of influence extended throughout the lands to the west of the Volta river in present-day Ghana. The Asante armies had subjugated the northern savannah states of Gonja and Dagomba, and in so doing had proved the supremacy of well-trained musketmen over the armoured horsemen of Muslim Sudan. This is often seen as a key moment in West African history, for it marked a shift in the balance of power, both military and economic, from the Sudanic states to the forest peoples of the south. Asante was ideally placed to control and benefit from trans-Saharan trade to the north and also from rapidly increasing trade with Europe along the Atlantic coast to the south.

The kingdom of Asante was initially a federation of existing Akan-speaking states, but it quickly expanded to include many non-Akan peoples. Asante supremacy was expressed in various cultural, military and political institutions, but above all in the person of the Ansantehene or divine king. Although the sword, along with other weapons, had been partially outmoded by the musket, the *afena* or state sword was the symbol of the authority of the Asantehene, and was recognised as such throughout the length and breadth of the kingdom.

Left Seventeenth-century bronze plaque showing soldiers of the southern Nigerian kingdom of Benin fighting against mounted enemies, possibly Ibos. The soldier in the centre holds a sword called an *opia.*

Below left Ivory lid of a vessel from Benin depicting a soldier armed with a loop dagger.

Opposite page, left to right
Two Yoruba ceremonial cutlasses, used in rituals connected with Ogun, god of iron. Blacksmiths and hunters set up personal shrines to Ogun, laying various cult objects on them, including ornate cutlasses such as these.

Kusu knife from central Zaire. The pommels of Kusu knives are extremely heavy, being made of solid steel.

Ceremonial sword or *ada* from Benin, southern Nigeria. Swords such as this were the property of the Oba or king of Benin and could only be carried in procession before him and before certain designated chiefs of the royal lineage.

A chief of Benin dressed in ceremonial costume imitating the skin of the pangolin or scaly anteater. He is holding an *eben* sword before him as a symbol of his authority.

For many centuries before the founding of the Asante kingdom the Akan states had been visited by Islamic traders from the kingdoms of Sudanic Africa. It is therefore not surprising that early European travellers noticed similarities between Akan and Islamic (Turkish) swords. In basic form, the Akan sword does not seem to have changed a great deal since the sixteenth century: the blade is curved, broad at the point and gradually tapering towards the tang, and the hilt is of wood encased in gold, with a cylindrical grip expanding into a sphere at both ends. The sheath is often fashioned from much-prized ray skin. On both hilt and sheath are gold castings called *abosodee*, which show the status of the sword bearer and of his master.

Abosodee are cast in a wide variety of forms which admit of an even wider variety of interpretations. To elaborate, to allude, to speak metaphorically and with innuendo are, in Asante, essential elements in discussing any matter in depth, although in the West we could consider this to be the very antithesis of 'plain speaking'. This style of discourse is translated into visual terms in the art of Asante and nowhere better than in the designs of some *afena*, in which the elaborate openwork of the blades and the interaction of the different types of creatures depicted both in *abosodee* and on the blade set up rhythm and counter-rhythm. A host of symbols – knots, kola pods, shells, human heads, various imitations of European-made objects – are points of departure for elaborate and fruitful graphic gymnastics, producing layers of meaning which, like a well-structured poem, can be understood and interpreted on many levels.

Messenger swords, *asomfofena*, were carried by the representatives of the Asantehene, men entrusted with the task of advising local chiefs and keeping them in touch with the wishes of the central government at Kumase. Seeing these swords, the vast majority of Asante subjects would recognize them as symbols of the authority of the Asantehene, but only a select few – perhaps the recipient chief and some of his counsellors – would appreciate the subtler messages communicated by the *abosodee* and other ornaments on the sword and sheath.

Keteanofena, the most important state swords in Asante, had a profound spiritual significance over and above their allusive and didactic qualities. They too were intimately associated with the Asantehene and seem to have had two parallel but separate personalities: *akrafena* were associated with the religious functions and spiritual well-being of the Asantehene and were carried on his right in procession, and *bosomfena* represented his political and secular authority, and were carried on his left. On another level, *akrafena* may be said to have represented the Asantehene's soul and *bosomfena* his ego or perceivable personality. *Akrafena* protected the king from evil while he slept and were also used in rites such as the 'soul washing' ceremony at which the Asantehene was ritually purified. *Bosomfena* on the other hand were used on special errands within Kumase and were associated with ceremonies at which the chiefs swore allegiance to the Asantehene. The most

Above A display of state swords or *afena* of the Asante people of Ghana. Golden sword ornaments known as *abosodee* decorate the sheaths and the hilts are covered with gold. Some of the sheaths are made of ray skin, others of antelope hide made to look like ray skin. Sword bearers' helmets are placed upon the swords.

Right The most important of all state swords, 'Mponponsuo', upon which Asante chiefs swear allegiance to the Asantehene. On the leopardskin-covered sheath a gold *abosodee* or sword ornament depicts a small antelope held in the jaws of a snake.

Opposite page, left and right
Wooden figure or *ndop* of King Shyaam a-Mbul a-Ngwoong of the Kuba people of Zaire. In his left hand he holds an *ikul* or peace knife, introduced into Kubaland in the early seventeenth century when the use of the *shongo* or throwing knife was forbidden.

Triple-bladed ceremonial sword or *afenatene* (literally 'long sword') of the Asante people of Ghana. Swords like this stand close to the Asantehene when he sits in state in his palace at Kumase. The wooden handles are missing from this example.

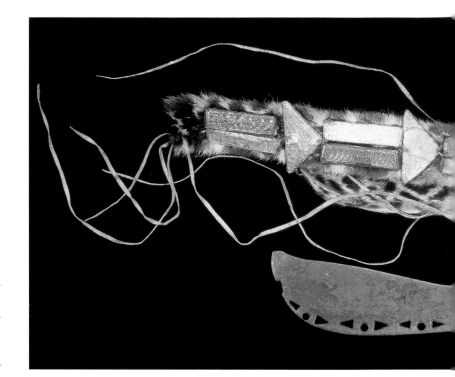

important of the *bosomfena*, and perhaps the most important of all Asante state swords, is 'Mponponsuo', a large and sumptuously decorated weapon upon which all the chiefs take their oath of allegiance. The most important of the *akrafena* is 'Bosommuru', upon which the Asantehene swears allegiance to the nation. He also dances with it at his 'enstoolment' as king, very much as the Oba of Benin 'dances' his *eben* at his investiture.

Many of the satellite states which made up the Asante kingdom had their own state swords, presented to them by various Asantehene as part of the acculturation process and arranged in a similar hierarchy to those belonging to the Asantehene himself. The Nafana of the northern province of Banda, for instance, have a large state sword known as 'Mponposon' upon which the subchiefs of Banda swear allegiance to their paramount chief or Mgomo.

Many *afena* can only be distinguished from one another by the types and functions of the different *abosodee* which adorn them. However, there is one type of ceremonial sword, the *afenatene*, which is structurally quite distinct from other *afena*. In its most elaborate forms it is far removed from the functional models from which it evolved. The blade usually has two distinct sections, a long narrow shaft and a broad flat terminal. The shaft is intricately fashioned to represent such things as the body of a snake, links of chain, or a series of knots; this then splays into a flat area upon which a variety of animals, birds and other proverbial motifs are depicted in delicate openwork. On some of the more 'baroque' examples, the shaft opens out into three broad blades like the petals of a flower.

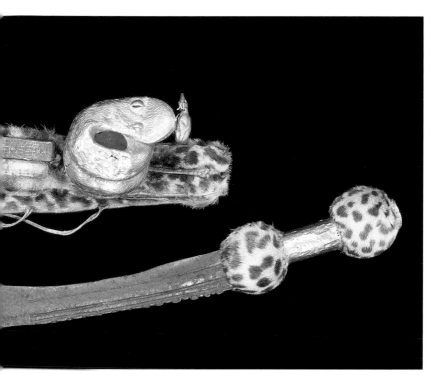

Afenatene do not seem to have been linked with any particular ritual or function, although they were closely associated with the Asantehene and stood beside him as he sat in state in his palace in Kumase. Perhaps they can best be understood as the ultimate expression of the verbal sophistication of the Asante within the material structure of the sword.

Although still widely used today, the symbolic power of the sword in Asante was largely snuffed out, along with its structural and functional development, by the advent of colonial rule in 1896. However, other important items of regalia such as staffs have continued to evolve.

The Kuba Kingdom

Fueled by the spread of iron technology in the first millennium AD, powerful states also grew up in eastern and central Africa, specifically around the great lakes of the Rift Valley, on the Zimbabwe plateau and in the iron-rich woodlands to the south and east of the Congo rainforest. In the great expanse of wooded terrain threaded by the southern tributaries of the Congo settled communities of agriculturalists came under the sway of itinerant hunters who were also skilled blacksmiths. Gradually, small settlements aggregated into larger and larger communities, and then into states. Modern-day Angola derives its name from the *ngola* – swords, knives and other iron objects – forged by the hunter-blacksmiths who set themselves up as kings of these newly-born states. In fact the region between the Upper Niari river and the Lower Congo is often referred to as 'the land of the blacksmith kings'. These states formed the nucleus of what was to

become, in the thirteenth century, the ancient kingdom of Kongo. By the seventeenth century, however, the kingdom was in decline and a series of smaller states grew up along the southern fringes of the Congo rainforest. One of these was the Kuba kingdom, centred on the Kasai and Sankuru rivers of present-day Zaire.

Although the Kuba benefited from the trade routes running between the northern Angolan ports to the west and the mouth of the Zambesi to the east, their culture remained relatively unaffected by Christian Portuguese or Muslim Arabs, and even during the colonial period they did not readily embrace European goods and materials, mainly because their own highly revered artefacts, and the materials of which they were made, could not be replaced by foreign imports.

The Kuba blacksmiths, if not actually kings themselves, wore the insignia of the royal family and were closely associated with divine kingship in every way. The swords and knives which they produced played a number of extremely significant roles within Kuba society and have been well documented by Emil Torday, a Hungarian-born ethnographer who made two expeditions to the region in the early years of this century. Torday divided Kuba knives into three basic categories: war knives, dance knives and knives intended only for show or for ceremonial use. It should be mentioned at once that war knives were also used in ceremonial and in dance, sometimes in versions made exclusively for these purposes.

In Kubaland, no man would appear in public without an *ikul*, a form of show knife, hanging at his right hip. *Ikul* blades vary

considerably in detail, but are generally leaf-shaped and mounted in a short hilt, usually with a circular pommel encrusted with inset metal designs. The combined length of blade and hilt is seldom more than 14 ins/35 cm. Some of the wooden Kuba king figures, *ndop*, depict the monarch holding an *ikul* in his left hand. It has been suggested that the knife was introduced by King Shyaam a-Mbul a-Ngwoong in the early seventeenth century as an emblem of peace and, rather more whimsically, that the design was inspired by a visit he made to Benin, where he was impressed by the *eben*, the ceremonial sword carried before Benin chiefs. King Shyaam was undoubtedly a great king, but not all the innovations attributed to him can be based on fact and we can safely dismiss the possibility of his ever having made a royal visit to Benin.

A knife which seems to have been used exclusively in ritual dances is the *ikulimbaang*. Its hilt is larger than that of the *ikul* and has a crown-shaped pommel. The iron blade is broad and leaf-shaped, narrowing to a thin point, and is often inset with one or more delicate circular designs in copper openwork.

The ultimate ceremonial knife was the *mbombaam*. Only the Nyimi (king) had the right to carry this, and even then in only the most important of ceremonies. It is the largest of all the Kuba knives, having a pointed, leaf-shaped blade decorated with incised longitudinal grooves, and a long hilt elaborately carved and inlaid with copper.

The *ngodip*, a war knife, is rather like a longer and thinner version of the *ikul*, the blade being narrower and more pointed, and the grip much wider. Another war knife, the *ilwoon*, may be an older weapon altogether than the *ngodip*. It has a highly distinctive blade, only about 1½ ins/4 cm wide where it joins the hilt but broadening to a blunt, chisel-shaped or even rounded point about 4 ins/10 cm wide. The hilt is richly carved and has a very broad, circular pommel. The introduction of this weapon is also attributed to King Shyaam, who decreed that because of its aggressive connotations it should never be carried in peacetime unless concealed beneath a cloth. This custom is still observed today.

Exact copies of all these types of knife were made in wood. This is most intriguing, and has led to to a great deal of conjecture. Although it has been suggested that they were simply worn after dark in place of metal weapons, the general consensus is that they were worn after dark only during the period of the new moon, when there is no moon in the sky. Other suggestions are that King Shyaam introduced the custom to prevent nocturnal brawls and accidents, that King Kot-a-Pey ordered it so as not to provoke evil spirits at the dangerous period of the new moon, and even that it was introduced to protect innocent citizens from attack by 'lunatics'.

The connection between the wearing of wooden replicas and the period of the new moon seems beyond doubt. This may in turn be linked to the Kuba belief that fertility is governed by the phases of the moon. Women are believed to be unable to conceive

Above Weapons of the Kuba people of Zaire: an *ilwoon* (left), the Nyimi's *mbombaam* (centre) and a *ngodip* with a copper-inlaid blade (right). All three have wooden hilts inlaid with brass and copper.

Above right King Kot-A-Mweeky III of the Kuba people of Zaire. He is dressed in ceremonial costume and in his right hand holds the *mbombaam*, the exclusive property of the Nyimi.

during the new moon, although their fecundity increases as the moon reappears and waxes. Another interesting piece in the jigsaw is that the main rituals of kingship among the Kuba take place during the period of the new moon, and all shiny objects of regalia are deliberately avoided. It may be that wooden knives are part of a symbolic order in which wood, dullness, moonless night and infertility are ranged against iron, brightness, moonshine and fertility.

There is one final type of Kuba knife which deserves mention and that is the *shongo*, a throwing knife from which the founders of the Kuba kingdom acquired their name Bushongo, 'the people of the lightning'. Throughout Africa there is a widespread belief that thunder and lightning have a physical form and to the Kuba the flashing flight of their throwing knife linked it indisputedly with lightning. The Dowayo of northern Cameroon refer to their throwing knives as the 'hands of the rain', 'hands' probably being a metaphor for forked lightning, and scatter them on the ground during rain-making rituals in the belief that they will transform dead females into ancestors who will have the power to fertilize the wombs of the living. Nilotic people widely believe that certain talismans and charms will turn bullets into raindrops, with the obvious connection between the flash, bang and metal projectile of a rifle and the rolling thunder and flickering lightning which falls to earth as iron. Unfortunately there are no extant examples of the *shongo* of the Kuba which was reputed to have been banned by King Shyaam and replaced by the *ikul* or peace knife. However, from the outline drawn in the sand for Emil Torday by the king of the Kuba, the *shongo* must have been similar to the multi-bladed weapons used by the Zande and related peoples who live to the north of the Congo rainforest. This would seem to fit in with the oral history of the Kuba which tells of a long journey from the north during which four great rivers were crossed, but as I have already mentioned, it is dangerous to draw conclusions about migration routes from the evidence of weaponry. Current opinion is that the Kuba came from lands only just to the north of their present location.

The African throwing knife

Ethnographers have labelled as 'throwing knives' a wide variety of weapons distributed over a vast area of the Sudan and central Africa. These weapons have been divided into two groups – the 'f' group and the 'circular' group – on the basis of their shape.

The 'f' shape knife is distributed over a wide area of the Sudan, from the southern Cameroon to Ethiopia, and deep into the Tibesti region of the Sahara. It consists of a narrow piece of iron about 30 ins/75 cm long, with a projecting spur about half way up. Below this is the shaft or shank, which is straight and blunt, and the grip which, if not of bare iron, is usually of wood or bound leather. Above the spur is the blade, often broader than the shaft and curving forward to form the upper portion of the letter 'f'. The weapon is often carried over the shoulder at its centre of balance in the angle between the spur and the shaft.

Knives of the circular kind have a number of blades radiating out from a central point on the shaft. They are generally found further to the south than the 'f' shaped variety, in a region stretching westward from the upper reaches of the White Nile across northern and central Zaire to the forests of Gabon and Cameroon.

Emil Torday lyrically describes Kuba throwing knives (of the circular rather than the 'f' shaped variety) in action: '. . . then all of a sudden, some objects, glittering in the sun as if they were thunderbolts, come whirling with a weird hum through the air. The enemy warriors raise their shields; the shining mystery strikes it, rebounds into the air and returns to the attack; it smites the warrior behind his defence with its cruel blades. A weapon which is capable of killing behind a shield cannot fail to cause a panic. . . .'

With one or two notable exceptions, the lack of first-hand accounts of throwing knives in action makes it very difficult to assess how effective they were as weapons. Attempts by eth-

nographers to test such things as the aerodynamic qualities of various knives must on occasions have been the cause of a good deal of mirth among watching warriors, to whom the idea of throwing their knives may have seemed the most insane indulgence. However, certain types of knife, even if they are not used as missiles today, were most certainly employed as such in the very recent past, and if Torday's description sounds a little farfetched, it does make two very important points. Firstly, if sent spinning into space with a final flick of the wrist, a circular knife

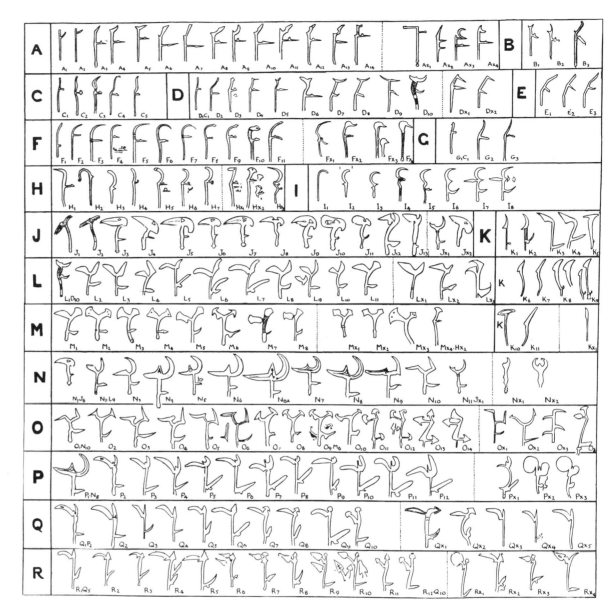

Above A spectacular variety of implements is shown in this early attempt at classifying African 'throwing knives'. Many of the objects illustrated were probably never intended to be thrown.

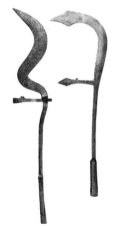

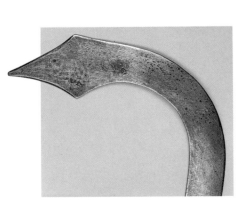

would tend to pivot about the point of whichever of its blades struck an opponent's shield first. It would then swing round the edge of the shield and strike the bearer in the face or side. Secondly, there was undoubtedly an aura of mystery and magic about such knives, which suggests that their capacity to wound and maim may have been secondary to their psychological effect.

Among the Zande of northeast Zaire and adjacent parts of Sudan, a battle would take the form of a large number of individual combats between opponents facing each other in two long lines, no more than a dozen yards apart. The throwing knife or *kpinga* could only be carried by members of the king's regular army and was considered to be *mara ngbanga* or 'court metal', to be used on the king's behalf to fight his battles. Therefore, before the weapon could be thrown, a warrior had to declare his intention of doing so to his opponent, lest he should be thought to be throwing away court metal out of fear. Given the great value placed on spears and throwing knives by the Zande, it seems possible that these highly ritualized martial encounters may on occasion have been an elaborate means of exchanging wealth.

In order to defend themselves against the throwing knife and other missiles, the Zande developed a large concave shield, rounded at top and bottom, which protected almost two-thirds of the body. Being of wickerwork, it was light enough to allow the bearer to leap into the air to avoid low-flying missiles and could be swiftly manipulated to deflect higher blows, provided they landed obliquely. Not being as rigid as a heavier shield, it did not allow circular throwing knives to pivot as they struck. An athletic dance of self-defence was performed by the Zande long after the colonial administration brought traditional warfare to an end.

If the Zande warrior's skill with the throwing knife was effective against men on foot, would it not have been devastatingly effective against mounted warriors? So much of the culture of Sudanic Africa has been shaped by the combined power of man and horse that it is not unreasonable to speculate that the throwing knife may have evolved as a means of resisting and counteracting this power, even that it acquired some of its magical qualities by serving this purpose.

The division of throwing knives into 'f' shape and 'circular' is a perfectly valid means of classifying them, but it has often resulted in any weapon with a hilt and blade which is neither knife, sword, axe or spear being labelled as a throwing knife and classified as belonging to one or other of these categories. It is often stated, for example, that the bird-headed *musele* is a throwing knife, albeit one adapted for use in a forest environment. In fact, it is as unlikely that the Kota would have thrown the *musele* as it is that the Kuɟu developed the pommels of their precious daggers to bomb their enemies from the branches of trees! The sickle-shaped knives of the Mangbetu of northeast Zaire and the bulbous-bladed knives of their neighbours, the Momfu, have also appeared in articles on the subject of throwing knives. Both types of knife were highly valued by their owners, the Mangbetu knife

being a symbol of kingship or high office, as the famous engraving of King Munsa in Schweinfurth's *Heart of Africa* shows. Since both types of knife are often fitted with beautifully carved ivory handles, it is most unlikely that either would ever have been thrown.

It has also been suggested that the 'execution knife' of the Ngombe of central Zaire is a derivation of the Banza throwing knife, but in fact it has much more in common with the *mugusu*, a billhook used to clear vegetation by the Lega of eastern Zaire and by many other lacustrine peoples as far to the north as Uganda. The Lega carve small ivory images of this knife for use in the Bwami secret society where it symbolizes diligence and the ability to cut through inextricable problems with the help of others. Only preceptors of the highest grade possess such images. Being such a useful implement, the *mugusu* would certainly have been traded down the river systems of the Lualaba and the upper Zaire to the land of the Ngombe. In fact blades of all sorts, particularly throwing knives, were used as items of currency throughout the Congo basin and in the savannah lands to the north. In 1887, the German explorer Nachtigal attempted to obtain grain at Baghirmi near Lake Chad, only to discover that throwing knives were the sole currency the traders would accept. Iron was an extremely valuable commodity before the wholesale introduction of European goods, although the estimated value of throwing knives and other items used for exchange must have been considerably higher than that of their metal content alone.

The blades and shafts of throwing knives are often embellished with incised designs. Among the Ingassana people of the Blue Nile Province of Sudan, throwing knives with incised decoration continue to be much in demand although they have long been obsolete as weapons. This may be because there is a relationship between the incised designs and the overall structure of these knives which gives them a deeper significance. Two varieties of throwing knife are produced by Ingassana smiths, *sai* and *muder*. Both are 'f' shaped and zoomorphic, the *sai* being in the form of a stylized snake and the *muder* in the form of a scorpion. The component parts of each weapon are described in anthropomorphic terms – the blade is the head, the spur is the breasts, the shaft the loins, and the handle the legs. On the blade are incised designs depicting harmful creatures such as the snake and the scorpion. Other parts of the weapon are decorated, again in stylized form, with harmless creatures such as the deer and the millipede. Between the blade and the spur is the neck, an area of cross-hatched incised lines imitating the traditional monitor-skin neckband worn by men and women. On a symbolic level, therefore, the *sai* and the *muder* reflect the world of man and the world of nature.

The fact that Ingassana knives are still made to traditional designs has suggested to one author that they are 'conceptual props', artefacts which in their structure and decoration reflect man's relationship with the natural world, and also, perhaps, the reconciliation of opposing elements within himself. Speculations of this kind, I feel, point the way to a very fruitful area in the study of African weapons.

An anthropologist recently told me, only half jokingly, that he wouldn't contemplate writing about weapons because he was a pacifist. Undoubtedly, traditional African weaponry represents a fusion of the destructive as well as the creative elements in the human character. Perhaps after all this is a healthier balance than our Western attempt to keep the two poles apart. Although such etiquette was by no means always observed by African peoples in traditional warfare, the Zande would avoid unnecessary losses by not completely encircling the enemy with the wings of their army, leaving a gap in the rear through which the vanquished foe could retreat. It might be said that the nature of our modern weaponry has closed that gap forever.

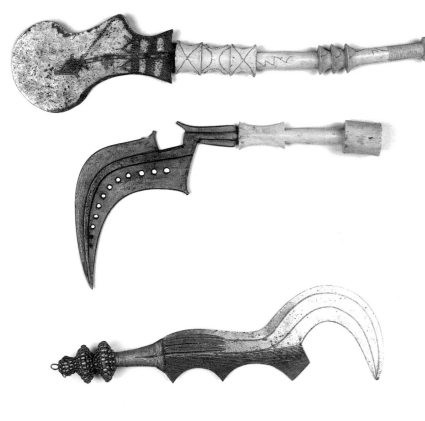

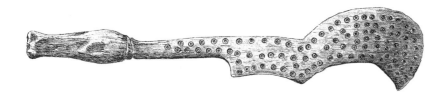

Left Ingassana man with a *muder* or 'scorpion' throwing knife. These knives are still made in large quantities by local smiths, but today no Ingassana would dream of throwing one.

Far left, top to bottom
Bulbous-bladed knife, Momfu people, northeast Zaire.

Sickle-shaped knife, Mangbetu people, northeast Zaire. Like the Momfu knife above, sickle-shaped knives often have finely carved ivory hilts and symbolize the status and authority of their owners.

'Execution knife' of the Ngombe people of Zaire. The sinister name is probably the product of an overactive European imagination inspired by the shape of the blade, which may be derived from the *mugusu* shown below.

Ivory replica of a *mugusu* or hill-hook, Lega people, eastern Zaire. The Lega carve these small ivory images for use in the Bwami secret society where they symbolize the owner's ability to cut through inextricable problems.

Opposite page, top to bottom
Throwing knives, *kpinga*, of the Zande people of northwest Zaire. Both are good examples of the 'circular' category of throwing knife and, unlike many 'throwing knives', their use as missiles has been well documented. The knife on the left is made of copper and may therefore be a ceremonial weapon or currency piece.

Two more throwing knives, the *sai* (left) and the *muder* (right) of the Ingassana people, Sudan. Both are variations of the 'f' shaped category of throwing knife.

Detail of the *muder* blade, showing the incised scorpion motif.

16 PRE-CONQUEST AMERICA

Michael D. Coe

Opposite page A Dene Indian of the Tanana tribe attacks a moose on the Yukon River, an engraving from *Travel and Adventure in the Territory of Alaska* (1868) by Frederick Whymper.

Below Tlingit dagger, Northwest Coast, southern Alaska. Fashioned from copper, wood, shell inlays, baleen, skin and rawhide, this is a substantial weapon measuring 20½ ins/52 cm overall. The pommel represents a bear, an important mythological animal.

Among the indigenous cultures of the New World, prior to the European conquest, edged weapons were very rare. This was largely due to the absence of metallurgy, the art of working metals and extracting them from their ores being limited to western South America, where the art was of considerable antiquity, Central America, where it was quite late, and a few isolated regions in North America. Most of the peoples of the New World managed perfectly well with a Stone Age level of technology until their 'discovery' by Columbus and his successors.

Even where metalworking was technically very advanced, as in Peru and Mexico, the making of metal artefacts was directed far less to utilitarian objects than to ornaments and items of status. Metal swords, daggers and knives were thus entirely unknown to the ancient peoples and civilizations of Latin America, including such great empires as the Inca and Aztec.

Of course, the want of metal weapons in most of the New World does not imply that edged weapons did not exist. In the tropical lowlands and in the West Indies there were trees whose wood was so hard and dense that it could be fashioned into extremely effective clubs and swords. The Aztecs also discovered that the edges could be slotted to receive incredibly sharp, prismatic blades of obsidian, a natural glass of volcanic origin. This produced a type of weapon much respected by the invading Spaniards. In fact Mexico was the one region of the New World where a Spanish soldier could be bested in hand-to-hand combat. Elsewhere, native armies and troops of warriors preferred to fight with long-distance weapons such as spears, darts, bows and arrows, blowguns and slings. Even so, the Aztecs were no match for European firearms, crossbows, war dogs and mounted troops.

North America

Although metalworking was a very ancient skill in North America, it was of sporadic appearance and underwent little indigenous development. The Old Copper Complex culture appeared as long ago as 3000 BC in Wisconsin, upper Michigan

and Ontario, and lasted until about 500 BC. Out of native copper nuggets from several sources in the Upper Great Lakes area, the Old Copper people fashioned knives and spear points, hammering, cutting and annealing them into shape. Their technology was therefore of a fairly rudimentary kind, and the objects they made, most of which have been found in graves, were probably used for hunting and skin preparation rather than fighting. Despite their name, these were Stone Age rather than Copper Age or Chalcolithic people. Nevertheless, Old Copper technology and access to sources of copper led directly to the copper bracelets, spiral finger rings and reel-shaped gorgets of the more advanced Adena and Hopewell cultures of the eastern United States during the early centuries of the Christian era.

One of the most interesting but least studied metallurgical traditions in the Western hemisphere is that of the early Northwest Coast. During the last decades of the eighteenth century, when the southern coast of Alaska and neighbouring British Columbia were first visited by Spanish, Russian and English explorers, most of these travellers, even those who considered themselves the earliest to visit the Northwest, found both copper and iron in use among the indigenous peoples. The copper was native, traded as nuggets from sources on the Coppermine River which cuts down to the Northwest Coast from the Alaskan interior following a line just west of the tribal lands of the Tlingit. However, metallurgical analysis by John Witthoft and Frances Eyman in the late 1960s points to other sources, as yet unidentified, in the interior. Originally, Northwest Coast iron may have been 'drift' iron, salvaged from Japanese wrecks and floating barrels stranded along the coast. Later, both copper and iron (including steel) were obtained from trade with European and American ships, and the anti-fouling copper plates which sheathed ships' hulls were quickly perceived by the Northwest Coast natives as a good source of raw material. Steel files and blades from Sheffield Bowie knives were also greatly prized trade items.

Technically, the Northwest Coast metallurgists were on no higher a level than the Old Copper people: detailed analysis of

Tlingit knives by Witthoft and Eyman showed that they knew nothing of smelting and that forging techniques were fairly rudimentary. Copper objects, for instance, were sawn out with stone tools, then hot-forged before chelation with fish oils, and then surface details were added using knives and gouges.

Nevetheless, the daggers and knives produced by Northwest Coast craftsmen, particularly the Tlingit, are truly astonishing in their artistry. They were probably very effective as weapons too. In the eighteenth century, Tlingit warriors fought in wooden armour made of vertical slats lashed together with rawhide and braided fibre twine (early explorers compared these outfits to ladies' stays!). Their heads were protected by elaborate visored wooden helmets, usually carved in the shape of animal crests. This equipment was worn in hand-to-hand combat, in which daggers were the offensive weapon.

Tlingit daggers or fighting knives of copper or steel can be up to 24 ins/60 cm in length, and generally have one or more spines running down one side. The hilts are often extremely beautiful, with animal horn pommels carved into the shape of animal heads and sheathed in copper, with abalone shell inlay, and grips lashed with caribou skin. On some fighting knives, the pommel is sharp-edged, designed to slash at an enemy when stabbing with the blade failed to have the desired effect. Given their technology and beauty of form, which owe little or nothing to early Euro-American models, these weapons seem to represent a very ancient indigenous tradition, possibly with its roots in northeastern Asia.

Even more mysterious are the metal knives produced by the Dene or Athapaskan-speaking peoples of northwestern Canada and the Alaskan interior. These were also examined by Witthoft and Eyman in their pioneering study. Prior to 1850, when steel weapons made from trade files began to appear, the Dene made their knives of native copper. These are highly forged, with frequent welds and forging folds; in technique, they are completely unlike the Stone Age products of the Tlingit or the Central Eskimo. Furthermore, the steel weapons which eventually replaced copper ones show an equal control of forge and hammer; in fact, daggers in both copper and steel show both heat treatment

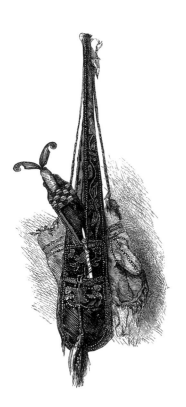

and stress hardening, and methods for controlling strength and hardness. They vary from just under 10 ins/30 cm in length to more than 24 ins/61 cm and have grips of caribou hide strips or vegetable fibre bound with twine, but the pommels are always in the shape of two flattened oppositely-curving volutes.

One is therefore obliged to conclude that there were two strongly contrasted traditions of metallurgy and weapon-making in northwestern North America, one technologically backward but artistically advanced, and the other technologically sophisticated but artistically less ambitious. Certainly there is nothing to match the the achievements of the Tlingit and Dene elsewhere in the native New World.

Mesoamerica

The term 'Mesoamerica' is applied by archaeologists and anthropologists to southern Mexico and neighbouring Central America, and comprises all those peoples in this region who were civilized at the time of the Spanish Conquest.

Certainly the most formidable weapon ever developed by the Mesoamericans, or by any other natives of the Western hemisphere, was the *macuauhuitl*, the terrible sword-club of the Aztecs. The name is Nahuatl, the official language of the Aztecs and of their empire, and is a compound of the words *maitl* ('hand') and *cuauhuitl* ('wood' or 'stick'). There are no known records, archaeological or otherwise, for the *macuauhuitl* prior to the early fourteenth century when the Aztecs rose to power, so there is every reason to believe that it was invented by the Aztecs and then adopted by their vassals and neighbours. In fact, it was first observed not among the Aztecs but among the Maya of the Yucatan Peninsula, which never fell under Aztec sway. On his fourth voyage of discovery (1502–04), Christopher Columbus, cruising off the Caribbean coast of Honduras, came across a great Mayan trading canoe filled with merchants and merchandise

probably from the Putun Maya enclave of Xicallanco on the other side of the peninsula. Among the goods, his chronicler son Ferdinand tells us, were '. . . long wooden swords with a groove on each side where the edge should be, in which cutting edges of flint were fixed with thread and bitumen (these swords cut naked men as if they were of steel).' While 'flint' (*pedernal* in Spanish) is given in the original text, the stone blades were almost certainly obsidian, a substance unlikely to have been known to Europeans.

In February 1519, Hernán Cortés and his small army of conquistadors left Cuba on an expedition which was to result, eventually, in the downfall of the Aztec Empire. Rounding the Yucatan Peninsula, they arrived at the settlement of Chanpoten, probably an enclave of the Putun Maya, where they were promptly attacked by the natives. According to Bernal Díaz del Castillo, one of Cortés' captains and the Boswell of the Spanish Conquest: '. . . they were well armed in their own manner with bows, arrows, and lances, some of them as long as our lances and some of them shorter, and shields and *macanas* and two-handed swords and slings and stones, and they wore cotton armour and carried trumpets and drums, and many of them had their faces painted black and others red and white.' The word *macana* is Arawak, and was brought by the Spaniards from the Antilles, where it referred to a flat wooden club with sharp edges; by 'two-handed swords' Díaz almost certainly meant the *macuauhuitl*.

The conquistadors encountered the *macuauhuitl* many times on the field of battle after they had entered the Emperor Motecuhzoma's realm, and had ample opportunity to observe its use. The Anonymous Conqueror tells us: '. . . they have swords of this kind – of wood made like a two-handed sword, but with the hilt not so long, about three fingers in breadth. The edges are grooved, and in the grooves they insert stone knives, that cut like a Toledo knife.'

Various illustrations in post-Conquest codices depict the *macuauhuitl*. The Codex Mendoza, preserved in the Bodleian Library at Oxford, was prepared for the first Spanish Viceroy of Mexico, and covers various aspects of Aztec life. One section deals with a citizen's rise through the warrior ranks as he gains military renown by taking captives. The illustration shows him grasping a prisoner by the hair; both victor and vanquished carry a round shield on one arm and a *macuauhuitl* set with obsidian blades in the opposite hand. In another illustration depicting early Aztec victories over rival cities in central Mexico, one combatant wields a *macuauhuitl*, while the other has a plain sword-club probably similar to the *macana* encountered by the Spaniards in the West Indies.

As we know from historical accounts of the Aztecs, the plain sword-club was no match for the *macuauhuitl*. A favourite form of sacrifice was to tie a captive to a great stone ring, and give him a shield and a sword-club (without the obsidian blades) with which to defend himself. He then had to face a great military leader armed with a *macuauhuitl*. However valiant his defence, the battle always ended with his death.

It seems odd that several feather-decorated round shields and five *atlatls* or spear throwers should have survived from Conquest times, but no Aztec *macuauhuitls*. There is not one, in any museum or collection. Fortunately, a very detailed watercolour drawing in the Codex Ixtlilxochitl, probably done by a European artist, gives a good idea of what this much-feared slashing weapon looked like. It shows the famous poet-king of Texcoco and close ally of the Aztec throne, Nezahualcoyotl, going to war in his Eagle Knight costume. He bears a feather-covered shield on his right arm and in his left hand he brandishes a *macuauhuitl*, clearly tied to his wrist; Fray Gerónimo de Mendieta, in his account of Aztec warfare, informs us that this was the custom so that the sword would not be lost when dropped from the hand as the warrior seized his captive.

The *macuauhuitl* was about 'three fingers broad', as the Anonymous Conqueror says, with at least eight obsidian blades down each side; the grip of the hilt seems to have been twine-wrapped. This weapon could inflict terrible wounds (in fact, fresh obsidian blades are so sharp that they are sometimes used in modern surgery). The Anonymous Conqueror writes: 'I saw one day an Indian fighting with a mounted man, and the Indian gave the horse of his antagonist such a blow in the breast that he opened it to the entrails, and it fell dead on the spot. And the same day I

Left Aztec gladiatorial sacrifice, a detail from the Codex Magliabechiano, an early colonial manuscript. A Jaguar Knight, a member of one of the military orders, attacks a captive. The victim is tied to a stone and equipped with a plain wooden sword-club decorated with eagle down, hardly a match for the obsidian-edged *macuauhuitl* wielded by his opponent.

Below Detail from the Codex Ixtlilxochitl depicting Nezahualcoyotl, the poet-king of Texcoco, attired as an Aztec Eagle Knight. In his left hand he wields a realistically depicted *macuauhuitl*; he defends himself with a feather-mosaic shield.

Opposite page, left to right
Volute-headed Tanana (Dene) knife with a ribbed blade, as drawn by Whymper in 1866, and a Tanana hunter's 'firebag' containing fungus tinder, a cord fire drill or flint-and-pyrites, and another volute-headed knife. The firebag was worn suspended from the neck.

Part of a page from the Codex Mendoza, painted for the first Spanish Viceroy of Mexico, showing progressively higher ranks of Aztec warriors, each grasping a captive. Victors and vanquished brandish *macuauhuitls*.

This page from the Codex Mendoza depicts the mythological founding of Tenochtitlan, the Aztec capital, symbolized by an eagle perched on a cactus. The lower panel depicts the first two conquests of the nascent Aztec state, personified by one warrior with a *macuauhuitl* and another with a plain wooden sword-club.

Right The Conquist-
adors capture the
Aztec capital
Tenochtitlan: initially
the Spaniards are
driven off and
Quauhtemoc is
proclaimed king
(top), but finally the
Spaniards take the
city (bottom). The
macuauhuitls of the
defenders are much in
evidence. From a
painting on mother-
of-pearl by Miguel
Gonzalez, Museo de
America, Madrid.

saw another Indian give another horse a blow in the neck, that
stretched it dead at his feet.'

During the fight between the conquistadors and the Tlaxcalans,
on the way to the Aztec capital Tenochtitlan, one Pedro de Morón
charged with his horse into the ranks of the enemy. In this
engagement 'the Indians seized hold of his lance and he was not
able to drag it way, and others gave him cuts with their broadswords [*montantes* in Spanish] and wounded him badly, and then
they slashed at the mare, and cut her head off at the neck so that it
hung by the skin, and she fell dead. If his mounted companions
had not come at once to his rescue they would have finished
killing Pedro de Morón.' Bernal Díaz del Castillo further records
that Pedro de Morón did not recover from his terrible wounds –
presumably they were beyond the skills of contemporary
surgery. Yet Aztec battlefield surgery seems to have been far
more advanced than that of the Spaniards – the Aztec wounded,
we are assured by Mendieta, were taken off by medical orderlies
to be treated by surgeons with special medicines.

A further development of the principle of the *macuauhuitl* was a
thrusting lance of wood, shown in the Codex Mendoza in the
hands of very high-ranking military officers. Somewhat taller
than a man, it had a slender shaft and a flat expanded head; the
latter was laurel-leaf shaped, with a central spine and slotted edges
fitted with obsidian blades. Shown in use against merchants
unlucky enough to have been waylaid on their journey by vassals
of a hostile foreign lord, it seems to have been a highly effective
weapon in close combat.

The invention and adoption of the *macuauhuitl*, an instrument
of war never before seen in Mesoamerica, may have allowed the
Aztecs to achieve crushing military victories over many
neighbouring peoples and to put together one of the great empires
of the American continent. When the Spanish invaders brought
their steel swords to Mexico, the resemblance between the two
kinds of weapon was immediately seen by both sides, and the
Aztec term *tepuzmacuauhuitl* ('metal macuauhuitl') was soon
applied to the import.

Human sacrifice is very old in Mesoamerica, and was probably
practiced among all pre-Conquest cultures, not just by the
Aztecs. The ritual form preferred by the ancient Maya, especially
during the Classic period (AD 300–900) was decapitation, often
after lengthy humiliation and torture, but during the Post-Classic
period (900–1521) the Maya and their Mesoamerican neighbours,
particularly the Aztecs, favoured heart sacrifice. This custom
probably reached its apogee among the Aztecs, with scores –
perhaps hundreds – of victims daily having their hearts plucked
out by priests as offerings to the gods in their capital,
Tenochtitlan.

Archaeological excavations in the remains of Tenochtitlan,
particularly in the ruins of the Great Temple, have brought to
light a fair number of large chipped flint blades. These were once
part of sacrificial knives, the wooden hafts having disintegrated

very rapidly in such damp conditions. Among the treasures that Cortés received from Motecuhzoma, and forwarded to the Holy Roman Emperor Charles V, were several magnificent sacrificial knives, with mosaic-encrusted handles. One of these in is the collection of the Museum of Mankind, London, and is hafted with the effigy of a crouching Eagle Knight. The chipped blade shows definite damage – it had probably opened more than one captured warrior's rib cage before it ended up in Cortés' hands.

If the climate of central Mexico has not been conducive to the survival of Aztec sacrificial dagger handles, far less favourable conditions for archaeological preservation are found in the humid, hot tropical lowlands inhabited by the Maya. Thus, a complete knife with a wooden haft of intertwined serpents in the Peabody Museum of Archaeology and Ethnology at Harvard is rare indeed. This was dredged up by Edward H. Thompson from the bottom of the Sacred Cenote at Chichen Itzá in Yucatan; the waterlogged conditions at the bottom of this natural sinkhole or 'well' had preserved the wood. As with the Aztec example in London, the edges of the blade, which has been fixed to the haft by resin, show nicks resulting from sacrificial use. It is difficult to put an exact date on objects recovered from the Cenote, but it is generally agreed that the Peabody knife belongs to in the Late Post-Classic period, when Mayan civilization was in decline.

It should be remembered that Mesoamerican sacrificial daggers were not offensive or defensive weapons in the combat sense. They were apparently used only against tied, held, or otherwise restrained victims.

South America

In the Andean area of South America – roughly the area covered by the Inca Empire in the early sixteenth century – metallurgy of sorts was known as early as 1500 BC. Over the centuries the Andean metalworkers developed a wide variety of sophisticated techniques, including smelting, casting and soldering, and produced gold, copper, silver and bronze objects in considerable quantity. In fact, it is likely that the peoples of Mesoamerica derived their knowledge of metallurgy from the Andean area some time around AD 900. Given such precocity and sophistication, it is somewhat surprising that the Andean civilizations produced no true offensive weapons in either copper or bronze.

Our best information on Andean warfare in pre-Inca times comes from the Moche civilization, which flourished in the narrow, desert-rimmed valleys of the northern Peruvian coast from the time of Christ until about 600. Moche artists produced a highly pictorial type of pottery, usually painted in fine red lines on a cream background, on which many facets of daily life and beliefs appear. Warfare is often depicted: battles were fought in the desert, the principal weapons being clubs with heavy expanded ends, mace-headed clubs, hand-hurled stones, and darts propelled with spear throwers or *atlatls*, to use the Aztec term. Moche warriors usually have a copper axe head tied to the

Top Aztec sacrificial knife with a mosaic-encrusted handle in the form of an Eagle Knight. This knife, which may have been part of a gift presented to Cortés by Motecuhzoma II, was forwarded to Charles V together with many other treasures.

Above Mayan sacrificial knife from the Cenote at Chichen Itzá, late Post-Classic period (AD 1150–1500). The handle is in the form of entwined serpents. Heart sacrifice may have been introduced into the Mayan area by the Toltecs of central Mexico; during the Classic period, decapitation was the usual fate of sacrificial victims.

Left Moche portrait vase, sixth–seventh century AD, depicting a crouching warrior with a shield and club. The details of his dress and armour have been achieved by the use of a cream slip and the application of iron oxide pigment before firing.

223

Below The Inca fortress of Sacsayhuaman, strategically located in the hills above the Inca capital of Cuzco. The Incas were skilled engineers and formidable warriors, and built the best-organized empire of the pre-Spanish New World.

Below right Gold and turquoise ceremonial knife or *tumi*, said to have been found in the Llimo district of Lambayeque, Chimú civilization, *c.*1100 AD. The elaborate hilt shows a deity. *Tumis* of this sort were probably never used in battle.

waist by two suspension holes. The purpose of these axes, of which a few actual examples survive, is very clear: they were employed to cut off enemy heads as trophies, a custom widespread over much of South America. These were edged weapons only in the narrowest sense, since the unfortunates they were used against would have to have been dead or secured in some way before their heads could be severed. Moche axe-knives, and their successors, the elaborate *tumi* knives of the somewhat later Chimú civilization of the Peruvian coast, are thus no more than butchering implements, similar in function to the sacrificial knives of Mesoamerica.

The Inca, the latest of the pre-Spanish peoples of the Andes to achieve civilization and found an empire, also fought with a kind of battle axe or halberd, made of a T-shaped axe head lashed to a shaft. The axe head was made of ground stone and sometimes had a metal edge.

Metals were largely unknown among the lowland cultures of the South American tropical forest. However, as mentioned earlier, edged weapons of a kind could be fashioned from hardwood trees. The Spaniards generally referred to such weapons as *macanas*. One of the earliest observations of *macanas* in action is by the sixteenth-century Spanish chronicler Gonzalo Fernández de Oviedo y Valdés. Describing the Arawak-speaking Taino Indians of the island of Hispaniola, he says: '. . . the Indians of this island fight with *macanas*, which are clubs some three fingers or less wide and as long as the height of a man, with two somewhat sharpened

edges; and at one end of the *macana* is a handle; and they use them like two-handed battle axes; they are made from very strong palm wood or from other trees.'

According to the Dominican Bartolomeo de las Casas, the related Ciguayans of the south coast of Cuba had a very similar club, which tapered from the handle to the straight distal end. *Macana*-like clubs or wooden swords were also widely used by the tropical forest peoples of the Amazon basin, the Guianas and Darien in Panama.

The sword-club of the highly cannibalistic Tupinambá of the Brazilian coast appears in the vivid account by the sixteenth-century German adventurer Hans Staden of his captivity among these people. The Tupinambá fought mainly with bows and arrows, and Staden fails to describe the use of the sword-club in war, although it was clearly a ceremonial object and highly decorated on important occasions. Whether its expanded head actually was flat and edged is uncertain from his text, but he saw it used to knock out the brains of a captive destined to be eaten in a cannibal feast.

The horse and the sword on a new continent

How did a few handfuls of Iberian adventurers manage to overthrow the Inca and Aztec empires, empires which possessed standing armies and held many millions of people in their sway? Certainly the steel swords, crossbow bolts and firearms of the conquistadors played a decisive role in this enormous human

tragedy, but while it is true that most of the New World prior to 1492 knew little of metallurgy, there is yet a puzzle as to why the Inca, with a long tradition of metalworking behind them, had no real swords with which to counter the Spaniards. Part of the explanation may lie in the absence of horses in pre-Spanish times, for much of the effectiveness of metal swords in the Old World depended on their use by mounted warriors.

Zoologists tell us that the horse evolved in the Western hemisphere and spread to Eurasia during the Pleistocene. The arrival of bands of Asiatic hunters in the previously unoccupied American continent spelled doom for many species of grazing animals, including the wild horse, through a combination of careless 'overkill' and broad-scale climatic change; the American horse was extirpated about ten thousand years ago.

There were no memories of wild horses in 1519 when Cortés and his troops landed on the shores of Mexico. The Indians were astonished at the sight of four-footed beasts which could be ridden by armed men. Writing only a few decades after the Conquest, Fray Diego Durán describes the inability of the natives to comprehend the reality of these creatures: 'In their ingenuous manner, they gave one turkey to each soldier and another to his horse, a basket of tortillas for the master and another for the animal.'

Spanish cavalrymen thus had an enormous technological and psychological advantage over the civilized nations of the New World, comparable in its way to America's possession, and use, of the atomic bomb in the war against Japan. Even so, scholars now believe that the ultimate weapon against the inhabitants of the New World was one over which the invaders had no control: disease. The natives had no resistance to epidemic diseases such as smallpox, cholera and typhoid. The viruses and bacteria imported by the conquistadors moved so swiftly that at times they ran well ahead of the 'front lines', ravaging and demoralizing Indian populations so severely that the struggle was often over almost before it began.

The outcome was conquest and subjugation. The conquistadors and their successors of course preferred to believe that it was their weapons and horses which enabled them to prevail. In a letter written to the Emperor Charles V by the Franciscan friar Toribio de Motolinia we read: '. . . now that many Indians are already using horses, it would not be a bad idea if Your Majesty would give permission to have horses only to the principal lords, because if the Indians became accustomed to horses, many would become cavalrymen and in time would be equal to the Spaniards. This advantage of horses and artillery is very necessary in this country, because it gives strength and advantage to the few over the many.' This from a friar generally considered sympathetic to the Indians! An English king once lost his crown for want of a horse, but seldom have entire civilizations perished through the same cause.

Below far left Tupinambá warriors of coastal Brazil, an illustration from Hans Staden's account of his adventures in this part of Brazil, published in 1557. Staden was a long-term captive of the Tupinambá, who were renowned cannibals, but managed to escape. The warrior on the left carries a ceremonially decorated club with an edge.

Below left The execution of Atahualpa, last emperor of the Incas, a woodcut by Guaman Poma de Ayala, c.1620. Even the mighty Inca Empire was no match for Spanish armour, artillery and other weaponry. Atahualpa was captured by treachery and executed by strangulation (Pizzaro ordered him to be burned but a last-minute conversion saved him from this fate). This illustration, done nearly a century after the event, wrongly shows him being murdered by decapitation.

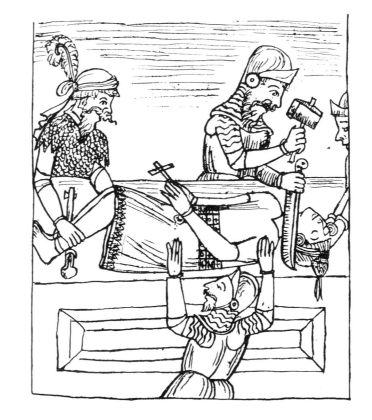

Major collections of hilt weapons

Austria
Abteilung Landeszeughaus, Graz
Heeresgeschichtliches Museum, Vienna
Historisches Museum der Stadt Wien, Vienna
Kunsthistorisches Museum
    (Waffensammlung), Vienna

Belgium
Koninklijk Museum voor Midden-Afrika/
    Musée royal de l'Afrique centrale, Tervuren
Musée de Porte de Hal, Brussels
Musée royal de l'Armée et d'Histoire militaire,
    Brussels

Canada
Canadian Museum of Civilisation, Ottawa
Royal Ontario Museum, Toronto

China
Museum of the Terracotta Army of Qin Chi
    Huang, Lintong
Palace Museum, Beijing

Egypt
Museum of Islamic Art, Cairo

France
Musée de l'Armée, Hôtel des Invalides, Paris
Musée de l'Homme, Palais de Chaillot, Paris
Musée de la Marine, Palais de Chaillot, Paris
Musée des Arts décoratifs, Palais du Louvre,
    Paris
Musée national des Arts africains et océaniens,
    Paris

German Democratic Republic
Historisches Museum, Dresden
Museum für Völkerkunde, Leipzig
Staatliche Kunstsammlungen, Dresden
Staatliche Museum zu Berlin
Staatliche Museum für Völkerkunde, Dresden

German Federal Republic
Bayerisches Nationalmuseum, Munich
Germanisches Nationalmuseum, Nürnberg
Jagd Museum, Munich

Römisch-Germanisches Zentralmuseum,
    Mainz
Staatliches Museum für Völkerkunde,
    Frankfurt

Great Britain
British Museum, London
Castle Museum, York
Fitzwilliam Museum, Cambridge
Glasgow Museums and Art Galleries
Museum of Antiquities, Edinburgh
Museum of Mankind, London
National Army Museum, London
National Maritime Museum, Greenwich
Pitt Rivers Museum, Oxford
Royal Armouries, H.M. Tower of London
Royal Scottish Museum, Edinburgh
Victoria & Albert Museum, London
Wallace Collection, London
Wellington Museum, Apsley House, London
Collection of H.M. The Queen, Windsor
    Castle

Greece
Archaeological Museum of Rhodes
Archaeological Museum, Thessaloniki
National Archaeological Museum, Athens

India
Andhra Pradesh State Museum, Hyderabad
Archaeological Museum, Red Fort, Delhi
Dr Bhau Daji Lal Museum, Bombay
Maharaja Sawai Man Singh II Museum, Jaipur
National Museum of India, New Delhi
Rajputana Museum, Ajmer
Victoria Memorial Hall, Calcutta

Italy
Ameria Reale, Turin
Museo Correr, Venice
Museo e Gallerie Nazionali di Capodimonte,
    Naples
Museo Archeologico Nazionale, Chieti
Museo Nazionale (Bargello), Florence
Museo Nazionale di Villa Giulia, Rome
Museo Nazionale di Castel Sant'Angelo, Rome
Museo Stibbert, Florence
Palazzo Ducale, Venice

Japan
Goto Art Museum, Tokyo
Kyoto National Museum
Sano Bijutsukan, Mishima City, Shizuoka
    Prefecture
The Sword Museum (Nippon Bijutsu Token
    Hozon Kyokai), Tokyo
Tokyo National Museum

Mexico
Museo de Antropología de la Universidad
    Veracruzana, Veracruz
Museo de la Cultura Huasteca, Madero
Museo Nacional de Historia, Mexico City

Netherlands
Koninklijk Nederlands Leger- en
    Wapenmuseum 'Generaal Hoefer', Delft
Rijksmuseum, Amsterdam
Rijksmuseum 'Nederlands Scheepvaart
    Museum', Amsterdam
Museum voor Volkenkunde, Rotterdam

Norway
Kunstindustrimuseet i Oslo
Universitetets Samling av Nordiske Oldsaker,
    Oslo

Peru
Museo Arqueológico 'Rafael Larco Herrera',
    Lima
Museo Nacional de Antropologia y
    Arqueologia, Lima

Poland
Czartoryski Collection (Muzeum Narodowe w
    Krakowie), Cracow
Muzeum Wojska Polskiego, Warsaw

Portugal
Museu Etnográfico da Sociedade de Geografia
    de Lisboa
Museu Militar, Lisbon

Spain
Instituto de Valencia de Don Juan, Madrid
Museo del Ejercíto, Madrid

Museo Naval, Madrid
Palacio Real de Madrid

Sweden
Livrustkammaren, Skolosters Slott, Stockholm
Hallwylska Museet, Stockholm
Statens Historiska Museet, Stockholm

Switzerland
Bernisches Historisches Museum, Bern
Historisches Museum, Basel
Schweizerisches Landesmuseum/Musée
    national suisse, Zurich

Taiwan
National Palace Museum, Taipei

Turkey
Türkiye Askeri Müzesi (Museum of the
    Janissaries), Istanbul
Topkapı Palace Museum, Istanbul

United States
American Museum of Natural History, New
    York
Freer Gallery of Art, Washington DC
Metropolitan Museum of Art, New York
Museum of the American Indian (Heye
    Foundation), New York
Museum of Fine Arts, Boston
Peabody Museum of Archaeology and
    Ethnology, Harvard
Philadelphia Museum of Art
Smithsonian Institution, Washington DC

USSR
Kremlin Armoury, Moscow
State Hermitage Museum, Leningrad
State Historical Museum, Moscow
State Museum of Oriental Art, Moscow

Bibliography

1 STONE, BRONZE AND IRON

Bianco Peroni, V. 'Die Schwerter in Italien', *Prähistorische Bronzefunde* IV.1. C.H. Beck, Munich 1970

Gonen, R. *Weapons of the Ancient World*, Cassell, London 1975

Gordon, D.H. 'Swords, rapiers and horse-riders', *Antiquity* 27, 1953

Jope, E.M. 'Daggers of the Early Iron Age in Britain', *Proc. Prehist. Soc.* 27, 1961

Maxwell-Hyslop, R. 'Daggers and swords in western Asia', *Iraq* 8, 1946

de Navarro, J.M. *The Finds from the Site of La Tène, Vol. I. Scabbards and the Swords found in them*, British Academy/Oxford University Press, 1972

Oakeshott, R.E. *The Archaeology of Weapons: Arms and Armour from Prehistory to the Age of Chivalry*, Lutterworth Press, Guildford 1960

Piggott, S. 'Swords and scabbards of the British Early Iron Age', *Proc. Prehist. Soc.* 16, 1950

Sandars, N. 'The first Aegean swords and their ancestry', *Amer. J. Archaeol.* 65, 1961

Sandars, N. 'Later Aegean bronze swords', *Amer. J. Archaeol.* 67, 1963

Schauer, P. 'Die Schwerter in Süddeutschland, Osterreich und der Schweiz, I., *Prähistorische Bronzefunde* IV. 2, A.H. Beck, Munich 1982

Snodgrass, A. *Early Greek Armour and Weapons, from the End of the Bronze Age to 600 b.c.*, Edinburgh University Press, 1964

Stary, P.F. 'Zur eisenzeitlichen Bewaffnung und Kampfesweise in Mittelitalien (ca. 9. bis 6 Jh. v. Chr.)', Marburger Studien zur Vor- und Frühgeschichte, Band 3, Zabern, Mainz 1981

Stead, I.M. 'La Tène swords and scabbards in Champagne', *Germania* 61, 1983

Wolf, W. *Die Bewaffnung des altägyptischen Heeres*, Leipzig 1926

Yadin, Y. *The Art of Warfare in Biblical Times in the Light of Archaeological Discovery*, Weidenfeld and Nicolson, London 1963

2 GREECE AND ROME

Bianco Peroni, V. 'Le Spade nell'Italia Continentale', *Prähistorische Bronzefunde* VI.1, C.H. Beck, Munich 1970

Cianfarini, V. *Antiche Civiltà d'Abruzzo*, De Luca, Rome 1969

Hatzopoulos, M.B. and Lokopolous,. L.D *Philip of Macedon*, Heinemann, London 1981

Jehasse, J. and L. 'La Nécropole Préromaine d'Aleria', *Gallia* Suppl. XXV

Oldenstein, J. 'Zur Ausrüstung romisher Auxiliareinheiten . . . aus dem zweiten und dritten Jahrhundert n. Chr.', Bericht der Römisch-Germanischen Kommission 57, 1976

Scott Anderson, A. *Roman Military Tombstones*, Shire Publications, Aylesbury 1984

Snodgrass, A.M. *Arms and Armour of the Greeks*, Thames and Hudson, London 1967

Ulbert, G. *Römische Waffen des 1. Jahrhunderts n. Chr.*, Limes Museum, Aalen 1968

Ulbert, G. 'Gladii aus Pompeii', *Germania* 47, 1969

3 BARBARIANS AND CHRISTIANS

Bruce-Mitford, R. *The Sutton Hoo Ship Burial*, Vol 2: Arms, Armour and Regalia, British Museum Publications, London 1978

Dufty, A.R. *European Swords and Daggers in the Tower of London*, HMSO, London 1974

Fillitz, H. *Vienna Kunsthistorisches Museum: Katalog der Weltlichen und der Geistlichen Schatzkammer*, Vienna 1968

Heath, I. and McBride, A. *Byzantine Armies 886–1118*, Men-at-Arms series 89, Osprey Publishing, London 1979

Laking, Guy F. *A Record of European Armour and Arms through Seven Centuries*, 5 vols., G. Bell, London 1920–22

Musée Rath *Armes anciennes des Collections suisses*, Edita Lausanne, Geneva 1972

Oakeshott, R.E. *The Archaeology of Weapons: Arms and Armour from Prehistory to the Age of Chivalry*, Lutterworth Press, Guildford 1960

Oakeshott, R.E. *The Sword in the Age of Chivalry*, Lutterworth Press, Guildford 1964

Oakeshott, R.E. 'Reflections upon some medieval swords from the Thames', Second Park Lane Arms Fair, 14–16 February 1985

Petersen, J. *Viking Antiquities in Great Britain and Ireland*, H.A. Schenoug, Oslo 1940

Peterson, H.L. *Daggers and Fighting Knives of the Western World from the Stone Ages till 1900*, Jenkins, London 1968

Royal Academy of Art *The Age of Chilvary: Art in Plantagenet England 1200–1400*, London 1987

Royal Armouries, H.M. Tower of London *Official Guide*, London 1986

Sewter, E.R.A. (trans.) *The Alexiad of Anna Comnena*, Penguin Books, Harmondsworth 1969

Wallace Collection *European Arms and Armour*, London 1962

The Ancient Art of Warfare, 2 vols, Barrie & Rockliff, London 1966

Zeitschrift der Gesellschaft für Historische Waffen- und Kostumkunde, 1987

Zylstra-Zweens, H.M. 'Of his array telle I no longer tale', *Aspects of costume, arms and armour in Western Europe 1200–1400*, Rodopi, Amsterdam 1988

4 THE RENAISSANCE SPIRIT

Blair, C. *European and American Arms ca. 1100–1850*, New York 1962

Boccia, L.G. and Coelho, E.T. *Armi Bianchi Itliani*, Bramante Editrice, Milan 1975

Norman, A.V.B. *The Rapier and Small-Sword 1460–1820*, Arms and Armour Press, London 1980

North, A.R.E. *An Introduction to European Swords*, HMSO, London 1982

Oakeshott, R.E. *The Sword in the Age of Chivalry*, Lutterworth Press, Guildford 1964

Seitz, H. *Blankwaffen*, 2 vols., Klinkardt & Biermann, Brunswick 1965

5 FROM RAPIER TO SMALLSWORD

Aylward, J. De *The Small-Sword in England: its history, its forms, its makers and its masters*, Hutchinson, London 1960

Boccia, L.G. and Coelho, E.T. *Armi Bianchi Italiani*, Bramante Editrice, Milan 1975

Dean, Bashford *European Court Swords and Hunting Swords*, Metropolitan Museum of Art, New York 1929

Hayward, J.F. *Swords and Daggers*, Victoria & Albert Museum, London 1963

Laking, Guy, F. *The Armoury of Windsor Castle*, Bradbury Agnew, London 1904

Norman, A.V.B. *The Rapier and Small-Sword 1460–1820*, Arms and Armour Press, London 1980

North, A.R.E. *An Introduction to European Swords*, HMSO, London 1982

Valentine, E. *Rapiers: an illustrated reference guide to the rapiers of the 16th and 17th centuries*, Arms and Armour Press, London 1968

6 SEVENTEENTH-CENTURY EUROPE

Dean, Bashford *European Daggers 1300–1800*, Metropolitan Museum of Art, New York 1929.

Frans Halsmuseum *Schutters in Holland*, M.S.D. Books, Haarlem 1988

Miller, Y. (ed.) *Russian Arms and Armour*, Aurora Art Publishers, Leningrad 1982

Oakeshott, R.E. *European Weapons and Armour from the Renaissance to the Industrial Revolution*, Lutterworth Press, Guildford 1980

Seitz, H. *Blankwaffen*, 2 vols, Klinkardt & Biermann, Brunswick 1965

Sloot, R.B.F. and van der Kist, J.B. 'Some facts concerning sword hilts at Hoorn around the year 1650', Leiden 1971

Stocklein, H. *Meister des Eisenschnitten*, Esslingen am. N. 1922

Wegeli, R. *Inventar der Waffensammlung des Bernischen Historischen Museums in Bern*, Bern 1920

Weyersberg, A. *Solingen Schwertschmiede des 16 und 17 Janrhunderts und ihre Erzeugnisse*, Solingen 1926

Schweizerisches Landesmuseum *'Barocker Luxus': Das Werk des Zürcher Goldschmieds Hans Peter Oeri*, Zurich 1988

Zygueschi, Z. *Bron w Dawne Polsce*, Warsaw 1975

7 EIGHTEENTH- AND NINETEENTH-CENTURY EUROPE

Annis, P.G.W. *Naval Swords: British and American Edged Weapons*, Arms and Armour Press, London 1970

Aries, C. and Petard, P. *Armes blanches militaires françaises*, Libraire Petitot, Paris 1965–70

Blair, C. *European and American Arms*, Batsford, London 1962

Bouchard, R. *Les Armes de Traite*, Collection Histoire populaire de Québec, Quebec 1976

Caldwell, D.H. (ed.) *Scottish Weapons and Fortifications 1100–1800*, John Donald, Edinburgh 1981

Dean, Bashford *European Court Swords and Hunting Swords*, Metropolitan Museum of Art, New York 1929

Held, R. *Art, arms and armour: an international anthology*, Vol. 1 1979–80, Acquafresca Editrice, Chiasso 1979

Mavrodin, V. *Fine Arms from Tula*, Aurora Art Publishers, Leningrad 1977

May, W.E. and Annis, P.G.W. *Swords for Sea Service*, HMSO, London 1970

Miller, Y. (ed.) *Russian Arms and Armour*, Aurora Art Publishers, Leningrad 1982

Moore, W. *Weapons of the American Revolution*, Promontory Press, New York 1967

Mowbray, E. Andrew *Arms and Armour, from the Atelier of Ernst Schmidt*, Providence RI 1967

Newman, G.C. *Swords and Blades of the American Revolution*, David and Charles, Newton Abbot 1973

8 COMBINATION WEAPONS

Blackmore, H.L. *Hunting Weapons*, Barrie and Jenkins, London 1971

Blair, C. *Pistols of the World*, Batsford, London 1968

Blair, C. (ed.) *Pollard's History of Firearms*, Country Life Books, London 1983

Carrington-Pierce, P. *A Handbook of Court and Hunting Swords*, Quaritch, London 1937

Diana Armi, 2 February 1988, Editoriale Olimpia, Florence

Dike, C. *Cane Curiosa*, Editions de l'Amateur, Paris 1983

Ducharte, P.L. *Armes de Chasse*, Office du Livre, Fribourg 1978

Frost, H.G. *Blades and Barrels*, Walloon Press, El Paso, Texas 1972

Schobel, J. *Princely Arms and Armour: a selection from the Dresden Collection*, Barrie and Jenkins, London 1975

Winant, L. *Firearms Curiosa*, St Martins Press, New York 1953

9 AMERICAN SWORDS AND KNIVES

Abels, R. *Classic Bowie Knives*, Robert Abels Inc., New York 1967

Albaugh, W. *Confederate Edged Weapons*, Bonanza Books, New York 1960

Dillon, R. *North American Indian Wars*, Arms and Armour Press, London 1983

Flayderman, N. *Illustrated Catalogue of Arms and Military Goods*, New Milford, Conn. 1972

Frost, H.G. *Blades and Barrels*, Walloon Press, El Paso, Texas 1972

Hamilton, J.D. *The Ames Sword Company 1929–1935*, Mowbray Company, Providence RI 1893

Hickox, R.G. *Collector's Guide to Ames U.S. Contract Military Edged Weapons 1832–1906*, 1984

Levine, B.R. *Knifemakers of Old San Francisco*, Badger Books, San Francisco 1977

Minnis, G. *American Primitive Knives*, Museum Restoration Service, Ontario 1973

Moore, W. *Weapons of the American Revolution*, Promontory Press, New York 1967

Neumann, G.C. *Weapons of the American Revolution*, Harper & Row, New York 1967

Neumann, G.C. *Swords and Blades of the American Revolution*, David and Charles, Newton Abbot 1973

Peterson, H.L. *American Knives*, Charles Scribner & Sons, New York 1958

Peterson, H.L. *The American Sword*, Roy Riling Books, Philadelphia 1965

Peterson, H.L. *Arms and Armour in Colonial America 1526–1783*, Bramhall House, New York 1856

Stephens, F. *Fighting Knives*, Arms and Armour Press, London 1980

Watts, J. and White, P. *The Bayonet Book*, Birmingham 1975

Weighley, R. *History of the United States Army*, Batsford, London 1968

10 WORLD WARS I AND II

Angolia, J.R. *Daggers, Bayonets and Fighting Knives*, James Bender Publications, Mountain View, Arkansas 1971

Atwood, J. *The Daggers and Edged Weapons of Hitler's Germany*, Berlin 1965

Buerlein, R. *Allied Military Fighting Knives*, The American Historical Foundation, Richmond VA 1984

Carter, A. and Walker, J. *The Bayonet*, Arms and Armour Press, London 1974

Hardin, A.N. *The American Bayonet 1776–1964*, Riling & Lentz, Philadelphia 1964

Johnson, T.M. *Collecting the Weapons of the Third Reich*, 5 vols. Columbia, South Carolina 1977

McClean, D. *American Small Arms Research in World War II*, Vol. I, Normont Technical Publications, Wickenburg, Arizona 1975

Peterson, H.L. *Book of the Continental Soldier*, Stackpole, Harrisburg, Pennsylvania 1968

Robson, B. *Swords of the British Army*, Arms and Armour Press, London, 1975

Young, P. *Commando*, Pan Books (Ballantine), London 1974

11 SWORDS OF ISLAM

Allan, J.W. *Nishapur: Metalwork of the Early Islamic Period*, Metropolitan Museum, New York 1982

Atil, E. *Art of the Mamluks*, Smithsonian Institution, Washington DC 1981

Buttin, C. *Catalogue de la Collection d'Armes anciennes européennes et orientales*, Rumilly 1933

Elgood, R. (ed.) *Islamic Arms and Armour*, Scolar Press, London 1977

Falk, T. *Treasures of Islam*, Sotheby Publications, London 1985

Historischen Museums der Stadt Wien *Die Türken vor Wien*, Vienna 1983

Jacob, A. *Les Armes blanches du Monde islamique*, Jacques Grancher, Paris 1985

Lenz, E. *Collection d'Armes de l'Hermitage impérial*, Hermitage Museum, St Petersburg 1908

North, A.R.E. *An Introduction to Islamic Arms*, HMSO, London 1985

Ricketts, H. and Missilier, P. *Splendour of Oriental Arms*, Acte Expo, Paris 1988

Rogers, J.M. *Islamic Art and Design 1500–1700*, British Museum Publications, London 1983

Smith, C.S. *A History of Metallography*, University of Chicago 1960

Stone, G.C. *A Glossary of the Construction, Decoration and Use of Arms and Armour*, Jack Brussel, New York 1961

Topkapı Palace Museum *The Anatolian Civilisations*, Istanbul 1983

Sotheby's/Philip Wilson *Treasures of Islam*, Musée d'Art et d'Histoire, Geneva 1985

Museum für Kunsthandwerk *Turkische Kunst und Kultur aus Osmanischer Zeit*, Frankfurt 1985

Wallace Collection Catalogues *Oriental Arms and Armour*, London 1964

12 JAPANESE SWORDS

Hawley, W.M. *Japanese Swordsmiths* (privately published) 1966

Robinson, B.W. *The Art of the Japanese Sword*, Faber & Faber, London 1961

Ogasawara, Nobuo *Japanese Swords*, Hoikusha 1970

Ogawa, Morihiro *Japanese Swords and Sword Mountings in the Museum of Fine Arts, Boston*, Museum of Fine Arts, Boston 1987

Sato, Dr K. *The Japanese Sword* Joe Earle (trans.) Japan Publications 1982

13 CHINA AND CENTRAL ASIA

Cotterell, A. *The First Emperor's Warriors*, The Emperor's Warriors Exhibition Ltd, London 1987

Gettens, R.J., Clarke, R.F. Jr and Chase, W.T. 'Two Early Chinese Weapons with Meteoric Iron Blades', *Freer Gallery of Art Occasional Papers*, 4.1, Washington 1971

Ghirshmann, R. 'Notes iraniennes XIII: Trois Epées sassanides', *Artibus Asiae* 26, 1963

Grancsay, S. 'Two Chinese Swords from A.D. 600', *Metropolitan Museum of Art Bulletin* 25, September 1930

Hubei Province, Institute of Archaeology CASS and CPAM, *Excavation of the Han Tombs at Man Cheng*, Wenwu Chubanshe, Beijing 1980

Janata, A. 'Zur Typologie chinesischer Stangenwaffen', *Archiv für Völkerkunde* 20, 1966

Loehr, M. *Chinese Bronze Age Weapons: The Werner Jennings Collection in the National Palace Museum, Peking*, University of Michigan Press and Oxford University Press 1956

Lvova, Z. and Semionov, A. 'On the principles of reconstruction of the Pereshchepina sword', *Arkheologičeskiya Sbornik* 20, 1985

Mao Yuanyi *Wubei Zhi*, Kyuko Shoin, Tokyo 1974 (facsimile of Japanese reprint of 1664; first printed in 1628)

Needham, J. *The Development of Iron and Steel Technology in China*, The Newcomen Society, London 1958

Nickel, H. 'About the Sword of the Huns and the "Urepos" of the Steppes', *Metropolitan Museum Journal* 7, 1973

Maenchen-Helfen, J.D. *The World of the Huns*, University of California Press 1973

Rawson, J. *Ancient China*, British Museum Publications, London 1980

Trousdale, W. 'The Long Sword and Scabbard Slide in Asia', *Smithsonian Contributions to Anthropology* 17, 1975

Werner, E.T.C. *Chinese Weapons*, Royal Asiatic Society North China Branch, Shanghai 1932

Yang Hong *Zhongguo Ge Bingqi Luncong*, Wenwu Chubanshe, Beijing 1980 (2nd enlarged ed. 1985)

Zhou Wei *Zhongguo Bingqi Shigao*, Sanlian Shudian, Beijing 1957

14 INDIA AND SOUTHEAST ASIA

Draeger, D. *Weapons and Fighting Arts of the Indonesian Archipelago*, Charles E. Tuttle Company, Tokyo 1972

Egerton, Lord *Indian and Oriental Armour*, Arms and Armour Press, London 1968

Gardner, G.B. *Keris and Other Malay Weapons*, Progressive Publishing Company, Singapore 1936

Rawson, P. *The Indian Sword*, Herbert Jenkins, London 1968

Solc, V. *Swords and Daggers of Indonesia*, Spring Books, London 1958

15 AFRICAN HILT WEAPONS

Agthe, Johanna *Waffen aus Zentral-Afrika*, Museum für Völkerkunde, Frankfurt 1985

Andersson, E. 'Contribution à l'Ethnographie des Kuta', I and II, *Studia Ethnographica Upsaliensia* 6 and 38, 1953 and 1974

Cabot-Briggs, L. 'European Blades in Tuareg Swords and Daggers', *Arms and Armour* 5, 1965

Cole, H.M. and Ross, D.H. *The Arts of Ghana*, University of California Press 1977

Evans-Pritchard, E.E. 'Zande Warfare', *Anthropos* 52, 1957

Fernandez, J. 'The exposition and imposition of order: artistic expression in Fang culture', in W. L. D'Azevedo (ed.) *The Traditional Artist in African Societies*, Indiana University Press 1973

Fischer, W. and Zirngibl, M.A. *African Weapons*, Prinz Verlag, Passau 1978

Jedrej, M.G. 'Ingessana Throwing Knives (Sudan)', *Anthropos* 70, 1975

Maes, J. 'Armes de jet des populations du Congo belge', *Congo* 1:2, 1922

Maes, J. 'Les sabres et massues des populations du Congo belge', *Congo* 1:3, 1923

McLeod, M.D. *The Asante*, British Museum Publications, London 1981

McNaughton, P.R. 'The throwing knife in African history', *African Arts*, 3:2, 1970

Northern, T. *The Ornate Implement*, Dartmouth College Museum and Galleries, Hanover 1981

Perrois, L. *Ancestral Art of Gabon*, Barbier-Mueller Museum, Geneva 1985

Phillipson, D.W. *African Archaeology*, Cambridge University Press 1985

Siroto, L. 'The face of the Bwiti', *African Arts* 1:3, 1968

Thomas, E.S. 'The African Throwing Knife', *Journal of the Royal Anthropological Institute* 55, 1925

Torday, E. and Joyce, T.A. 'Notes ethnographiques sur les peuples communément appelés Bakuba, ainsi que sur les peuplades apparentées – les Bushongo, *Annales du Musée royal du Congo belge*, série 4, vol. 2, 1910

Vaughan, J.H. 'Engkyagu as artists in Marghi society', in W.L. D'Azedevo (ed.) *The Traditional Artist in African Societies*, Indiana University Press 1973

Westerdijk, P. *The African Throwing Knife*, OMI, Utrecht 1988

Westerdijk, P. *African Metal Implements*, Greenvale, New York 1984

Zirngibl, M.A. *Rare African Short Weapons*, Verlag Morsak, Grafenan 1983

16 PRECONQUEST AMERICA

Anonymous Conqueror *Narrative of Some Things of New Spain and of the Great City of Temestitan Mexico* Marshall H. Saville (trans.) Milford House, Boston 1972

Díaz del Castillo, Bernal *The True History of the Conquest of New Spain*, 5 vols. Alfred P. Maudlsey (transl.) Hakluyt Society, London 1908

Durán, Diego *The Aztecs: The History of the Indies of New Spain*, Orion Press, New York 1964

Gunther, Erna *Indian Life on the Northwest Coast of North America*, University of Chicago Press 1972

Lovén, Sven *Origins of the Tainan Culture, West Indies*, Göteborg 1953

Mendieta, Fray Gerónimo de *Historia Eclesiástica Indiana*, 4 vols. Editorial Salvador Chávez Hayhoe, Mexico 1945

Métraux, Alfred *Handbook of South American Indians* Julian H. Steward (ed.) Bureau of American Ethology, Washington 1949

Morison, Samuel Eliot (trans. and ed.) *Journals and Other Documents on the Life and Voyages of Christopher Columbus*, The Heritage Press, New York 1963

Motolinia, Toribio de Letter in *Colección de Documentos para la Historia de Mexico*, Vol. I, Andrade, Mexico 1958

Staden, Hans *The True Story of His Captivity, 1557* Malcolm Letts (transl.) George Routledge & Sons, London 1928

Witthoft, John and Eyman, Frances 'Metallurgy of the Tlingit, Dene, and Eskimo', *Expedition* 11.3, 1969, The University Museum, Philadelphia

Photographs and illustrations

The publishers extend their sincere thanks to the many people – contributing authors, museum curators, private collectors, dealers, photographers and photographic librarians – who assisted in securing the photographs and illustrations reproduced in this book.

1 STONE, BRONZE AND IRON

p 8
Musée national du Louvre, Paris.
E 11517.
Photo Lauros-Giraudon

p 9
Anadolu Medeniyetleri Müzesi,
Ankara.
Photo James Mellaart.

p 10
Top Iraq Museum, Baghdad.
4307A, B.
Photo Scala, Antella.
Bottom left Egyptian Museum, Cairo.
JE 4666.
Bottom right British Museum, London.
EA 32577.

p 11
Left Photo Giraudon, Paris.
Upper right Istanbul Arkeoloji Müzeleri.
2345(m).
Lower right Egyptian Museum, Cairo.
JE 61584.
Photo Giraudon, Paris.

p 12
Left Musées royaux d'Art et d'Histoire,
Brussels. E 7359.
Photo A.C.L.
Right National Archaeological Museum,
Athens. Top: 8339; centre and bottom: 394.

p 13
Left Archaeological Museum, Nauplia.
Photoresources, Kingston, Kent.

Centre Archaeological Museum, Heraklion.
1019.
Photo Ecole française d'Athènes.
Right National Archaeological Museum,
Athens. 7325.
Photo T.A.P., Athens.

p 14
Left Nationalmuseum, Copenhagen. Left:
B 10600; right: A 17965-70.
Right Nationalmuseum, Copenhagen.
A 33093.

p 15
Top left Déri Museum, Debrecen.
SZ 1907/1204.
Bottom left Landesmuseum für Vorgeschichte,
Halle.
Bottom right Museo Lunense, La Spezia.
Photo Scala, Antella.

p 16
Prähistorische Staatssammlung, Munich. Left
to right: NM13/1421; HV 82; 1927,3; HV 205;
1983, 2094.

p 17
Top British Museum, London. Left to
right: 135054; 135055; 135476.
Bottom Anadolu Medeniyetleri Müzesi,
Ankara.
Photo Hirmer Verlag, Munich.

p 18
Top Landesmuseum Baden-Wurttemberg,
Stuttgart. V 86, 3.
Centre and bottom Landesmuseum Baden-
Wurttemberg, Stuttgart. V 86, 3

p 19
Left Musée cantonal d'Archéologie,
Neuchâtel.
Right Musée des Antiquités nationales, Saint
Germain-en-Laye. 28216.
Photo Musées nationaux, Paris.

2 GREECE AND ROME

p 21
Museo Archeológico Nazionale,
Naples. 10020.
Photoresources, Kingston, Kent.

p 22
Top Museo Archeológico Nazionale,
Naples. 81669.
Photo Pedicini, Naples.

p 23
Right Museo Archeológico Nazionale, Chieti.
4426.
Photo Soprintendenza Archeologica
dell'Abruzzo, Chieti.

p 24
Museo Arqueologico Nacional, Madrid.

p 26
Right Karl-Geib Museum, Bad Kreuznach.
Photo Römisch-Germanisches
Zentralmuseum, Mainz.

p 27
Right British Museum, London. PRB 1960.
4-5. 342.

p 28
Bottom left Landesuseum, Mainz. 5607.
Bottom right Museum of London. · 59.94/1.

p 29
Centre Istanbul Arkeoloji Müzeleri.
5826(T).
Right Museo del Duomo di Monza. 6.

*Artwork pp 20, 22 bottom, 23 left, 23 centre, 25, 26
left, 27 left and centre, 28 top and 29 left by Peter
Connolly.*

3 BARBARIANS AND CHRISTIANS

p 30
Nationalmuseum, Copenhagen. MDL
XXXI.

p 31
British Museum, London. MLA 1939 10-10
19 to 29.

p 32
Top Statens Historiska Museum,
Stockholm. 2194.
Bottom Statens Historiska Museum,
Stockholm. 19734.

p 33
Left Universitetets Oldsaksamling, Oslo.
Photo Werner Forman Archive, London.
Top right British Museum, London. MLA
81 6-23 2.
Bottom right Glasgow Museums and Art
Galleries. A 6617.

p 34
British Museum, London. MLA 93 7-15 1.

p 35
Left Kunsthistorisches Museum, Vienna.
Weltliche Schatzkammer XIII. 16.
Right British Museum, London. MLA 90
7-1 3.

p 36
Left Kunsthistorisches Museum, Vienna.
Weltliche Schatzkammer XIII. 5.
Right Musée de Tapisserie, Bayeux.
Photo © Michael Holford, Loughton.

p 37
Left Kunsthistorisches Museum, Vienna.
Weltliche Schatzkammer XIII. 17.
Top right The Burrell Collection, Glasgow
Museums and Art Galleries. Left 2/77, right
2/80.
Bottom right Musée national du Louvre, Paris.
Photo Giraudon, Paris.

p 38
Left British Museum, London. MLA 58
11-16 5.
Right Universitätsbibliothek, Heidelberg.
Photo Archiv für Kunst und Geschichte,
Berlin.

p 39
Top Photo Sotheby's, London.
Bottom left The Burrell Collection, Glasgow Museums and Art Galleries. 2/74; 2/75; 2/79.
Bottom right Museum of London. Left 52.12, right 8034

p 40
Toledo Cathedral Treasury.
Photo MAS, Barcelona.

p 41
Left Real Biblioteca de San Lorenzo de Escurial.
Photo Aldus Archive, London.
Right Palazzo Ducale, Venice. CX 1997.

p 42
Left Reproduced by courtesy of the Dublin Corporation.
Right Kunsthistorisches Museum, Vienna. Waffensammlung A 658.

p 43
Top left Royal Armouries, H.M. Tower of London. X 287.
Second from left Royal Armouries, H.M. Tower of London. X 4.
Third from left Robert Mottu Collection.
Photo Musée d'Art et d'Histoire, Geneva.
Fourth from left British Museum, London. MLA 94 2–24 44.
Upper and lower right Provinciaal Overijssels Museum, Zwolle.
Photo Rijksdienst voor het Oudheidkundig Bodemonderzoek, Amersfoort.

4 THE RENAISSANCE SPIRIT

p 45
Lambeth Palace Libarary. Ms. 6 f.243.

p 46
Left Royal Armouries, H.M. Tower of London. IX. 950.
Top right Metropolitan Museum of Art, New York. Collection of Giovanni P. Morosini, 1932. 32.75.225.
Bottom right Metropolitan Museum of Art, New York. Rogers Fund, 1932. 32.144.

p 47
Left Thyssen Bornemicza Collection, Lugano.
Photo Scala, Antella.
Right Metropolitan Museum of Art, New York. Gift of William H. Riggs, 1913. 14.25.1169.

p 48
Top Metropolitan Museum of Art, New York. Rogers Fund, 1904. 04.3.290.
Bottom Metropolitan Museum of Art, New York. Purchase, the Lauder Foundation Gift, 1984. 1984.73.

p 49
Left Alte Pinakothek, Munich.
Photo Scala, Antella.
Top right Metropolitan Museum of Art, New York. Rogers Fund, 1904. 04.3.21.
Centre right Metropolitan Museum of Art, New York. Gift of William H. Riggs, 1913. 14.25.1266.
Bottom Bayerisches Nationalmuseum, Munich.

p 50
Top Galleria Barberini, Rome.
Photo Scala, Antella.
Bottom The Wallace Collection, London. A623.

p 51
Top Philadelphia Museum of Art. Bequest of Carl Otto Kretschmar von Kienbusch. Left to right: 1977-167-578 a, b; 1977-1267-584 a, b.
Bottom Philadelphia Museum of Art. Bequest of Carl Otto Kretschmar von Kienbusch. Left to right: 1977-167-546/537/550.

p 52
Photo Archiv fur Kunst und Geschichte, Berlin.

p 53
Germanisches Nationalmuseum, Nürnberg.

p 54
Musée du Louvre, Paris. OA 7323.
Photo Musées nationaux.

p 55
Top left Philadelphia Museum of Art. Gift of Mrs Frederick Jordan. Bequest of Carl Otto Kretschmar von Kienbusch. Left to right: 1977-167-693; 1977-167-687; 303-1986-00l; 303-1986-002.
Top right Metropolitan Museum of Art, New York. Rogers Fund 1939. 39.159.1.
Bottom Galleria Nazionale, Perugia.
Photo Scala, Antella.

p 56
Left British Museum, London.
Photo Fotomas Index.
Top right Weltliche Schatzkammer, Munich. 233.
Bottom right Kunsthistorisches Museum (Waffensammlung), Vienna. A287.
Photo Marianne Haller.

p 57
Left Kunsthistorisches Museum (Waffensammlung), Vienna. A588.
Photo Marianne Haller.
Right Photo Archiv für Kunst und Geschichte, Berlin.

5 FROM RAPIER TO SMALLSWORD

p 58
Frans Halsmuseum.
Photo Tom Haatsen. 123.

p 59
Left Victoria & Albert Museum, London. M34-1948.
Right Metropolitan Museum of Art, New York. Fletcher Fund, 1970. 1970.77.

p 60
Top Victoria & Albert Museum, London. M73.1949.
2nd from top Victoria & Albert Museum, London. M93.192.
2nd from bottom Victoria & Albert Museum, London. M182.1921.

p 61
Top Private collection.
Bottom Wallace Collection, London. A628.

p 62
Top Victoria & Albert Museum, London. Private collection.
2nd from top Victoria & Albert Museum, London. M56-1947.
2nd from bottom Victoria & Albert Museum, London M124-11921.
Bottom Royal Armouries, H.M. Tower of London.

p 63
Left University Library, Amsterdam.
Photo Aldus Archive.

p 64
Top right Reproduced by gracious permission of Her Majesty the Queen.
Top left Royal Collection, Stockholm.
Bottom right Livrustkammaren, Stockholm. LRK 1946.
Photo Schmidt.

p 65
Top Reproduced by gracious permission of Her Majesty the Queen. L62WC.
Bottom Skoklosters Slott, Stockholm.

p 66
Victoria & Albert Museum, London. M153–1937.

p 67
Left Reproduced by gracious permission of Her Majesty the Queen. Laking 59.
Right National Portrait Gallery, London. 5948

p 68
Top Victoria & Albert Museum, London. M71-1947.
Centre Metropolitan Museum of Art, New York. Gift of Jean-Jacques Reube 1926. 26.145.236.
Bottom Peter Dale Ltd, London.

p 69
Peter Dale Ltd, London.

p 70
Cartier Museum, Geneva.

p 71
Top Victoria & Albert Museum, London. M48-1967.
Bottom Victoria & Albert Museum, London. M72-1947 and M29-1957.

6 SEVENTEENTH-CENTURY EUROPE

p 72
The National Trust Photographic Library.

p 73
Left Wallace Collection, London. A511.
Right Christie's, London.

p 74
Royal Armouries, H.M. Tower of London. IX.934.

p 75
Top Royal Armouries, H.M. Tower of London. IX.1248.
Bottom left Photo John Bethell.
Bottom right The Royal Hospital, Chelsea.

p 76
Top Royal Armouries, H.M. Tower of London.
Bottom Royal Armouries, H.M. Tower of London. IX.1096.

p 77
Top left Royal Armouries, H.M. Tower of London.
Top right Wallace Collection, London. A717.
Bottom right Victoria & Albert Museum, London. Private collection.

p 78
Top Castle Museum, Nottingham. 1966-23.
Bottom Victoria & Albert Museum, London. M610-1937.

p 79
Top Victoria & Albert Museum, London. Private collection.
Bottom centre Victoria & Albert Museum, London. M59-1947.
Bottom left Glasgow Museums and Art Galleries. A728.
Bottom right Royal Armouries, H.M. Tower of London IX.2156.

p 80
Top left National Museums of Scotland. LC15.
Top centre National Museums of Scotland. LC1.
Top right Collection Duc de la Force.
Photo Lauros-Giraudon, Paris.
Bottom Christie's, London.

p 81
Wallace Collection, London.
   Photo Robert Harding Picture Library,
   London.

p 82
Top left   Royal Armouries, H.M. Tower of
London.   X.688 and X.1359.
Top right   Victoria & Albert Museum,
London.   M34 and A1948; M.189-1951.
Bottom   Victoria & Albert Museum,
   London.

p 83
Galleria dei Uffizi, Florence.
   Photo Scala, Antella.

7   EIGHTEENTH- AND NINETEENTH-CENTURY EUROPE

p 85
Royal Armouries, H.M. Tower of
London.   IX.863.

p 86
Top   Glasgow Museums and Art Galleries.
154-118.
Centre   Royal Armouries, H.M. Tower of
London.   IX.1204.
Bottom   Victoria & Albert Museum, London.
Morrison Loan.

p 87
The National Trust for Scotland.

p 88
Top   Photo Archiv für Kunst and Geschichte,
Berlin.
Bottom   Royal Armouries, H.M. Tower of
London.   IX-1348.

p 89
Top   Etude Couturier Nicolay, Paris.
2nd from top   Bernard Croissy, Courbevoie.
2nd from bottom   Anthony North.
Bottom   Peter Dale Ltd, London.

p 90
Left   Château de Versailles.
   Photo Giraudon, Paris.
Right   Royal Armouries, H.M. Tower of
London.   IX.967.

p 91
Left   Victoria & Albert Museum, Wellington
Museum, Apsley House, London.
   Photo Macdonald/Aldus Archive.
Centre   Victoria & Albert Museum,
Wellington Museum, Apsley House,
London.   WM 1230-1948.
Right   Victoria & Albert Museum, London.
486-870.

p 92
Top   Musée de l'Armée, Paris.
   Photo Robert Harding Picture Library.
Bottom left   Museum of London.   IT 221a.

Bottom right   Royal Armouries, H.M. Tower
of London.   IX.717; IX.1854; IX.429.

p 93
Top   Christie's, London.
2nd from top   Peter Dale Ltd, London.
2nd from bottom   Victoria & Albert Museum,
Wellington Museum, Apsley House, London.
Bottom   Victoria & Albert Museum, London.
649-1889.

p 94
Top   Bismarck-Museum, Friedrichsruh.
   Photo Archiv für Kunst and Geschichte,
   Berlin.
Bottom   Philadelphia Museum of Art. Bequest
of Carl Otto Kretschmar von Kienbusch.
U977-167-659.

p 95
Top   Metropolitan Museum of Art, New
York. Purchase, the Sulzberger Foundation
Inc. Gift, 1987.   1987-161.
Bottom left   Imperial War Museum.   WEA
1233.
   Photo David Cripps.
Bottom right   Anthony North.

8   COMBINATION WEAPONS

p 97
Right   Historisches Museum, Dresden.   V.48.
Left   Historisches Museum, Dresden.

p 98
Left   Historisches Museum, Dresden.   V.48
(detail).
Right   Godeau-Solanet-Audap, Paris.

p 99
Top   Royal Armouries, H.M. Tower of
London.
Bottom left   Wallace Collection, London.
A1240.
Bottom right   Victoria & Albert Museum,
London. Private collection.

p 100
Left   Royal Armouries, H.M. Tower of
London.   AL22-Acquisition loans.
Centre   Anthony North.
Right   Archiv für Kunst and Geschichte,
Berlin

p 101
Top right   By gracious permission of Her
Majesty the Queen.   Laking.
Centre   Anthony North.
Bottom   Kunsthistorisches Museum
(Waffensammlung), Vienna.
   Photo Marianne Haller.

p 102
Left   Victoria & Albert Museum, London.
M118-1984.
Right   Glasgow Museums and Art
Galleries.   '39-65 nq.

p 103
Top   Glasgow Museums and Art
Galleries.   '39-65 no.
Bottom left   Victoria & Albert Museum,
London. Grosvenor Loan.   M63-1950.
Bottom right   Rijksmuseum, Amsterdam.
NM 6095.

Artwork pp 100 and 101 by Randy Macdonald.

9   AMERICAN SWORDS AND KNIVES

p 105
Left   Pilgrim Society, Plymouth, Mass.
Right   Connecticut Historical Society.

p 106
Left and right   The Mount Vernon Ladies'
Association of the Union, Virginia.

p 107
Pennsylvania State Capitol Collection.
   Photo Macdonald/Aldus Archive.

p 108
Bottom left and right   Photo Macdonald/Aldus
Archive.   24AB 16920.

p 109
Peter Newark's Military Pictures, Bath.

p 110
David Hayden-Wright Collection.

p 111
Buffalo Bill Historical Center, Cody,
Wyoming.

p 112
Top   Library of Congress.
   Photo Macdonald/Aldus Archive.
Bottom left and right   David Hayden-Wright
Collection.

p 113
Top   Pater Dale Ltd, London.
Centre and bottom   Macdonald/Aldus
Archive.   24AB 16920.

p 114
Top   Macdonald/Aldus Archive.
Bottom left and right   Gunshots, London.

p 115
Top   Peter Newark's Military Pictures, Bath.
Bottom   Royal Armouries, H.M. Tower of
London.

pp 116–117
Bettmann Archive, New York.

p 117
Library of Congress, Washington DC.
   Photo Macdonald/Aldus Archive.

p 118
Top   Peter Newark's Military Pictures, Bath.
Bottom   Peter Dale Ltd, London.

p 119
Peter Newark's Military Pictures, Bath.

p. 121
Top left and right   Gunshots, London.
Bottom left   Imperial War Museum,
London.   WEA 778 and WEA 646.
   Photo David Cripps.
Bottom right   Imperial War Museum,
London.   WEA 668 and WEA 672.
   Photo David Cripps.

10   WORLD WARS I AND II

p 123
Museo di Storia Contemporanea, Milan.
   Photo Scala, Milan.

p 124
Imperial War Museum, London. Left to right:
WEA 366; WEA 106; WEA 628; WEA 37;
WEA 124.
   Photo David Cripps.

p 125
Peter Newark's Military Pictures, Bath.

p 126
Top   Imperial War Museum, London.
Q 18972.
Bottom   Imperial War Museum, London.
Q 8434.

p 127
Top left   Imperial War Museum, London.
   Photo David Cripps.
Bottom   Imperial War Museum, London.
WEA 784; WA 614; WEA 676; WEA 655.
   Photo David Cripps.

p 128
Top   Peter Newark's Military Pictures, Bath.
Bottom left and right   Imperial War Museum,
London.   WEA 1100 and WEA 1097.
   Photo David Cripps.

p 129
Top   Imperial War Museum, London.
Q 46480
Bottom   Imperial War Museum,
London.   WEA 794; WEA 1073; WEA 1213.
   Photo David Cripps.

p 130
Top left   Imperial War Museum, London.
WEA 874.
   Photo David Cripps.
Top right   Imperial War Museum, London.
WEA 870.
   Photo David Cripps.

p 131
Imperial War Museum, London. Left to right:
WEA 843; WEA 843; WEA 844; WEA 845.
   Photo David Cripps.

p 132
Top left   Imperial War Museum, London. Left
to right: WEA 868; WEA 869; WEA 867.
   Photo David Cripps.

Bottom Imperial War Museum, London. Left
to right: WEA 1147 and WEA 1165.
 Photo David Cripps.

p 133
Top left Imperial War Museum, London.
H 204/10.
Top right Imperial War Museum, London.
H 26613.
Bottom Imperial War Museum, London. Left to
right: WEA 722; WEA 688; WEA 696.
 Photo David Cripps.

p 134
National Army Museum, London.

p 135
Left Imperial War Museum, London.
 Photo David Cripps.
Right Imperial War Museum, London. Left to
right: WEA 715 and WEA 718.
 Photo David Cripps.

11 SWORDS OF ISLAM

p 136
Photo Sotheby's, London.

p 137
Top Photo Howard Ricketts Ltd, London.
Bottom British Museum, London. WAA
129378.

p 138
Left Sonia Halliday Photographs, Weston
Turville.
Right Metropolitan Museum of Art, New
York. Rogers Fund, 1940. 40.170.169a–d.

p 139
Staatliche Kunstsammlungen, Kassel.
B 11 608.

p 140
Top left and bottom Victoria & Albert
Museum, London. I.S.3378.
Top right Topkapı Sarayı Müzesi,
Istanbul. 1/90.

p 141
Top left Wallace Collection, London. Left to
right: 1414; 1750; 1785; 1944; 1762; 1796; 1430.
Top right Victoria & Albert Museum,
London. 1060–1884.
Bottom Wallace Collection, London.
OA 1787.

p 142
Left Photo Howard Ricketts Ltd, London.
Centre Victoria & Albert Museum,
London. M47-1953.
Right Private collection.

p 143
Left Topkapı Sarayı Müzesi, Istanbul.
 Photo Giraudon, Paris.
Upper right Topkapı Sarayı Müzesi,
Istanbul. 2/3776.
 Photo Dr Oliver Watson.

Lower right Victoria & Albert Museum,
London. M964-1928.

p 144
Left Royal Museum of Scotland, Edinburgh.
Centre St Louis Art Museum, Missouri.
Museum purchase. 14.1922.
Right Victoria & Albert Museum, London.
I.S. 3471.

p 145
Left Chester Beatty Library, Dublin.
MS 144 f 20.
Right Victoria & Albert Museum, London.
585–1876 and 511-1874.

p 146
Left Photo Sotheby's, London.
Centre Państowe Zbiory Sztuki na Wawelu,
Cracow. Inv. 169.
Right Photo Sotheby's, London.

p 147
Left Victoria & Albert Museum, London.
574-1876.
 Photo © Michael Holford, Loughton.
Right Victoria & Albert Museum, London.
717-1889; 683-1889; 575-1876.

12 JAPANESE SWORDS

p 148
British Museum, London.

p 149
Kita-In, Saitumi.
Photo Werner Forman Archive, London.

p 150
Top Photo Okisato Fujisharo.
Centre British Museum, London. JA 1958
7-30 6.

p 152
Top Kita-In, Saitumi.
 Photo Werner Forman Archive, London.

p 153
Top Hinomisaki Shrine, Shimane Prefecture.
Bottom Victoria & Albert Museum, London.
 Photo Werner Forman Archive, London.

p 154
Top British Museum, London. JA 1958
7-30 158.

p 155
British Museum, London. JA Painting
Add. 324 and 325.

p 156
British Museum, London. JA 1984 7-23 1.

p 158
Right British Museum, London. 1958
7-30 64.

p 159
Top British Museum, London.

Centre British Museum, London. JA 1958
7-30 64.
Bottom British Museum, London. JA 1979
7-3 2.

p 161
Left British Museum, London. JA Painting
295.
Right British Museum, London. Left to right;
JA 1958 7-30 143; JA 1958 7-30 5; JA 1958 7-30
101.

p 162
Centre and bottom British Museum, London.
JA 1958 7-30 79.

p 163
Upper British Museum, London. JA 1958
7-30 87.
Lower British Museum, London. JA 1958
7-30 46.

p 164
Top British Museum, London. JA Painting
Add. 12.
Bottom British Museum, London. JA 1958
7-30 46.

p 165
Top British Museum, London. JA Painting
Add. 869.
Bottom British Museum, London. JA 1958
7-30 46.

p 166
Left Hulton Picture Library, London.
Centre British Museum, London. JA 1958
7-30 66.
Right British Museum, London. JA 1958
7-30 67.

p 168
Left British Museum, London. JA 1958
7-30 84.
Right Tokyo University Library.

p 169
British Museum, London. JA 1958 7-30 22.

p 170
British Museum, London. Left and centre:
JA 1958 7-30 156; upper right: JA 1981 1-27 49;
lower right: JA 1939 5-19 28.

p 171
British Museum, London. JA 1958 7-30 149.

*Artwork pp 150, 151, 152 bottom, 154 bottom, 156
extreme right, 158 left and bottom, 160, 162 top, 167
and 168 right by Philip Sutton.*

13 CHINA AND CENTRAL ASIA

p 172
Top right British Museum, London. OA
1948 10-13 4.
Bottom right British Museum, London. Left:
OA 1953 5-19 1; right: OA 1973 7-26 30.

p 173
British Museum, London. OA 1968 4-24 1
and OA 1986 2-22 1.

p 174
Left British Museum, London. OA 1940
12-14 281.

p 175
Top British Museum, London. OA 1911
4-7 25.
Bottom British Museum, London. OA 1978
12-18 1.

p 176
Metropolitan Museum of Art, New York. Gift
of George D. Pratt and gift of Clarence H.
Mackay. 30-65.1 and 30-65.2.

p 177
Top left Photo Hermann Historica O.H.G.,
Munich.
Left centre State Hermitage Museum,
Leningrad.
 Photo Werner Forman Archive, London.
Right Government Museum, Mathura.
Bottom British Museum, London. Above:
WAA 135158; below: WAA 135738.

pp 178–179
National Palace Museum, Taipei.

p 181
Top Edinburgh University Library.
Or MS 20 f 123v.
Bottom National Palace Museum, Taipei.

p 182
Royal Armouries, H.M. Tower of London.
XXVI 52S.

p 183
Top left Royal Armouries, H.M. Tower of
London. XXVI 190S.
Bottom left Royal Armouries, H.M. Tower of
London. XXVI 191S.
Top right Royal Armouries, H.M. Tower of
London. XXVI 58S.
Bottom right Royal Armouries, H.M. Tower
of London. XXVI 170S.

p 184
Left Royal Armouries, H.M. Tower of
London. XXVI 186S and XXVI 187S.
Right Private collection.
 Photo Claude Mercier.

p 185
Top Royal Armouries, H.M. Tower of
London. XXVI 36D.
Bottom Royal Armouries, H.M. Tower of
London. XXVI 50S.

14 INDIA AND SOUTHEAST ASIA

p 186
Victoria & Albert Museum, London.
 Photo © Michael Holford, Loughton.

p 187
Victoria & Albert Museum, London.
    Photo © Michael Holford, Lughton.

p 188
Top Victoria & Albert Museum, London.
    Photo © Michael Holford, Loughton.
Bottom Photo Gunshots, London.

p 189
Left Photo Sotheby's, London.
Right Photo Gunshots, London.

p 190
Royal Armouries, H.M. Tower of London.
XXVI 7S.

p 191
Top Photo Sotheby's, London.
Centre Royal Armouries, H.M. Tower of
London. XXVI 7S.
Bottom Photo Gunshots, London.

p 192
British Library, London.
    Photo © Michael Holford, Loughton.

p 193
Left Royal Armouries, H.M. Tower of
London. XXVI 4C.
Centre Royal Armouries, H.M. Tower of
London. XXVI 81S.
Right Royal Armouries, H.M. Tower of
London. XXVI 83S.

p 194
Royal Armouries, H.M. Tower of London.
XXVI 30D.

p 195
Top left Photo Sotheby's, London.
Bottom left Photo Sotheby's. London.
Top centre Royal Armouries, H.M. Tower of
London. XXVI 76D.
Top right Royal Armouries, H.M. Tower of
London. XXVI 74D.
Bottom right Royal Armouries, H.M. Tower
of London. XXVI 70D.

p 196
Musée Guimet, Paris.
    Photo Giraudon, Paris.

p 197
Top left Royal Armouries, H.M. Tower of
London. XXVI 5M.
Top right Photo Gunshots, London.
Upper centre Photo Gunshots, London.
Lower centre, bottom left and bottom right Royal
Armouries, H.M. Tower of London. XXVI
85S.

p 198
Top Royal Armouries, H.M. Tower of
London. XXVI 82D.
Bottom Pitt Rivers Museum, Oxford.
1968.23.55.

p 199
Top Pitt Rivers Museum, Oxford.
1948.7.15.
Centre Pitt Rivers Museum, Oxford.
Purchased from Stevens 1925.
Bottom Pitt Rivers Museum, Oxford.
Donated by T.M. Annendale 1900.

p 200
Left Photo Werner Forman Archive, London.
Right Photo Werner Forman Archive,
London.

p 201
Top left Pitt Rivers Museum, Oxford. Pitt
Rivers collection 1184.
Top right Pitt Rivers Museum, Oxford. Pitt
Rivers collection 1884.
Bottom left Pitt Rivers Museum, Oxford.
Purchased from Annendale 1902.
Bottom right Pitt Rivers Museum,
Oxford. 1945.6.63.

p 202
Top Photo Hans Hinz, Allschwil.
Bottom Photo Hans Hinz, Allschwil.

p 203
Top Pitt Rivers Museum, Oxford.
1925.59.1.
Centre Pitt Rivers Museum, Oxford.
1884.24.31.
Bottom Pitt Rivers Museum, Oxford.
Donated by R. Evans 1900.

15 AFRICAN HILT WEAPONS

p 205
Museum of Mankind, London. Top left: Ethno
9111; top right: Ethno 1949 Af 46 272; bottom
left (sheath and knife): Ethno 5736; bottom
centre: Ethno 1951 Af 24 3; bottom right:
Ethno 1956 Af 27 242.
    Photo Kirsty McLaren, London.

p 206
Top Museum of Mankind, London. Left:
Ethno 1939 1–18 2; right: Ethno 1904-113.
    Photo Kirsty McLaren, London.
Bottom left Worcester Art Museum,
Worcester, Massachusetts. 1922.145.
Bottom right Museum of Mankind, London.
Left: Ethno Af 1954 N23 (Box 141); right:
Ethno 1909 Ty 542.

p 207
Photo Museum of Mankind, London.

p 208
Left Museum of Mankind, London.
Ethno 1932 10-14 1.
    Photo Kirsty McLaren, London.
Centre Museum of Mankind, London. Left

(sword, baldric and sheath): Ethno 1955 Af 8 1;
right (sword and sheath): Ethno 1923 7-10 33.
    Photo Kirsty McLaren, London.
Right Photo Roger Balsom, Cambridge.

p 209
Left Museum of Mankind, London. Left
(sheath and dagger): Ethno 1934 12-8 4; centre
(sheath and dagger): Ethno 1943 16 8; right:
Ethno 1911 158.
    Photo Kirsty McLaren, London.
Right Museum of Mankind, London. Left:
Ethno 1904 6–11 30; right: Ethno 1949 Af 46
336.
    Photo Kirsty McLaren, London.

p 210
Right R.E. Bradbury.
Below Museum of Mankind, London. Left to
right: Ethno 1954 Af 23.218; Ethno 1954 Af
23.219; Ethno 1909 Ty 557; Ethno 1949 Af
46.166.

p 211
Top Museum of Mankind, London. Ethno
1898 1-15 49.
Bottom Museum of Mankind, London. Ethno
78 11-1 327.

p 212
Photo Doran H. Ross, University of
California, Los Angeles.

pp 212–213
Museum of Mankind, London.   Ethno 1900
4-27 7.

p 213
Left Museum of Mankind, London.
Ethno 1909 12-10 1.
Right Museum of Mankind, London.
Ethno Af 1978 N.22.

p 214
Left Museum of Mankind, London. Left to
right: Ethno 1909 5-13 184; Ethno 1909 5-13
192; Ethno 1090 5-13 191.
    Photo Kirsty McLaren, London.
Right Photo Eliot Elisofon. National Museum
of African Art, Eliot Elisofon Archives,
Smithsonian Institution, Washington D.C.

p 215
Earnest S. Thomas 'The African throwing
knife', *Journal of the Royal Anthropological
Institute of Great Britain and Ireland*, vol. 55,
1925, pp 136 and 137.

p 216
Top Museum of Mankind, London. Left:
Ethno 88.200; right: Ethno 98.205.
    Photo Kirsty McLaren, London.
Centre Museum of Mankind, London. Left:
Ethno 1928 4-9 2; right: Ethno 4388.
    Photo Kirsty McLaren, London.
Bottom Museum of Mankind, London.
Ethno 4388.
    Photo Kirsty McLaren, London.

p 217
Centre Museum of Mankind, London. Upper:
Ethno 98 159; middle: Ethno 98.174; lower
Ethno 98.149.
    Photo Kirsty Mclaren, London.
Right Photo Oswald Iten, Unterägeri.

*Artwork pp 210 left, 213 right and 217 bottom by
Christopher Spring*

16 PRE-CONQUEST AMERICA

Museo de America, Madrid.
    Photo Robert Harding Picture Library,
London.

p 223
Top Museum of Mankind, London. ST 399.
Centre Peabody Museum, Harvard
University, Cambridge, Massachusetts.
LO-71-20 c.6755.
    Photo Hillel Burger.
Bottom Museum of Mankind, London.
    Photo © Michael Holdford, Loughton.

p 224
Left Photo Tony Morrison, South America
Pictures.
Right Collection Señor Mujica Gallo, Lima.
    Photo © Michael Holford, Loughton.

p 225
Left The London Library.
Right Photo Tony Morrison, South America
Pictures.

p 218
Peabody Museum, Harvard University,
Cambridge, Massachusetts.
    Photo Bridgeman Art Library.

p 219
The London Library.

p 220
Top and bottom left The London Library.
Bottom centre Bodleian Library, Oxford.
MS. Arch. Feld A.12 f.2r.

p 221
Top Biblioteca Nazionale, Florence.
MS232 f.30r.
    Photo Pinerder.
Bottom Bibliothèque nationale, Paris.
MS Mex.65-71 f.106r.

*Photographs of weapons and other objects in
the collections of the Royal Armouries,
H.M. Tower of London, and of the
Victoria & Albert Museum, London, are
reproduced by kind permission of the Board
of Trustees of the Royal Armouries and of
the Trustees of the Victoria & Albert
Museum.*

Index

Page numbers in italics refer to illustrations.